TO COVET
HONOR

Alexander Hamilton

TO COVET HONOR

A Biography Of

Alexander Hamilton

by

Holmes Alexander

But if it be a sin to covet honor,
I am the most offending soul alive.
SHAKESPEARE: *Henry V*

Copyright 1977 by Holmes Alexander
All rights reserved
Published by Western Islands, Belmont, Massachusetts 02178
Library of Congress Catalog Card Number: 77-075276
ISBN: 0-88279-232-6

Printed in U.S.A.

To
MARY BARKSDALE ALEXANDER
"Forsaking All Others. . . ."

Contents

PART FOUR • THE INEVITABLE HOUR

Frontispiece: The statue of Alexander Hamilton by James Earle Fraser stands at the south front of the Treasury Department building in Washington, D.C. Photograph by courtesy of the Treasury Department.

PREFACE

Persons who have read my early biographies on Martin Van Buren (published 1935 and 1968) and on Aaron Burr (published 1937 and 1973) sometimes ask me:

"Why is it that as a young man you chose to write about two Americans in whom their countrymen could not have taken pride, but as a mature man turned to Alexander Hamilton whom you hold so high?"

I am not stumped for an answer. I have often thought it out. At age twenty-four, I was elected from rural Baltimore County and took my seat as an assemblyman in the Maryland legislature. At the time I was a preparatory school teacher by profession and a beginning author. I knew nothing of politics and very little of American history, having taken courses in ancient and European history while at Gilman School and Princeton, and studied English literature while a graduate student at Trinity College, Cambridge, England.

When I reached Annapolis, "the baby of the ticket," I soon learned that the men and women with "Hon." before their names were mainly exceptional for their affability. They liked people; they aimed to please those who put them in office—an abiding weakness of the democratic system, as Hamilton later would teach me. The average legislator is not a political thinker, and has little vision of public responsibility.

Like myself, most of the others were in office at the pleasure of some local boss who tried even harder to please the electorate—for a price. It was true then as now, in Sam Rayburn's homely cynicism, that "The way to get along is to go along." This wasn't for me. Without aspiring to be a reformer, I pulled off from the leadership and rode my own line. I decided that one four-year term would be enough. To me, politics was at times an exciting sport, and fun to play. But I wished to be an observer, not a participant. That way was personal freedom, and perhaps a public contribution.

Accordingly, continuing as a school teacher, I wrote two first-person articles about my political experiences, and sold them to *Harper's* Magazine. The first was "I Run for Office," and the second was "I Hold Office." They caused indignation and hilarity in Maryland political circles, and stirred some interest in me in literary New York. Cass Canfield of Harper & Brothers suggested I do a fictional political satire for the publishing house that he headed. I struggled with a novel and got nowhere. But in my search for ideas I discovered a better comic political hero than ever I could have invented—Martin Van Buren, eighth President.

In American history, Little Van stands between the sublime and the ridiculous. He succeeded men of stature—Washington, Jefferson, Madison, Monroe, the two Adamses and Jackson. He was followed into the Presidential office by men who created little stir in the world—Harrison, Tyler, Polk, Taylor, Fillmore, Pierce, and Buchanan. Though financially honest, Van Buren accomplished everything in politics by trickery. In his day he was called the Red Fox of Kinderhook, the Little Magician, the Northern Man with Southern Principles. "Vanburenish" became an adjective to denote polite evasion. That was how he won many offices, kept many friends, and acquired numerous and affectionate nicknames.

Two years after publication of the Van Buren biography I appeared with *Aaron Burr: The Proud Pretender*. Burr was rumored (with no evidence except their similarities) to have been the natural father of Marty Van. Gore Vidal made full use of this rumor in his best-selling novel, *Burr,* in which the protagonist was presented as a misunderstood, mistreated patriot. I saw Burr as an amoral, erratic, brilliant, scoundrel, possibly the worst American in history, a traitor but for Chief Justice Marshall's strict construction of the Constitution. Burr, however, had a ruthless Satanic charm, and I made the most of it in telling his story.

My publishers liked my performance in biography, and pressed me to continue. But I had a yen to try fiction, and sold them three novels before going off to World War II. When I returned, they again urged me to write lives instead of life; but I was not yet ready to write about Hamilton. I had many other projects in journalism and fiction, and I wanted to do a book on the coming Air Age.

But Hamilton never left my mind. The comparisons are modest, but I was a staff officer who had seen some combat—so had he, the individual hero of Yorktown. I was a Washington-based syndicated columnist from 1946 onward, and he was the most-read newspaper and pamphlet writer of his day—author-in-chief of the *Federalist Papers.* Moreover, in the 1940's, the United States had begun to accumulate allies by the dozens, as well as un-Constitutional obligations by the United Nations treaties—and Hamilton had warned against "entangling alliances."

Looking back, I can see that the experiences of military service and national reporting were what led me to this present biography. Hamilton, in promoting manufactures and export trade, instinctively put his own country first. He related religion to patriotism; he was suspicious of ultranationalism, which so readily becomes anti-nationalism. He was, by the definitions of the 1940's–1970's, a conservative. He was also a republican, a believer in the form of government guaranteed to us by the Constitution.

It may sound frivolous, but one of the factors which drew me to try a biography of Hamilton was the location of his statue. It stands on the south or rear side of the Treasury Department building, while the Jeffersonian Albert Gallatin stands high at the front of the Treasury building, overlooking Pennsylvania Avenue, the route of every heroic parade. Much that was wrong with the country, I thought, stemmed from the deference to Gallatin, a democrat, over Hamilton, a republican—using these terms in the nonpartisan sense.

Indeed, it would have been strange if any man, having lived my life, had not tended to turn from the Van Burens and Burrs to the Hamiltons of public life. Politics provides many subjects for satire and studies of the sinister, but the big stories of history are the heroic, often tragic ones. We sometimes have reason to think that the scoundrels outnumber us—that they are too clever for us, and must overcome the men of good will.

But it didn't happen that way to Hamilton. Dying, he drove Burr to flight and disgrace. Remembered, as I hope this book will show, he can make better Americans of us all.

INTRODUCTION

I

I intend not to add to the wasted ink which has been shed to discover Alexander Hamilton's true parentage, date of birth, and birthplace. The fact is that Hamilton chose all three, and his choices are at least as defensible as those of his biographers.

Hamilton's mother and father—whoever they really were—had little importance in his life. Teachers, employers, fellow-students, and fellow-officers influenced his formative years, but he had no real childhood, no real home, a strong desire to get away from his beginnings, and no inclination to return. It seems a biographical act of kindness to take him out of the West Indies as soon as possible, which I shall do, and establish him in New York City, where he chose to live.

Hamilton was illegitimate; and it is probable that his supposed mother was not the child of her own mother's husband. So much uncertainty exists on the maternal side that it is not very plausible to write, as has been done, that Hamilton's occasional gaiety, his sexual activity, and his passing concern for religious freedom and other civil liberties, resulted from his descent from French Huguenot refugees, whereas his serious side was a display of Scotch dourness, scholarship, and thrift. These assumptions are not beyond challenge, because their premises are questionable and arbitrary.

Hamilton's genes are said to have been brought to the New World in 1685 by John Faucette or Fawcett, who settled as a planter and physician at Charlestown, Nevis, British West Indies. Around 1714 Dr. Fawcett married a young woman christened Mary, surname and national origin uncertain. Two daughters, Mary and Ann, were born in due time. They became, respectively, the wives of Peter Lytton and Thomas Mitchell, both of whom had plantations on St. Croix, in the Danish West Indies. Hamilton always spoke of these ladies as his maternal aunts; they represented the well-to-do branch of his family.

Dr. Fawcett prospered and eventually retired with the gout to his town house, Gingerland. The trail grows faint just when the doctor is on the verge of being accepted in history as Hamilton's maternal grandfather. The biographer Broadus Mitchell thinks it possible that Fawcett married still another young woman named Mary, otherwise unidentifiable. In any event, the doctor was an old and ailing husband when his young wife surprised him by becoming pregnant. The biographer Nathan Schachner says that Fawcett thought himself a cuckold. Mother and child, a girl, left Gingerland, left Nevis, and went to live on another British island, St. Kitts. Meanwhile, a legal separation, rather than a divorce, had been worked out; Mrs. Mary Fawcett and the child Rachel, date of birth unknown, subsisted on an allowance from the estranged husband.

Rachel Fawcett is the woman whom Alexander Hamilton would inferentially accept as his mother without ever mentioning her name in correspondence known to this author. Since Rachel's paternity is in doubt, as well as her mother's surname and identity, there seems little point in speculating on her blood lines. But she was a lively young woman (who did not live long past thirty), and has long been irresistibly attractive to Hamilton biographers. Rachel is sympathetically presented as a victim of the household tyranny of her martinet of a mother. She was forced to learn foreign languages like a boy being prepared for the diplomatic corps, and she was given lessons in music and painting. Mrs. Mary Fawcett allegedly made Rachel the best educated girl in the islands, and also the loneliest. But her purpose was fulfilled when Rachel found a rich husband. Either in 1745 or in 1752, while she was still quite young, Rachel was married to the prosperous planter John Michael Levine of St. Croix, a Danish Jew who took the bride and her mother to Copenhagen for a lavish honeymoon.

Shortly after their return home, Rachel left both her husband and her infant son Peter, and moved back to St. Kitts with her mother. During the next several years Rachel had her fling with many men; she "went whoring in the Barbadoes . . .

whoring with everybody," according to the uncontested statements in the bill of divorce.

Alexander Hamilton claimed Rachel as his mother only by indirection. In 1782 he inquired vainly for mention of his name in a will by Rachel's legitimate son, Peter Levine, who Hamilton declared was his half-brother. He could not have been proud of Rachel. This supposed mother served some time in the Christiansted jail as a convicted adulteress. When she was divorced by Levine, Rachel went her mother one better—that is, she became a divorced wife, whereas Mary was only a separated one. It is impossible to believe that Hamilton held this woman dear as a mother.

While Hamilton understandably did not see Rachel as an object of admiration or affection, others did. In the 1920's Gertrude Atherton became the first writer to make the uncomfortable, vermin-infested trip to the West Indies for the purpose of putting together a Hamilton genealogy and biography. Mrs. Atherton searched the records of the court houses and churches on Nevis, St. Kitts, and St. Croix, his three most probable birthplaces. She blazed the trail of research which subsequent twentieth-century biographers would follow and sometimes alter. But she brought Rachel to life without violating the disputed borderline between factual biography and creative fiction. In *The Conqueror,* Atherton's fine biographical novel about Hamilton, his mother is tall, strong, and graceful, gifted with fair hair that gives off reddish glints. Her dark eyes and magnolia-white skin are the accouterments of love. She is a proud beauty of whom neighbors said that she "would look haughty in her coffin." Atherton conceived Rachel as a woman formed by destiny and nature to bring genius to the world. "The students of history know," the novelist wrote Byronically, "that while many mothers of great men have been virtuous, none have been commonplace and few have been happy."

Into Rachel's life, Atherton asserted, moved a suitably romantic love-mate, bringing with him the suitable vicissitudes. There were many Hamiltons in the British West Indies. One of them, Dr. Will Hamilton of St. Kitts—another physician-planter—was joined there in the early 1750's by James Hamil-

ton, a young kinsman. James Hamilton was the fourth son of
the Laird of Grange, Ayrshire, Scotland. Just past his twenty-
first birthday, he had hoped for an army commission; failing
that, for a university career and the life of a scholar. He had
an impetuous air and an elegant manner, carried his tall, spare
body well, and looked disdainfully upon the baked canefields
and tropical coconut groves of St. Kitts. There was that about
him, Atherton wrote, "which made him look best on horseback
and in white linen."

He had not gone so far from Scotland as to leave behind an
opportunity available to handsome, well-bred younger sons
everywhere. He might have found an heiress or wealthy widow
to marry. They were not scarce in the prospering West Indies,
nor in Spanish America, nor in the British colonies to the
north. But this charming drifter fell in love with the beautiful
cast-off wife. They set up a common-law household on Nevis,
where Rachel owned property. In time they had two or more
boys living at home who were supposed to be their sons.

Gertrude Atherton's research was diligent and her narrative
appealing, but there were discrepancies. The game of playing
with eighteenth-century documents is boresome and frustrat-
ing. Islands frequently changed imperial owners, and were renamed. St. Christopher, also known as St. Kitts, had nine other
designations under various regimes. The spelling of proper
names also was erratic. James Hamilton's consort was Rachel
or Rachael Faucette, Fawcett, Feacey, Faust, Faucet, or Fos-
sett. Her lawful husband was John or Johann Lavin, Lawin,
Lawine, Lawien, Lewine, Lèvin, Levine, Lowine, or Lovien.

Documents were often transferred to the European capitals,
or lost in fires, hurricanes, or at sea. When they survived they
often were embarrassing to researchers. For example, Atherton made Alexander Hamilton five years older than his brother
James. Henry Cabot Lodge in 1882 made the future statesman
"the only surviving child" of the irregular household, but later
mentioned the brother James in the appendix of *The Works of
Alexander Hamilton,* giving no date of birth. John Church
Hamilton, the statesman's biographer-son, says his father was
"the youngest" of "several" sons of James and Rachel.

Probate Court Document No. XXIX, St. Croix, February 19, 1765, confounds them all. It makes Alexander Hamilton two years younger than his brother James. The record reads in part:

". . . on the 19th of this month, Madame Rachael Lewine died, and whose effects were forthwith sealed up, in order now to take an inventory of them for subsequent distribution among the decedent's surviving children who are namely, Peter Lewine . . . also two other sons, namely, James Hamilton and Alexander Hamilton, the one 15 and the other 13, who are the same illegitimate children . . . born after the decedent's separation from the aforesaid Lewine. . . ."

By the time of Rachel's death, when Hamilton was eleven by his own count, this divorced wife of one man had become the deserted mistress of another. She had tried to set James Hamilton up in business, but he failed. He failed also when she got him work with her relatives at St. Croix. James Hamilton, after several shifts, left his family forever in the 1760's, and became a laborer on the British island of St. Vincent, where he was buried at the Georgetown cathedral in 1799, aged eighty-one.

Skepticism is always in order. There were no birth certificates for James's offspring, and there was Rachel's court-recorded reputation for fast living. Any male, present and potent, could have fathered her children, whose very number is not certain.

When Hamilton became famous, numerous men were nominated for the distinguished fatherhood. One was Dr. Will Hamilton; another was the planter Thomas Stevens, whose son Edward closely resembled Hamilton. Several royal governors of the Danish West Indies seem to have been thrown in for good measure. The most likely to deserve the claim of paternity were Christian Suhm and Baron C. L. B. von Pröcke, both of whom were in office during 1756, when Hamilton was presumably conceived. Some people would live to say that Hamilton had a Virginia look. Possibly this was because Martha Washington told a biographer that the General referred to Hamilton as "my boy." Lawrence and George Washington visited in Barbados during 1751–52, in Rachel's footloose days. And it is sometimes theorized that Hamilton was Levine's son, conceived shortly before Rachel left her married home.

Undisturbed by the genealogical mishmash, Hamilton asserted the unusual privilege of picking his own relatives. He had no ulterior reason for addressing James Hamilton as "father" and "honoured sir," although some biographers would say that he was social-climbing to a Scottish ancestry. But this could hardly be the motive of a teenage boy whose father had run off and become little better than a beachcomber. Hamilton also acknowledged James, junior, an unsuccessful carpenter, as his only brother. During the 1790's he sent these destitute men thousands of dollars, as well as repeated invitations to join him in New York.

Hamilton, quite indifferent toward Rachel, was very fond and generous toward a twice-married "cousin," Mrs. Ann Lytton Venton Mitchell. Writing in 1903, biographer Lodge interprets some correspondence of Hamilton as suggesting that the statesman was figuratively switched in the cradle, and that the supposed mother was really an aunt. "This letter," declares Lodge, "tends to show that, if the view there suggested is probable, Hamilton's mother was a Miss Lytton, and not Miss Fawcett." In that case, the well-loved "cousin" may have been Hamilton's sister.

Hamilton sorted out his relatives to suit himself, and also chose January 11, 1757, for his birthday. Others thought they knew better. The historian George Bancroft wrote that "the first trace of his existence is in 1766, when his name appears as witness to a legal paper executed in the Spanish island of Santa Cruz." Lodge corroborates Bancroft, "I have carefully examined an exact tracing of this signature. The handwriting is obviously Hamilton's."

This would discredit the chosen birthday. If Hamilton was old enough in 1766 to sign a legal document, other birth dates and other sires would have to be considered. But the editors of the Hamilton Papers, noting the comments of Bancroft and Lodge, point out, "The document has not been found." Generally speaking, Hamilton's detractors preferred to believe him older than he claimed to be. But three of Hamilton's friends—Nicholas Fish, Timothy Pickering, and John Mason—thought him even younger than he said.

Since the proof of it all was lacking, Hamilton was free to decide both when and where he was born. He had no difficulty in choosing a place of birth. His chief requirement was that it must make him an Englishman. Although he grew up on St. Croix and had reason to be grateful to many kindly persons there, he regarded Danish territory as alien soil; and St. Kitts, though British, was an insignificant place. He claimed, without the slightest proof, to have been born on the picturesque island of Nevis. Nevis's peaks were beautifully circled each night by the snow-white clouds which had inspired its name. Its coasts were graceful, studded with castles where families of the British court came to spend a fashionable season. And the rich cane-growing earth of Nevis made fortunes for English and Scottish landlords by the sweat of African slave-labor.

In the last year of his life, 1804, Hamilton went to the aid of "a near relative of mine, Mr. Alexander Hamilton, now a prisoner of war in Paris." He did this by writing to Prince Talleyrand, whom he knew well, identifying the namesake as "a Scotch gentleman of education and literary acquirements who [had] amassed a pretty fortune. . . ."

By this time, of course, Hamilton had become established as an ancestor in his own right. He had succeeded George Washington as president-general of the Society of the Cincinnati, an hereditary organization whose membership passes from father to eldest son. In the 1970's his descendant, the Reverend Alexander Hamilton, is a member. The *Dictionary of American Biography* includes Hamilton, one of his sons, and two of his grandsons.

But at best it was a makeshift family tree, a worry to the friends who outlived him. They knew he had made a name that stood by itself—the writer, the orator, the master of finance, the authority on foreign affairs, the leader of his party, the *bon vivant,* the scandalous lover, the ranking Army officer, the protégé and impresario of George Washington, a statesman of international fame in his own right.

He was to die at the hands of the Vice President of the United States in a duel too dramatic and pathetic ever to be forgotten. He would be buried with a public funeral never approached in early America for its panoply, and be mourned by the classes and masses of the city and nation. Beyond doubt, whatever the judgment of history, his memory would never die.

And yet his friends feared that he must be recorded as *filius nullius*. There was nothing they could do to prove the contrary. The most they could do was to certify the year of birth that he preferred. His tombstone at Trinity Church, New York, was marked: "He died July 12, 1804, aged 47."

II

I intend to refrain from joining Hamilton's battles with his contemporaries, or rather with their biographers. I am his partisan, but hope to do him justice without doing injury to others.

It can hardly have escaped attention that he had well-publicized quarrels with the leading figures of his day, with the men who served as the first five Presidents of the United States— Washington, Adams, Jefferson, Madison, and Monroe. There were other adversaries, and Hamilton was many times involved in challenges to the duel. It is beyond dispute that he was arbitrary and quick-tempered among his peers, but also worth noting that he was considerate of soldiers and other ordinary persons. He several times intervened against the death sentence in peacetime. He was popular enough so that some workers offered to build him a house; and he was successful on the only two occasions when he stood for public office.

Some persons who read and write about Hamilton today will be surprised and, I fear, unwilling to hear that he was anything except a militarist and a mercantilist, a womanizer and a philistine. I see no point in anticipating the reasons why the first Henry Cabot Lodge rated him as the foremost journalist of his day, or why his enemy Jefferson mounted Hamilton's bust at Monticello as a splendid trophy of their contest. It is better to admit that Hamilton threw a genuine scare into some of the early Americans. It was not that they feared for their liberties at the hands of Hamilton the miscalled "monarchist," but rather that they feared for the virtue of their republican society at the hands of Hamilton the inspired financier.

I did not fully understand this alarm that Hamilton caused until I read Richard R. Beeman's biography of Patrick Henry. "It was commonplace among nearly all Americans," Beeman writes, "that virtue was the element that held a republican society together." The infant United States had given up the disciplines of monarchical rule, established religion, a stern criminal code, and fixed traditions. The virtue of the citizenry would have to be the chief mechanism of social control.

Patrick Henry believed this, and at first opposed the Constitution, the national bank, the entire centralization of government. He changed his mind when he saw how fragile the republic was. In the end he joined with Washington and Hamilton against Jefferson and Madison. The threat to civic virtue was little more than the fear of something new. When it was seen that men could very quickly get rich, or go bankrupt, by the Hamilton-sponsored speculation, and that tariff-protected manufactures might become as salable as domestic crops and whiskey, there was fear—but it was only fear of change. Corruption in America did not await the coming of industrialism.

Nevertheless, Americans were shocked by the golden stream which flowed when Hamilton smote the rock. After his premature death, his enemies dominated the Age of Jefferson and did their worst against his memory. But even at that period such friendly survivors as George Cabot, Timothy Pickering, Noah Webster, Rufus King, and William Kent took his part. As the generations moved, other historians and other statesmen came along as revisionists: George T. Curtis, Richard Hildreth, the elder Henry Cabot Lodge, Theodore Roosevelt, and Arthur Vandenberg. Hamilton's ideas of energetic statecraft and government-encouraged enterprise have found political expression throughout American history. The footprints he left at the Treasury Department, the Supreme Court, and Columbia University have proven to be indelible.

But as a popular figure, Hamilton had fallen into oblivion until a lady novelist discovered him. Similarly, his statecraft did not come alive until it was brought into the open by the unlikely hand of a London merchant. In 1921, Gertrude Atherton did an admiring review of *Alexander Hamilton: An Essay on American Union,* by Frederick Scott Oliver. She assumed that the author was an English country gentleman at ease in the library of a stately mansion. The 400-page work had just such trappings. She laughed at herself when she learned that Oliver was manager of Debenham and Freebody's, one of London's big department stores, and that much of his book had been written on the Underground while commuting to and from his job.

Oliver wrote Mrs. Atherton, "I am *not* a man of letters, but a man of business—somewhat in the same line as old Nicholas Cruger. I am very well aware that it was an act of presumption on my part to write of Hamilton with so little real knowledge of history; but I was urged to do so because I thought my country needed to have the principles of his great statesmanship. . . ."

No matter; Oliver knew his handicaps and chose his subject for the best of reasons. He said he undertook the work because he was unable to discover any satisfactory account of Hamilton's career. Oliver paid all deference to "the learned and diligent American authors who have discoursed upon the topic . . . but," he added, ". . . their view of the man and his epoch is in every case too 'American.' " Oliver saw Hamilton as a master statesman who belonged to the past and present of the English-speaking peoples, and to the ages.

Oliver dipped into the well of Hamilton's own recorded thoughts. Had he lived and written his memoirs, Hamilton could have answered his enemies, expressed his philosophy, discoursed upon nation-building no more cogently than did this English shopkeeper. One word, repeatedly used by Oliver, tells all: "stewardship."

Everything was in that word for Hamilton. It rejected monarchy. "The divine right of kings," Oliver quoted from Disraeli, "may have been a plea for feeble monarchs, but the divine right of government is the keystone of human progress." Hamilton believed "with his whole heart," wrote Oliver, in the "right to enforce order and to compel men to live justly [under] the ordinances of God." When Hamilton used the word "empire," Oliver noted, "It is a synonym for a great nation in contrast with a small one." The charge of his being pro-British was absurd. "His foreign policy was . . . to keep his own country safe." As to Hamilton's ideas on government, Oliver believed that "The emotional spring or motive of his endeavors was not a love or pity for his fellow-creatures, but an overwhelming sense of duty toward his Creator, whose providence had appointed him to the stewardship."

But even if the Jeffersonians and other anti-Hamiltonians had had the benefit of Oliver's interpretation, it is unlikely that they would have disliked and distrusted the great Federalist less. Another word for "stewardship" is "paternalism." Americans have never cared for self-appointed or even God-appointed guardians, and formerly they cared much less than they do now. Hamilton was born to be a nation-maker, and the American spirit was not easily moulded to his ideas. From first to last, he struggled to do good for the country against its inclination.

III

Much is made of Hamilton's powerful intellect, but he had little claim to being an original thinker. He collected other men's ideas, applied them to immediate needs, and gave full credit to his sources. Another remarkable essay, *Philosophic Premises of Hamilton's Thought,* by E. P. Panagopoulos, shows how little Hamilton relied on inspiration and innovation, and how much on proven methods. A word he used frequently was "experience." Hamilton wrote that "experience alone can determine with certainty . . . experience only can decide . . . only can solve . . . is the parent of wisdom . . . [can] demonstrate . . . manifest . . . exemplify . . . regulate . . . justify . . . verify . . . guide . . . correct."

He recognized the limits of his own experience. He went outside of it for support of his programs of law-making, banking, finance, treaty-seeking, exposition of governing principles, and the pleading of court cases. He called upon "the experience of others . . . the experience of other countries . . . the experience of centuries . . . the experience of all times . . . the experience of the future."

By this last he meant that it sometimes paid to wait and see, to "test" a proposition. He felt this way about such diverse matters as forming branches of the National Bank, about duty-free importation of iron, and about suppressing the Whiskey Rebellion, as he originally advised Washington, "till further time for reflection . . . had served to correct false impressions. . . ." Before going to war with France, he wrote in *The Stand,* it was wiser to court "experience, sad experience . . . bitter experience" instead of being "untaught by . . . experience."

He also relied on a combination of the reasoning powers with the lessons of experience. Both "reason and experience," he wrote as he was leaving the Treasury Department, should warn the country of the "great mass of expense [which] proceeds from war." But experience should also caution the people against "dreamers or impostors" who go about "promising this country a perpetual exemption from war."

Along with reason and experience, he required "the conclusion of nature . . . the voice of nature . . . the principles of . . . natural justice." He defined "what is called the law of nature" as the will of God. He wrote that "the Deity . . . has constituted an eternal and immutable law . . . obligatory upon all mankind, prior to any human institution whatever."

Hamilton regarded "common sense" as one of God's gifts to man, not to be lightly considered. He said at the Poughkeepsie Convention, "Sir, we cannot reason from probabilities alone. When we leave common sense . . . there can be no certainty, no security in our reasonings."

As lawyer, writer, and orator he could never accumulate too many "facts." He was annoyed by persons "who constantly substitute hypothesis to fact, imagination to evidence." He believed that "fact is exemplified by experience," and that "abstract theoretic propositions" are worthless unless supported by "practical knowledge."

He had a high regard for "expediency." He did not mean cheap opportunism. He meant rather that there is a time for all things. In the New York Assembly, 1787, he opposed an amendment that would have disfranchised Tory privateers. He resisted the measure because it might punish "the innocent with the guilty," but he objected on grounds of "expediency" as well as "justice." He was concerned in this postwar period with keeping well-to-do merchants in the community. He asked, "Is it expedient to force, by exclusions and discriminations, a numerous and powerful class to be unfriendly to the government?" There are at least 165 uses of "expediency" in Hamilton's writings.

Very clearly, this is an extraordinary mentality, impossible to classify, difficult to assess except by what it accomplished; and the accomplishment itself is incalculable.

IV

St. Croix, Hamilton's boyhood home which he did not choose, was called "a rich man's heaven and a poor man's hell." In the seventeenth century the West Indies was the cockpit of sea power. After 1625, St. Croix belonged successively to settlers from Holland, England, France, and Spain. France ruled after 1651, under the Knights of Malta, in the name of the Sun King, Louis XIV. By 1695 things were going so badly in Versailles that the entire French colony on St. Croix was transshipped to the island of Martinique. For some time thereafter St. Croix was shown on maps and in texts as an abandoned island. Its coastline was almost impregnable because of growths of bush, mangroves, and coconut trees. Denmark bought it from the French in 1733.

Debtors and other dregs of Copenhagen were shipped out as colonists. They "died like flies" of malaria and hookworm, writes Waldemar Westergaard, historian of the Danish West Indies. The island lowlands were the site of sugarcane plantations. The uplands produced cotton. By 1740 the Danes erected a two-hundred-foot-square fort near the Basin on the north shore, and the capital and port-city of Christiansted grew up around it. Later Frederiksted was founded on the west shore. Both were "company towns."

The labor problem was solved when all import duties on African slaves were lifted. The blacks died of smallpox and exhaustion, but the supply seemed limitless. By 1754 there were 7,566 slaves, an increase of 162 percent since 1745. Manor houses with indoor servants were rising in the lush tropical countryside, which was fanned in season by the trade winds.

There had been a servile uprising on nearby St. Thomas, and an abortive one in 1746 at St. Croix. In 1759, when Hamilton was two years old, the Christiansted government got wind of trouble and acted with vigor. Waldemar Westergaard wrote of preventive action at St. Croix:

"The alleged conspirators were punished in exemplary fashion. Some of them 'confessed,' implicating themselves and others. Gibbet, stake, wheel, noose, glowing tong—all were employed to impress upon the community the sinfulness of rebellion. Of the fourteen condemned to lose their lives, one managed to escape by suicide, but his dead body was dragged up and down the streets, thereafter suspended by one leg from the gallows, and finally taken down and burnt at the stake.

"The remainder suffered from one and one-half minutes to ninety-one hours of torture. Ten others were condemned to be sold out of the island, fifty-eight were acquitted, and six were reported as being still at large—'free as birds.' "

In Hamilton's boyhood, an elegant colonial society had taken form. "White women," noted a Lutheran minister, "are not expected to do anything here except drink tea and coffee, make calls, play cards and at times sew a little." Men took their comfort in the billiard houses and taverns, consuming enormous amounts of liquor and creating much disorder, to the consternation of the governor and company officers.

Christiansted had its Bass-End Theater, as well as nondescript "houses of diversions." The *Royal Danish American Gazette* advertised tickets at twelve shillings to see the Leeward Islands players give performances at six-thirty of *Richard III*, *Hamlet*, and *King Lear*. As the night wore on the entertainment grew lighter, with such numbers as *The Virgin Unmaskt*, *Miss in Her Teens*, and *The Fair Penitent*.

Times were good during the 1750's and 60's. In a boom year

St. Croix produced 3,457 hogsheads of sugar, much of the cane being crushed in the local windmills. The slave trade prospered, bringing the black population to almost twenty thousand by 1766, doubled in a decade. In a single year, under the governorship of Baron von Pröcke, forty-five ships went from the colonies to the homeland, to say nothing of vessels to and from the English colonies of North America. Providence, Boston, and New York supplied St. Croix with flour, dried codfish, hoops and staves for barrels, shingles for roofs, mules for the treadmills and plantations, horses for the saddles and carriages of the island aristocracy. Historian Westergaard writes:

"When in the early seventies Alexander Hamilton was serving his apprenticeship as a counting-house clerk for the firm of Nicholas Cruger, he was near the economic center of gravity in the New World."

of Cuba, and deal $8,000 [in]to pesos, and at much to the time being engaged in the local commerce. The slave trade that period, bringing the slave population to about twenty thousand by 1700, doubled in a decade. In a very concrete [way] under the governorship of [Cassa] over, Puerto [Rico], the ships went being themselves to the mainland, over nothing of vessels to and from the British colonies of North America, though to [St. John] and Key West, supplied by [Cruz] and from Guadeloupe, [home] and gave the carrots, sugar and cocoa, coffee for the [tranquil] and plantations, horses [with] saddles and carriages to the island aristocracy, numerous merchant slaves.

When in [the early] seventies Alexander Hamilton [came] into life at [the age] of [a] flourishing commercial clerk for the firm of [Nicholas Cruger], he was one of the many thousand of persons in the New World.

PART ONE

ONE CROWDED HOUR

One crowded hour of glorious life
Is worth an age without a name.
Thomas Osbert Mordaunt

CHAPTER ONE

He Finds His Country

I
(1757–1772)

Girls he liked and always would. "We fondly sport and fondly play, and love away the night." The sing-song words were the final lines of a three-stanza ode that appeared in the *Danish Royal American Gazette,* Christiansted, St. Croix, April 6, 1771. He couldn't have been pleased. He had another piece in the same issue:

> Celia's an artful slut;
> Be kind, she'll kiss, *et cetera,* but . . .

Much better. He signed his initials, A. H., in a note to the editor, giving his age as seventeen, though he was only fourteen by his own count. He was later taken to be younger than his ambitions in college and the Army would warrant, and sometimes it would thwart him. But his youthful appearance and his flattering love letters in the coming days would please a number of American girls. He was small, spruce, compact, and durable. There is a reference to "the almost feminine rosiness of his cheeks." Another description speaks of "a bright, ruddy complexion; light-colored hair, a mouth infinite in its expression, its sweet smile being most observable and most spoken of." His eyes were deep-set, dark blue. The several artists who sculpted and painted portraits of him found his features dramatic and strong.

Some of the emphasis on his fair complexion came from exasperated relatives who resented the frequent description of him as a "Creole" or a "swarthy young West Indian." Dr. Allan McLane Hamilton, grandson and biographer, was offended because "One enthusiastic negro preacher, extolling his virtues as champion of that race during the Revolutionary War, when he favored the enlistment of black soldiers, recently went so far as to suggest, at a public meeting in the city of New York, that Hamilton's veins surely contained African blood."

Dr. Hamilton obtained a lock of hair, said to have been given to his grandmother by his grandfather in December 1780, and stiffly set the record straight.

"In reality," the physician wrote in 1910, "he was fair and had reddish-brown hair, and a specimen before me proves this to be the case. It has a certain glint which probably was more marked at an earlier period; but even now there is no difficulty in finding that it belonged to a person of the semi-blonde type."

One of the kindest things that Fawn M. Brodie, the biographer of Jefferson, said about Hamilton was that these antagonists both were red-headed.

"Markets are just about the same, excepting in the price of butter which is now reduced to 15 and 16 a firkin. Your Philadelphia flour is really very bad, being of a most swarthy complexion and withall very untractable . . . I have now the pleasure to acquaint you with the arrival of your new Sloop, Thunderbolt, commanded by Capt. William Newton, a fine vessel indeed, but I fear not so swift as she ought to be. . . . 70 Mules from the Main arrived two days ago." On another occasion, in 1771, the firm advertised a sale of "Three Hundred Prime Slaves."

Hamilton's basic prose had become the business letter. Beginning as a teenage clerk, promoted rapidly to acting manager of Beekman & Cruger, which was listed in New York as Kortwright & Cruger, he wrote endlessly about cargoes, voyages, prices, sales, and collections. Beekman had retired. Most of Hamilton's correspondence was addressed to Nicholas Cruger, an easy-going bachelor, member of an industrious German family, three generations in New York.

The letter-writing drilled the young man in turning out clear, colloquial, lively reports. "The Captain talks largely of dangers and difficulties upon the Coast, but no doubt exagger-

ates a good deal (by way of stimulation) . . . his Cargo was
stow'd very Hickledy-pickledy. . . ."

Hamilton (he was almost never called by his given name) was
off to a fast start and an assured career in business, but this
did not suit him. "I always had a strong propensity to literary
pursuits," he would remember. He had reason to know good
writing. Plutarch, Pope, and a French version of Machiavelli's
The Prince were among the thirty-four volumes auctioned off
when his home was closed at his mother's death in 1768. He
had access to many of the classics at the homes of wealthy
planters, and he also had a tutor, Dr. Hugh Knox, who would
be a lifetime encourager of his bent for writing. Knox, thirty
years older than Hamilton, was an apothecary, a newspaper
editor, and a Presbyterian minister who had been brought into
the church by the Reverend Aaron Burr, founder of the College
of New Jersey at Princeton and father of the Aaron Burr who
was Hamilton's contemporary.

Knox thought the young man showed talent and deserved a
formal education. An article in the *Gazette,* attributed to
Hamilton, was titled "Rules for Statesmen." It praised the British constitution and the office of Prime Minister, observing that
a man in that post could bring "honour" to his monarch and
achieve "enlargement of his own power."

This was much better stuff than listing cargoes. He dreamed
of steeds and swords and banners, and "would willingly risk
my life, tho not my Character to exalt my station," as he told
his friend Edward Stevens in November 1769, in a letter that
would become famous in the literature of biography. Stevens
had left St. Croix to study medicine at King's College, New
York. The rest of the letter is Alexander Hamilton in any
period of his life, self-revealed: ". . . for to confess my weakness, Ned, my ambition is prevalent. . . . I contemn the grov-
e'ling and condition of a Clerk. . . . I wish there was a war."

The letter from which the following is a brief excerpt was
addressed to his father at nearby St. Vincent island, and concerned a hurricane that struck the island of Nevis in 1772.

"Honoured Sir. . . . It began about dusk, at North, and
raged violently until ten o'clock. . . . Good God! What horror

and destruction—it's impossible for me to describe—or for you to form any idea of it. It seemed as if a total dissolution of Nature were taking place. The roaring of the sea and wind—the fiery meteors flying about in the air—the prodigious glare of almost perpetual lightning—the crash of falling houses—the ear-piercing shrieks of the distressed were sufficient to strike astonishment into Angels. . . ."

The Hurricane Letter appeared unsigned in the *Gazette,* September 6, 1772, but soon the author was revealed. Few writers were ever so well paid for an early effort, for at Dr. Knox's instigation, the young man's publisher, his employer, his maternal relatives, Ned Stevens' father, and probably the Danish Governor, Major General P. Claussen, made up a purse. They staked him to a passage to the continent and a college education there.

CHAPTER TWO

He Joins the Revolution

I
(1772–1773)

Hamilton was writing poetry again, this time with an elegiac tone, lamenting the death of Elias Boudinot's child.

> The unrelenting hand of death,
> Regardless of a parent's prayer
> Has stopt my lovely Infant's breath.

He was a part-time guest at the Boudinots' home, Boxwood Hall, in the village of Elizabethtown, New Jersey. He came well introduced by letters from Hugh Knox, and soon enjoyed the acquaintance of the first families of the state. This pretty town had a "fine church with steeple and chimes," as well as a good preparatory academy housed in a two-story wooden building topped by a cupola. The school's headmaster was Francis Barber, a graduate of Nassau Hall, class of 1767. Hamilton would fight nearly the whole Revolutionary War with Barber. He would serve in Congress with Boudinot, and in the Constitutional Convention with another new acquaintance, William Livingston, the state's wartime governor, sometimes called "the Whipping Post" because of his leanness. Hamilton's capacity for friendship, his attachment to letters, his thrusting ambition, had come with him from dockside in Boston, through New York, to Elizabethtown Academy, where his purpose was to cram on Latin, Greek, and mathematics. He intended to enter Nassau Hall as soon as he could pass the entrance examinations. By early 1773 he was ready.

When he first saw Nassau Hall, the College of New Jersey,

it was part of a small farming village, built of local brown stone and standing like a citadel "on the highest ground . . . which gives it a lofty appearance." It fronted the New York-to-Philadelphia highway across four and a half acres of nearly treeless campus, "walled in with stone and lime." Inside this impressive three-story oblong building, with its "three cross and one long entry on the first story," he faced a bust of Homer and portraits of the royal family. There was a modest library to which the college head had contributed three hundred of his own books brought from Scotland, a long hallway with a stage for plays and debates, and a tall Presbyterian pulpit. The dining gallery and the sleeping quarters were light-filled and pleasant, for "every chamber opens into these entries, rendering communication vastly more convenient."

Of the Reverend John Witherspoon, sixth president of the college, when he mounted the pulpit, one of his congregation wrote: "He is an intolerably homely old Scotchman and speaks in the true dialect of his country, except that his brogue borders on the Irish. He is a bad speaker, has no oratory . . . yet the correctness of his style, the arrangement of his matter and the many new ideas that he suggested, rendered his sermon very entertaining."

This stern pedant had set out to give the middle colonies an institution of learning the equal of Harvard and Yale in New England, and William and Mary in Virginia. He aimed to surpass these older colleges in reach and influence, and therefore openly solicited students from a distance. He had enrolled James Madison, Jr., and Henry Lee of Virginia, as well as several British colonials from the West Indies, to mingle with such New Jersey boys as William Paterson, Aaron Burr, and Philip Freneau. But Witherspoon also wished to prevent his college from becoming a playground for the sons of wealth and station, and he had set high and democratic standards for entrance.

Hamilton found all this to his liking, especially the Witherspoon Rule Book, in which it was written that "no school-master or others . . . may have reason to complain of advantage taken against them." Applicants were invited to bring along their tutors to insure just treatment. "By this means . . . all suspicion of unfairness and partiality will be effectively prevented."

With such encouragement, Hamilton tried for something better than routine admission. He called on Dr. Witherspoon, bringing along a New York sponsor, Hercules Mulligan, who recalled: "I went with him to Princeton to the House of Dr. Witherspoon . . . with whom I was well acquainted, and I introduced Mr. Hamilton to him and proposed to him to Examine the young gentleman which Dr. Witherspoon did to his entire satisfaction."

They met with the president in his house on the west corner of the college lot, which also contained the kitchen, the steward's house, the fire engine shed, and an outhouse. Witherspoon was heavily built, of medium size, blue-eyed and thick-browed. He had standard advice for politically minded students.

"Lads, if it should fall to the lot of any of ye, as it may do, to appear in the theater of public life, let me impress upon your minds two rules in oratory that are never to be departed from upon any occasion whatever—Ne'er do ye speak unless ye ha' something to say, and when ye be done, be sure and leave off."

After being examined, Hamilton requested that, if accepted, he be allowed to advance as fast as he could, and graduate as soon as possible. Dr. Witherspoon listened attentively "to so unusual a proposition from so young a person," said Mulligan. A fortnight later, Hamilton received a disappointing letter from Witherspoon, stating that the trustees declined the request as "contrary to the usage of the College and expressed his regret. . . ."

In point of fact, Hamilton's was not "so unusual a proposition." Madison "commenced" in 1771, having done the four-year course in two, and Burr graduated in 1772, having entered in the sophomore class. But the admissions were becoming formalized. Hamilton left no record of feeling ill-used. He returned to New York, forever after his home, which would love and honor him in life and death.

II
(1773–1776)

From shipboard in the bay, New York City struck one voyager as "altogether as fine and pleasing a view as I ever saw." It was a "well-filled town, with the many steeples of its churches, the turret of the statehouse and 'Change dispersed among its buildings, and a multitude of shipping with which it is perpetually thronged."

One who saw this harbor view in October 1762, a decade before Hamilton did, was the handsome twenty-six-year-old bachelor, the Reverend Doctor Myles Cooper, a schoolmaster second only to Hugh Knox in the influence and inspiration he was to bring to this student. Cooper, although orphaned early and left to make his own way, had been superbly educated at Christ College, Oxford University, and had come to America at the instigation of the Archbishop of Canterbury and the authorities at Oxford to be the second president of King's College, succeeding the aging Doctor Samuel Johnson. The youthful Anglican priest and teacher was as different as possible from the homely, dour Witherspoon, and very soon he and Hamilton became acquainted and "greatly attached."

King's College had received its first gift of land from nearby Trinity Church, under two absolute conditions. The college president must always be an Anglican, and the Church of England liturgy must be used in the morning and evening services at the college—forever. Students were required to attend these services daily, morning and evening. In addition, at the commencement and other ceremonial occasions there would be, in College Hall, "a short and elegant Latin speech by the Reverend President, from whence the students in their gowns and uncovered, proceeded to St. George's Chapel" on the campus.

Cooper had been moved when he first saw King's. He wrote that the gray stone college building, constructed between 1756 and 1760, "command[s] from the eminence on which it stands a most extensive and beautiful prospect of the opposite shore and country of New York, the City and Island of New York, Long Island, Staten Island, New York Bay with its islands, the

Narrows, forming the mouth of the Harbour . . . totally unencumbered by any adjacent buildings and admitting the purest circulation of air from the river, and every other quarter, [it] has the benefit of as agreeable and healthy a situation as can possibly be conceived."

Wealthy Episcopalians had subscribed generously to raise the building and to stock it well. The college president brought a large gift of books from Oxford and instructed an agent in England to solicit more. "Nothing but Libraries," he wrote this agent, "can make us learned; and nothing but learning can make us wiser than we are; and till we *are* made wiser . . . we can never be happy."

Cooper spent his own money to buy from John Singleton Copley of Boston a painting entitled, "The Nun with the Candle Before Her," and with this purchase started an art collection which he housed in the college library. Under his administration, ties with the Crown were further strengthened. Royal Governor Tryon endowed the chair for municipal law, and George III the Professorship of Divinity.

Hamilton applied to this dashing, self-confident cleric for admission on the same terms which had been rejected at Princeton. Other students, including John Jay in 1760, took written tests, but Hamilton apparently was admitted by oral examination. Jay had been required to render "the first three of Tully's orations and the first six books of Virgil's Aeneid into English, and the first two chapters of St. John's Gospel into Latin." He was to prove himself "well versed in Latin grammar and expert in Arithmetic as far as reduction." With only a limited tutoring in the classical languages from Knox and Barber, it is improbable that Hamilton could have passed such a severe test. However, he did pass the examination he was given, entered the most cultivated and royalist institution in America, and began, in his association with Cooper, a formative experience.

The acceptance into this classical and exquisite academic community was in itself formative. It fixed Hamilton's belief in personal privilege. He had been boarding with Mulligan, a fashionable men's tailor by trade; now he moved to the college dormitory. John Parke Custis, George Washington's stepson, lived there briefly in the same year, 1773, and he described the lodgings in a letter to his mother:

"I have a large parlour with two Studies or closets, each large enough to contain a bed, trunk & a couple of chairs . . . my chamber & parlour are paper'd with a cheap but very pretty Paper, the other is painted; my furniture consists of six chairs, 2 tables with a few paltry pictures. I have an excellent Bed, & in short every thing very convenient & clever."

Few store clerks from a distant island had such entrée as Hamilton was allowed in both New Jersey and New York. He was welcomed at King's by Ned Stevens, who looked enough like him to foster the rumor that they were brothers. Hamilton's roommate was Robert Troup, "a pleasant, laughing fellow." Troup wrote that Samuel and Henry Nichols were their "particular associates." Nicholas Fish, Marinus Willet, and Gulian C. Verplanck were new acquaintances who became lifelong friends.

Cooper's other students had aristocratic New York names, such as Livingston, Ramsen, Griswold, Reid, De Peyster, Philipse, Colden, Watts, Van Schaik, Skeene, Moore, and Ogden. They came from families which dined "in the English style, plain but plentiful, the wines excellent . . . the servants in livery."

Princeton would not have suited Hamilton nearly as well. Plain Presbyterianism was not for him, though Knox had brought him up in it and, some said, baptized him into that church. Many New York Tories attended Sunday worship at the college's St. George's Chapel. "This is a magnificent edifice," wrote a visitor. "The tower and steeple are larger and higher than any other in America. The inside of the church is very large. Some paintings and carvings."

Hamilton always regarded himself as belonging to the Anglican Episcopal Church. He never joined formally and never explained the omission to do so, except to regret it. But to feel part of such an institution was fully in character. A British writer would one day call him "an enjoying English gentleman."

He studied the regular courses of languages, philosophy, and mathematics. In addition, he took some anatomy, perhaps feeling inclined or obligated to return some day to practice medicine at St. Croix. But early in 1773 he wrote out a list of twenty-seven books in his possession, and they were works of history and philosophy; none were on medicine.

President Cooper lived among the boys, the better to guide their studies and enter their pranks in the Oxonian Black Book or Book of Misdemeanors, 1771–75. Often, it appears from Cooper's verses, favorite students—

> . . . Filled my peaceful cell
> Where harmless jest and modest mirth,
> And cheerful laughter, oft had birth
> And joy was wont to dwell.

At other times there was some fighting, drinking, pilfering, and wenching. A Scottish visitor noted "the entrance to this college is thro' one of the streets where the most noted prostitutes lived . . . a temptation to the youth."

Several close friends of Hamilton—Troup, Nicholl, Willet, Verplanck—made the Black Book, but Hamilton gained the president's attention in other ways. It is written in the *New York Historical Society Quarterly* that Cooper "rangled in the classroom" in political disputes with Hamilton. They were amicable contests, and the new student admitted "strong prejudices on the ministerial side" for a while. It is not remarkable that he was drawn by temperament and admiration to the opinions of this schoolmaster, whom Gulian Verplanck would call "a wit and scholar whose learning and accomplishments gave him a personal popularity and respect with his pupils and, of course, added authority to his opinions, and those were the opinions and prejudices of the high-toned English University Tory."

Cooper, along with the Reverend Samuel Seabury and other Loyalists, had a committee for "watching all that should be published, whether in Pamphlets or News-Papers, and for suffering nothing to pass unanswered, that had a tendency to lessen the respect or affection that is due to the Mother Country."

In the rough port city Hamilton also made contacts of a different sort. Two older men in particular excited his admiration. One was Alexander McDougall, son of an immigrant milkman, who had gone to sea as commander of two privateers, *Tyger* and *Barrington,* in 1756–63, and brought back a fortune to New York. When Hamilton came to know him in the 1770's, McDougall was a radical leader with "great fire and vehemence," more than once jailed for seditious pamphleteering, a member of popular committees, a presider at mass meetings.

The other was John Lamb, whose father had been transported to America as punishment for a daring burglary. Lamb manufactured mathematical instruments when not riding on raids with the Sons of Liberty and making himself generally "turbulent and troublesome" to the authorities.

These fresh acquaintances, the college president, the students, and the townsmen, all had much that Hamilton lacked —family, wealth, position, accomplishment. But he was made to feel at home in their company. They were attracted to him, as men would always be, by his smart looks, high spirit, and superlatively active mind, which he now again applied to writing.

III

(1774–1775)

Warmly received in New York by royalist and rebel alike, Hamilton's political sympathies might have taken any conceivable direction save one. He was not formed to be a neutral.

His writings show that his feelings moved ahead of his mind. Like a bold rider to the hounds, he threw his heart over the fences and followed hard behind. He joined the rebel cause with two long polemical essays published during 1774–75 in Holt's *New York Journal.* "A Full Vindication of the Measures of the Congress" and "The Farmer Refuted" were in rebuttal of Tory publications by Myles Cooper's associate, the Reverend Samuel Seabury. It was a duel of pseudonyms at first. Seabury, aged forty-six, signed himself "A Westchester Farmer." Hamilton rightly inscribed himself "A Friend to America."

He had been reading Locke and Montesquieu, as well as Blackstone, and these authorities assured him that God had written the laws of nature long before there were any man-made statutes. Hamilton was very devout at this time of his life. Troup says he began and ended each day on his knees. It was not cant for Hamilton to write that God intended man to be free, and that civil government was nothing but a voluntary compact between the rulers and the ruled. *"Civil liberty is only natural liberty, modified and secured by the sanctions of civil society."* The subdued poet in him almost broke bonds as he tried to express this conviction in newspaper prose.

"The sacred rights of mankind are not to be rummaged for among old parchments and musty records. They are written, as with a sunbeam, in the whole volume of human nature, by the hand of Deity itself, and can never be erased or obscured by mortal power. . . ."

He had also read Machiavelli and Hume, and they gave him a lifelong skepticism about the altruism of men and nations, especially as related to international alliances. "A vast majority of mankind," he wrote in the "Vindication" essay, "is entirely biased by motives of self-interest." But he used the measured logic of the business letter to refute the Westchester Farmer's argument that the colonists' military cause was hopeless.

"Our numbers are very considerable; the courage of Americans has been tried and proved. Contests for liberty have ever been found the most bloody, implacable and obstinate. The disciplined troops Great Britain could send against us would be but few. Our superiority in numbers would over-balance our inferiority in discipline. It would be a hard if not an impracticable task to subjugate us by force."

He would concede nothing to the Farmer's respect for British sea power. "Even this would not be so terrible as he pretends," Hamilton answered. "We can live without trade of any kind." An early believer in American self-sufficiency, he went on to list the indigenous resources for food, fiber, and leather. He proposed the development of an Oriental textile industry. "It would not be unbecoming employment for our daughters to provide silks of their own country. The silkworm answers as well here as in any part of the world." He ended the first essay with a salute to the Continental Congress: "May God give you wisdom . . . for the cause and virtue and mankind."

The Tory watchdog committee recognized talent and sought him out. Hamilton received "a most liberal offer by Myles Cooper to write for the royalist cause," but he ignored it. Patriot readers found the essays so good that they thought an experienced practitioner, John Jay perhaps, must have written them. When Jay disclaimed authorship, Hamilton was sometimes pointed out on the streets as the "collegian" who had composed those fifty thousand words of eloquence and logic.

He was the more easily identifiable because of his study-habit of walking alone and memorizing his lessons by murmuring them aloud. On the evening of July 6, 1774, some well-wishers hoisted him to a speaking platform in the "Fields," or park, at one of McDougall's rallies. Hamilton made the transition from writer to orator with a stirring address about "our brethren . . . now suffering in the common cause" at Boston, and about "the waves of rebellion, sparkling with fire and washing back on the shores of England the wrecks of her power, her wealth, her glory."

His speech was a popular success and often quoted. He had leaped to the same level of reputation that had been his in St. Croix—a young master in gallant control of the English language.

IV

(1775–1776)

Late in 1774 he signed up, along with Fish and Troup, with a cadre of volunteers, and drilled daily in the college's St. George's Churchyard.

Their training officer, Major Edward Fleming, "had been the Adjutant of a British Regiment . . . an excellent disciplinarian . . . ardently attached to the American cause." Hamilton soon became, his friends observed, "exceedingly expert in the manual exercise."

In the spring of 1775 the Continental Congress ordered New York to organize its militia, and Hamilton's cadre was incorporated into a battalion. By now he had undertaken serious study of artillery under his mathematics professor, Robert Harpur, whom he paid off for the special instructions much later, in 1783. The baptism of fire came in August '75 when *Asia,* a British man-o'-war of seventy-four guns, appeared in the harbor. Orders came for the Americans to remove some cannon which had been mounted on the Battery, and Hamilton went there by night under command of "that restless genius," Captain John Lamb.

Somebody fired at *Asia's* barge, at which the warship swung into place and loosed a broadside that sent shot skittering into the Battery and to nearby housetops. Mulligan remembers Hamilton tugging at cannon, "notwithstanding the firing continued." Troup recalled the barrage "during which Hamilton, who was aiding at the removal of the cannon, exhibited the greatest unconcern, although one of his companions was killed at his side."

His formal education virtually closed on this burst of gunfire. On April 4, 1776, General Thomas Mifflin, the Army quartermaster, requested of the Committee of Safety that "houses in an airy part of the city may be immediately prepared for a general hospital, capable of containing 800 sick." College authorities protested bitterly at their orders, but "the Students were dispersed, the Library, Apparatus &c &c were deposited in the City Hall, & the College was turned into an Hospital."

Hamilton may have continued some haphazard study, since instruction was carried on at the house of Leonard Lispenard, 13 Wall Street. Doctor Cooper was gone by now. On the night of May 10,. 1775, a mob of four hundred patriots had broken through the college gate, and "would certainly have committed the most violent abuse upon him if he had happily not saved himself by Flight."

He would hardly have made it without help from Hamilton, Troup, and Nicholas Ogden. As Troup told it later, Hamilton distracted the crowd with a speech, but Cooper in his night clothes mistook the purpose and bawled through the window, "He's crazy . . . crazy." The schoolmaster never did understand what Hamilton was trying to do for him, for he wrote a poem commemorating the adventure without mentioning his favorite student. "Stanzas written on the Evening of the 10th of May, 1776," appeared in the July issue of *The Gentleman's Magazine,* London:

> Hear me, Indulgent Heaven!
> Oh, may they call their arms away,
> To Thee and George submission pay,
> Repent and be forgiven.

With Cooper gone, the Reverend Benjamin Moore, assistant rector of Trinity Church, became the college president pro tempore. Moore would one day administer the last rites to the dying Hamilton.

The action at the Battery was something less than a battle, but it was a convincing forecast of battles to come. In January 1776, when the New York provincial congress called for the mobilization of an artillery company, Hamilton applied for the captaincy on the merit of his training and study. Colonel McDougall recommended the appointment, but his youthful appearance was a disadvantage to him. Hamilton was required to take an examination, which he easily passed.

"A Certificate of Stephen Badlam, Cap of Artillery, was read and filed. He thereby certifies that he has examined Alexander Hamilton and judges him qualified to command a company of artillery. Ordered: That the same Alexander Hamilton be and he is hereby appointed Captain of the Provincial Company of Artillery of this Colony."

He used the funds provided by his St. Croix backers to recruit and equip the company, and later was given a bounty for each new recruit. Known as the Corsicans, afterwards as the Hearts of Oak, his ninety-three-man command was turned out smartly in blue coats with buff cuffs and facings. They were armed with 12-pounder and 24-pounder cannon. He drilled the men hard, had them flogged into obedience, promoted some from the ranks, and developed a model unit. He gave personal attention to the rights of his men.

"Gentlemen," he addressed the Provincial Congress of the Colony of New York, "I take the liberty to request your attention to a few particulars. . . . The most material is respecting the pay. . . . My own pay will remain the same as it now is; but I make this application on behalf of the company. . . ."

Hamilton impressed his superiors and won special privileges. A standing order was issued to permit the boarding of any ship in the harbor to "make a strict search for any men who may have deserted from Captain Hamilton's Company."

CHAPTER THREE

War Is One Defeat After Another

I
(1776–1777)

On July 12, Hamilton's company was stationed at Fort George on the southern tip of Manhattan. Two British warships, *Phoenix* and *Rose,* sailed boldly through the narrows and into the harbor. They swept the town with broadsides, causing panic among the citizens. General George Washington, recently arrived from Boston, wrote Congress: "The shrieks and cries of these poor creatures running every way with their children, were truly distressing, and I fear they will have an unhappy effect on the ears and minds of our young and inexperienced soldiery."

Washington also reported that "a heavy and incessant cannonade was kept up from our several batteries here." These included Hamilton's company, enjoying the exhilarating experience of its first artillery duel. Little damage was done to the British ships, but one of the Hearts of Oak cannons exploded and blew the leg off a gunner's mate, William Douglas.

"He is therefore recommended," wrote Captain Hamilton, the model unit commander, "to the attention of those who have been appointed to carry into execution the late resolves of the Continental Congress, by which provision is made for all persons disabled in the service of the United States."

Hamilton marched the Hearts of Oak to Brooklyn Heights, where Washington planned to deny General Sir William Howe the high ground. Hardly sooner had the captain viewed the lay of the land than he decided it was untenable. He sent a note to that effect to General Washington. This was probably their first communication.

The Commander in Chief had already reached the same conclusion, and was lucky to get his main force back to Manhattan under cover of night and falling weather. Hamilton set up his guns at a little fort called Bunker Hill, but there was another American runaway when General Howe attacked. A few days later, Hamilton saw the rebels make a successful stand at Harlem Heights, where his men had raised breastworks to shield their guns. "At this place," wrote his son, "Hamilton first attracted the observant eye of Washington who, on inspection of the works he was engaged in throwing up, entered into a conversation . . . and formed a high estimate of his military capacity."

Washington fell back from Harlem Heights to White Plains, where on October 28 Captain Hamilton had the first real chance to distinguish himself. A history of the U.S. Field Artillery reads: "Concealed by the heavy foliage of trees and shrubs, Hamilton planted two field pieces on a ledge of rocks and commanded the place where the enemy were at work erecting a bridge across the Bronx [River]. He opened fire, killing several of the enemy and throwing the Hessians into confusion. The British rushed up the hill to capture the guns but were driven back. A second charge was more successful and the brigade and battery were forced to retire."

Unhappily, the Commander had left a garrison of 2,600 troops at Fort Washington, covering Harlem Heights, and these were deftly taken by the British. There commenced another disheartening retreat, with the depleted American army—down to three thousand men—fleeing into New Jersey, and General Cornwallis's army, eight thousand strong, on its traces.

At New Brunswick the Continentals were crossing the Raritan River when the British advance guard arrived; ". . . some of 'em are now in sight," Washington scribbled in a note to Congress. The Chief was relieved to hear "a smart cannonade" from a height looking down on the river. It was Hamilton's men. Their barrage covered Washington's retreat into Princeton on December 1, and this action won Hamilton a battle monument. On the campus of Rutgers University stands a metal plaque bearing the inscription:

"Here early in December 1776 ALEXANDER HAMILTON (graduate of King's College) with his battery of horse artillery covered the ford of the Raritan delaying the advance of the British across the river while WASHINGTON withdrew through Princeton to Trenton. By the class of 1899."

Washington, "charmed by the brilliant courage and admirable skill" of this artillerist, "sent to learn his name." Hearing that it was Captain Hamilton again, the Commander at the next halt "claimed him for his own," and the General's aide, Robert Hanson Harrison, gave the fighting captain a nickname—"the Little Lion."

Reputation had come quickly, and he was frequently recognized ". . . leading and pointing in the thick of a fight, or trudging contentedly at the head of his battery while his charger helped to drag the cannon." Both Washington Irving and Sir George Trevelyan would quote in their books from wartime memoirs:

"I noticed a youth, a mere stripling, slender, almost delicate in frame, marching beside a piece of artillery, with a cocked hat pulled down over his eyes, apparently lost in thought; with his hand resting on a cannon, and every now and again patting it, as if it were a favorite horse or a pet plaything."

On Christmas afternoon, 1776, Hamilton again covered a river crossing. Washington ordered his thin and shivering ranks, with horses and cannon, aboard barges at McKonkey's Ferry on the Delaware. The temperature fell with the darkness. A Connecticut man remembered that "as violent a storm ensued of hail & snow as I ever felt." Midnight approached, and a Delaware man lived to write, "The frost was sharp, the current difficult . . . the ice increasing . . . the wind high, and at eleven it began to snow."

But up to three thousand men and eighteen field pieces went across, Hamilton among the last. He came up fast to join the surprise attack on Trenton. Trevelyan picked him out. "Alexander Hamilton—who marched with the reserve, and was therefore the last to unlimber—discharged shell with deadly accuracy into the leading company of the Von Lossberg regiment as it emerged from Church Alley."

It was Washington's first field victory, netting him 918 prisoners. He retired across Assanpink Creek, a tributary of the Delaware, and on New Year's Eve moved out again, his objective the troops under Cornwallis at Princeton. At dawn on January 3, the Continentals entered the college town, where Hamilton impressed an eyewitness who furnished the account to Washington Irving:

"Well do I recall the day when Hamilton's company marched into Princeton. It was a model of discipline; at its head was a boy, and I wondered at his youth, but what was my first surprise when, struck with his diminutive figure, he was pointed out to me as that Hamilton of whom we had already heard so much."

Trevelyan finds him in action at the campus: ". . . young Alexander Hamilton, with the irreverence of a student from a rival place of education, planted his guns on the sacred grass of the academic campus, and fired a six-pound shot which is said to have passed through the head of George the Second's portrait in the Chapel."

The American version differs, saying that British troops had taken refuge in Nassau Hall, and that Hamilton ordered them out, and fired to expedite their decision to surrender. No matter the details, this terrible winter campaign had saved the Revolution, and the young captain who accompanied his Chief to quarters in Morristown had become a veteran. On January 20, 1777, Washington found time to dash off a letter which he entrusted to Harrison. "Be so good as to forward the Inclosed to Captn Hamilton." It was the formal invitation to join the Commander's staff.

II

(1777)

It was good to put on the epaulettes of lieutenant colonel, mount the green riband of an aide-de-camp, and get a pay raise to forty-four dollars a month. But he had mixed feelings about it all. He had already turned down two staff appointments, and meanwhile had made his name in combat. The Army was being reorganized with additional artillery, and there was a good chance for a regimental command. "Hamilton hesitated much," his son would write, with confirmation from Hamilton's correspondence, "before he decided to relinquish this advantage . . . but [was] influenced by the reputation of the commander-in-chief."

Morristown, the winter headquarters which lay between protective hills, described by one of the officers' ladies as "a clever little village," had three spired churches, two excellent taverns, some fifty dwellings, and the manor house of the wealthy Morris family, New Jersey branch. Oddly for a poet and journalist, Hamilton did not count the church spires, or name the taverns, or describe any of the Morristown buildings.

Stranger still, the author of the Hurricane Letter had, between the autumn of 1776 and the following spring, witnessed almost unbroken violence by man and Nature, and yet recorded none of it. As his artillery company staggered out of Manhattan in September, he could have looked across his shoulder and seen the New York wharfs afire, and the flames sweeping across Broadway, consuming Trinity Church and halting only at the open land in front of King's College. He had crossed the Hudson in darkness amid storm and gunfire, crossed the Delaware in a blizzard, made freezing marches, and fought a half dozen engagements from Long Island to Princeton, but he wrote nothing of it, and nothing about the gentler aspects of Nature in autumn and spring, in earth and sky.

Tom Paine, a volunteer with Brigadier General Nathanael Greene, composed and published *The Crisis* during the New Jersey campaign. Major Aaron Burr, with Brigadier General Israel Putnam, was keeping his sister Sally, his uncle Timothy Edwards, and his cousin Matthias Ogden posted on both his opinions and his adventures from Quebec to Morristown. But Hamilton was not ready to resume serious writing. His attention at first went to the General's correspondence and other military matters. Here at Morristown he presided at the General's table and flirted by letter with Catherine Livingston, the Governor's daughter:

"ALL FOR LOVE is my motto. You may make such comment as you please. . . ."

He grew bolder:

". . . I challenge you to meet me in whatever path you dare; and if you have no objection, for variety and amusement, we will even sometimes make excursions in the flowery walks, and roseate bowers of Cupid. You know, I am renowned for gallantry. . . ."

As warm days arrived, idleness became tedium in the camp. Men and officers gambled, quarrelled, malingered in hospitals to avoid boresome duties and to shirk dangerous ones, such as raids against the British to bring in provisions and intelligence. Drink took a toll. Washington believed that "the benefits arising from the moderate use of strong liquor have been experienced in all armies and are not to be disputed. . . ." However, ". . . there cannot be a greater failure in a soldier than drunkenness."

The aide felt a duty to spare the Commander needless bother. He intercepted a letter from Alexander McDougall, by now a Brigadier, and said of Washington, "I find him so much pestered with matters which cannot be avoided, that I am obliged to refrain from troubling him . . . especially when I conceive the only answer he would give, may be given by myself."

Hamilton yearned for cannon. He liked a model lately forged at Philadelphia and brought to Headquarters. "It weighs 227 lbs, carries a three pound ball," he noted. "The iron is wrought hooped and welded together. The General and others esteem it a great acquisition. It had been fired twenty times as fast as possible, and is supposed to be a thorough proof. For my part I am rather dubious of this matter, and have recommended 50 successive charges instead of 20. . . . We cannot have too respectful an artillery. . . ."

Brigadier General Henry Knox was chief of artillery, but Hamilton was making himself an authority. One of the resolutions of the Provincial Convention of New York, dated April 24, 1777, was this: "Resolved, That Major Lawrence and Capt. Rutgers be a committee with Colonel Robert Livingston on the subject of making field cannon out of wrought iron; and that the committee of correspondence be directed to write to Colonel Hamilton for his opinion on the usefulness of such artillery."

He read and wrote the General's letters, did some drinking,

and amused the ladies, but also resumed the life of the mind. The Morris family manor house contained an excellent library. The Commander gave him permission to explore it. The aide holed up there to study what he discovered, and possibly also what he had brought from King's College in his knapsack. He had with him Plutarch's *Lives,* Demosthenes' *Orations,* and Malachy Postlethwayt's *Universal Dictionary of Trade and Commerce.*

Two of Hamilton's military contemporaries also carried a luggage of books to war. In 1796, Colonel Arthur Wellesley, the future Duke of Wellington, set off for India with what biographer Longfurd calls "his small library." It included works of Julius Caesar, Locke, Paley, Plutarch, Rousseau, Adam Smith, and Voltaire. Napoleon Bonaparte somewhat later, in 1798, went to Egypt with Hanno, Livy, Polybius, Tacitus, Thucydides, and Virgil.

Of early American leaders, Samuel Eliot Morrison would write, "These men were not fitted for public responsibility by courses in civics, sociology and psychology, but by the study of Plutarch's *Lives,* of the orations of Cicero and Demosthenes and of Thucydides."

Hamilton filled 112 unused pages of his company paybook with items and comments. He wrote with a stream of consciousness that showed where his thoughts went. They went to sex, to Greek and Roman history, to what he called "political arithmetic," or economics. He copied out, among others, the legends of Phaedra, Theseus' wife, who felt a passionate love for her son Hippolytus; of Romulus and Remus, who were born when the daughter of King Tharsetius refused to lie with the god Priapus, and sent her serving maid instead; of the Spartan festivals, at which "the virgins should go naked as well as the young men, and in this manner dance in their presence."

Hamilton would keep his Notes and make use of them for the rest of his life. References to ancient history and biography embellished hundreds of his essays and orations. Many of his legislative measures and policy papers would reflect his knowledge of the remote past. He marked the liberalism of certain kings and the absolutism of others. He noted the practice in

Athens of allowing the magistrates to interpret the law. He
learned about land reforms, the redistribution of wealth, the
rise and fall of societies.

Many of the data in Postlethwayt's *Dictionary* were out of
date, but the economic theories generally held true. In coming
years Hamilton would adapt his Notes to current matters: public credit, useful manufactures, and a mint for the coining of
money. He was intrigued to read that Queen Elizabeth, whose
reign he admired on several counts, had ordered the beginning
of coined money in England. He wrote himself a query:

"Would it not be advisable to let all taxes, even those imposed
by the States, be collected by persons of Congressional appointment, and would it not be advisable to pay the collectors so
much per cent of the sums collected?"

The studies confirmed his conviction that the British order
government better than other nations. Englishmen with a
knowledge of trade and economics, the use of capital and application of force, made fortunes for themselves and prosperity
for their country. He saw how greatly England benefited by her
naval and merchant fleets, but also how necessary it was for
a mercantile country to maintain a measure of domestic self-
sufficiency. Everything earned above it was a national profit.
Postlethwayt wrote and Hamilton read: "The Spanish gave it
the name of the New World and not improperly, it being such
an immense tract that it exceeds any of the other three parts
of the old. . . ."

How enormous, then, were the opportunities offered by this
struggle for independence! Great exertions were required of the
patriots. In their minds, as well as in battle.

III

(1777)

In March Hamilton began to call for exertions, first from
civilian leaders, and through them from the people. It was
almost like writing those exhortations in Holt's *Journal,* when
he responded to the invitation of the New York Committee of
Correspondence, William Allison, Robert R. Livingston, and

Gouverneur Morris: "Gentlemen, With cheerfulness I embrace the proposal of corresponding with your convention. . . ."

Cheerfulness! He felt a duty to spread optimism among the politicians. He wrote the committeemen that the Army's daily skirmishes were wearing down the British forces, and that no day passed without a deserter coming into the American lines. It was learned from these sources, he declared, that the enemy regiments were riddled with discontent.

He salted his letters with rumors that France was on the verge of intervening. He quieted the committee's foreboding that General John Burgoyne might carry out an invasion of northern New York State, even make a juncture with General Howe that would cut the United States in two. The enemy would need midsummer weather, he declared, "before the roads will be fit for the transportation of Artillery, which is an essential instrument in their operations. . . ."

By April he was forced down off this plateau of calm assurance. He admitted his predictions to be "shaken" but not "overthrown." By May the Hudson country was throbbing with the march of 9,500 effectives under Burgoyne. The Delaware Bay region was in a dither over Howe's activities.

Hamilton's springtime optimism had miscarried, no doubt of that. Ticonderoga fell to Burgoyne on July 5. On July 23 a British fleet of 260 sail left New York and put Howe's troops ashore south of Philadelphia. Washington moved the headquarters to Wilmington, Delaware. Hamilton still would not feed defeatism to apprehensive men. He wrote the Committee of Correspondence:

"Our army is in high health and spirits. We shall, I hope, have twice the enemy's numbers. I would not only fight them, but I would attack them; for I hold it an established maxim, that there is three to one in favor of the party attacking."

Howe outnumbered Washington fifteen thousand to ten thousand in regular troops. The Chief drew up his army by a stream that flows past Wilmington and into the Delaware. Brandywine Creek would make the history books. Old Hugh Knox answered a long letter from Hamilton:

"Mark this: You must be the Annalist & Biographer, as well

as the Aide de Camp, of General Washington, & his Historiographer of the American War! I take the liberty to insist on this and hope you will take Minutes and keep a Journal! . . .

"This may be a new & strange thought to you; but if you survive the present troubles, I see few men will be better qualified to write the History of the present Glorious Struggle."

IV
(September–October 1777)

At Chadd's Ford, on Brandywine Creek, Hamilton heard the shells roaring overhead. The troops raised a cheer as the Commander strode by with his aides to inspect the lines. Had the enemy strength been known, the Continentals could have crossed in superior numbers. But this was the battle when intelligence broke down badly. Late in the day, trailed by Hamilton and other aides, Washington galloped toward the new sound of guns and encountered fugitives making for the rear. Trying to stop the runaways, a late addition to the staff, the Marquis de Lafayette, got a bullet in the leg. Hamilton and John Laurens pushed on to the front in time to see Major General John Sullivan "animating and encouraging the Men to their duty, but to no avail."

The line broke. Washington had lost another battle. He ordered retreat, but called for Hamilton and Captain Henry Lee of Virginia. Let them take a cavalry troop and destroy stores of provisions that were cached in mills along the Schuylkill. Off they galloped to the first of the mills. They saw it on the river bank at the bottom of a steep hill. Hamilton posted two lookouts at the crest with orders to fire their weapons and flee if the enemy showed up in force. He and Lee with several cavalrymen went to the mill, but before putting it to the torch, Hamilton confiscated a flat-bottomed boat near the bridge. He had hardly done so when the men on the hill opened fire and came racing down ahead of British dragoons.

Hamilton's horse was shot from under him. With four men he jumped into the boat and pushed off. Lee and others galloped across the bridge ahead of gunfire. The British lined the bank and discharged their carbines at the open boat, killing one man and wounding another. Lee and Hamilton each thought the other lost until they met back at headquarters. They had failed in their mission. Hamilton was disgusted with himself. "I did all I could to prevent this," he wrote, "but to no purpose."

He did better on his next try. He executed Washington's virtually open-ended orders to salvage the contents of Philadelphia. He advised John Hancock, president of the Congress, to get that body immediately out of town. He confiscated ("keeping an account and giving receipts") blankets, clothing, shoes, and horses, "except . . . those which are the property of needy persons . . . or persons who are on the point of leaving the city."

It was too late to save Philadelphia, and almost unthinkable that Washington could fight any time soon. By now there was divided opinion among those who followed the Commander. His officers discussed him.

"Before coming to the Army," said Timothy Pickering, "I entertained an exalted opinion of General Washington's military talents, but I have seen nothing since to enhance it." Nathanael Greene replied, "Why, the General does want decision." Johann De Kalb thought him "too slow, too indolent and by far too weak; besides he has a touch of vanity in his composition and overestimates himself." But Tom Paine, a soldier in the ranks, understood him best.

"Voltaire has remarked that King William never appeared to full advantage but in difficulties and in action; the same remark may be made on General Washington, for the character fits him."

Hamilton's opinion was closer to Paine's. The General was never so dangerous a foe as after he had taken a defeat. He was making plans to meet Howe at Germantown when great news came from the north. A French convoy of eight ships had brought arms and ammunition across the Atlantic and up the Hudson. On September 28 Major General Horatio Gates smashed Burgoyne at Saratoga and captured more than five thousand British troops. There had been little to cheer about in more than three years of war: Boston had been recovered by evacuation; Trenton and Princeton were blessed but minor victories. And now Saratoga . . . this ringing success in another theater, under another leader.

Washington showed no jealousy, only gratitude and exultation. He paraded his troops, fired the inevitable thirteen-gun salute, passed out rum, and prepared to fight at Germantown. This time he ransacked the countryside for information about its geography and place names. He examined intercepted letters, interviewed spies and prisoners. Washington would personally lead an offensive action for the first time since Princeton.

On October 5 fog rolled in from the sea, and soon was mixed with battle smoke as the guns opened up, and the Continentals advanced in low visibility on a wide front. Hamilton and Laurens rode forward with Washington, Pickering, and Knox. They came to the stone house of Benjamin Chew, which was held by British soldiers.

Knox tried to blow it down with artillery, but scored only glancing blows. Laurens brought straw from the barn and attempted to burn out the defenders. He went down with a bullet through the shoulder, the first of four wounds he sustained during the war, in which he would finally die in combat.

A precious hour was lost, as the weather worsened, before the Chew House was left behind. Then it happened as so often before. Fugitives came sweeping back from the front, those on foot first, followed by those driving or dragging artillery. Rumor had spread in the thickness of fog and smoke that Howe had executed a sweep and was at their rear. There was panic.

With defeat piled on defeat, a different sort of general would have withdrawn into positions of defense. Instead, Washington planned to strike Howe once more before winter set in. On October 29 the Chief called in five major generals and ten brigadiers for a council of war at Whitpain Township. He sent for Hamilton to take down the minutes. It was decided to draw twenty regiments from Generals Horatio Gates and Israel Putnam in New York State. These, along with Colonel Daniel Morgan's riflemen, who were already headed southward, would enable the Americans to outnumber Howe in a large way. The delicate business of calling on the victor of Saratoga, who had pointedly taken to reporting to Congress instead of to the Commander in Chief, seemed to require one of the general officers. But Washington jumped over rank and wrote to Hamilton, his twenty-one-year-old aide:

". . . I have thought it proper to appoint you to that duty, and desire you will immediately set out for Albany, at which place, or in the neighborhood, I imagine you will find Genl. Gates."

V

(1777–1780)

On a splendid white horse, but not as big as Washington's, wearing a long green cloak over his uniform, one end thrown rakishly over his shoulder according to an old print, and with Captain Caleb Gibbs as his aide, Hamilton set off on October 30 for the 254-mile ride from White Marsh to Albany.

Gibbs, seven years older than Hamilton, was commander of the Life Guards who were responsible for Washington's safety, a favorite of the General since the siege of Boston, and something of a Headquarters jester and entertainer. His added value to Hamilton on this trip was that he was known to have sung and drunk with General Israel Putnam. After a thirty-one-toast banquet in New York, Gibbs had written his wife Penelope:

"Our good General Putnam got sick and went to his quarters before dinner was over, and we missed him a marvel, as there is not a chap in the camp who can lead him in the Maggie Lauder song."

On the long trip Hamilton had time to ponder several factors in his mission. One was Washington's everlasting hopefulness, his sky-high expectation of a war-ending strike. The Commander had told his envoy that "the reinforcement . . . will in all probability reduce Gen. Howe to the same situation in which Gen. Burgoyne now is"—in sum, that of a humiliated captive.

Another factor was Washington's lack of information about

affairs in the north. For all he knew, Gates or Putnam might be planning something spectacular like an invasion of Canada or a strike at Clinton in New York. "If upon your meeting with Genl. Gates," read Hamilton's orders, "you should find he intends . . . some expedition [by which] the common cause will be more benefitted . . . it is not my wish to give any interruption to the plan." But if no action of magnitude were afoot, Washington continued with authority, "you are to inform him that it is my desire that the reinforcements, before mentioned, or such part of them as can be safely spared, be immediately set in motion to join this Army."

A third factor was the relative standing of the two generals. Despite Gates' sudden fame, Washington did not consider himself inferior. He was not a supplicant, nor was he sending Hamilton as such. Yet it was a fact that in the public and political mind Gates was a glorious winner and Washington a perennial loser. Congress had voted Gates a gold medal for the Saratoga victory and proclaimed a day of thanksgiving. All thirteen states had sent him resolutions of gratitude. Washington was low in the confidence of civilian leaders, notably John Adams, president of the board of war. Hamilton would always hold it against Adams that he considered Washington to be dilatory, dictatorial, and flattered by undeserved "idolatry."

On November 1, near New Windsor, Hamilton met units of the company of heroic Virginia riflemen who had distinguished themselves at Saratoga, and before that at Quebec. Their dynamic leader was the 200-pound, six-foot Daniel Morgan, who had been going into wars since at nineteen he signed on as a teamster for Major General Edward Braddock in the 1750's. Morgan had scornfully taken five hundred lashes for striking back at a British officer, and liked to say he was still owed one because he'd counted only 499. An Indian bullet had knocked out half his teeth. He had a bearing that was "exactly fitted for the toils and pomp of war."

"I told him," said Hamilton, "the necessity of making all the dispatch he could, so as not to fatigue his men too much," and this he promised to do. The forthright Morgan, apt to believe all men as honest as himself, assured Hamilton that all was well to the northward. He said that General Putnam at Fishkill had already decided to dispatch four thousand men to Washington; that General Gates, at Albany, had troops on the march down both sides of the Hudson.

Pleased at Morgan's disclosures, Hamilton believed he could "accomplish my errand without going any farther—unless it should be to hasten the troops that were on their march." He pushed on to the Putnam headquarters and found in Old Put, aged sixty-one, another veteran of the French and Indian War, but not otherwise very similar to Morgan. Putnam, six inches below six feet, jawed like a bulldog, was an illiterate farmer and tavern keeper, with several unbelievable legends attached to his name. He might not have strangled a wolf in its den, raced his horse down a flight of stone steps, or given the Bunker Hill order, "Don't shoot till you see the whites of their eyes." But he was a fearless fighter and British-hater. Hamilton found him so amenable that he asked Old Put to contribute a militia brigade as well as two Continental brigades.

"Your instructions," Hamilton wrote Washington, "did not comprehend any militia, but I concluded you would not disapprove. . . ."

This trace of self-satisfaction soon was wiped out. Upon leaving Putnam, Hamilton met an aide to General Gates, who said that the three brigades at Albany were not marching at all. Instead, along with a detachment of the Green Mountain Boys, they were settling down for the winter, and "barracks building for them."

Hamilton pressed on to Albany. Reporting there to Gates, he saw a short-coupled, overweight figure, fussy-mannered and wearing spectacles, no match in appearance for Washington, but supposedly being discussed as the latter's replacement. Hamilton heard something of the "cabal" from two fellow staff officers at Albany, James Wilkinson and Robert Troup, but did not let the rumors deter him from carrying out his main business. He put his proposition strongly. Since Gates had no better use for troops than to hole them up in winter quarters, there was no sound reason not to send all three brigades to the Delaware theater for the demolition of Howe.

Not unexpectedly, Gates demurred. With reduced forces, he could not "prevent the enemy from destroying this city and arsenal, whenever they please to make the attempt." The Albany arsenal had great value to the Revolution, containing at least three thousand stacks of arms and thirty brass cannon. Gates felt he might be called upon to defend New England against a British expedition. No, he told Hamilton, he must keep two brigades, but was willing to part with one. "I used every argument in my power to convince him," Hamilton reported, "but he was inflexible . . . that two brigades . . . remain."

Hamilton felt "infinitely embarrassed." It would be foolhardy to match the prestige of this victorious figure against that of the loser at Brandywine and Germantown. This was difficult to put into writing, but Hamilton tried in his next letter to Washington:

"General Gates has won the entire confidence of the Eastern States. If disposed to do it, by addressing himself to the prejudices of the people, he would find no difficulty to render a measure odious. . . . On the whole it appeared to me dangerous to insist on sending more troops. . . ."

This was before Hamilton learned from Troup that the brigade assigned to travel was the worst of the lot, under strength, with many enlistments about to expire. Fired by this show of bad faith, Hamilton returned to the argument with force. Gates relented and agreed to send two brigades instead of one. The aide commandeered vessels to carry one away, and started the other southward on foot.

He hadn't done badly with Gates, but on November 9 he returned to New Windsor to learn that Putnam was still encamped. "I am pained beyond expression to inform your Excellency that . . . everything has been neglected and deranged by General Putnam. . . ." The excuse was that New York was reportedly undefended and Putnam wished to move there. "As to attacking New York," Hamilton told him, the Commander "thinks [that] ought to be out of the question at present," the more so because "General Clinton's reinforcement is probably with Mr. Howe." Putnam's delay thwarted Washington's win-the-war strategy of smashing the enemy rather than capturing cities.

To make it all worse, Putnam's men hadn't been paid for nearly eight months, and a mutiny had already caused two deaths. Hamilton ended the pay dispute "by means of 5 or 6000 dollars which Governor Clinton was kind enough to borrow for me." He ordered Putnam, "by his Excellency's authority," to march.

Putnam complied, but Hamilton had succeeded too late. "Had the reinforcements from the northward arrived but ten days sooner," Washington wrote his brother, "it would, I think, have . . . rendered Philadelphia a very ineligible situation for them this winter."

By now Hamilton was deeply worried about his performance. The more he thought about it, the more he fretted. He was sinking into dejection. He felt it coming on. "I am afraid what I have done may not meet with your approbation. . . ." he'd written Washington on November 6. "I cannot forbear being uneasy lest my conduct should prove displeasing. . . ." On November 12, he wrote, "I have been detained here these two days by a fever and violent rheumatic pains throughout my body. This has prevented my being active in person for promoting the purpose of my errand. . . . Perhaps you will think me blameable in not having exercised the powers you gave me. . . ."

Frustration and anxiety overwhelmed him. He collapsed with aches and fever, and the kindly George Clinton, governor of New York, took him in. He rested, left his bed too soon, and fell into a relapse. "I arrived at this place last night," he wrote Washington from Fishkill on November 15, "and unfortunately find myself unable to proceed any further." Caleb Gibbs wrote both Washington and Washington's aide, Robert Hanson Harrison, reporting Hamilton "much worse than I expected, laboring under a violent nervous fever [but] this morning somewhat better."

For the first of several times, Hamilton was hit by a mental depression. His grandson, Dr. Allan McLane Hamilton, a neurologist, would write, "He undoubtedly possessed that form of nervous instability common to many active public men and characterized by varying moods, which was sometimes expressed by alternating depression on the one hand and gayety on the other."

Clinton got him back to bed and summoned a physician, who was delayed, and who at length arrived to find the patient in critical condition, according to Gibbs. "On the 25th in the evening he seemed to all appearances to be drawing nigh his last, having been seized with a coldness in the extremities & remained so for the space of two hours, then surviv'd. He remained calm and the fever not so high on the 26th. On the 27th in the morning the Coldness came on again, and encreased (he was then cold as high as his knees), insomuch the Doct'r thought he could not survive. He remained in this situation for near 4 hours, after which the fever abated very much, and from that time he has been getting better. The Doct'r now pronounces him out of danger."

Better medicine than the doctor's was a letter from Washington:

"I approve entirely of all the steps you have taken, and have only to wish that the exertions of those you have had to deal with had kept pace with your zeal and good intentions. I hope your health will before this have permitted you to push on. . . . I wish you a safe return. . . ."

It was not until December 22 that Hamilton felt strong enough to travel. He thanked God, and also thanked Clinton "for the interest you took in the restoration of my health and the safety of my person during my illness." A month before his twenty-second birthday, the aide saddled up and went to find the main force, not a difficult task that winter. As Washington told it, "you might have traced the Army from White Marsh to Valleyforge by the blood of their feet."

CHAPTER FOUR

He Winters at Valley Forge

I

(June 1777–December 1778)

To Hamilton, the winter immobility was a chance to get on with serious staff work. He wrote at length to Washington.

"There still exist in the army so many abuses . . . that, without a speedy stop is put to them, it will be impossible even to establish any order or discipline among the troops. I would therefore propose the following regulations. . . ."

He was working and walking around amid scenes of failure, degradation, and suffering; his mental withdrawal was such that he wrote almost nothing about the miseries of Valley Forge. Throughout most of his life, wrapped up in his preoccupations, he would be oblivious to natural and human surroundings.

"Here comes a bowl of beef soup full of dead leaves and dirt," wrote one of the surgeons. "There comes a soldier. His bare feet are seen through his worn-out shoes—his legs nearly naked from the tattered remains of an only pair of stockings—his Breeches are not sufficient to cover his nakedness—his Shirt hanging in strings—his hair disheveled—his face meagre."

A Frenchman "came into Camp, imagining to find an Army with fine uniforms, glittering Arms, flowing Standards . . . he saw soldiers wearing night caps under their hats, and some having for Cloaks or Great Coats, coarse woolen blankets. . . . These were our General Officers."

Hamilton never mentioned what he wore, how he kept his fingers warm enough to write, where he bivouacked. He did not command troops, but officers who did had orders "immediately to cause the men to be divided into squads of twelve . . . and set about to make a Hutt for themselves. . . . The soldiers'

Hutts are to be of the following dimensions; viz., fourteen by sixteen each. . . . The Officers' Hutts to form a line in the rear of the troops. . . ."

General Washington would not live better than his men did. At first they were in tents, and he also worked, ate, and slept under canvas. His impressive "marquee," eighty feet in circumference, stood on the hilltop called Mount Joy, the blue headquarters flag with thirteen stars whipping in the chill winds. He had a sleeping tent, eight feet long, as well as a baggage tent.

When the soldiers' huts were finished, Washington and staff took over the stone house of Isaac Potts, owner of the Forge. The working quarters were two small rooms on the ground floor; Washington's sleeping accommodations were straw, his pillow a bag of straw, his covers a single blanket piled with clothing. In mid-February, Martha Washington arrived, and the staff officers moved into out-buildings. On the twenty-second she gave a forty-sixth birthday party for the General, with music by the Army band, for which she paid fifteen shillings. Hamilton, Henry Knox, John Laurens, James Monroe, Nathanael Greene, and the Frenchmen made as merry as they could.

Among those privileged to occupy a farmhouse as his quarters was the gifted and magnetic Lafayette. Barely twenty years old, he was jumped on the Commander's order from volunteer to major general. At the battle of Brandywine when Lafayette took a slight wound, the Commander told the surgeon, "Treat him as if he were my son, for I love him as if he were."

Here Hamilton clearly had a rival for Washington's affections, but instead of the jealousy with which enemies-to-be would often charge him, there developed a lifelong friendship between the young men. Wealth and privilege, charm, and lucky success had seldom been bestowed so munificently as on the high-born French youth who had never heard a bullet hum until he reached America. Lafayette's one alleged foible, described by Jefferson as "a canine appetite for popularity and success," was the kind to endear him to Hamilton.

Another volunteer, though much older (actually two years older than Washington), was Baron Friedrich Wilhelm Augustus von Steuben. He quickly won Hamilton's notice and admiration. The amiable and profane German knew no English, but Hamilton and Greene translated his knowledge of army organization to the Americans and helped him drill the troops. Steuben remembered: ". . . the words company, regiment, brigade and division were so vague that they did not convey any idea. . . . I have seen a regiment consisting of thirty men, and a company of one corporal. . . . The arms at Valley Forge were . . . covered with rust . . . many from which a single shot could not be fired. . . . The men were literally naked. . . . With regard to their military discipline, I may safely say no such thing existed."

The camp had been chosen for strategy, not comfort. It was eighteen miles from Philadelphia, close enough to afford contact with the enemy and far enough away to avoid surprise. The layout was that of an ironclad triangle, easier to defend than attack, a maze of entrenchments and artillery emplacements.

The enemy was shut out, but not the hardships. Provisions failed and smallpox was rife. "A General cry thro' the Camp this evening among the soldiers, 'No meat! No meat!' The distant valleys echo'd back the melancholy sound, 'No meat! No meat!' Imitating the noise of crows and owls also, made a part of the confused music." Yet sometimes there were sounds of a violin and of men singing.

Washington wrote to Congress: ". . . unless some great and capital change suddenly takes place . . . this Army must inevitably be reduced to one or other of three things. Starve, dissolve or disperse. . . ."

In January, a Congressional committee met at Headquarters, and Hamilton was deep into a 2,500-word revision of the rules. They applied to general officers at the top, common soldiers at the bottom, and all ranks in between. Absence without leave would be subject to sentence by court-martial. An officer who overstayed his furlough was to "be cashiered and rendered incapable of ever holding a commission in the armies of the United States."

The use of enlisted men as servants had been abused, and Hamilton recommended strict limits. Major generals could have four servants from the ranks, brigadiers three, down to subalterns who could have one. Losses of arms and ammunition must be curtailed, and henceforth arms should not be issued to noncombatants, specifically, "generals and staff officers, waiters, waggoners, camp color men. . . ." Too many sentries diminished the fighting strength of the regiments, so sentries must be fewer but better trained. Officers of the guard must answer for whatever went wrong, "nothing being more disgraceful to the service, nor more dangerous for the army, than for the outposts to be surprised by the enemy."

The provost corps had not proved useful, so Hamilton proposed to rename and reform it. As an elite unit, the General Staff Dragoons should not be employed on any non-military duties, nor take orders from any other than a general officer, nor be sent to carry expresses more than twenty miles. This last was to keep the horses sharp and swift. Also, no dragoon horse was to be ridden by any except a dragoon.

Hamilton undertook all this writing as a voluntary contribution. Washington had requested his general officers, but not his aides, to submit their ideas for Army reform. When the generals responded, Hamilton doubled his labors by revising their observations into the Commander's report to Congress.

"Few men," runs the Hamiltonian philosophy in the Regulation for the Order and Discipline of the Troops of the United States, "are capable of making a continual sacrifice of all points of private interest and advantage, to the common good. It is in vain to exclaim against the depravity of human nature on this account, the fact is so. The experience of every age and nation has proved it, and we must in good measure change the constitution of man, before we can make it otherwise. No institution not built on the presumptive truth of these maxims can succeed."

He looked far ahead to a national military system that would be rendered permanent by half-pay, retirement pay, and pensions for next of kin. "When an officer's commission is made valuable to him, and he fears to lose it, then you may extract obedience from him."

Hamilton thought that American common soldiers responded to the same lure of self-advantage as everyone else. At first a fair number of units had volunteered for the duration. "We may fairly infer," he wrote, "that the country had been already pretty well drained of that class of men. . . ." The Continental regiments, therefore, must be filled by conscription from the state militias. "This is a disagreeable alternative," the report to Congress read, "but it is an unavoidable one."

Hamilton went on to propose an annual draft under which men would serve until January 1 of each succeeding year. On or before October 1, the conscripts would be offered a $25 bounty to sign up for another year. The plan permitted orderly bookkeeping. He also advised curtailing substitutions and enlarging the Continental cavalry to improve scouting and intelligence-gathering.

The Army emerged in the spring of 1778 much the better for its Valley Forge experience. Hamilton gave much credit to the man whom he pushed for the post of Inspector General. "Baron Steuben," he wrote Congressman William Duer, "who will be the bearer of this, waits on Congress to have his office arranged upon some decisive and permanent footing. It will not be amiss to put you on your guard. The Baron is a Gentleman for whom I have a particular esteem. . . . But I apprehend with all his good qualities, a fondness for power and importance. . . . Perhaps I may be mistaken in my conjecture. The caution I give will do no harm if I am. If I am not it may be useful."

Nothing that Hamilton did at Valley Forge resulted in greater benefit to America than his championship of the difficult Baron. The Prussian drillmaster pounded home the importance of punctuality, smartness, and accountability, but his best contribution to the cause was his introduction of bayonet practice. "The American soldier," a Steuben translator wrote for him, "never having used this arm, had no faith in it, never used it but to roast his beefsteak."

Teaching the Continentals to fight with steel as well as lead, Steuben changed the course of coming battles.

II
(February–June 1778)

"In the name of His Excellency General Washington and by virtue of His authority in me. . . ."

The proclamation, in Hamilton's Spencerian script, studded with capitalizations of pronouns that related to His Excellency and his authority, was the end product of a task that Hamilton carried on at Valley Forge from February till June. He had the assignment of recovering the 120 officers and 670 noncommissioned officers and privates who had fallen captive to the British in the campaigns from Canada to Germantown.

It was asked in the Congress, Why bother to bring back these men? America, with three million population, and growing, could raise soldiers far more easily than England could import them to this country. Better to bring in fresh recruits, and let the British go on guarding and feeding the American prisoners of war.

"Whatever refined politicians may think," retorted Hamilton in a letter to George Clinton, "it is of great consequence to preserve a national character. . . . And I would ask whether in a republican state and a republican army, such a cruel policy . . . can succeed. . . . I abhor such *Neroian* maxims."

Ethan Allen of the Green Mountain Boys had been taken at Montreal; General Charles Lee had been caught in his tavern just when Washington needed him most for the New Jersey battles of '76; the regimental surgeon Dr. James McHenry of Maryland had been left behind at the fall of Fort Washington. These were the celebrities of the lot. The nameless others, eighty of them in hospitals, were just as important, in Hamilton's estimation.

Another reason why he favored the trading of prisoners was democratic in nature. "The passions of the country and the Army are on the side of an exchange; a studied attempt to avoid it will disgust both, and serve to make the service odious."

Nothing was more important to governance than public opinion, thought Hamilton, and to flout it "will unquestionably have an ill-effect upon foreign negotiations and tend to bring the Government at home into contempt; and, of course, to destroy its influence."

Moreover, Hamilton saw the barter as a means of gaining *de facto* recognition of the United States by Britain. General Sir William Howe proposed that he and Washington trade "officer for officer of equal rank, soldier for soldier, citizen for citizen." Hamilton saw at once that the bargain would no longer be binding if either Howe or Washington ceased to command. The deal must be between the Congress and the Crown, and Hamilton so arranged it.

The British had Joshua Loring as commissary general of prisoners, and Congress named Elias Boudinot to the same position. Washington appointed a board of officers—Hamilton, Colonel William Grayson, and Lieutenant Colonel Robert Hanson Harrison. The three corresponding British officers were Colonel Charles O'Hara, Colonel Humphrey Stephens, and Captain Robert FitzPatrick.

They readily agreed upon a meeting place. Germantown, eighteen miles from Valley Forge, was chosen. The Americans would attend the opening session in style. Hamilton ordered a regimental colonel: "Send a corporal and six dragoons with a Trumpeter to Headquarters, without loss of time. They are wanted to escort the Commissioners on our part who are to meet on the subject of a general Cartel. You need not be told that they must be picked men and horses—must make the best possible appearance—must be very trusty and very intelligent."

The conference opened next day and dragged on for weeks. The young officers whiled away the time in drinking bouts that took a toll on Hamilton's digestion. The physician James McHenry warned him: "Water is the most general solvent—the kindliest diluent . . . I would therefore advise it for your table drink. When you indulge in wine let [it] be sparingly—never get beyond three glasses. . . . But in case you should fall into a debauch, you must next day have recourse to the pills."

The drinking made congenial enemies of the negotiators. "Now if I am taken prisoner," the jovial O'Hara exclaimed on a pleasant occasion, "I shall call on Colonel Hamilton, Colonel Harrison, and Colonel Boudinot, and I'll expect you'll immediately come to my aid and take care of me."

Perhaps there was something revealing in the jest and the British were losing their stomach for the long war. Hamilton was sure of this when one of the negotiators, Captain FitzPatrick, arranged to meet with him and Lafayette at "a friendly dinner at Germantown between the two armies." As Hamilton expected, "much political discussion took place." He said that "nothing short of Independency could be accepted by the United States." He was speaking for Washington, and Washington was speaking for the Congress. That body had resolved to receive no British commissioners "unless they shall, as a preliminary thereto, withdraw their fleets and armies . . . acknowledging the independence of said states."

In a move to break the stalemate over prisoners without making concessions, Hamilton drew up for study a Draft Cartel of Fourteen Articles. First captured would be first exchanged. Officers and men would be traded for those of equal rank. Where this could not be fully carried out, two or more inferior officers would be given for a superior. If a commander in chief were captured, 192 lesser officers would buy him back. The ratio continued downward through lieutenant general (ninety-six), major general (four), and ensign (one for one). But the meat of the cartel resided in its final paragraph, Article XIV, which made it a formal and binding state paper.

"This Treaty and Convention shall be and continue in full force throughout the present war."

By June 4, Howe was replaced by Sir Henry Clinton, and Hamilton sent him the formal Declaration of Prisoners. The British had been outtalked and outwaited. Their negotiators granted every substantive point, and Washington wrote to Hamilton, "I have therefore to desire you (Mr. Boudinot being absent from Camp) to hear any proposals Mr. Loring may have to offer . . . towards the execution of a general exchange of prisoners; and I hereby assure you that your proceedings in this instance will be ratified by me."

The honor of closing the deal went to the right man. The United States had won by conference a contest with the enemy state, not a usual event in Hamilton's lifetime or thereafter.

III

(June 1778)

On June 5, the day after Hamilton sealed the bargain on prisoners, Washington released exhilarating news from France. He had kept the secret since April 30. "I believe that no event was ever received with such heartfelt joy," he had told the Congress, and now he told his soldiers. "It having pleased the Almighty ruler of the Universe propitiously to defend the Cause of the United American States, and finally to raise up a powerful Friend among the Princes of the Earth to establish our liberty and Independence [upon] lasting foundations. . . ."

He ordered a complete turnout of troops, nearly naked as some were, and ragged as were most officers. Salutes were fired by cannon and musket in honor of the foreign officers. "Long live the King of France!" was the first huzzah. Then, "Long live the friendly European powers!" And finally, "To the American States!" The men disbanded and each received a gill of rum.

Hope! Salvation! Victory! Peace! All this could happen for America now, and her enemies knew it. Tories in Philadelphia scrambled to board ship for other parts. Sir Henry Clinton took alarm. On June 14 he evacuated the city and headed for New York with its protective Royal Navy. He lumbered across New Jersey, trailing a cumbersome baggage train, a fat and inviting target.

Never before had the odds so much favored the rebels. They were roughly twenty thousand patriots, against ten thousand redcoats. Clinton's army was the only substantial force opposing independence. If Sir Henry could be smashed, the war was over.

CHAPTER FIVE

He Learns About Generals

I
(June 1778)

On June 19 Hamilton rode out of Valley Forge at Washington's stirrup. Both of these optimists rejoiced in the turnabout of fortune: The French alliance a reality . . . Sir Henry Clinton on the run . . . another Saratoga in the making here in the Jersey lowlands!

Confidence was high in the Continental ranks. Perhaps Washington had not proved it yet, but he was far superior to Horatio Gates. He would never "hug himself at a distance and leave an Arnold to win the laurels for him," in Hamilton's words. Gates was known to be combat-shy, and Benedict Arnold was a Dutch-courage fighter, according to Anthony Wayne. The Continental Army had the better officers, and its Steuben-trained soldiers excelled the troops of the Northern Department, which had brought off the greatest victory of the war to date.

Find the redcoats and smash them. The sooner the better, before they got out of reach, before the Continentals' unreliable quartermastering and intelligence broke down in the sweltering unseasonable heat. But five days out of Valley Forge, Washington called a council of war at Hopewell, near Princeton, to learn the collective opinion of his officers. The meeting was "unwisely called," thought Hamilton, and Lafayette agreed. These two, along with Greene, Steuben, and Le Bègue de Presle Duportail, advised an immediate attack. But Major General Charles Lee, the Englishman who had served under Burgoyne, declared it folly to risk an encounter now that France had made the war as good as won. Better, said Lee, to build "a bridge of gold" to conduct Clinton out of New Jersey and across the water into New York. Henry Knox and William Alexander, called Lord Stirling, thought so too. Washington compromised between the two sets of opinion.

He chose discretion. He would go halfway. First, the enemy must be harassed, and he ordered "a number of militia to hang on and annoy their rear." He told Benedict Arnold, wounded at Saratoga and now commandant at Philadelphia, "We intend as soon as things are in train, to move toward them and to avail ourselves of any favorable circumstances that may appear."

Hamilton was dismayed. The council which had wrought such tactics "would have done honor to the most honorable society of midwives, and to them alone." General Lee, designated a field commander, still feared a major clash with the battle-wise enemy. He first relinquished his post to the eager Lafayette, then changed his mind.

Assigned as liaison officer to Lafayette, Hamilton went forward with the advance detachment, charged with maintaining a running communication between the Marquis and the General. At noon on June 26, under blistering skies, Hamilton wrote Washington from Allentown, "We have halted our troops at this place. . . . Our reason for halting is the extreme distress of the troops for want of provisions. . . ."

Not only had the commissary failed again, but the cavalry had lost contact with the British. "No horse was near the enemy, . . ." he reported back to Washington. "We are entirely at a loss where the [British] army is. . . ." He was desperate. This fateful opportunity was slipping away. "We feel our personal honor as well as the honor of the army and the good of the service interested, and are heartily desirous to attempt whatever the disposition of our men will second and prudence authorize. . . ."

Hamilton was just finishing his despairing note when Lafayette received the fourth letter of the day from Washington. The Commander was at last satisfied with the deployment. Let Lafayette complete the advance into Englishtown. Lee was en route with five thousand men. Washington himself would back the attack with an additional 7,800. They would catch Clinton at Monmouth. Hamilton answered with elation.

"This puts the matter on an entirely different footing. The detachment will march tomorrow morning at three o'clock."

Washington took the road early on June 28 with his large strike force. Cannon booms from Monmouth reassured him. At least, ten days after leaving Valley Forge, the Continentals had forced a battle. No matter if they were enervated by thirst, heat, and starvation, the "hand of Providence" which Washington always trusted would provide. Hamilton, in tireless motion between the Commander and the Marquis, was sent forward to report on Lee's expected assault. "I saw the enemy drawn up, and am persuaded there were not a thousand men. . . . However favorable this situation may seem for an attack, it was not made." Instead, he saw that Lee's men were "changing their position two or three times by retrograde movements." Hamilton raced back to the Commander, so distrait that he lost his hat. He warned Washington to move Nathanael Greene's troops into a holding position in case Lee should break into full retreat.

Retreat! A hateful word to Washington. But before parley, General Knox rode in. He did not like what he had seen up front. He confirmed Hamilton's report and repeated his advice. Angered by warnings from two favorite officers, Washington spurred ahead and beheld a replay of former spectacles in calamity. It was Long Island, Brandywine, Germantown all over again. The roadway ahead, and then the surrounding fields, swarmed with troops in flight.

Among them was Charles Lee. To Washington's indignant queries, Lee stammered excuses. His information was incomplete, his experience warned him not to meet British cavalry on level terrain, his prudence told him to beware of English surprise tactics.

Washington turned from him and assumed personal command. He managed to stem the retreat of the newly disciplined Continentals. He posted the men he had, and as many as his staff could collect, behind a hedgerow. Now the Americans must stand and deliver fire. They must prove themselves against the British cavalry, which now thundered in attack.

Suggestions had continued that Hamilton was gathering ma-

terial for a history of the Revolution. His old tutor harped on
the favorite subject: "Or are you so engaged in writing the
History of the American War . . . that you have no time to
write letters?" A Tory newspaper, Smythe's *Journal,* said that
"little Hamilton . . . is engaged upon a literary work which is
intended to give posterity a true estimate of the present rebellion and its supporters." If Hamilton took anything more than
mental notes, or commenced a manuscript, there is no evidence
of it. But he was agog at what he heard and saw.

He had seen two general officers caught on the horns of the
dilemma of indecisiveness. Before the battle Lee had wavered
and reversed himself on the question of whether or not to
assume his command. Washington had dillied and dallied over
what to do about a British army in front of him. Hamilton
thought Lee "childish," and was clearly disappointed in Washington.

But action would now test the men. Lee in flight presented
the same unprepossessing figure in the field as in the camp, but
Washington soon had Greene and Stirling in command of the
wings, with Steuben rounding up the fugitives. Hamilton now
was swept with awe at the feats of his Chief. "I never saw the
general to so much advantage," he recounted. "His coolness
and firmness were admirable. He instantly took measures for
checking the enemy's advance, and gaining time for the army,
which was very near, to form and make a proper disposition.
He then had the troops formed on a very advantageous piece
of ground. . . . America owes a great deal to General Washington for this day's work . . . he turned the fate of the day . . .
brought order out of confusion, animated his troops and led
them to success."

Hamilton himself chose to go where he could help the
most—to the units of cannon. He saw Colonel Henry Lee with
an aimless detail, "and strongly advised him to march to the
succor of the artillery. . . . I saw him, when at a small distance,
marching his detachment to do what I had recommended. . . .

"I saw some pieces of artillery pretty advantageously posted,
but destitute of cover and support. Myself and others observed
this to General Lee; no troops were sent that I know of by his

direction, but upon its being suggested that the cannon would certainly be lost if left there in so unsupported a condition, General Lee ordered them to be drawn off."

Here he lost sight of General Charles Lee, and rode to the rear, "where I found Colonel Olney retreating. . . . I pressed him to form his troops along a fence . . . which he immediately performed and had a smart conflict with the enemy. . . ."

Hamilton had been in the saddle since long before dawn, hatless under the merciless sun. His horse took a bullet and fell. Hamilton lay stunned, no more good for that day. He recorded the incident in restrained language at the subsequent court-martial of Charles Lee, calling himself "considerably hurt. This and previous fatigue caused me to retire." But McHenry did him justice in a letter to Boudinot:

"I am happy to have it in my power to mention the merit of your friend Hammy. He was incessant in his endeavors during the whole day—in reconnoitering the enemy, and in rallying and charging. But whether he or Colo. Laurens deserves most of our commendation is somewhat doubtful—both had their horses shot under them, and both exhibited singular proofs of bravery. They seemed to court death under our doubtful circumstances, and triumphed over it as the face of war changed in our favor."

On his own part, Hamilton gave generous praise to all except Charles Lee. "This man is either a driveler in the business of soldiership or something much worse." But, as he wrote Boudinot, ". . . a great number of our officers distinguished themselves this day. General Wayne . . . Col Stewart and Lt Col Ramsay . . . Lt Col Olney . . . Col Livingston . . . our friend Barber . . . the artillery acquitted themselves most charmingly. . . .

"I hope you will not suspect me of vanity when I tell you that one of them, Fitzgerald, had a slight contusion with a musket ball, another, Laurens, had a slight contusion also—and his horse killed—a third, Hamilton, had his horse wounded. . . . If the rest escaped, it was only to be ascribed to better fortune, not more prudence in keeping out of the way. . . ."

Nightfall at Monmouth ended the action, which had com-

menced before dawn. The Commander and his exhausted officers lay down in the open on their cloaks. While they slept the
enemy stole away, leaving 217 unburied dead and many more
badly wounded. All told, Clinton's forces were reduced by 1,200,
while Washington's casualties were 72 killed, 161 wounded,
132 missing.

"Our troops . . . behaved with more spirit and moved with
greater order than the British troops," wrote Hamilton. He did
not blame Washington for failing to chase Clinton across a
hundred miles of open sandy country—even if that had been
physically possible. At least, the Continentals were in possession of the field, with a victory that was the hinge of war.

II

(June–December 1778)

Some weeks after the battle, Hamilton, with Generals
Greene and Stirling, sat in the Quartermaster's office at the
Morristown headquarters. The common topic of soldiers' talk
these days was Monmouth and Charles Lee's conviction in
court-martial on three charges. He had disobeyed orders, mis-
behaved before the enemy, showed disrespect in subsequent
letters to General Washington. The trial, in which Hamilton
and Laurens were witnesses and Stirling was the presiding
officer, still awaited appraisal of its verdict by Congress.

Perhaps to influence that body, Lee talked and wrote in furious vituperation. He called Washington's formal letter of
charges "a most abominable, damnable lie." He said Hamilton
belonged to an "idolatrous set of toadeaters." The court's sentence was surprisingly mild, suspension of command for one
year, but Lee vowed to resign if finally convicted: "Aye, God
damn them, that he would."

Through the door of the office stepped one of General Lee's
aides, Major J. S. Eustice. He also had made public noises,
including a charge that Hamilton had "purjured" himself in
testimony, and a statement that this difference of opinion could
"be decided as he chose." These were actionable words under
the *code duello,* and they came in a period of many Army

challenges and duels. Steuben and Wayne had challenged Lee; Lafayette demanded "satisfaction" of Carlyle; Cadwallader had met and shot Conway.

Hamilton stood up and faced Eustice. By now Washington's aide had a reputation for temper. His confrontations with the senior officers, Generals Gates and Putnam, were well known. He and Troup had had words with James Wilkinson over last year's Conway Cabal to replace Washington with Gates. But now, surprisingly, Hamilton approached Eustice with outstretched hand.

"I took no notice of his polite intention," Eustice later declared, "but sat down without bowing to him or any of the clan."

Hamilton politely asked if Eustice had come from the camp. "No," said Eustice shortly, without "the usual application of Sir."

Hamilton remained standing. It was an awkward moment. Eustice rose and left the room, feeling "I could not treat him much more rudely." Later he boasted, "I've repeated my suspicions of his veracity on the trial so often that I expect the son-of-a-bitch will challenge me."

Hamilton maintained throughout his lifetime that he had religious scruples against dueling. He believed it glorious to engage in combat for his country, because in so doing he was fighting for ideals, ethics, and future generations. Personal combat did not have these reasons. There were alternatives to the field of honor. Offended men, or their seconds, could meet and thrash out their disputes. If this failed, there were military and civil courts, and boards of inquiry. He considered dueling not heroic but mock heroic; not an affair of honor but one of nonsense.

"We do not now live in the days of chivalry," he wrote. "The good sense of the present time has happily found out that to prove your own innocence, or the malice of an accuser, the worst method you can take is to run him through the body, or shoot him through the head."

About the same time that Eustice was goading him to fight, Hamilton gave cause for a challenge to another man. In October and November of 1778 he published three articles, signed "Publius," in which he scathingly attacked Congressman Samuel Chase of Maryland for buying flour and selling it at an inflated price to the French quartermasters. Chase waited until a legislative committee had cleared him, then sent Major William B. Giles to ask McHenry if Hamilton would acknowledge that he was Publius, which nobody doubted.

"You know the motives and the grounds for my charges against Mr. C——," Hamilton answered McHenry. "You know that I can have no personal enmity to him. . . ." Hamilton declined the fight on the high ground that "public good alone dictated my attack upon his conduct and character."

The incidents of Eustice and Chase show Hamilton in a thoroughly unheroic light, but he did not care if unheroic conclusions were drawn. He had often exposed himself in battle; he had the admiration of his fellow-officers and the adulation of women who understood what was expected of men at war. He spoke his mind freely, as he would always do. He did not feel that his contempt for the *code duello* cast any doubt on his honor as officer and gentleman.

In December of the same year there was another test of his scruples. General Lee published a "Letter of Vindication" in the *Pennsylvania Packet,* putting all his fulminations into print. John Laurens among others felt that "General Lee had spoken of General Washington in the grossest and most opprobrious terms of personal insult," and Laurens thought the matter demanded attention.

"An affair of this kind ought to be passed over in total silence," he told Hamilton, "or answered in a masterly fashion. . . . The pen of Junius is in your hand; and I think you will without difficulty expose . . . such a tissue of falsehood . . . and put him forever to silence. . . . Adieu, my dear boy. I shall set out for camp tomorrow."

Hamilton chose not to become involved, but Laurens sent Lee a challenge, which was accepted. On Christmas Eve the parties met on the edge of a wood near Philadelphia, with Hamilton as Laurens' second. Despite his disapproval of dueling, he evidently saw nothing wrong with assisting at it. There is an unverified suggestion that he had served as a second while still a youth at St. Croix. In an unfinished Hamilton biography Nicholas Fish made a note to find out if his friend "did receive a letter addressed to Mr. Cruger, containing a challenge; and as Mr. C's agent, offer to *adjust* . . . & . . . terminate the dispute happily."

Hamilton would always act as second when asked, because it put him in position to mediate the quarrel. When it was impossible to avert a duel in advance, it often was possible to do so after the men reached the field. If reconciliation failed at this point, it sometimes succeeded after a first volley had been exchanged.

This, in fact, did happen in the affair between Laurens and Lee. Hamilton wrote, and Major Evan Edwards, the other second, co-signed, an account of the meeting. "They approached each other within five or six paces and exchanged a shot almost at the same moment. As Col Laurens was preparing for a second discharge, General Lee declared himself wounded . . . then said the wound was inconsiderable . . . and proposed to fire a second time." Here was Hamilton's chance at intervention, and he made it good. The combatants agreed that their honor was satisfied.

Hamilton was in Philadelphia with Washington this winter of 1778–79 to urge on the Congress the Army reforms drafted at Valley Forge. The retaken capital was in no mood for serious business. Washington felt obliged to attend elaborate banquets given for him and Mrs. Washington, but complained of "idleness and dissipation" all about. "Our great Fabius Maximus," Greene wrote his wife, "was the glory and admiration of the city . . . but the exhibition was such a scene of luxury and profusion, they gave him more pain than pleasure."

Hamilton's feelings were the same, except that his disgust with the Congress was less restrained. He went the rounds of the taverns, where he undoubtedly said aloud what he was saying in print. It was not until later on, in July, when he was back in the field, that he heard himself quoted in a manner that brought him up short. An Army doctor, Major John Brooks, wrote him from West Point, saying he felt compelled to pass along "a piece of intelligence which affects many in some degree; but you, Sir, most intimately."

According to Brooks, somebody had said that Hamilton "had declared in a public coffee house in Philadelphia, that it was high time for the people to rise, join General Washington, and turn Congress out of doors." Not only that, it was "further observed that Mr. Hamilton could be in no way interested in the defense of this country; and, therefore, was most likely to pursue such a line of conduct as his great ambition dictated."

Who had said this? Brooks named Congressman Francis Dana of Massachusetts. Hamilton chose a second, Colonel David Henley, and sent him to Dana with a peremptory demand for explanation. Dana did not at first retract. He said he had got the story from the Reverend Doctor William Gordon. He added that Major Brooks may have "unintentionally blended conversations had at different times."

In other words, more than one person had heard Hamilton making intemperate remarks in public places where politicians and officers were drinking. Brooks undertook to refresh his memory and make sure that Dana had been one who quoted Hamilton. He "inquired of Colonels Marshall and Wesson who were present, and are as full and positive upon every circumstance as I am."

Hamilton's military career was at stake. He stood accused of insulting both the Congress and General Washington. The implication was that he had been drunk. Dana now denied that he had quoted the offensive remark. Old General Artemus Ward backed him up, saying that "the observation . . . was made by another gentleman then present."

Hamilton persisted in running the tale to its source. He next wrote to the Reverend Mr. Gordon, who said he heard the story from "a person of veracity [and] could not be mistaken." However, said Gordon, the place where Hamilton had spoken out was not a *coffee* house, "it was a *public* house." He was glad to hear, he told Hamilton, "that you have lost all remembrance of it; as it serves to show that it was the effect of a *sudden transport.*"

Hamilton demanded the name of the "person of veracity."

Gordon said he feared to give it, because Hamilton might challenge the man. In vain Hamilton declared his scruples against dueling, but would make no promises. Gordon proposed an investigation by Congress. This would never do for Hamilton. "I shall never expose myself to the ridicule of self-importance by applying to Congress for an inquiry."

The wordy correspondence dragged on. "I am ready to send all that has passed between you & me to be laid out before Congress," reiterated Gordon, "& so leave it to them. . . ." Hamilton was beside himself. A Congressional investigation or court-martial could ruin his career. A reprimand by Washington would be just as bad. This last seemed inevitable when Gordon sent the whole correspondence to the Commander at the Morristown headquarters. But there, fortunately, the matter got lost in the fluster of military trivia.

CHAPTER SIX

He Learns About Foreign Alliances

I
(1778–1780)

The French fleet had not thus far materialized. It was not there to support Washington at Monmouth, nor yet to cut off Sir Henry Clinton's retreat to New York. But at last, in late July of 1778, the splendid flotilla was sighted off the Jersey shore—six frigates and twelve ships of the line bearing heavy guns, and transports carrying four thousand infantrymen. Now the means existed to seal the Monmouth victory. New York must be stormed by land and sea, and the British utterly expelled from the rejoicing United States of North America.

Washington wrote the French Admiral, Charles Hector Théodat, Count d'Estaing, kinsman of Lafayette. "I am sending you Colonel Hamilton in whom I place entire confidence. He will be able to make you perfectly acquainted with my sentiments, and to satisfy any inquiries you may think to propose; and I would wish you to consider the information he delivers as coming from myself."

John Laurens, the other linguist of the staff, had previously been aboard, but Hamilton was somewhat acquainted with the waters around New York. He also had a smattering of sea-lore from managing the Cruger shipping business, and was quick with sympathy for d'Estaing's problems. Without knowing the channels and their depths, the Admiral was unwilling to dare the Manhattan Narrows. Besides, he'd had a rough voyage —eighty-four days at sea, an epidemic of scurvy among the crew, a shortage of fresh water. Hamilton, in his first venture into foreign relations, was so solicitous that d'Estaing entreated Washington not to confide secrets "to any person except Colonel Hamilton. His talents and his personal qualities have secured to him forever my esteem, my confidence and my friendship."

Hamilton meant to extend this promising beginning of the French alliance. On July 16 he was writing to a sea-pilot, Captain Patrick Dennis, bidding him "to go on board the Admiral as early as possible. . . . This letter, shewn to the Count d'Estaing, will be, I trust, a sufficient introduction of you." But the Admiral liked neither the shallow channels nor the frowning aspect of Lord Richard Howe's warships inside the harbor. "He has had the river sounded and finds he cannot enter," Hamilton reported to Washington on July 20. "He will sail for Rhode Island tomorrow morning."

Newport, Rhode Island, like New York, had been occupied since Independence, and would have to do as a less satisfactory target of opportunity. Almost anything would do, in Hamilton's opinion, to make use of the French fleet. But the Admiral had deep respect for British seapower, and was inventive in finding excuses. "He would sail immediately," said Hamilton, "but he awaits the arrival, or to hear, of a frigate . . . so that he fears his sudden and unexpected departure, before she arrives, might cause her to be lost."

Newport was held by Sir Robert Pigot with three thousand men, and Major General John Sullivan had an American command in Rhode Island of one thousand Continentals, with six thousand militia on call, and reinforcements of three thousand en route from Washington's main army. Still, the Admiral demanded extraordinary precautions, including "persons stationed along the coast and immediate expresses to facilitate the communication between them. Pilots will be a material article," Hamilton wrote his Chief.

Not surprisingly, the joint assault on Newport proved a fiasco. D'Estaing was buffeted by a storm and frightened by the approach of Admiral Richard Howe. He withdrew first to Boston, then to the safety of the West Indies.

In the disheartening anticlimax after Monmouth, patriotism gave way to profit-seeking. The greedy merchants and traders, Washington railed, were "murderers of our cause," and fit only for the gibbet. "The farmers," Hamilton wrote, "have got the game in their own hands." Tea in Philadelphia was selling at four dollars a pound, and stockings for a hundred dollars in the inflated Continental currency. Crops were hoarded and sold to the enemy or to agents for the French. Military morale dropped off, and the grand design for rebuilding the Army languished with the politicians.

Troops . . . troops. How thin the ranks seemed at a time when the pockets of British occupation waited to be wiped out. The war was moving south, and in March 1779 Hamilton sponsored a dip into an untapped reservoir of manpower—the southern Negro population. He wrote to John Jay, president of the Congress, saying that John Laurens was en route to South Carolina and would bring a recruitment plan to Philadelphia.

"This is to raise two, three or four battalions of Negroes, with the assistance of the government of that state, by contribution from the owners," said Hamilton. He anticipated "much opposition from prejudice . . . an unwillingness to part with property of so valuable a kind." But if Americans did not make use of Negroes, the enemy would, and "the best way to counteract the temptations they will hold out will be to offer them ourselves." He told Jay that the loyalty of Negroes could only be bought by promising what they most desired. "An essential part of the plan is to give them their freedom with their muskets."

Hamilton's opinions on slavery were quite unemotional. He had seen the institution at its worst in the West Indies, and he would own domestic servants after the war. He and Jay founded the Manumission Society in New York State. But the legislation by which they proposed to emancipate the slaves would show greater concern for the property rights of the slave owners than for the purely human rights of the slaves. He now was more interested in the fighting qualities of black men than in their freedom. Putting first things first, in war and peace, was Hamilton's way:

"It is a maxim with some great military judges that, with sensible officers, soldiers can hardly be too stupid; and on this principle it is thought that the Russians would make the best troops in the world if they were under other officers than their own. The King of Prussia is among the number who maintain this doctrine. . . ."

But Hamilton was having difficulty in convincing himself. He admitted to hearing it said that Negroes "are too stupid to make soldiers." He contended otherwise, although he ran into a problem unusual to him, that of choosing words. He first wrote that the Negroes' "want of cultivation" would be an asset. He struck that out, and substituted "spontaneity." He was not satisfied with that word, crossed it out, and tried "want of knowledge." Finally he restored "want of cultivation."

He sought to explain himself in a parenthesis: "(for their natural faculties are perhaps as good as ours)." Then he struck out "perhaps" and made it read "probably." On somewhat surer ground, he declared that their "habit of subordination . . . life of servitude" would make blacks "sooner become soldiers than our White inhabitants." He went on, "Let the officers be men of sense and sentiment, and the nearer soldiers approach to machines perhaps the better."

Again, there was a "perhaps" that betrayed his ambivalence. At any rate, he was positive on one score. "I will venture to pronounce that they cannot be put in better hands than those of Mr. Laurens. He has all the zeal, intelligence, enterprise and every other quality requisite to succeed in such an undertaking."

Negro enlistment failed as the French intervention had. He thought it useless in such an atmosphere to attempt to rally opinion by writing for the periodicals. Publication would "increase the evil of exposing weaknesses." For that reason he addressed many letters, some unsigned, to politicians. While still at Valley Forge the previous winter, he had resumed correspondence with Governor George Clinton. What was the matter with the Congress? "America once had a reputation that would do honor to any age or nation," he wrote. "The present falling off is very alarming and dangerous. What is the cause? What is the remedy? The great men who composed our first council, are they dead? Have they deserted the cause? or what has become of them?"

Hamilton answered himself in his letter to Clinton. "Very few are dead, and still fewer have deserted the cause—they are all, except for the few who still remain in Congress, either in the field, or in the civil offices of their respective states. The only remedy is to take them out of these employments and return them to the place, where their presence is infinitely more important."

Clinton could not have read this far without astonishment and perhaps some anger. Hamilton wrote as if the State of New York were inferior to the nebulous Confederation. The young man presumed to tell George Clinton his duty! Why, listen to this: "You should not beggar the councils of the United States to enrich the administration of the several members. Realize to yourself the consequences of having a Congress despised at home and abroad."

Hamilton was hardly more than a man-servant to the Chief! Yet he wrote, "I should with caution utter them except to those [in whom] I may place an entire confidence. But it is time that men of weight and understanding should take alarm. . . ."

So the little chap recognized his superiors!

". . . my own insignificance," Hamilton continued, "allows me to do nothing more than to hint my apprehensions. . . ." Yes, Clinton could see that the lieutenant colonel knew his place, even if he did deign to find fault with his betters. Clinton read on.

"As far as I can judge," Hamilton continued, "the remarks I have made do not apply to your state nearly so much as to the other twelve. You have a Duane, a Morris, and may I not add a Duer?"

Top men! All in Congress from New York! Didn't Hamilton know when to stop? "I wish General Schuyler was explicitly in the Army or in Congress." Clinton had just beaten Schuyler in the gubernatorial election and saw nothing very remarkable in him. But hold on! "For yourself, Sir," Hamilton ended, "though I mean no compliments, you must not be spared from where you are."

If Clinton was astounded at the young man's forwardness, he was also engaged by the earnestness and cogency of his argument. The Governor replied apologetically almost by return mail. He regretted being so busy "that I can hardly steal a moment to write to my friends." He urged Hamilton to continue the correspondence and not to be deterred if "I should not prove to be a very punctual correspondent."

From then onward throughout the war, Hamilton would write to almost anybody in a position to influence public affairs. Letters went out from Morristown, Middlebrook, or wherever the Headquarters sat, to Robert Morris, Gouverneur Morris, John Sullivan, James Duane. They ran into the thousands of words, and their common theme was the need for a bigger military, a sounder finance, better men in Congress—in short, a strong central government. It is not remarkable that he chose to express his ideas privately for a while. They were a mix of his own radical convictions and gleanings from foreign writers who would not have passed muster at this stage of history— John Law, Niccolo Machiavelli, David Hume.

John Law, a renegade Scot, had temporarily enriched King Louis XIV by establishing a combination bank and trading company which trafficked in raw materials from Canada to Louisiana. Issuing unlimited stock, generating lively income, the company ended in what was called the Mississippi Bubble of the early 1700's.

"Mr. Law," wrote Hamilton to one of his correspondents, probably Robert Morris, "who had more penetration than integrity, readily perceived that no plan could succeed which did not unite the interest and credit of rich individuals to those of the state. . . . It will be in our wisdom to select what is good in this plan. . . ." The not-very-busy staff officer of the Commander was proposing an artificial Bubble to raise money for the government.

"The only plan . . . is one that will make it the immediate interest of the monied men to cooperate with the government in its support. This country is in the same predicament in which France was, previous to the famous Mississippi scheme projected by Mr. Law. Its paper money had dwindled to nothing, and no effort of the government could revive it because the people had lost all confidence in its ability." Unhappily, "individuals in America are not very rich," but we must make do with what we have.

Machiavelli, a man born before Columbus discovered America, was Hamilton's model in all matters concerned with wartime Tories and foreign policy. In letters to Gouverneur Morris of New York and William Livingston of New Jersey, he was paraphrasing Machiavelli when he urged capital punishment. "If something is not done to strike terror into the disaffected, the consequences must be very fatal. . . . The Tories, emboldened by impunity, will be encouraged to proceed to the most daring and pernicious ends."

Machiavelli warned against half-measures, and so did Hamilton in a letter to the New York Committee of Correspondence. "The advice given by a certain general to his son, when the latter had a Roman army in his power, was certainly very politic. He advised him either to destroy them utterly or to dismiss them with every mark of honor and respect. By the first method, says he, you disable the Romans from being your enemies, by the last you make them your friends. . . . So with respect to the Tories."

Money was needed from France. He knew what Machiavelli would have said. "The most effective way is to tell France that without it we must make terms with Great Britain," he wrote to James Duane.

David Hume had been one of Hamilton's philosophic leaning-posts ever since college days, and now served to prop up the young officer's recommendations for authoritative government. "Political writers," Hume had written, "have established it as a maxim that, in contriving any system of government . . . every man ought to be supposed a *knave,* and to have no other end in all his actions but *private interests.* "Hume, followed by Hamilton, believed this a maxim "true in politics." Although men were often honest in private dealings, they could hardly be trusted in a public capacity. This formula was compounded in political assemblies, where a majority "acts as if it contained not one member who has any regard for public interest and liberty." For this reason, Hamilton did not like boards and committees, but preferred the single executive:

"There is always more decision, more dispatch, more secrecy, more responsibility where single men, than where bodies are concerned. By a plan of this kind we blend the advantages of a Monarchy and of a Republic in a happy and beneficial Union."

He wrote to Duane that the struggling government needed "the following great officers of state: A Secretary of Foreign Affairs, a President of War, a President of Marine, a Financier, a President of Trade." He proposed Philip Schuyler for War, Alexander McDougall for Marine, Robert Morris for Finance.

Also, Hume was strong for the national use of borrowed money to increase circulating cash, and so was Hamilton. "And why can we not have a national bank?" he demanded of Robert Morris. And a foreign loan? "I give you my honor that from our first outset I . . . wished for a foreign loan, not only because I foresaw it would be essential, but because I considered it as a tie upon the nation from which it was derived."

The reckless Law, the ruthless Machiavelli, the cynical Hume were radicals to agrarian, democratic, idealistic America. But Hamilton admired their practicality.

II

(1779–1780)

Philip Schuyler, often mentioned with favor by Hamilton, was frequently at Headquarters during 1779–80, as a member of the Congressional military committee. He was author of one of the few financial works of the time, *Causes of Depreciation of the Continental Currency,* which alone was reason enough for Hamilton's admiration. On March 17, 1780, Schuyler won passage of an act which devalued the Continental dollar at one-fortieth of its former worth, at one stroke dropping the national debt from four hundred million to ten million, at least on paper.

Hamilton liked the bony-faced, haughty man on many counts. Schuyler was rich, well-born, a military veteran, a financier, and an intimate of Washington. The Schuyler family fortune dated from 1650, when the first of that name had come from Holland to settle in New York with royal favors. Philip Schuyler, like Nicholas Cruger, increased his wealth by enlightened management. He ran a flax mill, a fishing fleet, lumber yards, and trading posts that were supplied with raw materials by Indian tribes with whom he cultivated friendly relations.

During a gay season in New York City, when Schuyler was twenty-one, he'd fallen in love with Catherine Van Rensselaer, whom he called "Sweet Kitty." The romance was interrupted in May 1755 by the outbreak of war between Britain and France. Captain Schuyler marched north to meet the enemy, but just before the battle of St. George, he received an urgent dispatch. He went galloping home and immediately married a very pregnant Sweet Kitty. Their first child, Angelica, was born five months later, barely missing illegitimacy. Thus Schuyler could hardly be snobbish toward the young aide, whose illegitimate birth was well known.

There was another affinity between the men. Hamilton's bad luck in wallowing in the backwater of war was matched by Schuyler's luck. He had missed his first battle, and would miss others. When the fighting broke out at Lexington and Concord in 1775, Schuyler felt that the British had gone too far in taxation and suppression, but that the colonies should fight only for better terms within the Empire. Already in the state assembly, Schuyler was sent to the Continental Congress, where he met Washington and became a major general, ranking third behind Greene. Chosen to command the invasion of Canada, 1775–76, he performed the planning superbly, but he got no farther north than Fort Ticonderoga, where he fell ill and had to be left behind.

His Tory politics made him unpopular. The doomed invasion, which cost five thousand lives, mostly of New Englanders, was blamed on him. From then onward he was hated in New England, and he cordially reciprocated the animosity. The antipathy heated up when Schuyler was named commander of the Northern Department, embracing New York and five New England states.

Schuyler at this point was the man picked to stop Burgoyne,

who came marching in July 1777. But the powerful Adamses
had no faith in him, and were reluctant to send him troops.
Washington bolstered him with two excellent brigadiers, Arnold and Wayne. He placed Major General Arthur St. Clair in
charge of Fort Ticonderoga. But everything went wrong at first.
Schuyler's planning was superb, his luck atrocious. Ticonderoga fell to the British. Schuyler turned over the command
to Gates, saying prophetically just before Saratoga, "The plan
of victory has been denied me, and it is left to you, General,
to reap the fruits of my labor." On top of all, he was accused
of embezzlement. The court-martial found he had actually contributed three thousand dollars to the preparations, and acquitted him with a citation for "honorable behavior."

Dogged by ill fortune, widely disliked for his cold manners
and Loyalist bent, trounced by Clinton for the governorship in
1777, believing very little in independence, he was far from
being a figure to whom a young officer might choose to hitch
his star. But Hamilton saw that Schuyler had much to offer
Congress, and had accepted appointment among unfriendly
men only as a matter of public service. Hamilton admired his
brains, his moral courage, his dedication, and was not put off
by his hauteur.

Schuyler brought along Sweet Kitty and the two youngest of their four daughters, Cornelia and Margaret, when he
joined Congress. He left Betsey in Albany with Angelica. After
getting part of the family settled at Philadelphia, he sent for
Angelica and Betsey, arranging for them to stay with his
sister, Mrs. John Cochran, wife of the Middle Department's
surgeon general. They would be living near the Morristown
camp.

Betsey must be closely chaperoned lest she do something
rash with some hard-drinking, hard-riding, amorous staff officer. As a further precaution, her father planned to steer her
toward a suitable husband, such as a titled foreigner. For that
reason he provided her with a letter of introduction to "one of
the most gallant men in camp," Baron von Steuben.

The Baron was not in camp when Betsey arrived, but Hamilton was.

CHAPTER SEVEN

The Arms of Love

I

(1780)

Hamilton's serious side coexisted closely with frivolity. On the very day, March 14, 1779, when he wrote Jay concerning Negro troops, Hamilton had a lighthearted note from Susanna Livingston, which he answered four days afterwards in like spirit. Susanna wanted a pass through the lines from New York for three of her girl-cousins, and Hamilton responded as an habitual flirt. "Had you appealed to my friendship or gallantry, it would have been irresistible."

In a letter to Laurens in April 1779, after solemn words about their friendship and the military situation, Hamilton again veered off into lightheartedness.

"And now, my dear [Sir], as we are upon the subject of wife, I empower and command you to find me one in Carolina. . . .

"She must be young—handsome . . . sensible . . . well bred . . . chaste and tender . . . of some good nature—a good deal of generosity . . . as to fortune the largest stock of that the better. . . . Mind you do justice to the length of my nose, and don't forget that I _____ [wench?]."

The joshing letter tells only that he had girls on his mind, and that his companions knew it very well. They twitted him about a conquest shortly after the staff withdrew from the Monmouth battlefield. At Morristown in January, 1780, they gibed at him about Cornelia Lott, who lived at her father's home near Headquarters. Some thought him engaged to Cornelia, and Colonel Samuel Webb teased him in verse about surrendering his bachelorhood ("What, bend the stubborn knee at last!").

He met Betsey Schuyler during his philandering with Cornelia. Around the camps this brunette daughter of General Schuyler was known as "the little saint," perhaps because her sisters were less than saintly. Tilghman observed that she had "the most good-natured lively dark eyes that I ever saw, which threw a beam of good temper and benevolence over her whole countenance." It was widely agreed that "she was the finest tempered girl in the world," language that men might use for a young woman they could not enthusiastically call beautiful.

At the time Hamilton also refrained from comment on her looks. The first thing he noticed about the new girl was that "she found out the secret of interesting me in everything that concerns her." Betsey's first letter from him was addressed to her and Catherine Livingston jointly, and concerned his intention to escort the two girls to a subscription dance. Shortly afterward, in February, in writing to Margaret Schuyler, he indulged with reckless abandon in the hazardous practice of praising one woman to another, albeit a sister:

"I should never have done, were I to attempt to give you a catalogue of the whole, of all the hearts she [Betsey] has vanquished, of all the heads she has turned, of all the philosophers she has unmade, of all the inconstants she has fixed. . . ."

He was still being flippant, but in March, while he was away on duty, he wrote back to Betsey as "My dearest girl," telling her to "take care of yourself and love your Hamilton as well as he does you. God bless you. . . ." The time for trivialities and verbal byplay had passed. By April it was time to inform her parents, and Hamilton did so in a note to Schuyler at the Morristown headquarters. He had already discussed his illegitimacy and poverty with Betsey, and these presented no impediment to the match. What worried General Schuyler was that the young couple might make a hasty marriage in camp, or elope.

Schuyler consulted with his wife, and wrote Hamilton from Philadelphia that "she consents to comply with your and her daughter's wishes." Hamilton was much in the saddle these days, and was just the kind of dashing officer for whom even a level-headed young lady of twenty-three might climb out of an aunt's window. "You will see the impropriety of taking the *dernier pas* where you are," Schuyler wrote. He then referred to the runaway marriage of Betsey's sister Angelica, who had literally climbed out of the window for the Englishman, John Church. "Mrs. Schuyler did not see her eldest daughter married. That also gave me pain, and we wish not to experience it a second time. I shall probably be in camp in a few days when we can adjust such matters."

The adjustments were that Hamilton would ask for a leave in the wintertime, when his duties were lightest, and that the wedding would be held at the gracious Schuyler mansion, to which Hamilton might invite as many friends as he liked. On April 12 Hamilton received a consenting letter from his future mother-in-law. Two days later he answered to express "my gratitude for your kind compliance with my wishes to be united to your amiable daughter."

"Hamilton's a gone man," Tench Tilghman had already observed; and now the engagement was formal.

II

(April–December 1780)

Between their betrothal in April and their honeymoon in December, the young couple came to know each other well. Betsey went back to Albany with her parents. Unlike her flighty sisters—all three of whom eloped—she was a homebody, sentimental and affectionate, and she would be understanding and worshipful of Hamilton till the end of her long life. She learned at once from his correspondence that he was filial, proud, mercurial. He could be as romantic and idealistic when buoyant as when despondent. He spoke of introducing her to James Hamilton, senior:

"I wrote you, my dear, in one of my letters that I had written our father . . . that I had pressed him to come to America after the peace. . . . I shall again present him with his black-eyed daughter, and tell her how much her attention deserves his affection and will make the blessings of his gray hairs."

Hamilton's devotion to a lost parent was more significant to Betsey than his bar sinister. She shared with him a confidence in good breeding. He would tell their children, "My blood is as good as that of those who plume themselves upon their ancestry." His pride yearned for accomplishment and recognition, and when these were withheld he turned gloomy. "Here we are, my Betsey, on our way to New York," he wrote on an abortive march to storm that city. "I hope we shall take it and hasten the happy period of our restoration to each other. Have no fears for me; for I can and will take care of myself."

Most of his Army friends were fighting in the South, and to her distress he was pulling all the strings to get a transfer. Another raid was planned but not executed, this one on Staten Island. "I made the application," he wrote, but added that Washington feared, "if an accident should happen to me, there would be a vacancy in the staff." Hamilton next proposed to lead an attack on some British posts at a future time when "my particular situation will, in any case, call me away from the Army." He was referring to the few December days of leave he would get for his marriage and honeymoon.

This inconstancy was more than any bride could bear with equanimity. Betsey never did understand that the reason he hungered so for glory was that his friends were feasting on it. The previous summer, 1779, Henry Lee had led a spectacular action at Paulus Hook, had been voted a medal by Congress, and was now galloping from one triumph to another in the South. Anthony Wayne in July of '79 had made his name by a stirring victory at Stony Point, and was a brigadier. Hamilton knew himself as good a combat soldier, and yearned to prove it.

But Betsey wanted him to leave the service. Her father had. Robert Hanson Harrison, called home by a death in the family, was returning to become chief justice of Maryland. "Meade has become engaged to a widow," Hamilton wrote, and "he has written a long letter to his widow asking her opinion of the propriety of quitting the service; and that if she does not disapprove it, he will certainly take his final leave after this campaign.

"You see," Hamilton continued, "what a fine opportunity she has to be enrolled in the catalogue of heroines. . . . I know, too,

you have so much of the Portia in you that you will not be
outdone in this line by any of your sex, and that if you saw me
inclined to quit the service of your country, you would dissuade
me from it."

He was teasing, of course, for he would never retire while
there was hope for battle. "It remains for you to show whether
you are a *Roman* or an *American* wife." He told her clearly,
"I could not with decency or honor leave the army during the
campaign."

Betsey's father tried to divert him from combat to diplomacy.
"You have been mentioned in private conversations," Schuyler
wrote from Philadelphia, "to go as Secretary to the Embassy
at the Court of Versailles." Lafayette also, at the capital, was
soliciting members of the Continental Congress to give the post
to Hamilton. "If you go, my dear Sir," wrote the Marquis, "I
shall give you all public or private knowledge about Europe I
am possessed of. Besides many private letters that may introduce you to my friends I intend giving you the *key* of that
Cabinet as well as of the societies which influence them. In a
word, my good friend, anything in my power shall be entirely
yours."

The foreign assignment would be an escape from the staff
and make an ideal honeymoon. But Hamilton already knew
that the post would go to John Laurens, who had generously
tried to get it for his frustrated friend. The rejection was de-
pressing. "Believe me, my dear Laurens, I am not insensible
of your affection in recommending me. . . . But I am a stranger
in this country. I have no property here, no connexions. If I
have talents and integrity (as you say I have), these are justly
deemed very spurious titles. . . . I am chagrined and unhappy
. . . disgusted with everything in this world but yourself and
a very few honest fellows, and I have no other wish than as soon
as possible to make a brilliant exit. . . . I hate Congress—I
hate the army—I hate the world—I hate myself."

This was a side of him which not many knew. Pessimism
could wrap him like a shroud, and so it would be the whole of
his life. Betsey received letters from him just as downcast and
self-castigating as those to his most intimate friends, Ned Ste-

vens and John Laurens, but she had the special power of love
to uplift him. If the war should be lost, he wrote, "in each
other's arms we cannot but be happy." They would go to live
in another land. "What think you of Geneva as a retreat?" His
spirits would plummet until he wished only for death in battle.
He would decide to stay alive, and they would rebound.

"I was once determined to let my existence and American
liberty end together. My Betsey has given me a motive to out-
live my pride. I had almost said my honor; but America must
not be witness to my disgrace."

She was hearing from a man with an open and trusting
heart, who held back no secrets. He spoke of his drinking habits. Washington had assigned him to another prisoner exchange meeting with British officers. "One of their principal
excellencies consists in swallowing a large quantity of wine
every day. . . ." He often mentioned the women he encountered. "A new mistress is supposed to be the best cure for an
excessive attachment. . . . Here we are, my love," he wrote
from a New Jersey stopping place, "in a house of great hospitality . . . a buxom girl under the same roof. . . .

"You see," he wrote on, "I give you an account of all the
pretty females I meet with; you tell me nothing of the pretty
fellows you see." He told of a dream he'd had, of finding her
"asleep on a green near the house, and beside you in an inclined
posture stood a Gentleman . . . one of your hands in his. . . .
I reproached him . . . and the dispute grew heated. This I fancy
awoke you . . . you flew into my arms and decided the conten-
tion with a kiss."

The fortunate bride-to-be received his letters as he rode with
the Commander over four states, counting the weeks until their
wedding. "How happy I am to find that one more month puts
an end to our long separation." Then she heard from him in
one of the most emotional episodes of his life. He wrote from
the New York Highlands, near West Point, disclosing "the
discovery of a treason of the deepest dye." Major General Benedict Arnold, commandant of that river fort, had been apprehended in an attempt to sell it to the enemy.

Arnold fled on horseback with Hamilton in distant pursuit.

The aide returned from the chase to find Arnold's wife, Peggy Shippen—the twenty-year-old former Tory belle of Philadelphia—in her bedroom, barely clad by some accounts, and in a transport of real or affected shock. Betsey soon was reading passages that revealed more of their author than his subject.

"I saw an amiable woman frantic with distress from the loss of a husband she tenderly loved. . . . It was the most affecting scene I ever was witness to. . . . One moment she raved; another she melted into tears; sometimes she pressed her infant to her breast and lamented its fate. . . . Her sufferings were so eloquent that I wished myself her brother, to have a right to become her defender."

A brother! As a woman, Betsey could see through Peggy's histrionics. She loved Hamilton all the more for finding him just a gullible male despite his worldly wisdom.

CHAPTER EIGHT

Into the Bonds of Marriage

I

(October 1780)

Going the rounds of the Headquarters at Tappan, downriver from West Point, was an ink-sketch—possibly several copies—that a young British officer had done of himself in uniform. He was Major John André, shown sitting casually at a rough table, his knees carelessly crossed, his right hand resting lightly near the ink-well. It was a picture of beautiful and aristocratic masculinity, depicting elegance, dignity, and repose. It was done in an inn that served as his prison, for the amusement of his visitors while the artist awaited military execution as a spy.

Hamilton was a frequent visitor to André, and apparently enclosed the sketch in a letter to Betsey on October 2. "I fear you will admire the picture so much as to forget the painter," he told her. His own admiration for André presents a portrait of himself. Hamilton desired for Betsey's sake to resemble the prince of gallantry that he saw in the debonair prisoner. André had everything that Hamilton revered—British officership at its gallant best, good looks, good blood, a private fortune, literary talent, and tragic grace.

"I wished myself possessed of André's accomplishments for your sake," he told her, "for I would wish to charm you in every sense."

André knew he was soon to be put to death, but he politely expressed to General Washington the hope "that I am not to die on a gibbet." The case against André was ironclad. He had been caught in civilian disguise, with Arnold's incriminating papers in his stockings, and had confessed all. Instead of ordering a drumhead court-martial, Washington appointed fourteen generals, topped by Nathanael Greene, to make a board of inquiry. Since the prisoner admitted his guilt, no witness was called, and the court found that "agreeable to the law and usage of nations . . . he ought to suffer death."

Washington knew the sentiment for André among his younger officers. Hamilton and Lafayette were sympathetic. Meade thought André's "conduct was such as did honor to the human race." Alexander Scammell pronounced him "perhaps the most accomplished officer of the age." Benjamin Tallmadge, whose troops had brought in the spy, confessed, "I can remember no instance where my affections were so fully absorbed in any man."

Washington was adamant. He stolidly ordered the sentence carried out "in the usual way," though he spared André the anguish of knowing in advance. The spy had sent to British headquarters for his full uniform. He donned the scarlet coat with green facings, bright buff breeches and waistcoat. A battalion of eighty files, with shrieking fife and heartbeat drum, escorted him, as did many new-found American friends.

Hamilton wrote, "In going to the place of execution, he bowed familiarly as he went along to all those with whom he had become acquainted." Suddenly, as the procession mounted a hill, the crude gibbet, a crosspiece between two poles, came in view. "He asked with some emotion," Hamilton recounted, " 'Must I then die in this manner?' He was told it had been unavoidable."

Living up to Hamilton's every expectation, André mounted the wagon, on which rested a coffin, placed the rope, used his own handkerchief to bind his eyes, and supplied another to tie his hands. His last words were to request that the onlookers "witness to the world that I died like a brave man." As Hamilton put it, "Among the extraordinary circumstances that attended him, in the midst of his enemies, he died universally esteemed and universally regretted."

The hanging did not turn Hamilton against his Chief, but it turned him against capital punishment. The beneficiary of his emotional experience in this death was the girl to whom he wrote his love letters. She learned what a compassionate heart he had, and how his spirits soared and plunged. In the eight

months of their engagement, she came to love him so well that
nothing he ever did afterward could change her feelings.

II

(April–December 1780)

Hamilton, infatuated as he was during the betrothal period,
which he spent mainly on horseback in Pennsylvania, New
Jersey, Connecticut, and New York, did not find his sweetheart
without fault. Neither then nor later did she write as often as
he, and he complained constantly of the neglect. "For God's
sake, my dear Betsey, try and write me oftener. . . ." He had
never had a home, and Betsey was very attached to her own.
She had so large a set of family and friends that she was not
lonesome when away from him, whereas he was painfully so.

While she was still at Morristown with her Aunt Cochran,
and he within calling distance at Amboy, Betsey asked Colonel
Samuel Webb to arrange a carriage ride into Philadelphia.
Hamilton's feelings were hurt that she missed him so little. "If
you should set out before I return, have the goodness to leave
a line informing me how long you expect to be there." He
wanted her to enjoy the trip, "though it will be a tax upon my
love to part with you so long. . . . Always remember your best
friend is where I am."

He worried much, and Betsey not at all, about the difference
in their finances. His ambition went to glory but not to gold.
"An indifference to property enters into my character too
much," he explained. Throughout the engagement he offered
her chances to reconsider. "Do you soberly relish the pleasure
of being a poor man's wife? Have you learned to think a home-
spun preferable to a brocade, and the rumbling of a waggon
wheel to the musical rattling of a coach and six?"

Betsey, snug in the family home, could comprehend the
meaning of poverty no more than that of loneliness. Hamilton
feared that he was trapping her by physical attraction, and he
asked if she felt the same for him when he was absent. He
wanted to hear from her "whether what seemed to be love was
nothing more than a generous sympathy." He would feel terri-

bly guilty if love did not survive the honeymoon. "The possibility of this frequently torments me." He did not want it on his
conscience that he had taken advantage of a wealthy girl who,
he admitted to Laurens, was "not a beauty."

Mindful of the letter he'd written to this friend about wife-
hunting, Hamilton tried to discount it. He very much wanted
to convince all his friends that he was not marrying this plain
girl for her money. It is doubtful whether he succeeded, but
they were all fond of her and she of them. "But mind," he
warned Laurens, "she loves you *à l'américaine* not *à la française.*"

He tucked this light-hearted admonition into a letter of war
news to Laurens, who was on parole after being captured at the
fall of Charleston in May. Sir Henry Clinton, supported by
Admiral Marriott Arbuthnot, with General Charles Cornwallis
second in command, had led the attack. In midsummer Sir
Henry was back in New York, weaker by land and sea, and a
new French general and admiral, Jean Baptiste Donatien de
Vimeur, Comte de Rochambeau, and Charles Louis d'Arsac,
Chevalier de Ternay, had arrived off the New England coast.

It was widely agreed among American leaders that, if only
the French would fight instead of *parlez vous,* the war could be
ended by the winter of 1780. Hamilton worked out an elaborate
proposal which he and Washington carried to Hartford for a
council of war with the Frenchmen in September.

"It is of great importance," ran his scheme for enticing the
French into battle, "that it should appear we are ready and in
condition to act; our allies not." If American weaknesses were
hidden and forces exaggerated, he argued, perhaps the allies
would seriously enter into the war. "As to operations," Hamilton wrote for Washington, "in my opinion we must propose
three plans. . . ." They were: "Take possession of the harbor
of New York . . . a landing in South Carolina . . . a winter
expedition into Canada."

Rochambeau and Ternay would think it over, and await still
more ships and troops. Stalemate in the north, difficulties in
the south, suggested that the war would drag on into another
year. Word reached the Commander's traveling headquarters

that Gates had been shamefully routed on August 16 at Camden. And on top of all, there was Arnold's treason.

"Whom can we trust now?" the Commander groaned, with tears in his eyes.

Hamilton's own affairs soon pushed the shocking West Point episode to the back of his mind. " 'Tis a pretty story indeed that I am to be thus monopolized by a little *nut brown maid* like you, and from a soldier metamorphosed into a puny lover. I believe in my soul you are an enchantress." He had a number of applications in channels for an assignment in the South, where Greene was rebuilding an army. Meanwhile the wedding day approached, and "I want to know whether you would prefer my receiving the nuptial benediction in my uniform or in a different habit. . . .

"Well, my love, here is the middle of October: a few more weeks and you are mine." He gave her a last chance to draw back. "Do you begin to repent or not? Remember you are going to do a very serious thing. . . . If you be disposed to retract, don't give me the trouble of a journey to Albany."

But neither of them for an instant considered turning back. She would have all her family around her. He would have many friends. "Be assured that we shall be happy to see the gentlemen you mention," Schuyler wrote, "and such others as you may bring with you."

He brought James McHenry and others from the camps. The Reverend Alexander Hamilton, a descendant, wrote the author on June 7, 1973: "I have always understood that the Hamilton-Schuyler wedding was a formal military affair. . . . Whoever was in Albany was there, I am sure. The Schuyler Mansion was the center of the social life of the day." It had been built to Schuyler's specifications in 1762, while he was in England on business. The family had lived there regularly since their country manor at Saratoga was burned down by Burgoyne. The house stood splendidly on a ridge at the city's southern edge, near the communal meadow, with the Helderberg Mountains in the background.

The young couple signed the register of the Reformed Church, Albany, on December 14, but they were married at the bride's home. The irrepressible McHenry wrote a long poem in celebration. He hailed the pageant for its graces of joy and family affections, its material luxuries and social dignity, but added his own "friendship voice" to warn:

> "Know, then, dear Ham, a truth confest,
> Soon beauty fades, and love's a guest."

General and Mrs. Washington sent congratulations. One of the guests later said of the bride that she "has a mild agreeable countenance," but that her brothers and sisters "are the handsomest . . . you can see."

Seldom does a wedding guest neglect to remark on the loveliness of the bride; much less does he give exclusive praise to other women present. Nobody, it would seem, thought Betsey beautiful, yet "I am the happiest of women," she wrote her sister Peggy. "My dear Hamilton is fonder of me every day."

CHAPTER NINE

The Road to Yorktown

I

(February–July 1781)

"Colonel Hamilton, you have kept me waiting at the head of the stairs these ten minutes. I must tell you, sir, you treat me with disrespect."

"I am not conscious of it, sir, but since you have thought it necessary to tell me so, we part."

Thus Hamilton tells of the break with his Commander at the New Windsor headquarters in February 1781. Back in his office, the aide sat stunned at the lightning episode, which "did not last two minutes." Then in less than an hour Tilghman entered with Washington's expression of regret. The General proposed reconciliation, "assuring me of his great confidence in my abilities, integrity, usefulness, etc., and of his desire, in a candid conversation, to heal a difference which would not have happened but in a moment of passion."

The greatest man of the age was apologizing to a subordinate, and Hamilton had the chance to be humble and generous in return. It was not to be. "Tell his Excellency, 1st—that I have taken my resolution in a manner not to be revoked," but he was willing to stay until a staff replacement could be found. In Hamilton's mind was the old aversion to meniality. This scene was the culmination of previous differences and the blank prospect of going through the rest of the Revolution without a unit to command. He wrote his father-in-law that he had always disliked the position of aide-de-camp, and had come to dislike Washington too. "At the end of the war, I may say many things to you concerning which I shall impose upon myself, till then, an inviolable silence. . . ."

Schuyler's own hurts from ill luck and military injustice made him kindly and wise. Instead of blaming Hamilton, he praised him as the one officer capable of being the General's *alter ego.* "Make the sacrifice," he advised, "the greater it is, the more glorious you."

Had Hamilton been movable, the appeal would have moved him, but his mind was set. There was no open breach with Washington, no sulking. In March Hamilton was in Newport, Rhode Island, to attend another conference with the French, and to write an address which Washington delivered to the town's inhabitants. The General invited him to attend a breakfast with Rochambeau, signing the note of March 7, "sincerely and affectly yrs." From Newport the aide rode to Albany for a fortnight's rest, before rejoining the headquarters staff at New Windsor, with Betsey. General and Mrs. Washington held a reception for the newlyweds, and later Betsey "served . . . tea with much grace" at the arrival of Baron de Closen-Haydenbourgh.

Throughout April Hamilton wrote letters for Washington to Rochambeau, to Pickering, to Greene, and to Sir Henry Clinton. He worked on another prisoner exchange and on new rules for punishment. He corresponded in his own name concerning artillery experiments at West Point by the French officer, Captain Lewis Granger.

All the while he was in touch with Greene and Lafayette, pulling strings for a field command, for "I shall hate to be [only] nominally a soldier." There were tantalizing clues that something was coming his way. On March 26 Robert Morris from Philadelphia addressed him as "Co. Alxr Hamilton of the Artillery." On May 18 he heard from John Church, Betsey's brother-in-law, who said, "Villemansey tells me he thinks you are to command a Body of Troops this campaign."

He asked Greene for "anything worth my while to do in the Southern army." He wrote Washington:

"Your Excellency knows I have been in actual service since the beginning of 76. I began in the line and had I continued there, I ought in justice to have been more advanced in rank than I am now. I believe my conduct in the various capacities, in which I have acted, has appeared to the officers of the Army in general such as to merit their confidence and esteem. . . ."

Washington would not grant assignments or promotions outside the chain of command. "I am convinced that no officer can with justice dispute your merit and abilities, . . ." he answered. "I beg you to be assured that I am only influenced by the reasons which I have mentioned."

There were many openings where Washington's reasons hardly applied. A note from Lafayette to Hamilton from Richmond a month after this latest rejection said, "I wish a reinforcement of light infantry. . . . I wish Laurens and Sheldon were immediately dispatched with their horse. Come here, my dear friend, and command our artillery in Virginia. I want your advice and exertions. . . ."

It was maddening. "As I cannot think of quitting the Army during the war," he remained on call, but other aides took up the General's letter-writing during May and June. Hamilton began to borrow books on economics and to resume his studies. During this transition period, Betsey was with him at Headquarters and in nearby villages where they took rooms, and sometimes at the Schuyler mansion. Now that she was a married lady, he thought she deserved a private servant, so he sold "a bill on France" to the Philadelphia trading firm of Stewart and Totten for "hard money" to purchase a female slave. Mrs. George Clinton had one for sale and Hamilton closed the deal with a letter of May 22 to the Governor, agreeing to send along "a sufficient sum to pay for the value of the woman Mrs. H. had of Mrs. Clinton."

Betsey didn't behave like a soldier's daughter, a soldier's wife, but there was somebody nearby who did. Angelica Church, Betsey's coquettish older sister, was thrilled by Hamilton's spirited desire for battle. As her husband told Hamilton, Angelica "is very anxious for your Happiness and Glory." This was the first manifestation of an ardent attachment that would end only with Hamilton's death.

II

(April–June 1781)

Hamilton's book-borrowing was a sign to Betsey that he had something else than fighting on his mind.

"Have you a tract written by Price? . . ." he asked Timothy

Pickering. "Have you Hume's Essays . . . or Postlethwaite?
Any of these books you may have, you will singularly oblige
me by the loan of them."

He wanted to get back into pamphleteering, and he warmed
up with a long letter to Robert Morris, who had been named
Superintendent of Finance. Betsey gladly helped him with the
copying, as she would do throughout his career. Hamilton
boomed away:

" 'Tis by introducing order into our finances—by restoring
public credit—not by gaining battles—that we are finally to
gain our object. 'Tis by putting ourselves in a condition to continue the war . . . that we shall bring it to a speedy and successful [end]."

That summer, without ceasing to dicker for the combat billet,
he resumed writing for publication. Since March of 1781, with
Maryland's ratification, the Articles of Confederation had
become the national charter—a significant step toward closer
Union. This was Hamilton's subject.

III

(July–September 1781)

His nom de plume, not Latin this time, was "The Continentalist." It expressed his theme: Think Continentally, More
Power to Congress. Samuel Loudon's New York Packet Company published the first four essays. He wrote that America
had begun the Revolution with a colonial mentality, and it is
"more to be wondered at that we have done so well than that
we have not done better." Townships, counties, states all had
local claims that endangered the common cause. This also had
led to "that defect which will be the object of these remarks—a
want of power in Congress." He urged that the central government be given the right to regulate trade, impose duties, levy
real estate and poll taxes, sell off public lands, and borrow large
sums of money. "Power, without revenue, in a political society,
is but a name."

When the Continentalist essays began to appear in July and
August, the long disease of military defeat was giving way.

Under General Nathanael Greene, the American forces down south were chipping away at Cornwallis. French ships off the Indies dared to challenge British vessels. The northern regiments were being reorganized and re-officered. At camp near Dobbs Ferry, July 9, Hamilton had business with Washington, but "nothing was said on the subject of a command." Perhaps Hamilton remembered his Machiavellian remark to Duane that the way to get money from France was to threaten to make a separate peace. He now tried the ruse on Washington:

"I wrote the General a letter and enclosed him my commission." No more staff work. No more fetch and carry. Let the Commander find another translator. The tug of war between these obstinate personalities suddenly went to the younger man, for the general gave way. "This morning," Hamilton wrote Betsey on the 10th, "Tilghman came to me in his name, and pressed me to retain my commission, with the assurance that he would endeavor by all means to get me a command. . . ."

IV

(July–October 1781)

Seeing was believing. General Orders on the last day of July: Two companies of light infantry and two of New York militia "will form a Battalion under command of Lieutenant Colonel Hamilton and Major Fish," the college mates. Better yet: "After the formation of the Battalion, Lieutenant Colonel Hamilton will join the Advance Corps under the orders of Colonel Scammell."

Not since the battle of Princeton had he commanded his own men. He must drill and equip them to be the best in the Army. Only two tents had been sent him, he notified Timothy Pickering, the new Quartermaster General.

"Will you be so good as to give an explicit order for two more?" he wrote on August 7. "We also want a Regimental order book and some regimental paper. . . . The camp kettles and pails you ordered for my use were not furnished. . . . We are unprovided with tents for the Adjutant Qr. Mr. and Surgeon."

Shoes, shoes—that perennial shortage. Tench Tilghman, still on the staff, thought that New York State should clothe its two militia companies, and Hamilton immediately went over his head to the Commander, writing, "Your Excellency is sensible that . . . the article of shoes is indispensible. If the men cannot be supplied, they cannot perform the duty required of them. . . . The state makes no provision . . . they must therefore be destitute if they have not a Continental supply."

Washington would not break out of channels. "Shoes will be issued to the State Companies under your command [by] the same mode . . . supplying the other companies." Inflexible officialdom! But Hamilton knew some tricks of his own. General Schuyler had long ago been Quartermaster to Sir Jeffrey Amherst, and John Church was getting rich with the French as a dealer in military equipment. With such sources, Hamilton would manage. He was jubilant to be with troops, and with Nicholas Fish. "I prize him both as a friend and an officer."

The French were sending still another admiral, François Joseph Paul, Comte de Grasse; but it was not known whether he would show up off New York harbor or the Chesapeake capes, whether his ships were well armed and well manned, whether he was a fighting seaman or a cruiseman.

Good news: Cornwallis had got himself penned up in Virginia between the York and James Rivers. Disturbing rumor: British Admiral Samuel Graves was sailing south to transport General Cornwallis back to New York and concentrate British strength there. Good news: Admiral de Grasse had sailed into Chesapeake Bay, with twenty-nine warships and three thousand troops. If Cornwallis could be marooned in Virginia, the allied forces would assemble with superiority that promised a war-ending victory.

When Hamilton was still in the headquarters family back in May, his friend, François Jean, Chevalier de Chastellux, had submitted an elaborate plan for deceiving General Clinton's New York garrison and simultaneously descending upon Cornwallis. Essential parts of the scheme began to materialize in mid-August. Secret agents spread word among the Tories of the vicinity that de Grasse was headed for Rhode Island, not Virginia, and that Continentals from all along the coast were concentrating in New Jersey. Washington ordered boats to be collected, as if for use against Staten Island. He deliberately displayed large bread ovens suitable for feeding French reinforcements.

General William Heath of Massachusetts was sent north along the Hudson. It was both a feint and a precaution. Next day, August 20, Washington's advance body started south. "The movement is critical," he wrote to Congress, "the opportunity precious, the prospects most happily favorable."

Hamilton divined what was stirring. He wrote Schuyler to "intimate" to Betsey that great events were afoot. Then, on August 22, he explained to her: "I used this method to prevent a surprise that might be too severe to you. A part of the Army, my dear girl, is going to Virginia. . . . I cannot ask permission to visit you. It might be thought improper to leave my corps at such a time and upon such an occasion. I cannot persuade myself to ask a favour at Headquarters."

Betsey was pregnant. He must be ever so gentle. His words of farewell must be of utmost tenderness, not revealing his exultation. He must discount the probability of a major engagement. "I am miserable because I know my Betsey must be so. I am wretched at the idea of flying so far from you without a single hour's interview to tell you all my pains and all my love." Odds were against a Virginia battle, he wrote, lying gallantly. "It is ten to one that our views would be disappointed by Cornwallis returning to South Carolina by land." Probably nothing would come of all the bustle. "At all events our operations must be over by the latter end of October and I will fly to the arms of my Betsey."

He was on the march soon after this. His battalion, in the midst of the tramping army, edged southward past Princeton and Trenton, into Philadelphia, where the City Troop rode forth to welcome them. There was no longer any purpose of deception. Washington held a parade and a reception to impress Rochambeau. Without the French, the Commander would face Cornwallis with no better than even numbers. Given Rochambeau, given de Grasse, he would enjoy odds of at least three to one, and the invaluable advantage of sea power.

At Philadelphia, John Laurens, fresh from France, joined up. Hamilton cashed a money order which Schuyler had arranged for him with Robert Morris. Out of the capital city, past Chester and Wilmington, on into Maryland where vessels awaited the troops at Head of Elk. From this bayside port, Hamilton wrote again. "My lovely wife. . . . Every day confirms me in the intention of renouncing public life, and devoting myself wholly to you. Let others waste their time and their tranquility in vain pursuit of power and glory; be it my objective to be happy in a quiet retreat with my better angel."

Meditations on the vanity of "power and glory" came easily aboard the troopship. The Continentalist Papers were running in the *New York Packet,* but would hardly make timely reading with all attention riveted on war news. His chances to distinguish himself in battle were cloudy. Cornwallis might escape the trap. The French rarely defeated the British at sea. Colonel Alexander Scammell, his immediate superior, was equally glory-starved after long administrative service. Courage without opportunity was a nullity. "How chequered is human life!" Hamilton wrote from Annapolis.

Disembarking with his troops at Williamsburg, September 28, Hamilton marched them the remaining ten miles through standing crops in sandy soil to the outskirts of the steepled village of Yorktown. He was hardly in position before the enemy breastworks when the British loosed a volley that killed one of his light infantrymen. Two nights later a death, sad but portentous, moved Hamilton higher up the ladder of command. Colonel Scammell went out on patrol and fell into an ambush. He was mortally wounded after his capture, to the indignation of the American camp. The vacancy meant that Hamilton and Lieutenant Colonel Chevalier Jean-Joseph Sourbador de Gimat each headed a corps under Major General Lafayette.

For the next three weeks Hamilton watched the familiar play of Washington's caution. The Americans, with troop superiority, with sea power for the first time in the war, with advantageous ground and experienced allied officers, could not afford to attack too soon or too late.

Delay was helpful because Cornwallis was short on rations and ammunition. Delay was risky because the British sea dogs, Admirals Samuel Hood and George Rodney, might show up at any time, perhaps bringing Sir Henry Clinton with them for an attempt to lift the siege. Perfect timing and a *coup de grâce* were essential, since de Grasse was under orders to leave before the end of October.

Move carefully in on Cornwallis. That was the plan. Baron von Steuben, following sketches by the French engineering officers, supervised much spade work. Hamilton's men, constantly under fire, dug trenches parallel to the enemy positions, dragged stakes, sticks, and baskets of dirt across open spaces. The plan was for American artillery to concentrate on two British redoubts, Number 9 and Number 10, the latter, flush against the York River, being the anchor of the British line. When these were deemed sufficiently reduced, they would be stormed by infantry. American ordnance had been hauled across New Jersey, barged down the Delaware River, carted across Maryland to the Chesapeake. Brought to bear at Yorktown were three 24-pounders and twenty 12-pounders, made of iron, and fifteen other pieces, made of brass. The French added their total of seventy-two howitzers and mortars.

An artilleryman at heart, Hamilton watched the most spectacular bombardment of the Revolution. It commenced theatrically on the afternoon of October 9. "General Washington himself put the match to the first gun," a journalist wrote; "a furious discharge of cannon and mortars immediately followed, and Earl Cornwallis received his first salutation."

After that, by day and night, it was a "sublime and stupendous scene," in the words of the watching Chevalier de Chastellux. "The bomb-shells from the besiegers and the besieged are incessantly crossing each other's path in the air. They are clearly visible in the form of a black ball in the day; but in the night they appear like a fiery meteor with a blazing tail, most beautifully brilliant. . . ."

Hamilton had eve-of-battle talks with Light-Horse Harry Lee, by now an illustrious hero. He told the Virginian, who put it down in his journal, about the rupture with Washington: "Hamilton had gone out in search of the courier, who had been long waiting, when accidentally he met the Marquis de Lafayette, who seized him by the button (as was the habit of this zealous nobleman), engaged him in conversation. . . . At length, breaking off from the Marquis, he reached the courier. . . . Returning he found the General seated by the table on which lay the dispatches. The moment he appeared, Washington with warmth and sternness chided him for the delay. . . . To this Hamilton answered, 'If your excellency thinks proper thus to address me, it is time for me to leave you.' " It made good soldiers' talk as the guns roared on.

"Thank heaven," Hamilton wrote Betsey on October 12, "our affairs seem to be approaching fast to a happy period. Last night our second parallel commenced. Five days more, the enemy must capitulate or abandon their present position; if they do the latter, it will detain me ten days longer."

He'd written her twenty letters, he declared, since leaving the North, and received only three from her in the seven weeks. At first he was testy in noting that she had far more time to write than he, but he quickly subdued the camp-life tensions:

"You think you have only to smile and caress and you will disarm my resentment, but you are mistaken. The crime is of too serious nature to be forgiven, except with one atonement which I am sure it will not be easy for you to make. This is to love me more than ever. . . ."

Prospective fatherhood, and battle fever, made him write archly. "I may compound for you one substitute. You shall engage shortly to present me with *a boy*. You will ask if a girl will not answer the purpose. By no means. I fear with all the mother's charms, she may inherit the caprices of her father, and then she will enslave, tantalize and plague one half the sex, out of pure regard to which I protest against a daughter. . . ."

Washington perceived he could stretch out the preparations no longer. The attackers must sweep forward, and no later than October 14. Hearing of the decision, Lafayette asked the honor of commanding the entire allied right wing, replacing General Benjamin Lincoln. The Chief would never grant so irregular a request, but he did assign Lafayette to the responsibility of assaulting Number 10 Redoubt, the key stronghold. One of Lafayette's lieutenant colonels should lead the storming party, and Lafayette picked Gimat on grounds that he "had made the whole Virginia campaign," while Hamilton was a late-comer.

Hamilton protested. On the date set for attack, he argued, he would be officer-of-the-day, technically Gimat's superior. Lafayette replied that the Commander must decide the point. Hamilton hurried to Headquarters to press his point. After a brief conference, he burst from Washington's tent and embraced Nicholas Fish, shouting:

"We have it! We have it!"

On the afternoon of October 14 Washington rode out to inspect Lafayette's position, which was some eight hundred yards from the enemy lines. The approach to Redoubt Number 10 (the Rock, as the soldiers called it) had been turned into an obstacle course by the defenders. Hamilton's men would have to get through an abatis, a barricade of bent trees with their branches sharpened like pikes. Engineers or sappers had orders to cut through this deadly barrier. There were ditches to cross and palisades to climb, and finally the parapet to scale under the direct fire of British muskets. Surprise was the best hope. In the councils of war it was decided that the Americans should attack by night, with empty guns. The assault called for bloody work with the cold steel of bayonet and sword, the tools of Steuben.

Washington gathered Hamilton and other officers for a rare battlefield entreaty. Let every man be resolute, he urged them. The attack on the redoubts would be decided by those whom he addressed, he said, and they held the fate of the battle. Did Washington's knees shake? One young officer said afterwards he wasn't sure whether the shaking knees were the Commander's or his own.

At eight o'clock that night Hamilton with his men waited in the trench. All was in readiness for the chance he had so eagerly sought. This was the war's climactic hour; small wonder

if legs were wobbly. One battle would end it. One charge could
decide it.

French cannon were to give the signal. The shots burst upon
the darkness. One . . . two . . . three . . . four . . . five . . . six.
It was his moment, and he leaped in front of his men. "Hamilton . . . rushed forward with impetuosity, . . ." wrote Light-
Horse Harry. "Pulling up the abatis and knocking down the
palisades, he forced his way into the redoubt."

Washington Irving wrote a spirited account of the charge:
"Hamilton, to his great joy, led the advance of the Americans.
The men, without waiting for the sappers to demolish the abatis in regular style, pushed them aside or pulled them down
with their hands, and scrambled over like rough bushfighters.
Hamilton was the first to mount the parapet, placing one foot
on the shoulder of a soldier, who knelt on one knee for that
purpose. The men mounted after him. Not a musket was fired.
The redoubt was carried at the point of the bayonet."

It was all over in ten minutes. Irving continued: "The loss
of the enemy was eight killed and seventeen taken prisoners.
Among the latter was Major Campbell who had commanded
the redoubt. A New Hampshire captain of artillery would have
taken his life in revenge of the death of his favorite, Colonel
Scammell, but Colonel Hamilton prevented him. Not a man
was killed after he ceased to resist."

Washington watched it all through a spyglass from an exposed position. He turned to Knox and said, "The work is done,
and *well done.*" He would praise the Hamilton charge in his
dispatches: "Few cases have related greater proof of intrepidity, coolness and firmness." Lafayette wrote the Commander
about Hamilton, "whose well-known talents and gallantry
were on this occasion most conspicuous."

Three days later, Cornwallis raised a flag of truce. Washington named the surrender terms. Enemy officers and men must
march in full regalia between parallel ranks of the Americans
and the French that stretched for a mile. The surrender would
be ceremonious, with banners and band music. It entailed the
handing over of a sword by the highest authority. But Cornwallis was sick with his defeat, and a heavy, jovial face appeared

at the head of the British party. Hamilton recognized his one-time drinking companion, Charles O'Hara, a brigadier, second in command.

"Now, sir," O'Hara called out to him, "perform your promise. . . . I had little thought that I should ever have the opportunity of requiring your performance of it."

Washington had never looked more cold. It was his right to receive the sword from Cornwallis and not a subordinate. He watched as O'Hara, unwilling to surrender to a rebel chief, offered the blade to Rochambeau and was directed back to the American line. Washington would not take the emblem from a brigadier; he nodded grimly to Lincoln, who received it and handed it back as required by the surrender terms. The British with their German mercenaries marched to the designated field and deposited their arms.

V

(October 1781)

It was the perfect battle, the total victory, the ultimate success. Hamilton had led a charge with brandished steel. He had seen a sword received in surrender, and had watched a laying down of arms. Color and music enlivened the scene, as the redcoat band played "The World Turned Upside Down." Washington entertained Brigadier O'Hara and his staff at dinner. Three days later the surrender terms were formally signed in the Hamilton-taken redoubt.

Now he could break away and ride to Betsey, but first he owed Lafayette a full report. He composed it the morning after the battle, attaching a casualty list that showed eight of his command killed and twenty-five wounded. He submitted this separately, so it did not clog his narrative account.

"Agreeable to your orders, we advanced in two columns with unloaded arms. . . . The rapidity and immediate success of the assault are the best comment on the behavior of the troops. . . . I do but justice to the several corps when I have the pleasure to assure you, there was not an officer nor soldier whose behavior, if it could be particularized, would not have claim to the warmest approbation. . . . Incapable of imitating examples of barbarity, the soldiers spared every man who ceased to resist."

Next day, the sixteenth, and again on the eighteenth, he wrote lovingly to his wife. Then, a week after the surrender, he left for Albany, and rode so hard that he wore out the horses, "and was obliged to hire others." It was the tenth year since his arrival on the mainland. The orphan boy had become a hero, acquired a doting wife, entered a family of singular warmth, and possessed himself of wealthy, influential, and famous friends; and by January he would have a son.

PART TWO

A SITUATION OF POWER

*Public life is a situation of power and energy;
he trespasses against his duty who sleeps upon
his watch. . . .*

Edmund Burke

CHAPTER TEN

The Young Congressman

I

(January–November 1782)

Hamilton was back in Albany among many Schuylers, for the General had five daughters and three sons. Since the previous spring Hamilton's mother-in-law, Betsey's sister Angelica, and Betsey herself had all produced babies. It was comfortable at the big friendly mansion, but he must soon set up a household and choose a career.

He might become a professional soldier. The Army wanted him to stay. In January 1782, Secretary at War Benjamin Lincoln specified that Hamilton be retained in service because of "superior abilities & knowledge." But Hamilton still smarted from the long neglect of his combat talents, and he wrote stiffly to Washington:

"The difficulties I experienced last campaign in obtaining a command will not suffer me to make any further application on that head. . . . I therefore renounce from this time all claim to the compensations attached to my military station during the war or after it."

With the British occupying New York City and Charleston, and a peace treaty still under negotiation, he did not wish to be out of any renewed action. "I shall accordingly retain my rank while I am permitted to do it, and . . . I shall at all times be ready to answer the call. . . ."

Inactive military service did not suit him. If he chose a business career, he could apply to the enterprising Cruger family or to John Church, who soon left for France to collect large sums for war materials. Perhaps Hamilton would study medicine. There had been physicians on both sides of his supposed family. He often heard from Ned Stevens, who thought him a

hero, and concluded his letters, "Believe me to be, My dear
Ham, *Yours inviolably.*" Hamilton had no inclination to the
other gentlemanly pursuits of farming, teaching, and preach-
ing. Schuyler told him, "I should most earnestly wish you in
Congress"; but politics was not a paying profession.

There remained the law. His first moves in that direction
were listless. "I lose all taste for the pursuits of ambition," he
wrote Richard Meade.

"I sigh for nothing but the company of my wife and baby. The
ties of duty alone, or of imagined duty, keep me from renouncing public life altogether."

He came across the two unpublished "Continentalist" papers, and dispatched them to the *New York Packet.* They had
been "written last fall," he told the editor. It was as if he had
hung the pen behind his ear and gone off to meet the enemy
at Yorktown.

He was drifting in this phase of his life. He requested Nicholas Fish to make purchases for him at G. Duychink, 13 Water
Street, New York. "The articles . . .

"four dozen decanters, if to be had, if not, two Quarts will do.

"a dozen wine glasses.

"two ale glasses to hold about a pint each, if not to be had,
two tumblers.

". . . I shall not be able to give a friend a glass of wine to
drink 'till these arrive, for they are not to be had here."

He was without an earned income. The first date in his new
cash book as a civilian is March 1, 1782, but he does not show
any receipts until February 1784. One discouragement to his
entering the Law was a wartime provision by the New York
Supreme Court, dated April 1778, when he was at Valley Forge:
"No person shall be admitted to practice as an Attorney of this
Court unless he shall previously have served as a Clerk to an
Attorney of this Court for at least three years. . . ." On April
26, 1782, the Court relented "in favor of such young gentlemen
who had directed their studies to the profession of the Law, but
upon the breaking-out of the present War had entered the
Army. . . ."

Strictly speaking, Hamilton had not been a law student at
King's College, although his reading had included Coke and

Blackstone. But since General Schuyler was the conservative leader of the state senate, some dispensation was to be expected. The Court ruled: "Whereas Mr. Alexander Hamilton has in court declared that he had previous to the war directed his Studies to the Profession of the Law . . . he prayed the court that the said law . . . be further suspended until October term next." The prayer was granted.

This break gave him almost six months to prepare for an examination of admission. He rented a home for Betsey and the baby. Troup, already a certified attorney, moved in as a tutor. James Duane wrote, "I am much pleased to find that you have set yourself seriously to the Study of the Law. You are welcome to the use of any of my books. . . . I know I can depend upon your care of them."

Always gifted with concentration, Hamilton resumed his college habit of memorizing books by reciting passages aloud, "while walking to and fro." He did not outgrow the concentration. Some years later the story was told of his pacing the street in front of a store at Kinderhook, where he had gone to plead a case. "Apparently in deep contemplation, and his lips moving as rapidly as if he were in conversation with some person—he entered the store, tendered a fifty-dollar bill to be exchanged."

When the storekeeper refused and was asked why, he said: ". . . I have seen him walk before my door for half an hour, sometimes stopping, but always talking to himself, and if I had changed the money and he had lost it, I might have received blame."

He aided his memory by abstracting what he learned into a manual of 177 manuscript pages. This manuscript, *Practical Proceedings in the Supreme Court of the State of New York,* was not published in his lifetime, but was copied out by fellow-students and may have earned him some money. He drove himself hard, aiming at examinations that would admit him as an attorney in July, and to the higher rank of counselor in late October. It was not an extraordinary pace under the prejudice allowed for veterans. Aaron Burr, in Albany at the time, moved about as fast as Hamilton, and so did John Marshall in Virginia.

Possibly Hamilton's first client, and one somewhat indicative of his coming career, was the seventeen-year-old British Guardsman, Captain Charles Askill, whom General Washington condemned to death by hanging in May 1782. Askill had been chosen by lot from among captured enemy officers to die in retaliation for the death of an American captain who had been hanged by Loyalists in this twilight season between war and peace.

Askill's sentence seemed monstrously unfair to Hamilton. He looked back on the execution of André "as an act of *rigid justice,*" he told Henry Knox, but for Washington to repeat such an act in peacetime, he thought, "will have an influence particularly unfavorable to the General's character. . . ." He begged Knox to intercede with the Commander. Washington, whose mercy was also besought by the young captain's mother, turned the matter over to Congress, which granted clemency. Hamilton's part was minor, but it marks the first of many cases in which he served for simple justice without a fee, or for far less than a delighted client offered to pay. "Such was his professional character," wrote Robert Troup.

II

(April–November 1782)

During his studies that spring Hamilton began getting various communications from Robert Morris, the Continental Financier. Morris had induced Congress to call upon the states to deliver eight million dollars in specie to meet national expenses for 1782. The state quotas were to be paid to loan commissioners in each capital, but little money was forthcoming. Morris tried a circular letter to the governors. The few who bothered to reply gave "evasive and unsatisfactory" answers. As a further resort, the Financier decided to appoint in each state a Receiver of Continental Taxes, and in May he wrote to Hamilton:

"The intention of this letter is to offer you that appointment. . . . For the trouble of executing it, I shall allow you one fourth percent on the monies you receive."

New York's quota was $370,598, and for any chance of collec-

tion it might as well have been that many million. "I am now
engaged in a course of studies . . . ," he replied to Morris.
"Time is so precious to me that I could not put myself in the
way of any interruptions unless for an object of consequence
to the public or myself. The present is not of this nature . . .
does not afford a sufficient inducement. . . ."

He regretted refusing any favor to Morris, who was quick to
sense this feeling. Morris tried again. "I see with you that the
office I had the pleasure of offering will not be equal to what
your abilities will gain in the Profession of the Law." As a
follow-up the Financier said he would pay Hamilton a fee for
the full amount of the state obligation, whether collected in
whole or part. This would put about nine hundred dollars in
Hamilton's pocket, "without more attention than you could
spare from your studies. . . . I should be happy in your acceptance, and will leave the matter open until I have the opportunity of hearing from you. . . ."

Hamilton was tempted more by the challenge than by the
fee, which he later waived. He agreed to accept the appointment "to advance the public interest," if Morris understood
that his studies came first. These would end with an examination in late July. "In the mean time," he wrote on June 21, "I
shall be happy to receive your instructions. . . . A meeting of
the Legislature is summoned early in the next month at which,
if I previously receive your orders, it may be possible to put
matters in train."

Morris promptly sent him a commission, professing himself
to be "very happy to find you have determined to accept the
office. . . . I must request you to exert your talents in forwarding with your Legislature the views of Congress. Your former
situation in the Army, the present situation of that army, your
connections in the state, your perfect knowledge of men and
measures, and the abilities which heaven has blessed you with,
will give you a fine opportunity to forward the public service. . . ."

Hamilton still had not taken the examination, but the Legislature went into session, and he boarded a ship for Poughkeepsie, at that time the state capital. He requested of Governor

Clinton "that I may have the honor of a conference with a committee of the two houses." Though not yet twenty-five years old, and with little residence in the state, he had good credentials, as Morris had foreseen. The Continentalist Papers and their plea for a stronger Congress had made an impact. Hamilton met first with a senate committee, then with an assembly committee, and the astonishing result was a "Resolution of the Legislature Calling for a Convention of the States to Revise and Amend the Articles of the Confederation."

Two days after final passage, Hamilton wrote Morris saying, "It is of indispensable importance that I leave this place immediately to prepare for an examination." During the six-day stay, "I urged the several matters contained in your instructions. . . . I found every man convinced that something was wrong, but few that were willing . . . to consent to the proper remedy." Nevertheless, in addition to the Resolution for a national convention, he obtained the appointment of still another committee to make a recess study of the tax structure "and to communicate with me on this subject."

On the same date as this letter, July 22, the Legislature named him as one of five delegates to serve the one-year term in Congress, "from the first Monday in November next ensuing."

He needed to prepare himself for the new post as well as for his law career. He asked the Governor to send him printed volumes of the Laws of New York. Clinton had to reply that "only those for particular purpose" had been published, but that he had requested the printing committee "to furnish you with a set, which I doubt not will be complied with. . . . I shall, however, be happy to give you every aid in my power. . . ." Hamilton pursued his quest for source material, noting to Clinton that he also needed: "History of New York, [History] of England since the Revolution to the last peace—[which] entails history of the late war."

His friends received word of his election with mixed reactions. John Laurens, still trying to raise Negro troops, this time for an assault upon Charleston, thought Congress only a way station toward his "becoming a Minister plenipotentiary for peace. . . ." James McHenry, now a Maryland state senator on a salary "that might perhaps defray about two-thirds of one's expenses," made an oblique reference to Hamilton's financial support by Schuyler, remarking, "I find that to be dependent on a father is irksome. . . . I hear you have been chosen a delegate to Congress; will you forgive me for saying that I wish you had not been chosen . . . a few years practice at the bar would make you independent. . . . By pushing your studies to a conclusion, you at once perfect your happiness."

Lafayette chaffed him from Paris for being a laggard correspondent. "Dear Hamilton, however silent you may choose to be, I will nevertheless remind you of a friend who loves you tenderly. . . . Now let us talk politics. The old Ministry have retired and Lord North is not sorry. . . . This stroke of Count de Grasse has greatly deranged my schemes. I hoped for [Charleston]. . . ."

The last word, in code, told Hamilton that Lafayette's plans to send the French fleet to South Carolina had come apart, along with much else. De Grasse had left Yorktown, clashed with Admiral Rodney off the West Indies, and been decisively beaten on April 12, '82. The episode gave Hamilton a lifelong conviction that if there were to be European ties, they had better be with a nation of sea power. In addition to losing another naval battle, France was withdrawing Rochambeau's men and also its financial support of the young country. "Your ministers ought to know best what they are doing," Hamilton answered Lafayette, "but if the war goes on. . . ."

That thought bothered him. "These states are in no humor for continuing exertions; if the war lasts, it must be carried on with external succors. I make no apology for the inertness of this country. I detest it; but since it exists, I am sorry to see other sources diminish."

Hamilton joked with Lafayette about married felicity and "the little stranger" in the crib. "I have been employed for the last ten months in rocking the cradle and studying the art of fleecing my neighbors." In mid-August he was exhorting Laurens: "Quit your sword, my friend, put on the toga, come to Congress. We know each other's sentiments, our views are the same; we fought side by side to make America free, let us hand to hand struggle to make her happy."

The letter never reached this best of friends. Laurens had been dancing at a Carolina mansion when word was brought of a British foraging body in the area. He mounted and galloped, at the head of his cavalry troop, directly into a fatal ambush. Hamilton learned the bad news while still in Albany.

No man was ever closer to his heart than John Laurens. They had the compelling affinity of young men who had suffered. Hamilton's flawed childhood was matched by a mysterious and tragic marriage which the young Laurens had made while studying law at the Middle Temple in London. His wife's death had left him with a melancholia that approached a death wish. Washington thought Laurens had an "intrepidity bordering on rashness." Greene said of him, "The love of military glory made him seek it upon occasions unworthy of his rank."

Once, in berating Laurens for not writing, Hamilton said to him: "But like a jealous lover, when I thought you slighted my caresses, my affection was alarmed and my vanity piqued. I had almost resolved to lavish no more of them upon you and to reject you as an inconstant and ungrateful ____."

The affection was as extravagantly expressed as Lafayette's for Hamilton: "I feel within myself a want to tell you that I love you tenderly." Such devotion between men of the Revolution will not be understood by a reader unable to comprehend deep, chaste, masculine love. Laurens' death was the harder to bear for being so inappropriate. "How strangely are human affairs conducted," Hamilton brooded.

Somehow the examinations in July and October were taken and passed, and somehow he managed to make some collections before closing his accounts for Morris. Hamilton was appointed Receiver on July 13, resigned on August 28, and turned in $6,250, of which he declined to accept any part. He was going into politics in a mood that would never change. He wrote to Richard Meade:

"Experience is a continuing comment on the worthlessness of the human race. . . . [As] a member of Congress . . . I do not expect to reform the state, although I shall endeavor to do all the good I can."

III
(November 1782–March 1783)

Hamilton set out in mid-November for Philadelphia, borne by two "free and gentle" horses, gifts from his father-in-law. Crossing the river at Fishkill, he wrote back to Betsey, whom he had left behind with the baby: "Remember your promise; don't fail to write me by every post. I shall be miserable if I do not hear once a week from you and my precious infant."

He was soon among new and old friends at the boarding house and at the state house, the latter accommodating both the Pennsylvania Executive Council and the Congress of the Confederation. There was close contact with Robert and Gouverneur Morris; with James Madison of Virginia; with Elias Boudinot, now president of Congress; with James McHenry, who arrived in May 1783. On his first day in session, November 25, Hamilton was able to do something for the memory of Laurens. That beloved comrade had been Captain-General of Prisoners after Yorktown, when his father, Henry Laurens, a diplomatic commissioner, was captured at sea and imprisoned in the Tower of London. Because Madison had quarreled with Henry Laurens, he was interested when Hamilton told of Washington's agreement to exchange Lord Cornwallis for this American prisoner. Madison, who meticulously kept a journal, made note of the new member's intimate contribution to the discussion. It is the first evidence of an acquaintanceship which would take many turnings in times to come.

In 1782, at thirty-two years of age, Madison was not long recovered from a nervous illness, identified as epileptoid hysteria by his best biographer, Irving Brant. It had kept him from military service, but not from becoming an ardent revolutionary, and his invalidism allowed him the leisure for study and reflection at Montpelier, his home in Orange County, Virginia. Diffidence caused him to avoid public speaking until he was thirty years of age, by which time he was profoundly read in law, history, and philosophy.

Hamilton knew something about nervous disorders, and could have felt only admiration for Madison's courageous recovery of health by mental discipline and physical exercise.

Called "Jemmy" by close friends who appreciated his "vein of quiet humor," Madison comported himself with deep reserve toward such casual associates as Hamilton was at this time.

But their minds had a magnetic attraction for one another. On November 26, the second day of the session, Hamilton entered a petition for the states to negotiate for raising money to support the central government. "One consideration suggested by Mr. Hamilton, . . ." Madison recorded, "was that it would . . . tend to cement the union."

Federal taxes would do that, but the states were unready to call a common assembly, or to act in concord. Pennsylvania, far from donating money, was demanding settlement of a debt owed by Congress. "On the motion of Mr. Hamilton, . . ." wrote Madison, "Resolved: that a committee be appointed to confer with the legislature of Pennsylvania."

Vermont, which the Green Mountain Boys had put together with lands claimed from New York, New Hampshire, and Massachusetts, was independently declaring statehood. A Hamilton resolution declared Vermont's peremptory attitude "highly derogatory to the authority of the United States and dangerous to the confederacy." He favored Vermont statehood, but there should be order and formality in the proceedings.

Rhode Island refused to go along with the other twelve states in agreeing to a federal tax on imports. Under the Articles of Confederation, all such matters required unanimous consent. Hamilton moved that a delegation be sent to Providence "urging the absolute necessity of a compliance. . . ."

He was indefatigable. He was brilliant. He was named to committees on finance and military affairs. On December 16 he composed a 3,000-word Report which lectured the Rhode Island Assembly "for refusing their compliance." By now he was more than ever dismayed concerning the prospects for nationhood. "God grant the union may last," he wrote John Laurence of New York, "but it is too frail now to be relied on, and we ought to be prepared for the worst."

He advised Governor Clinton to introduce legislation giving land to all officers and soldiers willing to become citizens of New York. The increase in the military-minded population of the state seemed important. "It is the first wish of my heart that the Union may last, but feeble as the links are, what prudent man would rely on it? Should disunion take place, any person who will cast his eye upon the map will see how essential it is to our state to provide for its own security." With troops to repel invasion from Canada and elsewhere, he added, "all we shall have to do will be to govern well."

Fearing that the states would go their separate ways, he was also apprehensive that the Continental Army, which was camped at Newburgh under Washington and Knox, would develop a rough will of its own for collecting back pay. Philadelphia was holding receptions and banquets, dances and race meets, but Hamilton made no mention of joining in these festivities. He became so lonely that he asked Betsey to make plans to bring the child and join him:

"There never was a husband who could vie with yours in fidelity and affection. I begin to be insupportably anxious to see you again. . . . I wish you to take advantage of the first good snow that promises to get you through. . . . Take the advice of your friends about the route. . . . For God's sake take care of my child on the journey. . . . God bless my lovely Betsey and send her soon to me."

The river was impassable during much of December and January, and the young husband burned with loneliness and desire. "I have borne your absence with patience till about a week since," he wrote on January 8, 1783, "but the period we fixed for our reunion being come, I can no longer reconcile myself to it. Every hour in the day I feel a severe pang on this account and my nights are sleepless. Come, my charmer, and relieve me." But not until the spring did Betsey get through for a short visit.

Pennsylvania's demands subsided, but Virginia joined Rhode Island in nullifying a federal import tax. Vermont still demanded admission to the Confederation, but Congress could not move without consent of all the states. Hamilton wrote Clinton "on the idea of compromise." There was no chance, he now believed, of recovering all the seized land, so why not call a meeting of New York, New Hampshire, and Massachusetts commissioners to work out a bargain with Vermont? "If you agree with Massachusetts and New Hampshire, or with one of them, the agreement will, I think, meet with support here.

"Every day proves more and more the insufficiency of the Confederation, . . ." he continued to the Governor. Revenue was the crying need. Hamilton proposed that the states cede the public lands to Congress, which would then levy taxes to pay war debts. Madison, increasingly impressed with the young New Yorker, gave him much space in his journal. He copied out Hamilton's motion for federal taxation:

"That it is the opinion of Congress that: Complete justice cannot be done to the creditors of the United States, nor the restoration of Public Credit be effected, nor the future exigencies of the War provided for, but by the establishment of permanent & adequate funds to operate generally throughout the United States, to be collected by Congress."

This Motion said it all. To show agreement between New York and Virginia, Madison submitted a nearly identical resolution with all the key words, but it was voted down on February 12.

Next day Hamilton took his cause to George Washington. With the tensions of war far behind them, each man was better able to understand their break.

At the Philadelphia Convention of 1787 a story was told, in several versions, of how Hamilton bet Gouverneur Morris a good supper that he wouldn't dare clap Washington on the shoulder and give a familiar greeting.

"The challenge was accepted. On the evening appointed, a large number attended; and at an early hour Gouverneur Morris entered, bowed, shook hands, laid his left hand on Washington's shoulder and said, 'My dear General, I am very happy to see you look so well.' Washington withdrew his hand, stepped suddenly back, fixed his eye on Morris for several minutes with an angry frown, until the latter retreated abashed, and sought refuge in the crowd. The company looked on in silence. At the supper provided by Hamilton, Morris said, 'I have won the bet, but paid dearly for it, and nothing would induce me to repeat it.' "

Hamilton, hot for glory in wartime, had often felt rejected

by Washington, but by now their stiffness had relaxed, possibly helped by their common grief over the death of Laurens. The Commander bent his rule against eulogizing dead soldiers: "The death of Colonel Laurens I consider a very heavy misfortune, not only as it affects the public at large, but particularly so to his family and all his private friends. . . ." That sort of unbending appealed to Hamilton. His many letters to Washington at this period carried a warm, respectful, confident reliance on the General's ability to reach and influence the whole people. They expressed a corresponding disappointment when the General did not make the desired effort.

"It is of moment to the public tranquility and Your Excellency should preserve the confidence of the Army without losing that of the people."

Everybody surmised that the Commander in Chief was the Army's spokesman, but his intimates (Hamilton was not the only one) knew of the General's disinclination to put himself forward. He had already, "with abhorrence and . . . severity," spurned Colonel Lewis Nicola's suggestion of advancing from Commander in Chief to King of America. There was fear in some quarters that he might become a dictator in spite of himself. Hamilton had misgivings in another direction. He feared, as did others, that Washington would not make full use of his military leadership.

Admittedly the Army had just complaints, had weapons to rectify them to some extent, and for these reasons was a threat to the shaky Confederation. Hamilton wanted the General not to discount or ignore these dangerous forces, but "*to take the direction of them.*"

This has been read by anti-Hamiltonians as a call for dictatorship. That was not in his mind at all when he underscored the provocative clause. He was seeking Washington's influence for the rejected Madison-Hamilton tax measure.

"The great *desideratum* at present is the establishment of general funds, . . ." Hamilton went on. "This is the objective of all men of sense; in this the influence of the Army, properly directed, may cooperate."

Shortly afterwards, February 20, Hamilton attended a meeting of six concerned delegates and revealed the tenor of his appeal to the General. A new uneasiness had spread in Congress. There were rumors that Washington might step aside and that the disaffected Army would then turn to some radical leader "as the conductor of their efforts to obtain justice." Madison's journal recorded Hamilton's reaction:

"Mr. Hamilton said that he knew Genl. Washington intimately and perfectly, that his extreme reserve, sometimes mixed with a degree of asperity of temper, both of which were said to be increased of late, had contributed to the decline of his popularity; but that his virtue, his patriotism & his firmness would, it might be depended upon, never yield to any dishonorable or disloyal plans into which he might be called; that he would sooner suffer himself to be cut into pieces; that he [Mr. Hamilton] knowing this to be his true character, wished him to be the conductor of the Army in their plans for redress, in order that they might be moderated & directed to proper objects & exclude some other leader who might foment and misguide their councils. . . ."

Hamilton was finding Congressional service much like warfare. Beckoning opportunities collapsed. Tensions mounted and fell off into boredom. Some men disappointed, others satisfied. Washington was Fabius Maximus once more. His lengthy answer to Hamilton's last letter conceded the financial crisis, the political impotence, the military emergency, and the fact that "the blood we have spilt in the course of an eight-year war, will avail us nothing [unless solutions can be found]."

"Be these things as they may," he nevertheless concluded, "I shall pursue the same steady line of conduct which has governed me hitherto."

Hamilton was stopped. Washington would do, in a word, nothing. Only Madison, or none so much as Madison, came up to expectations, and showed the bold initiative that the time demanded.

IV

(March–June 1783)

By now, Madison and Hamilton were joined in a linkage which historians would call the American Enlightenment. A

669-page book by that title published in 1965 chose five men as representative of the national awakening—Franklin, John Adams, Jefferson, Madison, and Hamilton.

Persons living through an epochal period do not always know it, but in post-Revolution America the leaders did. Indeed, there was a world-wide awareness that something altogether new in history was taking place in the new nation.

"The epoch has become one of total fall of Europe, and of transmigration into America," wrote the Abbé Fernando Galiani of Naples in 1776 to a friend. "This is not a jest. . . . I have said it for more than twenty years, and I have constantly seen my prophecies come to pass. Therefore, do not buy your house in Chaussée d'Antin; you must buy it in Philadelphia."

George Washington, not given to philosophy, nevertheless dispatched his remarkable Circular Letter of June 1783 from Newburgh to the thirteen governors. Hamilton and Madison, both nearby in Congress, later wrote for Washington, but neither claimed any part in the Circular Letter. Yet its phraseology was more like theirs than his.

"The foundation of our Empire was not laid in the gloomy age of ignorance, but at an Epoch when the rights of mankind were better understood and more clearly defined than at any former period; the researches of the human mind after social happiness have been carried to a great extent. . . . At this auspicious period the United States came into existence as a Nation, and if their citizens should not be completely free and happy, the fault will be entirely their own."

In times ahead Hamilton and Madison would take strolls together, and discuss the country's future. That degree of intimacy seems not to have developed at this Congress, but it was in the making. Both men were blue-eyed, short but erect of stature. Both were religious at heart, but free-spirited and stand-offish toward orthodoxy. One was volatile and the other staid. They shared the confidence of Washington and of Princeton's John Witherspoon.

Hamilton throughout the 1780's maintained a correspondence with the Princeton schoolmaster, who at least once visited his New York home. It was Witherspoon, also an immigrant, who coined the word "Americanism." He defended American

usage of such words as "clever" and "fellow countrymen."
Witherspoon, together with other friends of Madison and
Hamilton—Philip Freneau and Noah Webster were outstand-
ing—formed a cult which sought an American identity in
literature as well as politics. Cultural independence from Britain was a perennial object of enthusiasm with Witherspoon.
Americans, he wrote, should not "be subject to the inhabitants
of that island, either in receiving new ways of speaking, or
rejecting the old."

This spirit of intellectual freedom would extend to a defiance
of the classics. Nathaniel Ames, the almanac-maker, denounced Homer's "Grecian lies" and "silly gods." T. G. Fessen-
den, a poet of Hamiltonian persuasion, would turn upon
French literature as "vile fricassees of foreign trash . . .
trumpery novels." Noah Webster summarized the post-Revolution feeling when he insisted that "America must be *independent* in literature as she is in *politics.*"

Madison and Hamilton were alike in that they had no European experience, and that American public life was their natural habitat. Neither of them cared to earn a fortune; the father
of one, the father-in-law of the other, bore much of their living
expenses. Neither one was visionary. Hamilton scoffed at utopi-
anism, and Madison said, "That government is best which is
the least imperfect." Fittingly, they would be collaborators in
the sole masterpiece which came out of the American Enlightenment, *The Federalist.*

They came together in Philadelphia at the precarious time
when the victorious young nation had no precedents to guide
it. The Declaration of Independence was frighteningly unique,
and the Confederation Congress was a novice in the experience
of peace. Perhaps America would be pulled into the orbit of the
European power struggle. There was real and present danger
that the states would spin off into separatism or, to avert that,
decline into dictatorship. Success, too, had its dangers. America's vast undeveloped resources presented a blueprint for
materialism that would not at all accord with the Enlightenment. This blurred picture, in fact, held the shape of these two
men's future relationship and its rupture. Hamilton's idea of

"empire" had strong economic lines. Madison's view of nation-hood showed him chiefly an expanded Virginia of contented agrarians and colleges for the advancement of letters and science.

It was a time for meeting a host of challenges. The long marches and the humiliating occupation, the gunfire and the blood-letting, were over for a while at least, and the nation struggled to reach upward and soar like the eagle which had become its symbol.

V

(June–October 1783)

Hamilton was despondent as the winter passed, and as the coming of spring led to the summer recess of a barren session, everything that he and Madison had attempted in Philadelphia had come to naught. He had achieved neither progress for the country, nor fame for himself. Schuyler came down for a visit, and brought with him an eye that saw Hamilton's mission and achievement better than Hamilton did. Schuyler wrote home to Betsey about "my beloved Hamilton":

"He affords me satisfaction too exquisite for expression. I daily experience the pleasure of hearing encomiums of his virtues and abilities from those who are capable of distinguishing between real and pretended merit. He is considered, as he certainly is, the ornament of his country. . . . In short, every true patriot rejoices that he is one of the great council of these states."

VI

(March–July 1783)

Captain Joshua Barney of Maryland, a naval hero, arrived on March 12 in the happily named ship *Washington,* with the provisional peace treaty. Doctor Franklin and the other commissioners had signed it in Paris on November 30, 1782. Like the announcement of the French Alliance amid the miseries of Valley Forge, this news was great medicine for sunken spir-

its, even though it did not remove every anxiety. On the face
value of the terms, the victors of Yorktown had received rich
rewards.

In Article One, "His Britannic Majesty acknowledges the
said United States . . . to be free, sovereign, and independent
States." Article Two set the national boundaries, and Article
Three ensured offshore fishing rights. Article Four agreed to
the full recovery of all bona fide debts, and Articles Five and
Six bade Congress to deal justly with the civil rights and the
property rights of Tories.

Article Seven proclaimed that "all hostilities, both by land
and sea, shall from henceforth cease," that all prisoners "shall
be set at liberty," and that His Britannic Majesty shall with
"all convenient speed" withdraw his forces, without commit-
ting any destruction "or carrying away any Negroes or other
property."

Article Eight promised "free and open" navigation of the
Mississippi River, and Article Nine called for the restoration
of any territory captured by either side after the arrival in
America of these provisional articles.

Hamilton agreed with most of the provisions, but had misgivings about his country's ability to cope with the liberty it had
won. "I congratulate Your Excellency on this happy conclusion
of your Labours," he wrote Washington. "It now remains to
make solid establishments—in fine to make our independence
truly a blessing." Again he urged the Commander to assert
leadership before some unworthy person did so. It was a call
to avert some form of despotism, not to institute it. For himself,
Hamilton declared, he did not believe in force, but "I confess,
could force avail, I should almost wish to see it employed."

This correspondence alarmed the General. He answered, "I
. . . contemplated the picture it had drawn with astonishment
& horror. . . . The idea of redress by force is too chimerical to
have a place in the imagination." The Army, said the General,
"is a dangerous instrument to play with," and "every possible
means . . . should be essayed to get it disbanded without
delay."

To Hamilton, this was restating an obvious problem without

offering any solution. Plainly disappointed in Washington, he looked elsewhere for help, and his attention was drawn to another wartime acquaintance, Robert Morris. Hamilton saw, or soon would see, that to disband the Continental Army in fairness, without violence, was a task of the purse rather than the sword, a crisis to be solved by a financier rather than a commander.

VII

(January–June 1783)

Hamilton's preceptors had been Nicholas Cruger, Hugh Knox, and Myles Cooper; and now there was Robert Morris. Foreign-born (in Liverpool), clerk in a counting house at Philadelphia, rising to a partnership by extraordinary merit, radiant in spirit, accessible in friendship, intensely patriotic, and twenty-three years Hamilton's senior, Morris stood second only to Washington in prestige and authority.

From the spring of 1781, when he had been unanimously elected to be sole executive of the Office of Finance, Morris did somewhat as Hamilton wished Washington to do. The Financier demanded and accumulated power in a fully legal manner. He consolidated the bureaus of the Marine, the Admiralty, the Hospitals. He appointed and dismissed employees of these agencies at will. He made overseas purchases and had charge of loans from abroad. This gave him a strong hand in foreign policy. He wrote directly to American ministers in Europe and consulted with European agents in Philadelphia.

Morris worked hard and was well paid. Acting as his own broker, with full consent of Congress, he acquired large profits from the benefits he gave the country. He was business manager of the Yorktown campaign. When it ended, both Morris and the country were better off by the arrival of two hundred thousand dollars in specie from France, by the spoils of battle collected on the field, by the reduction of men under arms from a high of ninety thousand in 1776 to thirteen thousand in 1783.

It often was asked: Was Morris financing the Revolution, or was the Revolution financing him? Hamilton had to ponder these questions. They now became a phase of his education in statecraft. Morris was visible proof that whoever held the purse strings held the power. The Financier confirmed a two-part thesis which had already taken shape in the younger man's mind and writings. It was (a) that the American cause could not survive without the good will of moneyed men, and (b) that rich individuals would most willingly support policies that allowed their fortunes to prosper. In the time ahead Hamilton would incorporate this thesis into his plan of national finance— with one important exception. He would never use public policy to enrich himself. And to the consternation of his enemies, then and now, they have never been able to show that he even tried to do so.

As he watched Morris in action, Hamilton saw a man who used authority without abusing it. Setting January 1, 1782, as his effective date of office, the Financier disavowed all previous obligations toward the Army. If Washington's men and officers were to be paid, Congress must requisition sums from the states, which in turn must deliver. Morris was not without money, some his own, some belonging to Congress. He used it to settle with merchants and contractors, but not with soldiers. He contended that current income must be applied to current expenses, and that past obligations such as military pay required special handling. Public credit of the government must be preserved. It was the "inestimable jewel." Hamilton would never forget nor neglect that precept. "Public credit" would be a Hamiltonian watch-word.

Hamilton saw the amiable, strong-willed Morris slowly gaining the ascendancy. The troops stayed in place, and their presence was an asset to Morris. A majority of Congress balked at interfering in the affairs of their respective states, and this stubbornness also worked for Morris in the long pull.

But it was a punishing ordeal. The newspapers and the legislatures railed against the Financier. He had lined his own pockets, they declared, but cared nothing for the public good. He had turned the people against the troops, who would be left in the camps to starve. "I will feed them," Morris coolly declared. Then why didn't he borrow money and pay them off?

"To increase our debts, while the prospect of paying them diminishes, does not conform with my ideas of integrity," he answered. "I must therefore quit a situation which becomes utterly intolerable."

He set his resignation for the end of May, and this raised more howls of abuse against the indispensable man of the time. But he had won the struggle of wills. Congress voted three months' back pay for the soldiers, and five years' half-pay for the officers in lieu of pensions.

Morris stayed on at his post in order to oversee the disbandment, for "I will never be the minister of injustice." He issued the whole amount of $750,000 in "Morris notes." This was personal money, bills in denominations of twenty and one hundred dollars, signed by himself. The requisitions would be payable to the bearers in six months' time. By then, Morris hoped, the entire issue of notes would be covered by a Dutch loan or, preferably, by the federal taxation which Hamilton and Madison were seeking.

Meanwhile most of the soldiers began to drift out of Newburgh and nearby camps. They went without violence, without ceremony, carrying their weapons and their dubious certificates. It was a heart-rending sight to Washington, who wrote, "The sensibilities occasioned by the parting scene, under the circumstances, will not permit of description."

As for Hamilton, he had received an object lesson that taught him much about the opportunities and dangers of being a finance minister.

CHAPTER ELEVEN

Days of Doubt

I

It was not over. Not yet. Some of the dismissed soldiers refused to go home. The void of military leadership left by Washington would be filled by small men, by pygmies, as it turned out. In mid-June "a board of sergeants," chosen from the 500-man garrison at Philadelphia, sent to Congress what Hamilton termed "an insolent and threatening message." A few days later word came that some eighty soldiers, also led by sergeants, were marching from their Lancaster camp to demand pay.

Named chairman of a three-member military committee, Hamilton ordered Major William Jackson, Assistant Secretary at War, to intercept the "mutineers" at once. "You will please proceed to meet them and to endeavor by every prudent method to engage them to return to the post they have left." He authorized Jackson to promise furloughs, provisions, and pay, but only if the marchers turned back. This they refused to do.

Hamilton had feared an armed uprising, and now it was building. He called upon John Dickinson, president of the Pennsylvania Council, to bring out the militia and prevent the marchers from joining up with the men in Philadelphia barracks. Dickinson demurring, Hamilton's committee resolved that if matters turned worse, Congress should move to New Jersey, and ask the Commander in Chief to take action "for suppressing the present revolt. . . ."

On the day before the resolution was put to paper, June 20, the insurgent forces united and surrounded the state house. Elias Boudinot, president of Congress, wrote to Washington:

"The mutineers sent in a paper . . . [but] neither Congress nor the Council would take any measures while they were so menaced."

The firmness was admirable. Madison, inside the chamber, calmly kept his journal. "The soldiers remained in their position without offering any violence . . . but it was observed that spirituous drink from the tippling houses adjoining began to be liberally served out to the soldiers. . . . About three o'clock, the usual hour, Congress adjourned; the soldiers, though in some instances offering a mock obstruction, permitted the members to pass through their ranks. . . ."

This did not meet Hamilton's standards for military discipline and the security of a governing body. He sent a report to Dickinson on June 24 demanding "vigorous measures." He appealed to General Arthur St. Clair to "take order for terminating the mutiny." When nothing was done, Hamilton's committee recommended that Congress wait "as long as they could be justified in doing it," and then reconvene elsewhere. The members voted to move to Princeton.

Hamilton considered Dickinson's conduct "weak and disgusting," but he was inclined to treat the incident as finished business. "Fortunately no mischief ensued," he reported to Governor Clinton on June 29, and perhaps an opportunity had been opened for transferring the national capital to New York. "To your Excellency," he continued, "I need not urge the advantages that would accrue to the state from being the residence of Congress."

Hamilton hardly noticed it, but his service in the Congressional session, now nearing its close, had not been universally admired. Almost nobody accepted the implicit Hamiltonian creed that a strong central government must rule the nation. Washington had objected to using the Army as "an instrument." Madison thought Hamilton's message to Rhode Island was in harsher language than Congress should use to a sovereign state. A good many delegates did not like Hamilton's demand for an armed force to subdue soldiers who were not without a grievance, and to quell an uprising that never rose above loud talk and intoxicated bravado. Immensely proud of his reputation for cool judgment and valor, Hamilton was enraged when unflattering comments reached him at Nassau Hall.

"It is insinuated," he wrote Madison about the removal to Princeton, "that it was a contrivance of some members to get them out of the state of Pennsylvania . . . and I am told that this insinuation has been pointed at me in particular."

As Madison had been a witness to the whole transaction, Hamilton asked him to write a testimonial. "I do not mean to make public use of it; but through my friends to vindicate myself. . . . I think you will recollect that my idea was clearly this: that the mutiny ought not to be terminated by negotiation; that Congress were justifiable in leaving . . . but . . . it was prudent to delay it till its necessity was apparent. . . ."

The letter was too long, protested too much, and Hamilton compressed it and wrote again a week later, July 6, telling Madison, "I will thank you in your letter to me to answer the following question. What appeared to be my ideas and disposition respecting the removal of Congress? Did I appear to wish to hasten it, or did I not rather show a strong disposition to procrastinate it?"

By ill luck the letter failed to reach Madison for nearly four months, and the vindication was not forthcoming. Displeased with politics, and having once in May and twice in June asked Clinton to be released "to my private occupations," Hamilton nevertheless sat down and began an essay, "Defense of Congress," intended for a Philadelphia newspaper, but never finished and unpublished.

Congress was not infallible, he wrote, "and a servile complaisance to its errors would be as dangerous as despicable; yet it must be allowed that an opposite extreme may be little less pernicious." He had noted that when meritorious acts were performed by Congress, the credit went to certain members, and these "good deeds of Congress die or go off stage with the individuals who were the authors of them."

He was arguing for a government of laws, not of lawmakers. Congress was a continuing body. Like the King of England, it "never dies," he wrote. He was promoting, as usual, the idea of a strong central government. He saw the Confederation as

a hopeless tangle of executive and legislative functions. It
needed separation of powers. It needed a stronger head than
the president of Congress, who served only a one-year term.
Worse, the Confederation Congress was subservient to the state
legislatures, and, in fact, to the strong-willed, multi-term governors and their organizations. At the same time and place that
Hamilton "defended" Congress, he also drafted a Resolution
Calling for a Convention to Amend the Articles of the Confederation.

Despite all irritations and setbacks, Hamilton was doing
work that his talents and disposition had shaped him to perform. He was the only one of New York's five delegates who
was in constant attendance at the Congress. New York was one
of only six states that reported to Princeton, although the Articles required that nine states be represented in order for Congress to conduct any serious business. He grumbled to Clinton
about having to stay, and kept promising Betsey to hurry home.

But when Congress returned from Princeton to Philadelphia,
he had two reasons for being there. He wanted to debate and
put his signature on the definitive Treaty of Peace, and he
wanted to get action on his call for a convention to change the
Confederation. He did not realize either of these desires. Congress couldn't raise a quorum, so the Treaty was put off till the
next year, when Thomas Jefferson would be a signer. The resolution for a Federal Convention had to be abandoned, Hamilton
noted, "for want of support." Nevertheless, his Congressional
experience was not barren. A close look shows that at least
three enduring American doctrines were influenced by his
presence and ideas.

First, he stressed in debate the obligation which a treaty
imposed on the United States, and he demanded high ethical
standards in diplomacy. Such criteria did not exist in Europe.
English, French, Spanish, and Russian diplomats routinely
used bribery and perfidy as ploys in the international game.
Hamilton wanted the United States to have a reputation for
honest dealing. He was displeased to learn that the American
negotiators in Paris had made a separate peace with Britain.
They had violated a pledge by not informing France until after-

wards. In debate, he admitted that France and Britain were notorious cheaters, but declared that this did not excuse American trickery. "He highly disapproved of the conduct of our Ministers in not showing the preliminary articles to our Ally before signing them," noted Madison.

There were other irregularities, but Hamilton did not wish to hold up the treaty. "He thought a middle course best," wrote Madison. This amounted to accepting the terms of the treaty, but deploring the duplicity used by Benjamin Franklin to get an agreement. Hamilton's viewpoint was not so much that of a moralist as of a hard bargainer. He believed that by observing high standards the United States could command better terms.

Second, while conferring with Robert Morris and two Congressmen on ways to save military funds, Hamilton conceived the idea of an unarmed border with Canada. He proposed on May 15, 1783, as a condition to the peace treaty, that the two nations "stipulate that neither party will keep any naval force on the lakes on the Northern & Western frontier." A decade later, as part of the Jay Treaty of 1794 with Britain, he tried to arrange for "diminishing or wholly withdrawing all military forces from the Border . . ." because "mutual justice, confidence & goodwill [are] sufficient Barrier. . . ." Although never formalized into a pact, these ideas of Hamilton when he was a young Congressman became and have remained Canadian-American policy.

Third, Hamilton was an early exponent of the doctrine to be known as "splendid isolation." In June of 1783, a committee on which he served with Oliver Ellsworth and Madison considered an invitation by the Dutch government to join the League of Armed Neutrality, an international organization to enforce freedom of the seas. This was the first of many times when Hamilton opposed "entanglements" (Tom Paine had used the term before him) by military alliance. The committee reported on June 12, 1783:

"The true interest of these states requires that they should be as little as possible entangled in the politics and controversies of European states."

Hamilton ended his Congressional term in a mood of mixed

satisfaction and disappointment. This is normal enough. Genius is always enchanted by the calling which it answers, and is always disillusioned by imperfections which are never overcome. His correspondence of the time expressed both moods. Shortly before heading home, he wrote to Betsey:

"I give you joy, my angel, of the happy conclusion of the important work in which your country has been engaged."

Three days later he wrote John Jay in London to say that the negotiated peace "is all the more agreeable, as the time was come when thinking men began to be seriously alarmed at the internal embarrassments and exhausted state of this country."

II

(August–December 1783)

Back at the Schuyler home in Albany, Hamilton's law practice got off to a slow start. A prominent insurance man of Boston retained him to represent a suit. Mrs. Schuyler had real estate business in New York. He accompanied her there and had the opportunity to see the British evacuation in progress. It disturbed him to observe "a spirit of emigration" among Tories, who were frightened by "some violent papers sent into the city." Many were merchants "of no political consequence, each of whom may carry away eight or ten thousand guineas. . . . Our state will feel for twenty years at least, the effects of the popular phrenzy," he wrote to Robert R. Livingston on August 13.

More shocking still was the September issue of the *Pennsylvania Gazette,* in which John Dickinson, the chief executive officer of that state, accused the Hamilton committee "of confounding facts and sentiments . . . extreme inaccuracy," and of ruthlessly "pursuing the object of having the soldiers in their power."

Hamilton answered furiously. "I take up the matter individually because . . . it happened to be my lot as Chairman principally to conduct the conference on the part of the Committee." He called Dickinson's statement "willfully discoloured" and an act of "self-justification" in which "material facts [were] either suppressed or denied."

Dickinson looked back on the brief insurrection as a legitimate petition for the redress of wrongs. Hamilton called it "a deliberate mutiny of an incensed soldiery carried to the utmost point of outrage short of assassination." Dickinson, he pointed out, had judged the militia unreliable for the defense of Congress, yet the very next day had mobilized it to protect the Bank of North America. For himself, Hamilton said, he had opposed the withdrawal of Congress until it was evident that the delegates remained "at their extreme peril."

Self-doubt and dejection settled upon him. He needed reassurance. At the past session he had drafted an elaborate prospectus for a peacetime army and navy. But when names were recommended for a new officer corps, his name was missing. He didn't want to serve, but he wanted to be asked. He thought an offer of a renewed commission and a promotion was due him "as an honorary reward for the time I have devoted to the public," as he informed Washington. He reminded the General of the Yorktown assault, and pointed out that a French officer, Baron Antoine Charles du Hoax de Vioménil, "who acted in a similar capacity in another attack made at the same time . . . has been handsomely distinguished in consequence of it. . . ." Vioménil had been made a Commander of the Order of Saint-Louis and promoted to lieutenant general.

Hamilton would have loved a medal, and told the General, "There are several examples among us where Congress has bestowed honors upon actions, perhaps not more useful nor apparently more hazardous" than his own. Congress had given decorations to Light-Horse Harry Lee and Mad Anthony Wayne, but had neglected the Little Lion. He hoped for a diplomatic appointment, and wished to carry distinction with him. "As I may hereafter travel, I may find it an agreeable circumstance to appear in the character I have supported in the Revolution."

Washington answered that he was willing to help "with my testimonial to your Services," but was advised against it by

"your particular friends." They declared, said Washington,
that the peace establishment would be built on "fresh appointments; so unless you wished to come into actual command
again (which none supposed), they saw no way by which you
could preserve your rank." As a consolation, Washington sent
him the certificate of a brevet colonel, a temporary and mini-
mal promotion.

Hamilton's yearning for fame and glory had made him forward and gauche. His failure to get recognition deeply depressed him. Luckily there came a welcome letter from Madison, who was belatedly answering Hamilton's appeal of the
previous June about the flight to Princeton. Madison assured
him: "Even after the delay that has taken place, my recollection enables me with certainty to witness that the uniform
strain of your sentiments, as they appeared both from particular conversations with myself, and incidental ones with others
in my presence, was opposed to the removal of Congress except
in the last necessity; that when you finally yielded to the measure, it appeared to be more in compliance with the peremptory
expostulations of others than with any disposition of your
mind. . . ."

This was something. Hamilton needed still more, and evidently asked McHenry to comment.

"I obey you," the Marylander answered. "The homilies you
delivered in Congress are still recollected with pleasure. The
impressions they made are in favor of your integrity, and no
one but believes you a man of honor and republican principles."

McHenry had not exactly pronounced him fit for larger responsibilities, but Hamilton read on.

"Were you ten years older and twenty thousand pounds
richer, there is no doubt that you might obtain the suffrages
of Congress for the highest office in their gift."

Since he would certainly grow older and richer, Hamilton
could take this as a prophecy of greatness-to-be. What followed
was more circumscribed.

"You are supposed to possess various knowledge, useful—
substantial—and ornamental. Your grave and your cautious
—your men who measure others by the standard of their own

creeping politics, think you sometimes intemperate, but seldom visionary, and that were you to pursue your object with as much cold perseverance as you do with ardor and argument, you would become irresistible."

Hamilton hadn't yet heard what he wanted to hear—unqualified encouragement and approval. But another letter arrived that fall from "Yours Unalterably, Hugh Knox." The old tutor chided him humorously. "Three years have now elapsed since my last from you, though I have wrote you frequently in that time. . . . When you were covered with the dust of the Camp, & had cannon balls whistling about your ears, you used to steal an hour's converse with an old friend every 5 or 6 months. . . . Since your marriage to the amiable Miss Schuyler are you so loss'd in [love] as to render you forgetful of your other friends? [Or] are you grown too rich and proud to have a good memory? Or are you engaged in writing the History of the American War?"

Actually, Hamilton had not written for publication for over a year. His Cash Book showed some entries, but his law practice in Albany went at a creeping pace. He began at this time to take in law students for pay, one of them being John Adams' scapegrace son, Charles. Hamilton was impatient to have the redcoats move out of New York, "on which event," he told Nathanael Greene, "I shall set down there seriously on the business of making my fortune."

That was his ambition, then, he thought—a fortune. Whatever else, no politics! He had not been sufficiently appreciated. When, late in December, friends nominated him for the state assembly, Hamilton sent a note to the *New York Packet* declining the honor.

CHAPTER TWELVE

The Alexander Hamiltons of New York

I
(1783–1785)

There was a charming red-brick house, with a view of the bay, at 57 Wall Street, and Betsey discussed it with Aaron Burr while Hamilton was away. Burr handled the property for a client, and Hamilton advised his wife to take it. First she rented, then she purchased, and it became the home of this privileged couple, whose wedding was remembered as a grand event of the Revolutionary period.

Society blossomed after Evacuation Day, November 25, 1783. The Alexander Hamiltons exchanged entertainment with the elite of the town. John and Sarah Jay moved into the city. She was one of the Misses Livingston with whom the young staff officer had once flirted. The other Livingstons, the New York branch, some of the Clintons, the Isaac Roosevelts, the Van Cortlandts, the Wattses, and the Webbs were in the circle. So were the many Schuylers and their widespread relatives— Schaicks, Piesterses, Slichtenhorsts, Van Rensselaers. The William Duers came to town. She was Lady Kitty, Lord Stirling's daughter, and her husband, as a guest reported somewhat later in the decade, ". . . lives in the style of a nobleman. I presume he had not less than fifteen sorts of wine at dinner, and after the cloth was removed, besides most excellent cider, ports and several other kinds of strong beer."

Hamilton was glad to be out of uniform, and to have the means to dress well. His English biographer, Frederick Scott Oliver, notes that he was far different from the typical student of Lincoln's Inn or the Temple, where young British barristers made their start. At twenty-five, Hamilton was ". . . this strange smiling boyish figure, with the fine lace ruffles, who had already played the part and borne the responsibilities of a man in the affairs of a great war, who had dealt with statesmen in the high matters of politics, and conducted with tact and firmness the diplomacy between the commanders of America and France."

Hamilton would always be well turned out. He liked his blue coat, bright buttons, white waistcoat, silken small-clothes and stockings, and the gay parties where he displayed them.

Since 57 Wall Street was both home and office, people came on both pleasure and business. Betsey's part of the house was exquisite. She had the long living room appointed with spindle-legged tables and bibelots sent from Europe. She chose a decor of rose-tinted brocade and red mahogany pieces. She worked at yarn and embroidery in her own drawing room, and served large dinners with a rich collection of silver and glass.

She loved being called into her husband's study, as she often would be throughout their lives together. He would try out his ideas and speeches on her, and let her talk with the law students. She enjoyed his pride in the growing collection of volumes which came in from New York's eleven book stores, Boston's forty-two, Philadelphia's fifty, and from overseas. He saw his clients in the law office, of course, but also used the study, and sometimes the whole house, for political discussions.

"He loved society and rejoiced to meet his enemy at any gate," writes Oliver. "His house was open to all men without distinction of politics. His hospitality was splendid in its simplicity and kindliness. Men were put off guard by his wit and gaiety. They were disarmed by his enthusiasm. His eloquence took them prisoners."

And yet there was something that made him withdrawn. Many persons would mention his moods of abstraction, when he walked about in a daze and murmured to himself, memorizing and constructing arguments for court. He had no diversions at this time of life. Work was his obsession, his lock-in. His escape was through social drinking and philandering. Friends noted and lamented his "liquorish flirtation" and "his pleasures." His enemies tattled and excoriated. A social history of the day makes allowance for his "extraordinary genius," and says:

"It is true that Hamilton was something of a roué, but his gallantries were subject to a certain law of honorableness which even in such affairs is not altogether impossible. . . ."

Unhappily, his favorite relative would live abroad for most of his life, and only brighten New York, Albany, and Philadelphia with irregular visits. Angelica, conceived before her parents' marriage, love-child in all but the law, was already married when Hamilton met her, else he might have chosen a different Schuyler. A year older than Betsey, Angelica was lovely, chic, coquettish, intelligent, much that Hamilton's wife was not. From a portrait, she had her father's bony nose, but round merry eyes and flaxen curls. James McHenry met Angelica Church in Baltimore, August 1782. "She charms in all companies. No one has seen her, of either sex, who has not been pleased, and she has pleased everyone. . . ."

Hamilton's qualities were perfect complements to hers. He was handsome, fashionable, amorous, and not very strong at resisting temptation. She wrote from shipboard at their first separation, "Adieu, my dear Hamilton . . . adieu mine *plus cher.*" Once when he pleaded for her to cross the ocean to him, she called him "my dear and naughty brother," and she sent her love to him "*à la française.*" From London and Paris, where she was the toast of the American colony, Angelica sent him an unbroken stream of lively and affectionate letters, which were answered in kind.

When she and Hamilton were together in company, they did not bother to hide their attraction to each other, and there was talk inside and outside the family. On at least one occasion he and Angelica were together in Philadelphia, while Betsey was in Albany with a sick child. "My brother seemed very sad yesterday," Angelica wrote her sister, "and when I questioned him, I was sorry to find little William's health to be the cause of his dejection, his sensitivity suffers from the least anxiety to you or your babes." Perhaps Angelica knew that the true cause of his melancholia was his wife and family. Perhaps it was the sadness of illicit love or guilt, which John Adams plainly called "incest."

But all of Betsey's sisters treated Hamilton like a famous older brother who became a romping playmate at home. "Assure them of everything my heart is capable of feeling for the lovely sisters of a lovely wife." Angelica candidly acclaimed Betsey's sparkling catch, and wrote the lucky matron, "Embrace poor dear Hamilton for me, it is impossible to know him and not wish him health and pleasure, and then I am so proud of his merit and abilities, even you, Eliza, might envy my feelings." Angelica had a pagan jest with Betsey while there was an ocean between them:

"Ah, Bess . . . if you were as generous as the old Romans, you would lend him to me for a little while."

These postwar years were the period of Hamilton's family building. He and Betsey would have eight children of their own, and one adopted daughter. Philip, born January 22, 1782, was followed by Angelica (September 25, 1784), Alexander (May 16, 1786), James Alexander (April 14, 1788), John Church (August 22, 1792), William Stephen (August 4, 1797), and Eliza (November 20, 1799). The first Philip was killed in a duel in 1801, and a new son (June 2, 1802) was named for the dead brother. In the autumn of 1787, Colonel Edward Antil came to New York to seek aid from the Society of the Cincinnati. He died penniless, leaving several children, and Hamilton took Antil's infant daughter into his household, where she grew up, later to become Mrs. Arthur Tappan.

Hamilton liked to have his children around him. He often rehearsed them in their lessons at the breakfast table. It was a rare letter to his wife in which Hamilton did not send messages of love and concern for their boys and girls. He told Philip "a promise must never be broken," and reminded Angelica that "the best way to act is with so much politeness, good manners and circumspection as never to have occasion to make any apology." He taught the children to be devout and to trust in Divine Goodness.

From the beginning Philip was prepared for his father's alma mater, which became Columbia College by act of the state legislature in 1784. In June of the same year Hamilton was pointing the college toward greater contributions to the state and nation. He wrote to Paris to his learned friend, the Marquis de Chastellux, for the purpose of introducing Colonel Matthew Clarkson, who was on a special mission of culture. Clarkson was authorized by the trustees of Columbia to solicit and purchase "such philosophical apparatus for the College as Dr. Franklin, Mr. Adams and Mr. Jefferson, Ministers of the United States, should advise." Hamilton recommended Clarkson to de Chastellux "as the messenger of Science . . . for the benefit of a Seminary of learning. . . ."

Hamilton continued, "Learning is the common concern of Mankind; and why may not poor republicans be sent abroad to solicit the favors of her patrons and friends?"

His growing family made him less cavalier about his due for military service. In February 1784, he petitioned the New York legislature to pay $3,525 that he felt was owed him. He said that "from scruples of delicacy," he had relinquished all claims for his service after 1781, but felt that expenses incurred before that date should be recompensed. "With full confidence in the equity and generosity of the Legislature, your memorialist respectfully submits his prayer." His petition was referred to committee and was never heard of again.

Hamilton concentrated on winning every case he entered. In January 1785 James Kent saw him in legal action at the Supreme Court in Albany, opposed to the eminent Robert R. Livingston. "Hamilton was then at the age of twenty-seven, and had never met and encountered at the Bar such a distinguished opponent. His eyes and lips were in constant motion, and his pen rapidly employed during his opponent's address to the Court. He rose with firmness and dignity and spoke for two hours . . . marked by a searching and accurate analysis of the case, and a thorough mastery of all the law and learning. . . ."

His friends would always wonder why he worked so hard. "Your matrimonial connection, I should think," wrote Hugh Knox, "might enable you to live at your ease. . . . As a gentleman of independent fortune [you are situated] to pursue studies

more pleasant to yourself and more profitable to the Commonwealth and to posterity. You guess at the meaning of this hint."

Dr. Knox wanted Hamilton back in public affairs. He still
wanted his brightest pupil to write, not just pamphlets, but
searching dissertations like those of Burke and Hume, and
interpretive history like Gibbon's, or perhaps clever comedy
such as was turned out by the English and French statesmen,
Richard Brinsley Sheridan and Pierre Augustin Caron de
Beaumarchais.

"Perhaps camps and marches & hardy deeds of war may
have a little fortified and steeled your constitution (which used
to be rather delicate and frail). But beware that you do not
enfeeble & impair it again by plunging into intense studies and
the anxieties of the Bar."

III

(1784–85)

Hamilton did not tell his tutor this, but he was learning that
the hardest way to make money is to marry it. In these years
the industrious attorney was also the factotum of the Schuyler
family, especially its ladies. Angelica Church had a slave
named Ben whom she had lent to William Jackson, and now
she wrote from London to her sister Margaret Van Rensselaer
to get him back. The transaction fell to Hamilton, who had to
take time from his practice to communicate with John
Church's Philadelphia agent, John Chaloner:

"Mrs. Rensselaer has requested me to write to you concerning a negro Ben, formerly belonging to Mrs. Church who . . .
is desirous of having him back again; and you are requested,
if Major Jackson is willing to part with him, to purchase
his remaining time for Mrs. Church, and to send him on to
me."

Angelica had shipped some presents to Betsey and their
mother, and Hamilton was again pressed into service, writing
in masculine puzzlement to the agent:

"There is *sheeting* for Mrs. Hamilton. There is another of
garden seed, and another with what Mrs. Church calls a Bea-

trice for Mrs. Schuyler. If you can distinguish these boxes, you will oblige the ladies by sending them to me."

Chaloner went to the warehouse and found two boxes other than those with export merchandise intended for sale by the Church interests. "I suppose that these must contain the several articles wanted by the ladies . . . if by examining the contents of them, they or either of them should turn out to contain things different from what was intended for the ladies, will you please to have them taken care of for Mr. Church.

"Major Jackson declines to part with Ben, but says when Mrs. Church returns, he will let her have him should she request it."

It all made tedious, trivial, and interrupting work, but Angelica made amends by sending him books from the London shops as well as her charming letters. She paid a visit to New York in 1785, and allowed him to take care of the paper work and luggage. He escorted her to Philadelphia without Betsey on her return to England, and bade her farewell with a pang. This exquisite and vivacious lady called him her "*petit fripon*" (little rogue), and extracted many a yearning sigh from the hero of Redoubt Number 10.

"You have, I fear, taken a final leave of America and of those that love you here. I saw you depart from Philadelphia with a particular uneasiness, as if forboding you would not return. . . . Judge the bitterness it gives to those who love you with the love of nature, and to me who feel an attachment to you not less lively. . . ."

Angelica's husband had a thriving two-continent business, and Hamilton was not far above the condition of a clerk. Church wrote him, "I sent you . . . a machine for the purpose of copying writings with paper, ink and everything belonging to it. I wish you may find it of use to you." This apparatus, evidently for printing certificates, was addressed to Hamilton in care of the merchant Nathaniel Shaler. Hamilton was continuously dealing through several middlemen to oblige Church and Church's partner, Jeremiah Wadsworth. In February 1784, Hamilton drew up the charter of the Bank of New York, and was soon able to make Wadsworth its president. As a director, Hamilton limited himself to a single share of stock, which he sold when he became Secretary of the Treasury.

None of this work was agreeable to him. He wished to be more in life than a fetch-and-carry manservant for wealthy relatives. But it was difficult to say "No" to the Schuylers and their in-laws. Besides, as he wrote to Gouverneur Morris in February 1784, ". . . legislative folly has afforded so plentiful a harvest to us lawyers that we have scarce a moment to spare from the substantial business of reaping."

Yet he had to admit that wealthy clients, a profitable marriage, and a standing in the community were not the worst lot that could befall a man. He recalled that he was the son and the brother of men who had never been able to cope with the world. The two James Hamiltons were destitute. "The situation you describe yourself in gives me much pain," he wrote to James Jr., in St. Croix. "I will cheerfully pay your draft on me for fifty pounds sterling, whenever it shall appear. I wish it were in my power to desire you to enlarge the sum; . . . but although my prospects are of the most flattering kind, my present engagements would make it inconvenient for me to advance you a larger sum. My affection for you, however, will not permit me to be inattentive to your welfare, and I hope time will prove to you that I feel all the sentiment of a brother."

Advising James, a carpenter, to take employment and avoid marriage, Hamilton offered to bring him to America and settle him on a farm. "But what has become of our dear father? It is an age since I have heard from him or of him, though I have written him several letters. Perhaps, alas! he is no more. . . . My heart bleeds at the recollection of his misfortunes and embarrassments. . . ."

He had compassion for the underdog, but this would never be of central concern unless related to some high principle. The Law, his jealous mistress, could not hold him much longer. Knox was right about him: Service to the commonwealth, the lure of nation-building, was in his blood. He was not just a practicing attorney, but one who must turn justice into legislation, pleas into philosophy, courtroom clashes into the molding of public policy.

IV

(1784)

Among the patriots who had fled the taken city of New York in the summer of '76 was Mrs. Elizabeth Rutgers, a widow who had inherited a dilapidated brewery in Maiden Lane.

One of the Loyalists who remained behind in the enemy-held city and collaborated with the occupying forces was Joshua Waddington, British merchant and subject, who came into possession of Mrs. Rutgers' brewery and thereby into history.

Hamilton signed up as chief counsel for the defense of Tory Waddington. The Trespass Act, under which the poor widow sued the rich merchant for eight thousand pounds, was one of a battery of anti-Tory statutes that disfranchised Loyalists, confiscated their property, "stayed" debts owed to them, and threatened them with the punishment of banishment or death.

The law seemed ironclad for Mrs. Rutgers' convenience. Under it, if upheld, Waddington had made unlawful use of the brewery even if acting by "military order or command of the enemy." The case for the defense would be an uphill try, against popular prejudice, against the entrenched position of the Governor and the legislature, against state sovereignty and postwar Anglophobia.

Hamilton thought it out, and decided to plead his case in print. In January, when he was preparing for several similar cases, he wrote and published the first instalment of "A Letter from Phocion to the Considerate Citizens of New-York." In April, when *Rutgers v. Waddington* went to court, his publisher, Samuel Loudon, released the second instalment. Hamilton would appeal to the community, attack his adversaries, assault the credibility and justice of their position.

He chose the nom-de-plume of Phocion with studied audacity. In Plutarch's *Lives,* Phocion was the stormy petrel of Athens. He reveled in going contrary to convention. He espoused "the cause of those who differed most from him." He was the advocate of those banished for offending decency and law. Instead of courting the people, Phocion "thwarted and opposed them." If by chance he gained general applause, he would ask his friends, "Have I inadvertently said something foolish?" Athenians called him "the Good," but at the end they forced him to drink hemlock.

Hamilton reeled off the two-part essay in top polemic form. He was writing while the legislature sat, in its January session, on a bill to strip the Tories of citizenship. All these anti-Tory acts, notably the pending one on "Alienism of Persons therein described," he denounced as contrary to the state constitution and the Treaty of Peace. New York's constitution declared that no person "shall be disfranchised or defrauded of any of the rights or privileges sacred to the subjects of this state." The Treaty in its sixth article provided that "there shall be no future confiscations made nor persecutions commenced against any person . . . by reason of the part . . . taken in the present war." Men who incited the people against such pacts "advise us to become the scorn of nations," he wrote.

Hamilton never varied from his belief that men and nations are governed by self-interest, and it was to this that his essays appealed. His style became colloquial as he warned the mechanics against creating a scarcity of labor. Drive out fellow-workers and others will come from nearby states. Drive up wages, and "those classes of the community who are to employ you will make a great many shifts rather than pay the exorbitant prices you demand."

This was writing for people at the level of their shops and sidewalks. He told the tailors that "a man will wear his old cloaths so much longer before he gets a new suit." He told the cobblers that their customers "will buy imported shoes rather than those made here at a dear rate." He said to the carpenters that "the owner of a house will defer the repairs as long as possible, and he will only have those which are absolutely necessary made. . . ."

These homely appeals, happily phrased, paved the way into popular confidence. The legislature could not lawfully amend the Treaty, for Congress was "representative of the United States" in dealing with foreign powers. He pleaded for good faith, as he had in Congress when criticizing Franklin and other negotiators of the Treaty. Shall we invite the British to rescind their concessions on our fishing rights and access to the Mississippi? he asked, and answered the question: "Breach of the Treaty on our part will be a just ground for breaking it on theirs."

Besides, there were laws outside the statute books. Throughout the Phocion Letters he made reference to "common law . . . law of the land . . . laws of war . . . laws of nations." These would become important when he pleaded Waddington's defense.

Hamilton mounted to rhetoric as he closed the Letters. "What shall we do to perpetuate our liberties and secure our happiness? The answer would be 'Govern well. . . .' The world has its eye on America." We must put forth our best appearance, because " 'Tis with governments as with individuals, first impressions and early habits give a lasting bias to the temper and character. Our government hitherto have no habits. How important to the happiness not of America alone, but of mankind, that they should acquire good ones."

CHAPTER THIRTEEN

The Courts of Law

I

(April–August 1784)

Hamilton had pierced a hornets' nest. The reaction to each of the Phocion Letters was a swarming attack upon his probity and loyalty. A writer under the name of Mentor stirred such resentment that a group of patriots planned to challenge Hamilton to successive duels and prevent his coming to court. The Second Phocion Letter was partly a retort to Mentor, whose pamphlet he called "a feeble attempt . . . a group of absurdities."

Since he was out to make converts, and to separate Clinton from his adherents, Hamilton softened his language as he went along. He conceded that he had used "expressions of too much asperity." He was trying to win over the populace from which jurors and voters are drawn. In the Second Phocion Letter, Hamilton composed what might be called a personal Bill of Rights. He took pains to state that he was drawing on codes "as old as any regular notion of government among mankind . . . the law of the land . . . the common language of this country at the beginning of the Revolution . . . essential to its future happiness and respectability."

His Bill of Rights named five:

"First, That no man can forfeit . . . any right to which, as a member of the community, he is entitled. . . .

"Secondly, That no man ought to be condemned unheard. . . .

"Thirdly, That a crime is an act . . . in violation of a public law.

"Fourthly, That a prosecution is . . . an inquiry . . . whether a particular person has committed or omitted such act.

"Fifthly, That duties and rights . . . are reciprocal; or in other words, that a man cannot be a citizen for the purpose of punishment, and not a citizen for the purpose of privilege."

Mentor, identified as Isaac Ledyard, recognized what Hamilton was driving at, and caused the challengers to disband.

With so much advance notice, *Rutgers v. Waddington* drew capacity crowds at the Mayor's Court. The widow and her son were represented by Robert Troup and William Wilcox, with Egbert Benson, the attorney general, as counsel for the State of New York. Hamilton brought in two associates, Brockholst Livingston and Morgan Lewis, but would do most of the speaking himself. Since he had already put his arguments into the Letters, he carried only notes into the courtroom, but these outlined his case.

"Congress have made a Treaty. A breach of that would be a breach of their constitutional authority. . . . As well a county may alter the laws of a State as a State those of the Confederation. It has been said, legislatures may alter laws of nations. Not true. . . . If such a power does exist in our government, 'tis in Congress. . . .

"But how are the JUDGES to decide?

"Answer: . . . the law of each State must adopt the laws of Congress. . . . All must be construed to stand together! . . .

"We have seen that to make the defendant liable would be to VIOLATE the laws of nations and forfeit character, to violate a solemn Treaty of Peace and revive a state of hostility, to infringe Confederation and endanger the peace of this Union.

"Can we suppose all this to have been intended by the legislature?

"The Law cannot suppose it.

"And if it was intended, the [Trespass] act is void."

II

(June–December 1784)

Rutgers v. Waddington was the main event of the season, and lesser events must await the results. Action ground to a halt in test cases for other anti-Tory laws. Hamilton himself had at least sixty-five such cases. On a larger front, the British government let it be known that it would stop and watch the game. Despite pledges of the Treaty, London had retained possession of forts at Niagara, Oswego, on the St. Lawrence, and on Lake Champlain, to see how the Tories fared in America. Pleas were filed in April, and verbal arguments postponed till June 29. Although the records were lost in a subsequent fire, the legal debate may be roughly reconstructed.

Attorneys for the Plaintiff, Mrs. Rutgers:

The Trespass Act did not contravene the common law, as defense counsel contended. It was remedial legislation and must be liberally construed. The Act clearly applied to the trespass on the brewery property, and it specifically forbade Tory Waddington to plead that he had military permission to trespass.

Hamilton and Associates for Defense of Tory Waddington:

When a state law is in violation of the law of nations and the laws of war, it is void. The right of a military captor to use abandoned property is indisputable. Waddington occupied the brewery as the agent of the British commandant.

Attorneys for Plaintiff:

This court has no power to act upon anything except the state laws, and that disposes of counsel's reliance on the law of warring nations and on the Peace Treaty. The Articles of Confederation gave Congress power to make war, peace, and treaties, but not to interfere with state laws.

Hamilton for the Defense:

If the legislature had intended the Trespass Act to override the Peace Treaty, the legislature would have provided that the Act go into effect notwithstanding any international agreements made by Congress.

Attorneys for Plaintiff:

The legislature was elected by the people, and their law is supreme authority. This court's magistrates, servants of the people, may not consider common law or national law, only state law.

Hamilton for the Defense:
Congress also was a creation of the people, and the people had given Congress the duty of making peace. Every peace treaty, unless otherwise stipulated, implies a general amnesty. Whatever Waddington had done in wartime must be considered as expunged when Congress ratified the treaty in the name of the states.

Attorneys for Plaintiff:
This court could not repeal the Trespass Act. Only the legislature can repeal.

Hamilton for the Defense:
This court must find certain parts of the Act to be void. It must set the national law above the state law, the Treaty above the Trespass Act.

III

(June–December 1784)

Having heard arguments, the Mayor's Court requested counsel to submit briefs for closer study of the points. On August 17, Mayor James Duane delivered judgments. On August 18, he went into explanations; and by December a jury had fixed the penalties. Mrs. Rutgers' claim of damages was cut from 8,000 pounds to 791 pounds, with odd shillings and pence, and this amount was reduced still further by a settlement between the principals. It was a victory for Hamilton.

He had contended that Waddington had occupied the brewery during part of the time in question under authority of the civilian commissary, and during another part, under that of the British commandant. It was his plea that these two periods of time should be considered separately. The court agreed, ruling that Waddington could be required to pay rent for only two years, instead of five. This was another success for Hamilton.

Hamilton won a big point when Mayor Duane declared that

the case involved "questions, which must affect the national character:—questions whose decision will record the spirit of our Courts to posterity. Questions which embrace the whole law of nations!" The magistrates of the Mayor's Court agreed that a state may not violate a national treaty. They sustained Hamilton.

Public reaction fell along predictable lines. Clinton's followers were enraged. When the legislature met, it resolved that the reasoning of the Mayor's court was "subversive of all law and good order, and leads directly to anarchy and confusion . . . and therefore will end our dear-bought rights and privileges, and the legislatures become useless." A committee of nine leading citizens, including highly regarded lawyers, wrote a four-column letter in the *New York Packet and American Advertiser*. They found it outrageous that "the Mayor's Court have assumed and exercised a power to set aside an act of the state."

But there was strong reaction in the opposite direction. The Continentalists, the party that would soon be called the Federalists, hailed Hamilton's work as a long step toward nationhood. General Washington saw that a blow had been struck for centralized government. He congratulated Mayor Duane, saying, ". . . reason seems very much in favor of the opinion given by the Court, and my judgment yields a hearty assent to it." John Jay, Secretary for Foreign Affairs, and a Peace Commissioner, expressed gratitude that the Treaty had been upheld.

Hamilton had turned a damage suit into a gain for Federal Union.

IV

(1785–1786)

Rutgers v. Waddington was a victory for principle. Hamilton had dealt a blow against the tyranny of the majority, established defenses for the people against the mastery of government, and set in motion forces that would soon obtain repeal of all the anti-Tory Acts, and in so doing had made his name and arguments known to the working classes.

Men with an eye to American statecraft and jurisprudence

saw Hamilton as a brilliant achiever for civil rights and national unity. Others saw that this fashionably clad, well-connected wrangler and writer had displayed an affinity for the moneyed and propertied classes. The city merchants and the up-country landlords brought their business to him, and the parallel columns of his Cash Book marked "Dr" and "Cr" grew longer. Where there had been entries of 10 pounds 12 shillings 8 pence, he was now writing such figures as 768 pounds 5 shillings 9 pence (paid to him by Alexander McCauley, merchant and shipowner). Receipts from related transactions between January and June of 1786 came to more than six thousand pounds.

He was in demand, but he kept his fees modest, and often served gratis, as shown in the two-volume collection, *The Law Practice of Alexander Hamilton.* He would charge five pounds for a court appearance in the city, a little more if he had to travel. He made nominal charges for consultation and for drawing legal documents. The big payments came when he won lucrative judgments. If he stayed at this work, he would become one of those "monied men" about whom he had mixed feelings of respect and contempt.

Unexpectedly, he had gained adherents among the mechanics, tailors, and carpenters whom he had familiarly addressed in the Phocion Letters. In April 1785 he found his name on a list of candidates for the Assembly. His appointment to Congress had been by favor of his father-in-law and Governor Clinton, who was now alienated; but this time he was lifted by a ground swell. He entered a third-person note in the *New York Packet:* ". . . being sincerely desirous of declining public office at the present juncture, thinks it proper to declare his wishes on this head. . . ." It was the second time he had refused to run.

Hamilton was not really a man of the people. This was stressed during a public clamor against the Society of the Cincinnati, which called its first general meeting in May 1784. The Society had been formed at West Point in 1783. Washington was its president-general; Hamilton was secretary of the New York chapter, and a very active member. The Society's purposes were patriotic and charitable. Funds were raised for out-of-pocket officers and their next of kin. Membership was limited to officers with three years of honorable Revolutionary service, eligibility passing from father to eldest son. Chapters were organized in the thirteen states and France. There was unmistakable Hamiltonian language in the Society's statement of overall intent:

"To promote and cherish between the respective states that Union and National Honor, so necessary to their happiness and the future dignity of the American Empire."

But not everybody was enchanted by this high ideal of Honor and Empire. Persons excluded by the eligibility clause called the Society militaristic and aristocratic. Adams and Jefferson, civilians throughout the war, stigmatized the Society as a threat to civil liberties. It was denounced in speech and writing as "a race of Hereditary Patricians." It was said to be the nucleus of a monarchist political party.

Hamilton dismissed all the jealous and surly criticism. To him the Society was an arrangement made in heaven. He had no legitimate father, but membership in the Cincinnati certified his aristocracy. It provided a precious legacy to hand down to his son. It perpetuated his status as an officer and a gentleman of the Army that had turned the world upside down.

Opposition and doubts concerning the Cincinnati were not, however, confined to envious outsiders. George Washington himself held serious reservations. The General had no son and no need to prove his social standing. Any controversy that threatened to disunite the American people, he wrote Hamilton, must be avoided or removed. Had the French officers not been invited to join, the General declared, he would demand an outright disbandment of the Society. He completely favored revision of the charter to eliminate the objectionable father-to-son membership. He proposed that the charitable funds be turned over to the state legislatures for distribution. When Hamilton remonstrated, saying that the tempest of popular disapproval would blow over, the General was unmoved.

"It is a matter of little moment," Washington wrote on, "whether the alarm which seized the public mind was the re-

sult of foresight—envy & jealousy—or a disordered imagination, the effect . . . would have been the same. . . . The fears
of the people are not removed; they only sleep, and a very little
matter would set them afloat again."

His own inclination, like Hamilton's, would be to speak out
and "to convince the narrow-minded part of our countrymen
that the *Amor Patriae* was much stronger in our breasts than
theirs—and that our conduct through the whole business was
actuated by nobler & more generous sentiments than were
apprehended." But the General had no hope that the people
would accept the Society in its present form and acknowledge
"the purity of its intentions." If the members "mean to live in
peace with the rest of their fellow-citizens, they must submit
to the alterations. . . ."

Hamilton's tactics in the face of this formidable opposition
were those of strategic delay. He called meetings, he wrote
reports, he referred decisions to committees, he allowed the
waters of two years to run under the bridge. At last, in a committee report to the New York Society, July 6, 1786, he was
able to write that "the alternatives proposed" had been "attentively considered" and the motives "highly approve[d]," but
that "it would be inexpedient to adopt them." Thanks to Hamilton's Fabian marches, the Society would never change its aristocratic ways.

Of itself, membership in the Cincinnati did not mark any
man as antidemocratic. Other members, like Clinton and Burr,
were accepted as friends of the people. But Hamilton's relationship to Schuyler, his activity in the Bank of New York, his Tory
clientele, were indicative of his sympathies. Even so, he was not
an easy man to label.

"I am aware," Hamilton wrote in April 1786 to an iron-
monger, Nathaniel Hazard, who was petitioning the legislature
for a stay of prewar debts, "that I have been represented as an
enemy to the wishes of what you call your corps." But he was
pleased that Hazard called him fair-minded. "The good opinion
of liberal men I hold in too high estimation not to be flattered."
He agreed to intercede for Hazard at the legislature, asserting
that merchants who had contracted debts to the British prior

to 1776 "have been in a great measure victims of the Revolution." He could feel for persons who were locked into debt. The idea that he was indifferent toward them, or biased in favor of their British creditors, "does not do Justice either to my head or to my heart," he told Hazard.

For a full year, since last declining to run for the assembly, he had noted alarming trends that made it difficult for him to devote full attention to money-making. A landlord client, Robert Livingston of Livingston Manor, had asked him to bring suit against Robert R. Livingston, Chancellor of the University of the State of New York since 1784, and Hamilton's friend, regarding a family quarrel over water rights and grist mills.

"The law is with you," Hamilton answered, "yet you know my sentiments as to the uncertainty of the event. Much will depend on the whim of a jury. . . ."

He advised his client to make a friendly settlement, and then veered off into politics. He was "concerned for the *security of property*," wrote Hamilton. He thought it time "to put men in the Legislature whose principles are not the *levelling kind*," because "a number of attempts have been made . . . to subvert the constitution and destroy the rights of private property." He urged Livingston to back candidates who would watch the interest "of all those who have anything to lose . . ." and to "take care that the power of government is entrusted to proper hands."

Livingston replied that he also was alarmed about "the politics of the present dangerous times . . ." and about "the need to prevent ourselves & country from ruin, which we clearly [see] rapidly descending on our heads." But he assured Hamilton that something was being done about it outside the city.

"By uniting the interests of Rensselaer, Schuyler & our family, with other gentlemen of property in the County . . . we carried this last election . . . and I trust we shall have like success provided we stick close to each other. . . ." Livingston closed by saying that he and other landholding conservatives "most cordially desire your interest and influence in [the] future. . . ."

There was much here to set Hamilton thinking. Property

rights were not separate from human rights. If they were worth preserving, they were worth a political fight. Much could be done by joining with men of common interests, picking suitable candidates, and backing them with money and organization. True, it was easier to do this in the up-state counties, where the great families could pool their wealth and prestige. In the city it would be difficult to bring together men of wealth and business; they were temperamentally apathetic to politics and were much outnumbered by men of the other kind, though there were property restrictions on the right to vote.

Still, a beginning must be made. When his name was put up as a candidate for the third time, in the spring of 1786, Hamilton did not remove it. He stood for the Assembly, and finished fifth among the nine who were elected from the city and county of New York.

V

(September 1786)

Public business was beginning to interfere with his social life, as well as with his law practice. The new legislature would not meet till January, but there were other obligations. On September 1, he cancelled a dinner engagement with Richard Varick because "this is the day of departure," and "Mrs. Hamilton insists on my dining with her." As a married man himself, Varick "will know that in such a case implicit obedience on my part is proper."

Hamilton was off to Annapolis, having been appointed back on May 5 as one of five New York State commissioners to a thirteen-state convention on trade and commerce. Madison had called this meeting after a previous one between Virginia and Maryland at Mount Vernon, regarding traffic on the Potomac. So little regarded was the Annapolis gathering that three of the New York commissioners backed out, and Hamilton set forth accompanied only by Egbert Benson, "a prophane bachelor" with no home life to neglect.

At Newark, Hamilton sent back a note to John Lansing, Jr., calling off an appearance in court "at the intended trial at

which Mr. Rensselaer is concerned." He made other postpone-
ments. By winning election to the Assembly and accepting the
appointment in Maryland he was giving hostages to political
service. He would not be a full-time lawyer again for nearly a
decade.

Madison and Edmund Randolph of Virginia waited in Annapolis at George Mann's Inn, where lodging and a servant
could be had for a shilling and sixpence a night. By September
7, Delaware, New Jersey, and Pennsylvania produced delegates, but the host state of Maryland and the eight others of
the thirteen sent nobody. It was a sorry showing, and sorrier
still when the twelve men sat down to compare what their
legislatures had empowered them to do. There was no unifor-
mity in their instructions. The dispirited group would have
broken up if Abraham Clark of New Jersey had not proposed
calling a new convention to try again. Hamilton was named to
draft a resolution to that effect, but before getting to work on
it, he wrote to Betsey on September 8:

"In reality my attachments to home disqualify me for either
business or pleasure abroad; and the prospect of detention here
for eight or ten days fills me with an anxiety, which will best
be conceived by my Betsey's own impatience. . . . Kiss my
little ones a thousand times for me. . . . Think of me with as
much tenderness as I do of you, and we cannot fail to be always
happy."

He set to work at composing a suitable Address from the
Annapolis Convention to the state legislatures. While he was
in the midst of that assignment, on September 11, farmers at
Concord, Massachusetts, broke up a court hearing in a revolt
over taxation. Captain Daniel Shays, a Revolutionary hero, was
head of a movement that demanded "the abolition of debts, the
division of property and reunion with Great Britain." Hamilton's wartime comrade, Light-Horse Harry Lee, now in Congress, thought Washington should take his presence and influence to New England to back up a call for order. Other
delegates asked whether Continental troops should not be sent
to support the Bay State militia.

Hamilton would support any proposition that called for ener-

getic, centralized decision-making. Since 1780, as soldier, revenue collector, member of Congress, he had been composing
appeals to scuttle the Confederation and establish a national
authority.

He had a kindred spirit in Madison, whom he knew quite well
by now. That blue-eyed, ruddy-faced scholar, "no bigger than
a half-piece of soap," had a reputation at Princeton for ribald
humor. Not yet deprived of personality by prudish biographers
and by a sobersidedness that increased with age, Madison still
had a residual sparkle at Annapolis. Hamilton found him brim-
ming with grand ideas and capable of picturesque language.

Such traits were needed if the Annapolis gathering was to
lead to something better. Interstate agreements on trade and
commerce were all very well, but they did not approach the
heart of the problem. The disarray of the Confederation was
ludicrous. Seven states printed their own money, which was
hopelessly mingled with foreign currency. Nine had their own
navies to catch cross-border smugglers, expeditions as futile as
swatting summer flies. Governor Clinton had just refused to
call a special session for considering a Congressional request
to levy and collect imposts. Vermont was negotiating to become
a Canadian province. In Massachusetts the Shays rebellion
would not be put down for another five months; finally General
Benjamin Lincoln smashed it in a pitched battle at Petersham.

To be sure, crops grew, wagons moved, and ships sailed, but
the relative well-being of the states would never grow into
prosperity without national cohesion. Hamilton and Madison
saw New York and Virginia as logical partners in unification,
but there was a hitch. Randolph, tall and portly at thirty-two,
his state's attorney general and governor-presumptive, tempered his ambition for a great career with excessive caution.
The elders of the Old Dominion were divided on the issues at
Annapolis; Patrick Henry and George Mason were at odds with
Washington. Randolph was growing popular by being inoffen-
sive, and he would never put his name to a trumpet-call mani-
festo. Madison warned Hamilton:

"You had better yield to this man; for otherwise all Virginia
will be against you."

So Hamilton wrote out a pussy-footing message to the legislatures. He and the other delegates "humbly beg leave to suggest . . . the appointment of Commissioners to meet at Philadelphia on the second Monday of May next, to . . . render the Constitution of the Federal government adequate. . . ."

It was a tame enough document to earn the signatures of all twelve attendants. Hamilton headed home, where, he said, "In the bosom of my family alone must my happiness be sought. . . ."

VI

(January–May 1787)

Luckily for his convenience, the New York State General Assembly rotated its sessions between temporary capitals, and in 1787 it met in New York City. He could attend regularly, and he did. By his thirtieth birthday, January 11, he had formed impressions of state legislative life. It promised to be dilatory. Ten days passed without a quorum. The session had an agenda of large matters and relatively small ones. He was in the lair of the Clintonians and could hardly expect to turn the majority around.

On January 19 he made an impressive address. The point at issue was a motion by Speaker Richard Varick to express "approbation" of Clinton's prior refusal to convene a special session at the request of the Confederation Congress. "Free deliberations" would be impaired, the Governor contended, if the legislature were at the beck of a monarchical Congress.

Hamilton scoffed at Clinton's attempt to draw an analogy between a lifetime king and a one-year Congress. He did not contend that the Governor was obliged to make the call, but only that the Assembly should not praise his refusal and his wrong-headed reasoning. To approve Clinton's rationale of defiance would set a bad precedent for future governors, and bring "the councils and powers of the Union into universal contempt."

Hamilton lost his motion, with only nine members supporting him. Another leftover matter soon turned up before the

Assembly. Secretary for Foreign Affairs John Jay asked the legislature to repeal all laws inconsistent with the Treaty of Peace. This proposition had been pending since *Rutgers v. Waddington.* Hamilton introduced a sustaining resolution and backed it with a stirring appeal that won the day in the Assembly. The state senate did not concur, but the path for repeal of anti-Tory legislation had been opened. Before the session ended a Hamilton bill expunged the most offensive clauses of the Trespass Act.

He turned to the subject of federal taxation at the waterfront, but his exhortations to "continental thinking" could not again crack the disciplined majority. On state taxes he did better. He introduced a measure to abolish the old method of arbitrary assessment. "Today an assessor, my friend, taxes me at ten pounds. Tomorrow one less my friend will tax me four times the sum . . . great inequality results and all is uncertainty."

Of course, he acknowledged, "The present bill does not pretend to reach absolute equality. No human plan can attain it. . . . but the principles of the present bill will approach much closer to equality . . . it will have the great advantage of certainty."

He would tax bachelors, who have no family to maintain, and give a bounty to maiden ladies. He would make a charge for seals on legal documents, using the revenue to pay judicial salaries, so that judges would not be beholden to the legislatures. He would levy upon specified possessions that were found only among families most able to pay, and most concerned with having a stable and proficient state government.

"He asked," reported the *Daily Advertiser,* "on whom did the tax on carriages, on servants, on marble chimney pieces, stucco and papered rooms, fall; where were the houses that in general would pay for six rooms? Did not the merchant pay a duty on his ships, and many other things on which people in the country paid nothing?"

He found inequities in the county tax quotas. Albany County with seventy thousand persons paid the state seventy thousand pounds, but Suffolk with fourteen thousand population paid only forty-five hundred pounds. His own New York City and County were overcharged. "He believed that every gentleman who could lay his hand on his heart and vote according to his conscience, would declare that one-fourth part of the taxes was too great a portion for New-York." In the voting which followed, Albany's share was increased and New York's was lowered.

He kept broadening his reputation. The attorney for the wealthy was the taxer of luxuries. The Continentalist was solicitous of back-home interests. The city banker proved to be an authority on county quotas. The man who had married a rich wife believed that families in carriages had responsibilities to go with their privileges.

Hamilton was incredibly painstaking. Appointed, together with the Clintonian Samuel Jones, to arbitrate a boundary dispute with Massachusetts, his brief had a voluminous appendix, "Notes on the History of North and South America," which traced land titles to Columbus, Amerigo Vespucci, and Sebastian Cabot.

He was unbelievably objective. Although it offended the big landlords, he introduced an Act Acknowledging the Independence of Vermont; this would cede thousands of acres belonging to the State of New York. He held that since the people of Vermont had formed a viable government that had existed since 1777, Vermont's statehood should be recognized.

"Policy demands it, and justice acquiesces. . . . The first object is drawn from the great principle of the social compact— that the chief object of government is to protect the rights of the individual by the united strength of the community."

Again, he overwhelmed the Assembly majority. New York became the first state to invite Vermont into the Union, though the invitation was not binding and the Governor still balked.

To his colleagues, and to the *Advertiser* and the *Packet,* which covered Assembly debates, this new member was disturbingly unpredictable—and yet not inconsistent when his habits of thinking became familiar.

There was an election bill to allow poll inspectors to explain the ballot to illiterate persons. Hamilton opposed it. He said it tended "to increase rather than prevent an improper influence. . . . For though the inspector takes an oath that his conduct shall be impartial . . . the consequence will be that inspectors will have the disposition of the votes of all unlettered persons. . . . Here then is more of a concerted influence over the illiterate and uninformed part of the community than they would have been subject to if left to themselves."

After two Hamilton speeches on the subject, his position was accepted against opposition by the Governor's party. The Governor's floor leader, Samuel Jones, spoke for another election bill, this one to require a loyalty oath abjuring fealty to any ecclesiastical leader. It was anti-Catholic, and Hamilton beat it down. "Why should we wound the tender consciences of any man?" he demanded.

Still another election bill called for destruction of all ballots for governor and lieutenant governor when the ballots in the district exceeded the number of eligible voters. "This was shewn by Mr. Hamilton to be a very great injustice to the district, as it was in the power of a clerk or any officer, by putting in an additional ballot, to set aside the votes of 500 persons." He moved that where there were more ballots than eligible voters, the excess ballots should be destroyed by lot. His motion was adopted.

He also opposed a bill to deny seats in the legislature to any person holding office in or receiving a pension from the central government. He abominated discrimination against pensioned war veterans. He suspected all arbitrary limitations on civil rights. "Let us on our part be cautious how we abridge the freedom of choice. . . ." The state constitution did not authorize preclusion of any class of citizens. "I am uniformly opposed to every innovation not known in the provisions of the constitution. I move that the clause be struck out." His motion was carried.

On another day he altered the law that fined and imprisoned the scavengers of shipwrecks. The English penalty was "death without benefit of clergy," which he found too severe. Instead of capital punishment, he demanded "corporeal punishment at the discretion of the court, so as not to affect life or limb."

He had always stressed "due process," and he applied this to a bill that would have required a woman giving stillbirth to prove herself innocent of murder. "He expatiated feelingly on the delicate situation it placed an unfortunate woman in." She might have no witnesses to the birth, might wish to conceal her dishonor, and in any event was entitled to the presumption of innocence. "The operation of this law would compel her to publish her name to the world." His motion that the clause be "obliterated from the bill" was adopted.

He pushed through a strict divorce law, making adultery the only cause and forbidding the guilty party to remarry. He opposed the British primogeniture system, which secured inheritance of property to the eldest son. He favored equity of inheritance, saying it "will melt down the great estates which, if they continued, might favor the power of the few." He supported a bill for "erecting an University within this state," which included the incorporation of colleges.

By mid-April, as candidate for office, as delegate to the Annapolis convention, as member of the Assembly, he had devoted virtually a full year to politics, and dealt with scores of topics. His writings and speeches provided an index to his philosophy. He was protective toward the unfortunate and demanding toward the privileged. He was a fundamentalist who opposed "innovation" and respected the status quo. He was an idealist who sought improvements without insisting on perfection. He believed in equity but not equality.

He had been named, back in March, as a delegate to the Federal Convention at Philadelphia, but he was not satisfied with the selection method. He thought five delegates better than three, as the legislature had determined. He had seen how absenteeism stultified deliberative gatherings. He saw better promise of getting a man or more of real ability among five than among three.

Despite its previous rejection, he re-introduced a motion for the enlarged panel. He went further on the chamber floor and named some individuals. He nominated Robert R. Livingston, chancellor of the University and former secretary for foreign affairs; Egbert Benson, attorney general and judge; James

Duane, Mayor and magistrate; and the very experienced John Jay—"particularly the latter," he added.

This time he did not win. Two of the Governor's henchmen, Lansing and Yates, and himself as Schuyler's choice, were appointed by the legislature for the "sole and express purpose of revising the Articles of Confederation."

This was not what Hamilton had in mind. He was convinced, and knew that Madison was too, that only a completely new Federal charter would do.

CHAPTER FOURTEEN

The Making of a Government

I

(May–June 1787)

Hamilton was no longer the "boy" of great events. He was now in his thirty-first year. At what Philadelphia called the Grand Convention (the city, that May, played host also to general meetings of the Cincinnati, the Pennsylvania Society for the Abolition of Slavery, the Presbyterian Synod, and a Baptist gathering), at least four delegates—Jonathan Dayton, John Mercer, Richard Spaight, and Charles Pinckney—were under thirty.

Hamilton's maturity was recognized at the outset. He was chosen, with Henry Knox and Elias Boudinot, to wait on Washington as representative of the Society of the Cincinnati. They found the General embarrassed at his dual role of heading an elite corps and also seeking to promote a republican government. It was arranged for Thomas Mifflin, the Society's vice president, to attend its meetings.

Characteristically, Hamilton was blasé about the historic atmosphere. Though he had served as Congressman and now as delegate in the state house, which later Americans would call Independence Hall, he expressed no awe and sent home no descriptions. More impressed than Hamilton, another visitor called the state house "a noble building; the architecture is in a richer and grander style than any public building I have seen before."

The Convention was using the chamber of the legislature, which was in recess, but the three justices of the Pennsylvania supreme court could be seen across the arched and pillared hallway. The other visitor wrote in his diary: "Their robes are scarlet, the lawyers' black. The Chief Judge, Mr. McKean, was sitting with his hat on, which is the custom, but struck me as being very odd and seemed to derogate from the dignity of the judge." Hamilton was not noticing. Several delegates would write vivid character sketches of the Constitution makers, who were bound to become Founding Fathers if they succeeded. Hamilton didn't bother. He was thinking governance.

His serious handsome presence, however, did not go unnoticed. Who could "look at his features and not see that they are ineffaceably stamped by the divine hand with the impress of genius?" Other delegates must have been good-looking too, but—

"Mark the fairness of his complexion and his rosy cheeks. Watch the play of his singularly expressive countenance; in repose, it seems grave and thoughtful; but see him when spoken to, and instantly all is lighted up with an intelligent vivacity, and around his lips plays a smile of extraordinary sweetness."

When the Convention found its quorum, twelve days off schedule, he was elected to the important three-man committee on "standing rules and orders." Its chairman was George Wyeth, law professor at William and Mary College, the teacher of Jefferson and Monroe. Charles Pinckney of South Carolina completed the panel. Hamilton sought influence. William Temple Franklin, the Doctor's grandson, was the sentimental favorite to become Secretary to the Convention, but Hamilton nominated William Jackson, the borrower of Angelica's slave. His candidate defeated young Franklin by the vote of five states to two.

By then Washington had been elected President of the Convention, and Hamilton was quartered with eight other delegates at the Indian Queen, close by the Hall. Among these was James Madison, steadily improving in health by riding and tramping, and even capable of wearing a ruffle and of varying his black attire with one of buff and blue.

The two men were now friendly, and becoming close friends. Hamilton recalled "a long conversation which I had with Mr. Madison in an afternoon's walk." It concerned the problem of the enormous debt of the states. Hamilton felt that the new central government, when and if formed, should take it over.

"I well remember that we were perfectly agreed in the expediency and propriety of such a measure; though we were both of the opinion that it would be more advisable" to approach it through legislation afterwards rather than write it as "an article of Constitution, from the impolicy of multiplying obstacles to its reception on collateral details."

The delegations at the Queen were comfortably housed. Another guest who visited the Convention put up there, and he wrote: "It is kept in elegant style. . . . As soon as I inquired of the bar-keeper . . . a livery servant was ordered immediately to attend me, who received my baggage from the hostler and conducted me to the apartment assigned by the bar-keeper, which was a very small but handsome chamber (No. 9), furnished with a rich field bed, table with drawers, a large looking-glass, neat chairs and other furniture. Its front was east and, being in the third story, afforded a fine prospect toward the river and the Jersey shore. The servant that attended me was a young, sprightly, well-built black fellow, neatly dressed —blue coat, sleeves and cape red, and buff waistcoat and breeches, the bosom of his shirt ruffled and his hair powdered. . . .

"Being told while I was at tea, that a number of the members of the Continental Convention . . . lodged in the house . . . I sent into their Hall (for they live by themselves). . . ."

On May 28, the Rules Committee made its first report: "The said rules were once read throughout, and then a second time one by one; and upon the question [being] severally put thereupon, two of them were disagreed to. . . ." The committee's work was of a continuing nature, depending on problems that arose. On the 29th, in an attempt to keep a quorum intact, the committee added, among other new regulations:

"That no member be absent from the House so as to interrupt the representation of the State without leave.

"That Committees do not sit whilst the House shall be, or ought to be, sitting."

Philadelphia was "a mere oven," Doctor Franklin had written Susanna Wright back in 1753, and this summer was said to be the hottest one since. Hamilton went out in company for

some morning strolls. The streets were filled with women at
the open food markets. Those who sold the wares often brought
their children and kept their infants in their arms, while those
who purchased were usually accompanied by a servant with a
basket. It was a cosmopolitan town, with many immigrants,
and forty-five foreign-language printers who turned out a variety of almanacs, sermons, broadsides, and pamphlets, as well
as newspapers. The morning bustle surprised a New Englander. "What would the delicate Boston ladies think if they
were to be abroad at this hour?" he exclaimed.

Convention sessions began at ten o'clock and ran till late
afternoon. Madison and Randolph, now governor of Virginia,
had brought along their state's plan for a Constitution, and
William Paterson his New Jersey version. The struggle would
swirl around these two proposals, one to abolish the Confederation and start anew, the second to preserve but liberalize the
Articles. Most of the delegates agreed with Hamilton that they
were not bound by their legislatures' instructions, since the
states would ratify or reject whatever the Convention proposed.

With sentries at the doors, with members enjoined to secrecy,
it would prove a tight little conference. Of the seventy-four
delegates, from all states except Rhode Island, only fifty-two
would attend, and those not regularly.

After some early skirmishes, the two major proposals becoming familiar, Madison noted, "Col. Hamilton cannot say he is
in sentiment with either plan." Hamilton had one of his own
that he presented to the Committee of the Whole on June 18.

He spoke from notes for nearly six hours. Madison, Yates,
Lansing, and Rufus King of Massachusetts wrote down his
words. Editors of the Hamilton Papers call it "perhaps the most
important address ever made by Hamilton—if its influence can
be measured either by its use in subsequent evaluation of
Hamilton's political philosophy, or by the controversy about it
during his lifetime. . . ." It was a dissertation on governance
and an outline of "his" Constitution.

"To deliver my sentiments on so important a subject," he
began, according to the Yates version, "when the first characters of the Union have gone before me, inspires me with the

greatest diffidence, especially when my ideas are so materially dissimilar. . . . My situation is disagreeable, but it would be criminal not to come forward on a question of this magnitude."

With that he fired a jolting volley into the ranks. The unicameral Jersey plan had the merit of doing away with one-state-one-vote, and providing some central taxation at the ports. But Hamilton could not accept any charter "so long as state sovereignties do, in any shape, exist." The Virginia plan for a two-chamber legislature, a chief executive, and a judiciary suited him better, but caused him "great doubts." It retained the integrity of the states and, much worse, betrayed overconfidence in the people.

His own Plan for Government would get away from confederation, as well as federation. He favored a "national government" under which the states would be reduced but not obliterated, and the people checked by an "energetic" authority.

The delegates were all emissaries of their states, and some were devotees of democracy. They never once interrupted this day-long oration. Hamilton's plan had not a snowball's chance in the stifling closed-door chamber. Washington, temporarily out of the chair, sat silently among the Virginia delegation. Madison's pen moved stolidly abreast of Hamilton's words, which fired pointblank at the sovereign states.

"The great question is 'What provision shall we make for the happiness of our country?' . . . The States have constantly shewn a disposition rather to retain the powers delegated to them than to part with more. . . . The ambition of the demagogues is known to hate the control of the Gen. Government. . . . All the passions . . . of avarice, of ambition, interest . . . fall into the current of the States and do not flow in the stream of the Genl. Government."

Hamilton leveled his guns at democracy with its impossible promise of equality. "In every community where industry is encouraged, there will be a division of it into the few & the many. Hence separate interests will arise. There will be debtors & creditors. Give the power to the many, they will oppress the few. Give all power to the few, they will oppress the many.

. . . Both therefore ought to have power, that each may defend itself against the other."

Robert Yates, making his own notes, caught Hamilton saying of society, "The first [the few] are the rich and well-born, and the others the mass of the people. The voice of the people has been said to be the voice of God. . . . It is not true in fact."

He was driving at something that approximated the English system: a powerful head of state, a central parliament, a high judiciary, and, below the level of important government, minor shires and local magistrates. Madison followed him with care.

"He hoped Gentlemen of different opinion would bear with him. . . . The English model was the only good one on this subject. The hereditary interest of the King was so interwoven with that of the nation . . . that he was placed above the danger of being corrupted. . . . What is the inference from all these observations? That we ought to go as far in order to attain stability and permanency as republican principles will permit."

A hereditary monarch would never do in America, as Hamilton knew well. He proposed an elected chief executive to serve for life or good behavior. He wanted a senate, not hereditary like the House of Lords, but with members chosen for life. "Is this a republican system?" he asked in the Yates version of his remarks, "It is strictly so, as long as they remain elective." He wanted the lower chamber to have a popular base and be chosen in state districts. "It is essential to the democratic rights of the community that this branch be elected by the people."

At this point, wrote Yates, "Mr. H. produced his plan." Had it been accepted, a patent impossibility, the American charter, in condensed form, would have been as follows:

The Supreme Legislature would make "all laws whatsoever, subject to the *negative* hereafter mentioned." The lifetime senators would be picked by electors, and thus be once removed from the people. The Supreme Executive, called Governor, would be chosen "by Electors chosen by electors, or appointed by the legislatures," thus twice removed from popular suffrage.

The Governor would have a negative over all laws, both state and national. He would appoint state governors as well as Cabinet officers and ambassadors, with Senate approval. He would be commander in chief. While the Governor would have the "direction of war" once begun, only the Senate could "declare" war. On the "death, resignation or removal of the Governor," the president of the Senate would succeed him.

The Supreme Judiciary would be composed of twelve good-behavior judges "with adequate and permanent salaries," and all state laws would "be utterly void" if found to be contrary to statutes of the General Government. No state would have land or naval forces, other than militia, the officers of which would be appointed by the General Government.

Impeachment of any national official for "corrupt conduct" would be tried before the Supreme Court sitting with the chief judges of all the states.

"Then adjournment," wrote Yates when Hamilton finished.

II

(June 1787)

Hamilton's plan of government had gone too far for his own good. Some delegates, oversimplifying his remarks, would call him a monarchist, hater of democracy, hedger on republicanism, abolitionist of statehood. Some historians and biographers would follow this line and condemn him as anti-American and royalist.

But Hamilton knew what he was doing, which was making a strong case for an energetic central government. "I am aware that it goes beyond the ideas of most members. . . . I do not mean to offer the paper I have sketched." He did hope to be understood in what he had said, and not to be misquoted. For that reason he went to Madison, read over the Virginian's transcript of his remarks, and verified it.

He was willing to stand on that, and Madison also was pleased. The Virginian understood perfectly that his friend intended only to make the Convention do some thinking. The speech was meant "to suggest amendments . . . to the plan of Mr. R[andolph] in the proper stages of its future development." Only one delegate, George Read of Delaware, actually supported the Hamilton plan. Read "wished it to be substituted in place of that on the table," which was the Randolph plan.

Hamilton never intended his address to do more than get the Convention out of the deadlock in which it had hung for four weeks, in danger of fizzling out as the Annapolis meeting had done. There is no doubt that he jolted the Convention in the direction that it eventually took, but his audacity cost him dear.

There was much misunderstanding of what he had said, and the clarifications were long in catching up. George Mason of Virginia thought that Hamilton's Governor would be "more powerful than the British king." Abraham Baldwin of Georgia jumped to the same conclusion, but backed away. Baldwin at first called Hamilton's plan "King, Lords and Commons." But three months after the Convention closed, Baldwin, a graduate of Yale College, wrote to Yale President Ezra Stiles to give him an account "of the whole process in Convention." By this time Baldwin had served on the committee that wrote the section creating the Presidency. He assured Stiles that no "Member in Convention had the least idea of insidiously laying the foundation of a future like the European or Asiatic monarchies, either ancient or modern. But were unanimously guarded & firm against everything of this ultimate tendency."

But Hamilton had recklessly placed himself at the mercy of political foes and hostile writers, contemporary and to come. They branded him a would-be king-maker. In 1922, however, a precise historical researcher, Louise Burnham Dunbar, wrote a searching monograph with the explanatory title, *A Study of Monarchical Tendencies in the United States from 1776 to 1801.* She found a number of early Americans who wished to rejoin the British Empire or to import a European monarch. None of them, however, was named Alexander Hamilton. Of him the author wrote:

"His real desire seems to have been to combine the separation of powers and the stability of the British form with the representative feature of a republic and the popular participation consistent with democracy, and thus to meet the peculiar needs of America."

III
(June 1787)

It was Madison, and only Madison, who caught some spiritual overtones in the address. "I chose a seat," he later wrote, "in front of the presiding member, with the other members on my right and left hand. In this favorable position . . . I was enabled to write out my daily notes during the session or within a few finishing days after its close." This diligent, objective, cogitative note-taker was determined to make an exact record of the proceedings, so far as was humanly possible, and also to catch nuances that would instruct his well-informed mind.

Madison's intimate admiration of Jefferson could be the reason he heard an echo of the sacred phrase "pursuit of happiness" in the New Yorker's opening passages. Three times Hamilton referred to "happiness" as the purpose of the state. He was repeating Jefferson, but also Aristotle's dissertation on the Good Life as the purpose of all political organization.

Hamilton told the delegates in his first paragraph that duty required "every man to contribute his efforts for public safety & happiness." He added, according to Madison, that "we owed it to our Country to do, in this emergency, whatever we should deem essential to its happiness." He opened his second paragraph: "The great question is what provision shall we make for the happiness of our Country?" These Madison-recorded lines do not appear in the outline from which Hamilton spoke. It is evident that the speaker improvised them as a flourish, an oratorical tie-in with the Declaration of Independence.

Aristotle, he went on, had traced the formation of the state from the family unit to the combining of communities for ends that were thought to be good. When communities expanded into villages and villages united, according to Aristotle, "the state came into existence, originating in the effort to obtain the bare necessities of life, but continuing in the effort for the sake of a Good Life. . . . The state is thus a natural creation, and man is by nature a political animal."

Like the Athenian schoolmaster, Hamilton recognized economic prosperity as essential to the enjoyment of spiritual values. His address grouped together national "revenue . . . commerce . . . agriculture." He believed that "money is, with propriety, considered as the vital principle of the body politic." Both the Athenian and the New Yorker spoke out for political discipline. Aristotle wrote, "Yet it is liberty that goes along with obedience to law." Hamilton told the delegates that "the goodness of government consists in a vigorous execution."

Like Aristotle, he was concerned with longevity of the state. He judged that a country would best endure if it had authority backed by popular participation, which was what he proposed for the House of Representatives. Hamilton expressed an Aristotelian scorn for Utopia, or for a visionary society based on aspirations alone. In the Federalist Papers he rejected any proposition that promises "an exemption from the imperfections, the weakness and the evils incident to society in every shape."

Madison was much in sympathy with these views. It is an allowable assumption that their co-authorship of the Federalist Papers became possible at this time. The Virginian did not object to Hamilton's division of society into classes and masses. In this same year Madison wrote, "All civilized societies are divided into different interests and factions, as they happen to be creditors or debtors—rich or poor—husbandmen, merchants or manufacturers. . . ." Both Hamilton and Madison apparently were borrowing from John Adams' London-published book, *Defence of the Constitutions.* This volume was being distributed in Philadelphia during the Convention by a Boston bookshop. In his work Adams dwelt at length upon the inequalities of men. "These sources of inequality which are common to every people can never be altered by any because they are founded in the constitution of nature; this natural aristocracy among mankind . . . is a fact. . . ."

Madison and Hamilton believed, as the latter wrote in another place, that "to establish substantial and permanent order . . . to increase the total mass of industry and opulence, is ultimately beneficial to every part" of society. They both had the same regard for seeing liberty and prosperity united with justice and cohesion. They would not part company until they fell out over the means to accomplish that desirable end.

Neither Madison nor Hamilton had any liking for Aristotle's attachment to the "city-state," which was at odds with the concept of union. They both agreed strongly with the philosopher's belief in private property, which was in sharp contrast with Plato's ideas of collectivism. They were of one mind that the Constitution, whatever its details, must produce a government which citizens would support because they cherished it. As matters stood, Hamilton declared, "Men will see their fortunes secured, their persons protected, offenders punished by State laws and State magistrates—they will love the Govt. that is thus immediate." He desired to transfer that immediacy from the States to the Federal government, which would then deserve the people's love.

That was also Madison's purpose. He saw much more in Hamilton's long speech than its emphasis on centralized power and economic stability. His New York colleague did not rhapsodize about "equality," and did not equate it with liberty. But Madison perceived that the spiritual element of the people's "happiness" was there.

IV
(June 1787)

On the day after Hamilton's speech, the Convention again dissolved itself into a Committee of the Whole, and turned to debating the Jersey and Virginia plans. James Wilson of Pennsylvania made a glancing reference to "some gentlemen" who wished to "swallow up the state governments." Considering that he had mentioned state governors, state chief judges, and state legislatures, Hamilton felt misrepresented. He took the floor to answer "Caledonia James," as they called Wilson because of his Scotch burr.

"I did not intend yesterday a total extinguishment of state governments. My meaning was that a national government ought to be able to support itself without aid or interference of the state governments, and therefore it was necessary to have full sovereignty."

It was a useless effort. Hamilton would have to live with the accusation that he wished to dissolve the states. He drew little comment at the Convention hall, but he became the talk of the inns and boarding houses. William Pierce of Georgia called him "rather a convincing speaker than a blazing orator," and likened his style to Bolingbroke's and Sterne's. Connecticut delegate William Samuel Johnson, new president of Columbia College and son of its first president when it was King's College, said that Hamilton spoke "with boldness and decision . . . praised by everybody . . . supported by none." Johnson overlooked George Read of Delaware, Hamilton's one overt supporter.

Johnson, invariably addressed as Doctor, was one whose approbation counted for much. He "is about sixty years of age," noted Pierce, "possesses the manners of a Gentleman, and engages the hearts of Men by the sweetness of his temper, and that affectionate style of address with which he accosts his acquaintances." The Doctor was so impressed by Hamilton's speech that he long remembered the plan it proposed. Years later he discussed its "substance, though I cannot give the exact words," with Chancellor James Kent of New York.

Johnson told Kent that "if the Constitution should prove to be a failure, Mr. Hamilton would be less responsible than any other member, for he frankly pointed out to the Convention what he apprehended to be its infirmities; and that, on the other hand, if it should operate well, the nation would be more indebted to him than to any other individual, for no one labored more faithfully than he did, nor with equal activity, to give the Constitution a fair trial, by guarding against every evil tendency, and by clothing it with all the attributes and stability requisite for its safety and success, and compatible with the principles of the republican theory."

Another favorable commentator was Gouverneur Morris, Hamilton's wartime correspondent, a fellow Columbian, a reprobate scholar who was now on a wooden leg because of a carriage accident in 1780. Morris said Hamilton's speech was "the most able and impressive he had ever heard."

This opinion was worth many others put together, for Morris dazzled his fellow delegates. Pierce wrote that Morris "is one of those Genius's in whom every species of talents combine. . . . He winds through all the mazes of rhetoric, and throws about him such a glare that he charms, captivates and leads away the senses of all who hear him. With an infinite stretch of fancy he brings to view things . . . that render all the labor of reasoning easy and pleasant. . . . No man has more wit—nor can any engage the attention more than Mr. Morris."

With Morris's seal of approval, Hamilton could bear the criticism with better heart. His fellow New York delegates, Lansing and Yates, disapproved, as well they might, since their legitimate mission in Philadelphia was to block a consolidated government. To do them justice, Hamilton's colleagues were more than mere cat's-paws and marplots. Yates was a judge in the state supreme court, and Lansing was mayor of Albany. They both outranked the junior member of the delegation. They were the majority of the New York delegation, and together could cast the state's vote with or without him, while his vote in the Convention was of no consequence without theirs.

The Convention pressed forward on its zigzag course. Hamilton had an improved place on the Rules Committee, from which the chairman had departed on June 4 to go home. He spoke on many subjects before the Committee of the Whole. He was determined that the House of Representatives should not be merely an extension of the state political organization. Here he collided with the Southern delegates, customarily men of the organization. In particular, he differed with Brigadier General Charles Cotesworth Pinckney of South Carolina, whom in times ahead he would try to make President of the United States.

A big-boned, broad-shouldered, Roman-nosed lawyer-planter of forty-one, C. C. Pinckney had much that associated him with Hamilton. The Carolinian's family fortune had been made in the West Indies. He somewhat resembled Hamilton's father-in-law, Philip Schuyler, in looks and manners, and also in military bad luck. Educated in England at Westminster School and Oxford University, trained in the law in the Middle Temple and admitted to the English Bar, Pinckney had also attended the French royal military academy at Caen, and he had a great deal to offer the Revolution.

When soldiering was dull in the South, Pinckney rode north and flung himself into the battles of the Brandywine and Germantown. As a volunteer officer, he had no troops and no assigned duties, and he found no glory. He returned south to some desultory campaigning, and was at Charleston in May 1780, when the British attacked by land and sea. Colonel Pinckney favored a fight to "the last extremity," but was voted down. Then he was taken prisoner, much to his disgust. He spent most of the remaining war years under parole, but was exchanged, rejoined the army, and was brevetted brigadier general just before the close.

Pinckney had come to Philadelphia as an unapologetic spokesman for wealth and property, notably property in slaves. He wanted a strong central government, as Hamilton did, but wanted South Carolina to send to Congress representatives who spoke for the great families. He concurred with his colleague Pierce Butler that "Money is power," and thought that "the States ought to have weight in the Government in proportion to their wealth."

Hamilton disagreed with some of this. He was against excessive influence over Congress by state houses and governors, whether or not the wealthy were overrepresented. "The views of the governed are often materially different from those who govern," he said. The people were less apt to resent a central power than the local politicians were. He spoke in opposition to motions that the Representatives be paid by the state: "It is a general remark that he who pays is the master." He supported the Virginia resolve that both representatives and senators "receive fixed stipends to be paid out of the national treasury."

He debated the optimum duration of a representative's term. State assemblymen in New York were elected for one year, and members of the House of Commons for seven years. "There is a medium in everything," Hamilton declared. The short term was too short. "Frequency of elections tended to make the people listless to them, and to facilitate the success of little cabals." The long term was too long, yet in England "the democratic spirit of the constitution had not ceased." As a compromise, wrote Madison, "Col. Hamilton urged the necessity of 3 years."

He kept coming back to the British mode. The royal executive was "a check" between conflicting interests within Parliament, and something of the sort was needed here. The American government needed means to bring its "influence" to bear. David Hume called it "corruption," the bestowal of patronage by the king for political purposes. Hume, Hamilton said, "had pronounced that all influence on the side of the crown, which went under the name of corruption, [was] an essential part of the weight which maintained the equilibrium of the constitution."

Madison thought his friend had used an unfortunate quotation. He wrote that "[by] influence—he did not mean corruption, but a dispensation of those regular honors and emoluments which produce an attachment to the government." But in times to come, Madison's closest friend, Jefferson, would make much of those two words—monarchy and corruption—so readily twisted out of Hamilton's context.

The debate reached a motion to make House members ineligible for other offices for a year after their time in Congress. Nathaniel Gorham of Massachusetts smelt venality in giving salaried posts to former legislators, their friends and relatives. Hamilton agreed that any patronage system bred jobbery and conflict of interest, but said that "there are inconveniences on both sides."

"We must take man as we find him, and if we expect him to serve the public, must interest his passions in so doing. A reliance on pure patriotism has been the source of many of our errors." He would not rule out sinecures for deserving supporters of the Federal government.

He agreed with Madison that "the use of the Senate is to consist in its proceeding with more coolness, with more system & with more vision than the popular branch." This purpose would be furthered by giving senators long service, seven or nine years, Hamilton agreed, since the Convention was not disposed to life terms.

In all, said Hamilton, "he concurred with Mr. Madison in thinking that we were now to decide forever the fate of republican government; and if we did not give that form due stability and wisdom, it would be disgraced & lost. . . ." He was leaning toward Madisonian republicanism, but asking for a government with authority to command revenue and suppress rebellion. Madison wrote: "He professed himself to be as zealous an advocate of liberty as any man whatever. . . ."

By the end of June he had made up much of the ground lost by the mid-month speech. The debates modified his position about a lifetime President. "His opinion essentially changed," wrote James Kent in his *Memories of Alexander Hamilton,* "and he became satisfied that it would be dangerous to public tranquility to elect, by popular elections, a Chief Magistrate with so permanent a tenure . . . his subsequent plan gave to the office of President a duration of only three years."

Though Hamilton would never convince his critics about this change of mind, Madison now regarded him as a convert to the Virginia plan. Washington thought him consistently with the forces for consolidation, and saw that he had outdistanced his New York colleagues in acceptability of ideas. Lansing complained that the Convention had scuttled the instructions which had called it together. Yates called the Virginia plan "utterly unattainable, too novel and complex."

Without doubt, the delegates were confused. Dr. Franklin addressed the chair, saying he knew the reason for the "small progress we have made after four or five weeks close attendance." In this very room, he went on, the Continental Congress had achieved the Declaration of Independence, but had only done so through divine providence. "Our prayers, Sir, were heard, and they were graciously answered . . . the longer I live, the more convincing proofs I see of this truth—*that God governs the affairs of men.*"

Franklin proposed that sessions thereafter be opened with prayer, "and that one or more of the clergy of this city be requested to officiate in that service."

Roger Sherman of Connecticut seconded the Doctor's motion, but Hamilton—"and several others," Madison wrote without naming them—opposed giving the public any reason to feel that the delegates had reached an impasse. Funds were lacking to pay a chaplain, but this could not have been as strong a reason as the one cogently urged by Hamilton.

The Convention pulled itself together on July 27–28–29 to debate and accept the main resolves of the Virginia plan. This brought about a natural interlude. "Some private business calling me to New York, I left the Convention for a few days," Hamilton recalled a year later, "and . . . I was absent 10 days."

Max Farrand, who spent ten years, ending in 1912, collecting and editing the material of the Convention, speculated that Hamilton's decision to depart was strengthened by the "harangue" of Luther Martin. Later known as "Lawyer Brandy Bottle," the tiresome Marylander occupied the floor for two whole hot days, June 27–28, and "might have continued two months," Oliver Ellsworth wrote, "but for those marks of fatigue and disgust you saw strongly expressed on whichever side of the house you turned your mortified eyes."

Hamilton may have meant that he was absent ten business days. The Convention did not sit on Sundays. It took a two-day break over July Fourth, and a ten-day recess, July 26 to August 6, when Washington and others went fishing and revisited Valley Forge. Lansing and Yates left in early July and did not return at all, explaining to the Governor, in a joint letter:

". . . before we left the convention, its principles were so well established as to convince us that no alteration could be expected to conform it to our ideas of expedience and safety."

Hamilton, much to Madison's and Washington's relief, did not give up so easily.

V

(July–September 1787)

He had left the Convention city, but not the Constitution, which he promoted en route and at home. "In my passage through the Jerseys and since my arrival here," he wrote

Washington on July 3 from New York, "I have taken particular
pains to discover the public sentiment. . . . I have conversed
with men of information . . . and they agree that there has
been an astonishing revolution for the better in the minds of
the people."

He found, as expected, that state office-holders were opposed
to change. The only thing feared by "thinking men," he said,
was that the delegates "will not go far enough." This didn't
mean, he cautioned Washington, that "the people are yet ripe
for such a plan as I advocate." Still, they might accept one
"equally energetic, if the Convention should think proper to
propose it."

His optimism may have lifted Washington's spirits. "I *almost*
despair . . . I am sorry you went away. I wish you were
back. . . ."

Hamilton promised to return "if I have reason to believe that
my attendance at Philadelphia will not be a waste of time." He
was there on July 13–14–15, according to the diary of Manasseh
Cutler, pioneer, missionary, botanist, and proprietor of the
Ohio Company. Hamilton and Cutler had met previously when
Hamilton was a Congressman, and had discussed the chartering of this company and development of the Northwest Territory.

From the first Hamilton saw the western lands as a source
of national revenue. Soldiers' bounties could be paid off in
acres, settlers could be sold large lots at small prices, and the
Ohio Company in good hands would become a useful corporation. Another of Hamilton's interests would be served through
the Reverend Mr. Cutler.

"Brother, . . ." a delegation of the Oneida tribe would address Hamilton later, "we write you in particular because
some of us know you. We have all heard that you are a friend
of everybody—Indians as well as White people."

Undoubtedly, these matters were under discussion between
Hamilton and Cutler. "We sat up until half past one," Cutler
wrote, of a session that included Hamilton, Madison, and others. On July 13, Cutler recounted that he visited Franklin, who
showed him "a snake with two heads, preserved in a large vial.

He was going to mention a humorous matter that had that day taken place in Convention . . . but the secrecy of Convention matters was suggested to him, which stopped him, and deprived me of the story."

On the fifteenth, Hamilton and six other delegates got up at five in the morning in order to take Cutler across the Schuylkill River to visit the botanical garden of John Bartram, and to be back at the state house when the session opened.

The Convention was debating apportionment for the House, and a three-fifths head count for Southern Negroes. Hamilton made no recorded speeches. Back in New York by the 20th, and having in mind how the Phocion letters had broken the way to success in *Rutgers v. Waddington,* he again put his hand to pamphleteering.

A two-part polemic signed "Caesar" was injuriously said to be his, and he was charged with writing the statement therein: "For my part, I am not much attached to the majesty of the people." The Hamilton Papers mark these essays as "erroneously . . . attributed to H." The language sounded Hamiltonian, but the pseudonym did not. All of his known noms-de-plume throughout his lifetime were the antithesis of Caesarism. But now he posted his name with the printer of the *Daily Advertiser,* and boldly struck out at New York's foremost opponent to the Convention:

". . . Governor *CLINTON* has, in public company, without reserve, reprobated the appointment of the Convention, and predicted a mischievous issue of that measure." There followed a nine-point bill of particulars.

It was risky business, attacking a prominent man by name, adding emphasis with upper-case print and italics. A counterattack disparaging "a certainly lordly faction" and giving Hamilton as the offender against Clinton appeared over the signature, "A Republican," in an opposition paper. Hamilton fired back a third-person volley in the *Daily Advertiser,* saying:

"Mr. Hamilton to avoid the appearance of ostentation, did not put his name to the piece . . . [but] in fixing that publication upon him, there is certainly no mistake."

He was making his identity available for the Governor's convenience. Clinton "had his choice of two modes of vindicating himself from the aspersion." He could do so by "a simple and direct denial to it in the public prints," or by "a personal explanation on the subject with the writer," who would prove the facts or "retract the imputations."

Hamilton did not mention the other recourse in a quarrel between gentlemen, but it must have been in his mind, for during that third week of July he was engaged in preventing a fight between two gentlemen of his acquaintance. "I can never consent to take up the character of a second in a duel 'til I have in vain tried that of a mediator," he wrote William Pierce of Georgia, who was challenging one of Hamilton's mercantile clients, John Auldjo.

This trouble was dispelled with a partial apology. "Be content with *enough* for *more* ought not to be expected," Hamilton successfully urged. Some weeks later he was jolted by an insult past ignoring. A writer signing himself "Spectator" in the *New York Journal* made a sneering allusion to Hamilton's war record.

"I have known an upstart attorney palm himself off upon a great and good man for a youth of extraordinary genius, and under the shadow of such a patronage, make himself known and respected. But being sifted and bolted to the brann, he was at length found out to be a superficial and self-conceited coxcomb, and was of course turned off and disregarded by his patron."

Upstart attorney! Self-conceited coxcomb! Those were fighting words. Instead of answering in kind, Hamilton sent the correspondence to Washington, who responded by return post:

"It is with unfeigned concern I perceive that a political dispute has arisen between Governor Clinton and yourself. For both of you I have the highest esteem and regard. . . . It is insinuated by some of your political adversaries and may obtain credit that you palmed yourself upon me and was dismissed from my family; and you call upon me to do you justice by a recital of the fact. I do therefore explicitly declare that both charges are entirely unfounded."

Nearly four months elapsed between these various exchanges, which were part of a continuous barrage in the news-papers as tension mounted. Hamilton had to consider his family, his law practice, his never-suspended work for the Constitution. He would not let himself be enticed into a physical encounter, which was plainly the intention of his enemies.

The Convention was all. He went back for the week of August 6–13. He got in a strong speech against a proposal by Elbridge Gerry to confine House members "to Natives," and one by Hugh Williamson to stretch eligibility to nine years of residence. Hamilton had liberal views on immigration. Madison wrote:

"Col. Hamilton was in general agst. embarrassing the Government with minute restrictions . . . the advantage of encouraging foreigners was obvious & admitted."

Afterwards he went home again, but wrote to Lansing and Yates that "if either of them would come down, I would accompany him to Philadelphia." Twice in August he requested Rufus King to keep him informed as to the wind-up, "for I would choose to be present at that time."

Although traveling the court circuit, he knocked down a fraudulent rumor which connected the Society of the Cincinnati and himself to a Tory scheme of reunion with the British Empire. The plan was to bring over the Duke of York, who was also the secular Bishop of Osnaburgh, to be the American crowned head. Colonel David Humphreys of Connecticut, formerly also on the Commander's staff, helped Hamilton to expose the mischievous fiction—"not a novel idea among those who were formerly termed Loyalists," wrote Humphreys. He gave Hamilton a cheer. "Go on & prosper."

By early September Hamilton was back at Philadelphia for the wind-up. "Whether he speaks or writes," it was noted, "he is equally great. He can probably endure more unremitted and intense mental labor than any man in this body."

Hamilton now swung over to the Virginia position that there must be a considerable measure of democracy in the republican form of government. He spoke for increasing the number of representatives, for "he held it essential that the popular branch of [government] should have a broad foundation." He seconded Madison's motion for amending the Constitution by a three-fourths vote of the states, "as the people would finally decide the case."

Hamilton held that liberties would be protected by separation of the powers of the government. For that reason he said that the proposal to have the President elected by the Federal Congress would create "a monster" of concentrated power. He accepted the Electoral College system as a way of getting the President of the United States elected by the states. He suspected that many Electors would be chosen by faction-controlled state legislators, but he saw no way to avoid this. Several years later, after some bad experience with the system, he would advocate placing the responsibility of choosing Electors "on the shoulders of the people." He still thought the states too powerful, but "he meant to support the [Virginia] plan to be recommended as better than nothing."

Historians who wrote that Hamilton shirked did not consult their sources. Max Farrand's *The Records of the Federal Convention* shows that he was among the fourteen delegates who spoke one hundred times or more. Even when away from Philadelphia he was working and writing for the Constitution, urging its adoption and attacking its enemies.

The delegates did not think him a shirker. They had assayed his ability on the floor and on the Committee on Rules. When he returned in September they elected him to the elite five-member Committee on Style and Arrangement. Its task was to pull together the twenty-four "resolves" and to "write" the American Constitution. In addition to Hamilton, the Convention elected William Samuel Johnson, the college president; Rufus King of Massachusetts, "natural, swimming and graceful . . . ranked among the Luminaries of the present Age"; and Gouverneur Morris, who had made 173 speeches here, even more than Madison, the fifth member, who had made 161.

Hamilton may well have thought he had another "Yorktown" in the making, a late-coming chance for single glory at a climactic moment. None of this select group had published so early, so often, and to such response as its youngest member and most seasoned pamphleteer. But when the committee sorted out the mass of material, and came to face the need of an eloquent prologue, they turned to another penman. As Madison later declared, the man who displayed the wit and sagacity to give the document its stylish "finish" was not Hamilton, but Morris.

Hamilton's draft began, "The people of the United States of America do ordain and establish this constitution. . . ." A five-member composite commenced, "We the undersigned delegates of New Hampshire, Massachusetts . . ." and on through the states, from north to south.

Too awkward by far! Morris wrote, "We, the people of the United States. . . ." The treason clause was difficult. Could there be treason against one state (as in the Shays Rebellion) that would not be treason against the nation? Morris had no instructions, but deftly shifted from the singular to the plural pronoun in referring to the United States. "Treason against the United States shall consist only in levying war against them. . . ." Nowhere else was the plural used, observed the Convention's best historian, Catherine Drinker Bowen. She also notes that Morris marshaled some of the noblest verbs of the language:

". . . in order to *form* a more perfect union, *establish* Justice, *insure* domestic Tranquility, *provide* for the common defense, *promote* the general Welfare, and *secure* the Blessings of Liberty to ourselves and our Posterity, do *ordain* and *establish* this Constitution. . . ."

Hamilton was no match for this superb draftsman. If his hand shows at all, it is in Article VI. The suggested language of "shall be the supreme law of the respective states" was revised into "shall be the supreme Law of the Land." This satisfying phrase belonged to nobody, as it went back to Magna Carta, but Hamilton had Americanized it in *Rutgers v. Waddington.*

On the afternoon of Monday, September 18, 1787, the delegates lined up in geographical order. Rhode Island was still absent. There would be, in Washington's words, "the unani-

mous assent of 11 States and Colo. Hamilton from New York,"
which in the absence of Lansing and Yates lacked a delegate
majority.

But the people must know that the states had created the
United States as a Federal Union, and Hamilton took it upon
himself, in his own hand, to write out the names of the twelve
from New Hampshire through Georgia. He made a last plea
for signatures. Madison, floor leader and ringmaster of the
whole performance, recorded it:

"Mr. Hamilton expressed his anxiety that every member
should sign. A few characters of consequence, by opposing or
even refusing to sign, might do infinite mischief. . . . No man's
ideas were more remote from the plan than his were known
to be; but is it possible to deliberate between anarchy and Convulsion on one side, and the chance of good to be expected from
the plan on the other?"

Hamilton waited behind Roger Sherman of Connecticut and
ahead of William Livingston of New Jersey, and then signed
his name. "The business being closed," Washington set down
that night in his diary, "the members adjourned to the City
Tavern. . . ."

VI

(October–December 1787)

Hamilton returned to New York, where his Wall Street home
was filling with children—now four including the adopted orphan; and Betsey was expecting another in the spring. His
practice flourished. He was representing clients as far apart as
Boston and Charleston. He later expanded his quarters by obtaining the house next door, Number 58.

To stay home and enjoy his success and his family! With that
in mind he had already declined re-election to the Assembly.
It was rotating to Poughkeepsie "which renders it impracticable for him to serve . . . the ensuing year," he posted notice
in the *Daily Advertiser.*

If not to stay home, then to take a trip abroad with Betsey!

There were clients he could visit on the Continent and in England. He had frequent and affectionate letters from Lafayette in France, and from John Church, who was about to win a seat in Parliament. Revolutionary America was being honored overseas. Hamilton's relatives in Scotland would doubtless receive him well. There was a further incentive.

"You have every right, my dear brother, to believe that I was very inattentive to your last letter," Angelica wrote from London on October 2, "but I could not relinquish the hopes that you would be tempted to ask the reason for my silence, which would be a certain means of obtaining the second letter. . . .

"Indeed, my dear Sir, if my path were strewed with as many roses as you have filled your letter with compliments, I should not now lament my absence from America. . . ."

He answered "your invaluable letter" by observing, "I seldom write a lady without fancying the relation of lover and mistress. It has a very inspiring effect. . . . If you read this letter in a certain mood, you will easily divine that in which I write it."

A tantalizing separation, a mutual infatuation, an impossible love. He would not say that Betsey joined him in sending regards. " 'Tis too old fashioned." He despaired of ever seeing Angelica in America, and "my only hope is that a jumble of events will bring us together in Europe. . . . Wherever I am, believe always that there is no one can pay a more sincere or affectionate tribute to your deserts than I do—Adieu, my *chère soeur*. . . ."

VII
(October–December 1787)

There was no way he could turn his back on the Constitution, an unfinished business until ratified by the states. Governor Clinton was disinclined to ask the Legislature to call for a ratifying convention. The issue hung fire amid a renewed war of words. Clinton could not be moved except by moving the earth of popular opinion under his feet. Hamilton knew from

his Phocion experience how to go about that. On an October
evening in the cabin of a sloop traveling from Albany to New
York, he began:

". . . it seems to have been reserved to the people of this
country, by their conduct and example, to decide the important
question, whether societies of men are really capable or not of
establishing good government from reflection and choice, or
whether they are forever destined to depend for their political
constitutions on accident and force."

The essay was addressed "To the People of the State of New
York," and it appeared on October 30 in both the *New York
Packet* and the *Daily Advertiser*. Hamilton signed it "Publius,"
as he had signed other writings. Much of what he set down was
repetition, though never before so well expressed. It was what
he had stood for these many years.

Considering how it was addressed, how it was written, what
it was about, this first of the eighty-five Federalist Papers
hardly left its authorship in doubt. What was not known for
a while, with two and three Papers appearing each week, was
that some were written to New Yorkers by a Virginian, James
Madison. A few others, on foreign policy, were the work of John
Jay. By December 22, when No. 26 of the series appeared,
James Kent wrote to a friend:

"You may praise whom you please, and I will presume to say
that 'Publius' is a more admirable writer and wields the pen
of party dispute with justice, energy and inconceivable dexter-
ity. The author must be Alexander Hamilton who . . . in genius
and political research, is not inferior to Gibbon, Hume and
Montesquieu."

Kent couldn't have been the only reader to see through the
pseudonym. Hamilton was writing under stress, several times
a week, in between court appearances. He would gladly have
had more than two collaborators. He tried Gouverneur Morris
and James Duer, but could not engage their attention. Luckily,
Madison was sometimes in New York where Congress sat. At
other times he was available in the Virginia Convention at
Richmond.

Although it went against Hamilton's competitive grain, he

chose not to attack personalities in these Papers. As a result, *The Federalist* managed to be both a work of special pleading and a far-ranging treatise on governance, Hamilton's forte. By the time the last essay was published, on May 28, 1788, the immediate purpose was near accomplishment, and book publication in English and French during 1788 amounted to the birth of a world classic.

Hamilton and Madison lived to know they had struck off a masterpiece, and in time they became as jealous about their respective contributions as authors commonly are. But during the serialization, they had eyes only for the political result. The executive, the legislature, and the courts of New York State had been powerless for five months to bring the Constitution before the people. But there was a fourth estate of government. The press, acting through these three Federalist authors, lent a hand.

CHAPTER FIFTEEN

His Brightest Hours As Orator

I

(January–July 1788)

In January the Legislature elected Hamilton to Congress, which conveniently sat in New York. By then, conventions in Delaware, Pennsylvania, New Jersey, Georgia, and Connecticut had met, debated, and ratified the Constitution. They were five of the necessary nine states. New Hampshire convened and recessed, but was on the verge of ratification.

New York would never join the procession if Governor Clinton and his party had their way. It was easy to call Clinton obdurate, backward, demagogic, "a designing croaker," as the opposition press was doing, but he also was consistent and warmly supported at home. His opposition to the Constitution made Clinton a member of a respected school of thought that included Richard Henry Lee, Luther Martin, Elbridge Gerry, Patrick Henry, and George Mason. All these believed, as did Martin Van Buren later, that the Grand Convention was "unlawful" in exceeding its authority; illiberal in failing to adopt a Bill of Rights; "squinting at monarchy," as Patrick Henry put it.

Attending Congress very irregularly at the 1788 session, Hamilton voted to postpone Kentucky statehood; to demand release of an American prisoner in France and return of fugitive slaves who had escaped from Georgia into Spanish Florida. His attention was directed to the Poughkeepsie-based Legislature where, in January, bills were pending to call a state convention to accept or reject the Constitution.

Congress had recommended the call, but it was by no means a command performance. The Assembly agreed narrowly, by two votes, the Senate by three; and the Governor signed a measure that was unique in its day. For the first time in the state's history, an election was to be thrown open to what was viewed as universal suffrage. Property qualifications were waived. All male citizens could participate in choosing delegates to the state convention. Hamilton helped put together an impressive slate, and accepted nomination to be one of the nine representatives of New York City.

The Federalist Papers had reached No. 77 on election day. Hamilton's propositions and his popularity were squarely on the line. John Jay drew 2,735 votes, Richard Morris 2,716, Hamilton and John Hobart 2,713, and five other pro-Constitution candidates trailed but were chosen. Hamilton was now acknowledged as head of the party called Federalist, and Clinton was head of the Antis. The results of the state-wide tallies came in over the weeks until May, when they were certified. The Clintonians counted forty-six delegates and the Hamiltonians only nineteen.

"I believe," a citizen remarked, "that there has not been a time since the Revolution in which the Well Born, who are the leaders of that party, have felt and appeared so uninfluential . . . the number of the Antis astonish the Federalists, and they look on their case as desperate."

This commentator might have been reading Hamilton's mind. "My dear Sir, . . ." he wrote Madison in June, "the elections have turned out, beyond expectation, favorable to the anti-federalist party. They have a majority of two-thirds in the Convention and, according to the best estimate I can form, of about four-sevenths in the community."

Fearing the worst as usual—"eventual disunion and civil war"—Hamilton needed support from other states. He told Madison, "Communicate to me by express the event of any decisive question in favor of the Constitution, authorizing changes of horses &c with an assurance to the person sent that he will be liberally paid for his diligence."

John Sullivan in New Hampshire, Rufus King in Massachusetts, and Henry Knox in New York City, received similar instructions about rushing news to Poughkeepsie, the convention site. "I shall with pleasure defray all expenses, and give a liberal reward. . . ." Luckily, General Schuyler, though not a delegate, would attend the convention with his purse open.

Into Poughkeepsie, George Clinton's home town in his stronghold of Dutchess County, the delegates straggled by river and roadway. Massachusetts, Maryland, and South Carolina made the sixth, seventh, and eighth states to join the Union that spring. Only one more was needed, and it was conceded that New Hampshire was sure to be Number Nine. Two doubtful joiners remained, Virginia, largest of the states, and New York, only fifth in population but geographically central. Without these two the union would be feeble and fragile.

Poughkeepsie was a singularly pleasant setting for a political battle. There would be no such heat as delegates had suffered last summer in Philadelphia. No secrecy was imposed; visitors were welcome. Coverage by stenographic reporting was assured by Francis Childs, publisher of the New York *Daily Advertiser,* and in addition several delegates would keep notes. The meeting place for conventioneers and onlookers was the court house, completed only a year before at a cost of 4,800 pounds. Its court room easily accommodated the sixty-five delegates and up to two hundred of the public.

Since both opposing factions believed time to be on their side, there was no hurry when the roll calls began on June 17. Governor Clinton, chosen to be the presiding officer, headed an experienced corps of advisors—Yates, Lansing, Melancton Smith, Samuel Jones, John Williams, Gilbert Livingston. The Antis, Hamilton had told Madison, "resolve upon a long adjournment as the safest and most artful course to effect their final purpose."

On June 20, Robert R. Livingston opened for the Federalists with a time-eating resolution. He proposed that the Constitution be discussed article by article. Melancton Smith, the witty Clinton floor leader, had no objection. He said that the question here "was not whether the present Confederation was a bad one, but whether the proposed Constitution was a good one." The debate began methodically. First up for consideration was

the proposed House of Representatives. Some called it not large
enough for democracy. Then came the Senate. Some said it was
too aristocratic. There were demands that U.S. senators be
limited to a single term, and be recallable by their legislatures.

Thus the central issues were drawn, and the principal actors
soon emerged. Smith would speak forty-five times, Lansing
thirty, Clinton eleven, Gilbert Livingston seven. Hamilton,
who was allowing others to take the lead, would eventually rise
thirty times, Jay eighteen, R. R. Livingston twelve. But before
the heavy artillery could be decisive, there was an intervention, not unexpected but dramatic. On June 24, an express
rider dashed into town with a message from John Sullivan.
New Hampshire had ratified. The ninth state was in. The
Confederation was dissolved.

Clinton and Smith refused to quit. The debate must continue.
"We acknowledge," Lansing declared, "that our dissent cannot
prevent the operation of the government. Since nine states
have acceded to it, let them make the experiment . . . which
is dangerous to liberty."

Hamilton thought the Clintonians strengthened by the challenge to fight on. He gloomily wrote Madison next day that New
York's fate depended on Virginia, which had been in convention for three weeks.

"Our chance of success here is infinitely slender, and none
at all if you go wrong."

He signed himself "Yrs. affy" to the friendly Virginian.

II

(June–July 1788)

Governor Clinton, presiding while Hamilton spoke, was also
writing a letter to John Lamb. "I steal this moment while the
Convention is in Committee, and the little Great Man employed in repeating over parts of Publius to us."

The Clintonians sprang their trap. In that reckless six-hour
speech at Philadelphia, they declared, Hamilton had proposed
to abolish the states and establish monarchy. The accusation
was intended to swing the Federalist leader by the heels. "Mr.

Lansing . . . made an appeal to Judge Yates, who had taken
notes in the Federal Convention, for proof. . . ."

Hamilton hotly "accused Mr. Lansing's insinuation as improper, unbecoming and uncandid, . . ." the *Daily Advertiser*
reported. "This produced some disorder . . . and the Chairman
was obliged to call to order. A motion for adjournment put an
end to the altercation."

Next day the uproar continued. There was a retraction by
Yates, and an apology by Hamilton. "My exertions have already exhausted me," he declared on the floor. "I have no design to wound the feelings of any one who is opposed to me."

But he could not overlook insinuations that there were some
who would "derive peculiar advantages from this Constitution.
. . . If the gentlemen reckon me among the obnoxious few, if
they imagine that I contemplate with an ambitious eye the
immediate honors of the government; yet, let them consider
that I have friends—my family—my children. . . ." These
were more to him than any rewards government could give.
"Gentlemen ought not to presume that the advocates of this
Constitution are influenced by ambitious views. The suspicion,
Sir, is unjust; the charge is uncharitable."

His speech, with others, brought applause from the galleries.
Melancton Smith complained about "the entertainment of the
ladies and gentlemen without the bar." Hamilton was beginning to swing votes. His "reasoning was so conclusive that it
seems to have carried conviction to every mind," R. R. Livingston declared. But when Smith offered to end debate and let
the Convention decide on ratification then and there, the
Hamiltonians refused to accept the risk. Wait for the next
break!

It came in the afternoon of July 2, with Clinton in the midst
of a speech. He was interrupted by a "buz through the House."
A dispatch rider had flung from the saddle outside the door,
and handed Hamilton a message. The rider had worn out three
horses in the eighty-two miles from New York City. He brought
stirring news—Virginia had ratified!

Hamilton walked in with a letter from Madison and a certificate from Edmund Pendleton, president of the Richmond con-

vention. The tenth state! Jay moved for adoption, but Thomas
Tredwell for the Clintonians answered that "the proposed plan
is certain destruction of liberty." On with debate.

III

(July 1788)

Both Hamilton and Madison were now signing themselves
"Yours Affectionately" in various abbreviations. Victorious as
a Richmond delegate, Madison came to New York to take his
seat in Congress. His authoritative advice would now be more
accessible to Hamilton. "We yesterday passed through the Constitution," Hamilton wrote on July 8, meaning that the article-
by-article consideration was finished. He felt that the opposition was splitting up; ". . . our opponents are not agreed, and
this affords some ground of hope." He was not displeased to
report a political riot in Albany on Independence Day. "The
antifederalists were the aggressors, and the Federalists the
Victors."

He hoped for the same passions and the same results in
debate. The Clintonians began to offer crippling amendments,
and to renew their slurs. He was called "an ambitious man, a
man unattached to the interests and insensitive to the feelings
of the people; and even his supposed talents had been wrested
to his dishonor, and produced as a charge against his integrity
and virtue."

The *Daily Advertiser* presented him as an heroic figure, and
outdid itself in colorful reporting. "He opened with a beautiful
exordium in which he described . . . the various ungenerous
attempts to prejudice the minds of the Convention against him.
. . . He called on the world to point out an instance in which
he had ever deviated from the line of public or private duty.
The pathetic appeal fixed the silent sympathetic gaze of the
audience, and made them all his own."

It was Hamilton's brightest hour as a popular orator. With
the galleries "all his own," he showed that his opponents had
the natural right of every freeman "to adopt . . . reject . . .
recommend," but had "none to dictate or to embarrass the
Union. . . . Mr. Hamilton, after recapitulating his arguments

in a concise and cogent manner, entreated the Convention in a pathetic strain to make a solemn pause and weigh well what they were about to do."

He was pummeling the Antis into submission. "They sickened at the splendor of his triumph," the *Daily Advertiser* recounted. "Inspired by jealousy and wounded by conscious disgrace, they retired with malice still more embittered, and an obstinacy more confirmed than ever."

None was more enraged than George Clinton, "the man who of all others should set the first example of magnanimity," observed the *Advertiser*. The Governor waited until the daily recess and then publicly explained, "I see the advocates of the Convention are determined to force us to a rejection. We have gone great lengths and have conceded enough—but nothing will satisfy them. If convulsion and civil war are the consequence, I will go with my party." But the *Advertiser,* publishing four days after the debate, left no doubt that Hamilton had got the better of it:

"The orator . . . received from every unprejudiced spectator the murmur of admiration and applause."

Nonetheless, the Antis were advancing conditions on ratification that had to be answered with more than rhetoric. One, by Melancton Smith, man of dry humor and imperturbable aplomb, had a deceptive plausibility. He proposed ratification with the proviso that another Federal Convention be called to weigh amendments offered by the states. Among the amendments would be a Bill of Rights, sacred to American hearts, and hardly considered at Philadelphia. Hamilton contended that these rights were inherent in the Federal Constitution, and should be left for enactment by Congress. But he needed to give the delegates an unassailable reason for neglecting to secure such protections as freedom of press, assembly, and religion. The Antis were ready to enter the Union on the proposition that they could secede if Congress did not provide a national Bill of Rights. Hamilton turned to Madison:

"You will understand that the only qualification will be the *reservation* of the right to secede in case our amendments have not been decided upon . . . within a certain number of years, perhaps five or seven. . . . This will satisfy the more consider-

ate and honest opposers of the Constitution, and with the aid
of time will break up the party." What did the sagacious Virginian say to that?

Madison in New York received the query on a Sunday, July
20. He answered "this instant" when Hamilton's letter came
to hand. He wrote that "a reservation of the right to withdraw
if amendments are not decided upon . . . is a *conditional* ratification that does not make N. York a member of the New Union,
and consequently . . . she could not be received on that plan.
. . . The Constitution requires an adoption *in toto* and *for ever.*
. . . Know my fervent wishes for your success & happiness."

It was all that Hamilton needed. His amazing little friend
had turned the tide. Hamilton took the floor on the morning
of July 24, "proposed to read a letter—read it," and the deed
was done.

Melancton Smith gave up. Years later John Fiske, historian
and essayist, praised the Anti floor leader as Hamilton's most
formidable opponent. "He must have been a man of rare candor, too, for after weeks of debate, he owned himself convinced." Lansing made a desperate attempt to insert the words
"upon conditions," but this was amended to read "in full confidence" that a Bill of Rights would be forthcoming. The five-
week struggle ended with adoption on July 26 by a vote of
thirty to twenty-five.

Victory had come very late in the game. Several states and
cities had already celebrated the Federal Union on the appropriate date of July 4. Three days before the final vote, Nicholas
Cruger and other Federalists in New York City had launched
a huge parade. It featured a horse-drawn float in the shape of
a frigate with the name "Hamilton" on the prow. But Hamilton
was too busy in Poughkeepsie to attend his own triumph, glory-
lover though he was.

Instead, he waited for the ratifying document to be engrossed, and headed for New York and his seat in the waning
Confederation Congress. Noted the *Albany Journal,* August 4,
1788, "Col. Hamilton, who has brought with him the ratification of the Constitution . . . will have the honor, this day, to
present it to Congress."

CHAPTER SIXTEEN

The Chores of Statecraft

I

(August–December 1788)

By August Hamilton had seized upon new projects in Congress. He would serve out the tail-end of this one-year session; the Legislature had replaced him with a Clintonian delegate for the next meeting. It was the only election Hamilton ever lost, if losing was the name for it, considering what he had done at Poughkeepsie to abolish the Confederation Congress.

He aimed to set up the new Congress of the Constitution in style. He and other lawmakers of the Confederation had been meeting in the old City Hall on Wall Street, within sight of his home. Built in 1700, the Hall had a certain grace under its cupola and tall chimneys, but the Common Council now engaged Major Pierre Charles L'Enfant as chief architect "to purchase materials & superintend" remodeling "for the accommodation of the Genl. Government."

Hamilton was well acquainted with him. Trained to be an artist, this tall, dignified Frenchman at first did sketches of Washington at Valley Forge, and made the transition to an engineering officer. L'Enfant suffered a painful leg wound and was captured in the Southern campaign with John Laurens.

Work on the Federal building was "nearly at a stand for want of funds," Hamilton noted to City Recorder Richard Varick when he came to the aid of "my poor bantling"—his brat, the Constitution. "Another thousand by the corporation will relieve all our difficulties." He arranged this loan of one thousand pounds to the City Corporation by the Bank of New York. L'Enfant went ahead with elaborate plans for the renamed Federal Hall.

As it took shape, citizens beheld an impressive front of "four

massy pillars . . . four Doric columns and a pediment." Above
the second-floor balcony was a frieze "ingeniously divided to
admit thirteen stars in the metopes," surmounted "with the
American Eagle . . . the 13 arrows and the olive branch
united. . . ."

Inside the ground-floor entrance was the marble-paved vestibule topped by a skylight, "which is decorated with a profusion of ornament in the richest taste." The House of Representatives, on the first floor, was "a spacious and elegant
apartment" with high windows and four chimneys. The Speaker's chair, raised by several steps, faced the two semicircles of
members' chairs, each with a small desk, the whole room standing below the second-floor visitors' galleries.

Vestibule stairways, the left one for the public, the right one
for officials, led up to the second-floor Senate chamber, just
behind the Wall Street balcony. L'Enfant spread his considerable talents for the incoming senators. Their chamber, noted
the *Massachusetts Magazine,* "is decorated with pilasters . . .
the proportions are light and graceful, the capitals are of a
fanciful kind . . . for amidst their foliage appears a star and
rays, and a piece of drapery below suspends a small medallion
with U.S. in a cypher. . . . The President's chair is at one end
of the room, elevated about three feet from the floor, under a
rich canopy of crimson damask."

Such was the splendor that awaited the First Federal Congress, as yet unelected when Hamilton returned to New York
from Poughkeepsie. Also unchosen were the members of the
Electoral College, who would be named in each state on the first
Wednesday of January 1789. On the corresponding Wednesday
of February, the Electors were scheduled to meet and cast their
votes here at Federal Hall. The two men picked to be President
and Vice President would be inaugurated here on the first
Wednesday of March, if the schedule held, which seemed unlikely.

In the dying Confederation Congress, Hamilton pushed for
the Residency Bill, which would name the permanent site of
the Federal Government. Seven votes were needed.

"Six states and a half prefer New York," he noted, "five and a half Philadelphia."

How to get the other state vote? He thought of Rhode Island, which was in the expiring Confederation but not in the Union. Among his wide acquaintance of national leaders was Jeremiah Olney of Providence, to whom he wrote on August 12:

"We have a question of very great importance pending in Congress, in which the vote of your state would be decisive. . . . Every effort must be made to induce a representative of your state to come forward without loss of time."

Two obstacles barred the way. The Rhode Island delegate, Jonathan Hazard, had left Congress and gone home. Also, Hamilton admitted to Olney, "A doubt might perhaps be raised about your right to vote under the present circumstances." Rhode Island had repeatedly snubbed the Union, but Hamilton contended that under the Constitution "the non-adopting states stand on the same footing with the adopting." If the chief author of the Federalist Papers said so, it must be true. Quickly, quickly send a delegate. "If any difficulty about expense should arise, I will with pleasure accept a draft on me."

But Hazard had just become a member of Rhode Island's legislature, and declined to hurry back to an expiring Congress. Rhode Island could not give New York the capital city. Hamilton thought of Vermont. He had befriended the Green Mountain experiment, but the state was outside both the Confederation and the Union. Even so, Hamilton sent off a letter to the Federalist leader in Vermont, Nathaniel Chipman of Newphane, with whom he had helpfully corresponded about the Vermont Grants.

Chipman consulted with Governor Chittenden and members of the Vermont assembly. All agreed "that the terms suggested are good; that it will be highly in the interest of Vermont to accede."

Kentucky and Vermont statehoods were tied together. The Southern delegates would not yield unless the Northerners did. Time was running out on Hamilton's plans to place the national capital in New York. Meanwhile other cities—Lancaster and Baltimore—were proposed. The Confederation Congress set aside the Residency Bill and left the matter for the Federal Congress to decide.

There was a still more urgent matter. Who was to be first President of the United States? All eyes, of course, turned to George Washington, and Hamilton wrote him at Mount Vernon on August 13:

"I take it for granted, Sir, you have concluded to comply with what will no doubt be the general call of your country in relation to the new government."

Washington's answer was evasive. He congratulated Hamilton on the publication of the Federalist Papers as a book—"that work will merit the notice of Posterity." He next alluded with disapproval to Clinton's part in the Poughkeepsie Convention. Down at the finish of his letter Washington got around to "the delicate subject." He said, "It is my great and sole desire to live and die, in peace and retirement, on my own farm."

Hamilton knew the man's sincerity, pride of reputation, patriotism, and his indecisiveness too. All these had to be addressed. "The caution you observe in deferring an ultimate determination," Hamilton answered, "is prudent." He also knew the key-words that would summon Washington. It would be "inglorious in such a situation not to hazard the glory . . . previously acquired." There is still greater hazard to "fame . . . in refusing your future aid to the system."

Washington thanked him warmly. He also showed another worry. He might not be the winner. For, he submitted, if "friends to the Constitution" believed he would bring it strength, "is it not probable that the adversaries of it may entertain the same ideas?" He feared their opposition.

So did Hamilton. The Constitution had a "defect." The candidate with the most Electoral College votes would be President, the runner-up Vice President. It would be unthinkable for any aspirant to defeat, or even to finish close to, the nervous and sensitive hero at Mount Vernon, who was already being called "father of his country." But Hamilton would see to it that nothing went wrong.

Meanwhile, on October 10, his term in Congress expired. He

had served 128 days and been absent forty-three, and he sent a bill to the "State of N.Y." for 153 pounds 12 shillings.

II

(October 1788–February 1789)

"We are making efforts to prepare handsome accommodations for the session of the new Congress," he wrote Theodore Sedgwick of Massachusetts. When arrangements lagged, he prodded Mayor James Duane. "The Philadelphians are endeavouring to raise some cavils on this point."

By November, sending Betsey's "affectionate remembrances to Mrs. Washington," he added a postscript to a casual letter to Mount Vernon. "I feel a conviction that you will finally see your acceptance to be indispensable. . . . I think circumstances leave no option."

John Adams and Clinton were leading aspirants for second place in the government. "On the subject of Vice President," Hamilton wrote Sedgwick, who was speaker of the Massachusetts House, ". . . I believe Mr. Adams will have the votes of this state. He will certainly, I think, be preferred to the other gentleman. Yet certainly is perhaps too strong a word."

He had not forgotten Adams' wartime criticism of the Commander, and brought this up with Sedgwick: "He is unfriendly in his sentiments to General Washington. . . . Consider this. . . . What think you of Lincoln and Knox? This is a flying thought." He was disturbed to hear that Madison leaned toward a Washington-Clinton combination. "I cannot believe that the plan will succeed," he wrote his friend in Virginia.

What worried him most was that "defect which renders it possible that the man intended for Vice President may in fact turn up President." For example, if all Electors voted for the second man, and just one withheld a vote for Washington, the ticket would be turned upside down. There could even be a tie vote for the Presidency. Perhaps, he hinted to Madison, it was a mistake to unite behind a powerful figure, like Adams. To do so raised "the possibility of rendering it doubtful who is appointed president. . . . It would be disagreeable even to have a man treading close upon the heels of the person we wish for President."

The solution, he decided, was to flood the field with Vice Presidential prospects. Sedgwick wrote that he thought highly of Adams and considered it too late to push Knox and Lincoln; he brought up John Hancock's name. Hamilton's wide-ranging correspondence showed that James Wilson of Pennsylvania and John Rutledge of South Carolina were also in the running.

To his embarrassment the Clintonian legislature was slow in choosing Electors. This prevented New York from casting its eight votes in this first Presidential election. Rhode Island and North Carolina also were non-voters. As late as January 25, with most of the Electors chosen but unpledged, he wrote his anxiety to James Wilson. "There is a chance of unanimity in Adams. . . . Men are fond of going with the stream. Suppose personal caprice or hostility to the new system should occasion half-a-dozen votes only to be withheld from Washington—what may not happen? Granted there is little danger. If any, ought it to be run?"

He knew what Machiavelli would have done in such a case. With the success of the incoming government at stake, it was no time for qualms. Hamilton confided in Wilson, whose compliance he needed. "Hence I conclude it will be prudent to throw away a few votes, say 7 or 8: giving these to persons not otherwise thought of. . . . For God's sake, let not our zeal for a secondary object defeat or endanger a first."

Hamilton kept his eye on the first objective—to make Washington the first American President by an impressive majority. A number of "persons not otherwise thought of" divided the Vice Presidential vote: John Jay, Robert Hanson Harrison, John Hancock, John Rutledge, George Clinton, Samuel Huntington, John Milton, James Armstrong, Edward Telfair, and Benjamin Lincoln. Hamilton got the Washington-Adams ticket that he wanted, with the General taking all first-place ballots. Final results: Washington sixty-nine, Adams thirty-four. Adams was furious, but didn't yet know how it had happened: "Is not my election to this office, in the scurvy manner in which it was done, a curse rather than a blessing?"

III
(January–April 1789)

Madison and Theodore Sedgwick were elected to the new House of Representatives. "As to me this will not be the case, I believe, from my own disinclination," Hamilton noted. He might well have won in the city, which had elected him to both the Assembly and the Poughkeepsie Convention. He was proposed by friends as a candidate for the governorship against Clinton, but "he steadily rejected the idea in the most explicit manner."

A more appropriate position, instantly accepted, was offered to him "at a numerous and respectable meeting of citizens at Bardon's Tavern" on February 11. He was named Chairman of the Committee of Correspondence for the spring elections. Another member of the twelve-man Committee was Aaron Burr.

In effect, Hamilton was the Federalist campaign manager —an appropriate post in view of his management of Washington's election. Hamilton's talents of persuasion, selection, organization, writing, and speaking were what the Federalists needed—statewide, of course, but interstate also, and in the national government. He began by picking a slate of candidates.

For Congressman from the city he wanted a lawyer who served the merchants and who would help to retain New York as the national capital as long as possible. "Our representative should be a man well qualified in oratory to prove that this city is the best station for that honorable body," he declared at a political meeting, in nominating John Laurence. "Mr. Laurence is well acquainted with the mercantile laws, and closely attached to the real interest of his commercial fellow citizens— therefore a very proper person to represent us."

In order to gain two United States Senators, the Hamilton faction must capture a legislative majority, since some combination of the state assembly and state senate would appoint the men. If Hamilton was planning to win and was thinking ahead, which seems probable, he must have foreseen that General

Schuyler would get one of the Senate seats. For the other vacancy, an unexpected but welcome candidate appeared in
Rufus King of Massachusetts. The dark-haired, musical-voiced
lawyer, prominent in both the adoption and the ratification of
the Constitution, was nevertheless passed over for advantages
at home.

King moved to the New York City home of his wealthy fa-
ther-in-law, John Alsop. On April 5, 1788, Hamilton and Henry
Knox were sponsors at the baptism of the Kings' infant son,
Episcopal Bishop Samuel Provost officiating. King was warmly
received by his adopted home state. The New York Supreme
Court, waiving customary requirements, admitted him at once
to the state bar. "Friend Hamilton," as King addressed him,
put the newcomer's name in nomination for the state assembly.
King was thirty-four years old, and had served in both the
Massachusetts Assembly and the Confederation Congress. Like
Hamilton, he had married into a prominent family with a considerable name. He had all the qualifications that Hamilton
desired in a United States Senator.

For Governor, or more accurately for a candidate to defeat
George Clinton, Hamilton looked for a different sort. A militant
Federalist would not do, since that party was still in a minority
position throughout the state. "It appears therefore," he reasoned, "most advisable to select some man of the opposite
party, a coalition figure capable of drawing bipartisan support."

He picked Judge Robert Yates, his uncooperative colleague
at Philadelphia. Yates had opposed ratification at Poughkeepsie, too, but since then he had instructed a jury in the strongest
terms that the Constitution, now being the law of the land,
must be upheld. Such instructions "entitle him to credit . . .
as a man likely to compose the differences of the State," wrote
Chairman Hamilton. Moreover, during the Poughkeepsie debates, Yates had admitted under questioning by Hamilton and
Jay that "Col. Hamilton's design did not appear to him to point
at a total extinguishment of the State governments, but only
to deprive them of the means of impeding the operation of the
Union."

   Yates was Hamilton's personal choice, agreeable to his Committee, but not the only person willing to take on Clinton.
Pierre Van Cortlandt, lieutenant governor since 1777, posted
notice in the *Daily Advertiser* "to offer myself as a Candidate
for Governor." It would never do to divide the anti-Clinton vote,
and Hamilton wrote Van Cortlandt that the present organization had one purpose—"removal of the present governor." To
that end he invited Van Cortlandt "to yield . . . and withdraw," and to accept as a reward the Correspondence Committee's nomination for lieutenant governor on the ticket with
Yates.
   It was a neat arrangement, duly announced in print by "A.
Hamilton, Chairman." Political language had not yet adopted
the useful word "boss," else it would certainly have been applied to both Hamilton and Clinton in the New York elections
of 1789. They were the partisan captains, opposed head to head
for control of the governorship, the Congressional delegation,
and the Legislature, which, in turn, would choose two United
States Senators. Hamilton traveled to many towns and counties, giving speeches and holding meetings, issuing releases to
the press. As the campaign turned hot, he wheeled up the
artillery, of which he was a past master. His barrage took the
form of sixteen stinging essays in the *Daily Advertiser*. Clinton
was the unspared target, under a code of "all's fair in political
warfare."
   Hamilton signed himself H. G.; it was later guessed that the
initials stood for the Scottish family title, Hamilton of Grange.
The disguise, however, whatever it implied, was stylistically
transparent. Readers soon perceived that H. G. had appeared
before as Continentalist, Phocion, and Publius. Same author;
different product. He used the devastating device of addressing,
as "Dear Sir," a fictitious Suffolk County farmer, and of casti-
gating George Clinton by name.
   "That Mr. Clinton is a man of courage, there is no reason to
doubt," he wrote. But cheering the Governor's war record,
H. G. asserted, "is mere rant and romance." Serving both as
brigadier general and governor, Clinton was never slow to call
out the Revolutionary militia and to put himself at the head

of them. But here Clinton's "praise as a soldier ends." Clinton's only combat experience was at Fort Montgomery, where "the Governor made a well-timed retreat (I mean personally, for a great part of the garrison was captured)." Then Hamilton, as H. G., delivered the coup of sarcasm. "It was undoubtedly the duty of the *Brigadier* to provide in season for the safety of the Governor."

He went on without mercy. The word for Clinton was "cunning," and Clinton's forte was "obstinacy." Clinton's entire career was "either negative or mischievous." H. G.'s summary was rendered with emphasis: *"I do not recollect a single measure of public utility since the peace for which the state is indebted to its Chief Magistrate."*

Running from January into April, Hamilton's barrage of vituperation drew furious denials of his facts, threats of a challenge, veiled slurs about his birth, and other scurrilities that the *Advertiser* finally refused to publish. This sort of electioneering was unprecedented and its outcome unpredictable. The Federalists were being rallied, but so were defenders of the Governor. Yates was called a "cat's-paw" of the aristocratic families, and he almost disappeared from notice as an individual. The campaign was Hamilton's personal vendetta. It was also a recruitment of rank-and-file voters. He aimed to form a political party that would outnumber the entrenched Clintonians.

An impossible venture—or almost. He came within 431 votes of displacing Clinton, whose prestige never fully recovered. He seated Laurence and three other Federalists in the House of Representatives. He won Federalist majorities in both houses of the Legislature. And he put the two men he wanted, King and Schuyler, into the U. S. Senate. In July '89, they reported to Federal Hall and drew lots for the seats. King's good fortune still holding, he got the six-year term. With his perennial ill-luck, Schuyler had to settle for the short term of two years.

Hamilton's political victory was impressive, if incomplete, and there were losses. Aaron Burr, denied a Senate seat, abandoned the Federalists and was appointed Attorney General of

New York by the Governor. Yates drifted back to the Antis.
James Duane was miffed. At one point he had had the votes
to reach the Senate. "I immediately," said Hamilton, "set about
circulating an idea . . . that some very unfit character would
be his successor" as Mayor of New York. Morgan Lewis, who
had married into the powerful Livingston family, grumbled
that King's appointment was "very generally disapproved of."
Hamilton, as in Philadelphia, had gone too far. It smacked too
much of royal patronage to send a relative and a parvenu,
though both were worthy men, to the Federal Senate.

IV

(April–September 1789)

On the Federal Hall balcony above Wall Street, April 30,
1789, Robert R. Livingston, Chancellor of the University of the
State of New York, administered the oath of office to George
Washington. The General wore a suit of brown broadcloth
made in Hartford, a deliberate promotion of American products. On that glorious day New York revelled in the colors,
sights, sounds, and personalities of the Revolution. Many Continental officers were in uniform. Bands played, troops
marched, guns saluted, flags flew high, the multitude cheered.
Washington stepped from the balcony into the Senate chamber
of Federal Hall to address both houses of Congress. Representative Fisher Ames noted:

"Time had made a havoc of his face . . . it was a very touching scene and quite of the solemn kind. His aspect grave, almost
to sadness; his modesty, actually shaking; his voice deep, a little
tremulous, and so low as to call for close attention. . . . I sat
entranced."

Hamilton, with a group of friends, watched the ceremonies
from the balcony of his home directly across the street. Within
a week the new president was asking suggestions on "etiquette." Hamilton advised him to "steer clear of extremes" of
kingly remoteness on the one hand and "notions of equality"
on the other and offered specifics about giving and attending

dinners. Washington sent "unfeigned thanks for your friendly communications of this date," and added, "Permit me to entreat a continuation."

On July 4, honored by the presence of the First Lady (Washington was too tired to come), Hamilton delivered a eulogy to the late General Nathanael Greene before the Society of the Cincinnati at City Tavern. It seemed a safe enough undertaking, but Hamilton's speech recalled how the Southern militia at Guilford Court House had broken ranks and run away. This was too much for Aedanus Burke, a fiery South Carolina Congressman, who sent a challenge. Hamilton positively would not fight. He held that no offense could properly be taken when none was intended.

Hamilton could not doubt that he would be part of the Administration, nor that he was qualified to fill any of the four cabinet posts. If appointed Attorney General, he would be the government's lawyer, and would also continue in private practice. His absorption in military matters would make him an excellent choice as Secretary of War. He had the linguistic facility to fit him for Secretary of State, and many times in the past he had represented Washington as a military diplomat. The Chief Justiceship did not interest him at all. The appointment that was most congenial to him, and to which Robert Morris advised Washington to name him, was that of Secretary of the Treasury. It was the one position wholly indispensable to the success of the Union.

As Hamilton saw American peacetime policy, it was identical with the policy of wartime. The struggle for independence from Europe merely took a different form. He had in mind total national freedom. He and the President were in full accord about despising the forces that drew some of their countrymen toward England and others toward France. This continued dependence on Europe would not soon be ended, but its earliest termination—its fullest suppression—was to Hamilton's mind a paramount duty of American government.

Hamilton undertook the personal responsibility of educating the American people, most especially the Congress, to the full meaning of independence. He would do this throughout the rest of his life by writing hundreds of essays and letters on politics and economics, by shaping legislation in Congress and policy in the Cabinet.

He was working from a master plan. Frederick Scott Oliver, the London department storekeeper, understood it earliest and best. Oliver wrote of Hamilton's "threefold policy . . . for . . . getting rid of all influence from without, not only direct but indirect, not only political in the strict sense, but general." The three phases of independence in Hamilton's policy had to do with finance, foreign policy, and industry.

That was the order of their priority. First, Hamilton wished to free the nation from external creditors, and from unwarranted "gratitude" for wartime loans. One advantage of the states' ceasing to be colonies, he believed, was the throwing off of exploitation and usury from abroad.

Second, he sought freedom from foreign intrigue and secret diplomacy. He favored rescinding the treaty of alliance with France at the propitious moment, and making no other treaties except for trade and territorial rights.

Third, and over a longer period, he wanted America to cast off dependence on European imports and to become self-sufficient in manufactured products. That would be difficult. The new nation was predominantly agricultural and a good many political leaders wished to keep it so. Almost all items except foodstuffs were cheaper to buy from European ships than at home; but Hamilton had plans to change that. He intended to encourage useful manufactures, to subsidize them by various forms of bounty, and to protect them by tariffs.

Since he could not hold all the Cabinet portfolios at once, he naturally hoped for the one which had most to do with government—that is, with finance, foreign policy, the promotion of industry. This department ought to have the prestige of seniority. He should be the first-appointed of Washington's ministers. Once in office, he would see that his was the busiest department, with the most assistants and clerks and the widest responsibility.

If his threefold policy was successful, and rather quickly, he anticipated that the new government would rapidly enlist the support of wealthy men, and also of the working classes, since everybody benefited from prosperity, peace, and productiveness.

He had won two elections since the war and had experienced spectacular success at the Poughkeepsie Convention and also in leading Federalist candidates to victory, but popularity was never his ambition. He was not a climber, but a nation-builder. He expected success for his three-part plan to be rapid and conspicuous. He hoped it would bring respect, even reverence, to the government, and give rise to patriotic pride in America.

Social events clogged the wheels of government as Washington's administration settled into place. It was not until September 11 that the President sent the Senate "the following nominations for the Treasury Department:

"Alexander Hamilton (of New York) for Secretary. . . ."

He was the first-named of the first Cabinet. His nomination was unanimously confirmed on the same day.

CHAPTER SEVENTEEN

The American Prime Minister

I

(May 1789–February 1790)

Angelica was back in America for a visit. She returned in May and Hamilton announced her arrival to the doting father, who responded: "Your anxiety that the harmony of the family should be compleat affords me the most pleasing sensations. . . ."

There had been some quarrel between Angelica and General Schuyler, and Hamilton played the mediator. It was a duty sweetly rewarded in dividends of increased affection. "Let neither politics or ambition drive your Angelica from your affections," she begged; ". . . you said I was as dear to you as a sister; keep your word, and let me have the consolation to believe that you will never forget the promises of friendship you have vowed." How she loved him—"*mon très cher.*" How he loved her back—"Amiable Angelica! Dear Angelica!"

In early November he put her aboard a packet and took sad leave; then, he wrote, "I hastened home to soothe and console your sister." As soon as Betsey was composed, Hamilton with young Philip and Steuben (who was a guest) "walked down to the Battery." Perhaps her ship was still in sight. Yes, "with aching hearts and anxious eyes, we saw your vessel in full sail, swiftly bearing our loved friend from our embraces. Imagine what we felt. We gazed, we sighed, we *wept.* . . ."

He was writing only a few hours after the farewells. He continued to mediate the quarrel between father and daughter over "the unexpected step you took," whatever that may have been. "The arguments I have used with him will go far toward reconciling." She wrote back from London that "my father's letters have relieved me from the dread of having offended him."

There seemed endless ways for her to tell him how much she cared. When she disclosed that her father "speaks of you with so much pride and satisfaction," she added that "if I did not love you as he does, I should be a little jealous of the attachment." She vowed that she could not be consoled even by the three letters which arrived from Hamilton in a single post. "I lament the loss of your society," she told him. "I am so unreasonable as to prefer our charming families to all the gaieties of London. I cannot relish the gay world . . . —but do not let me pain your affectionate heart. . . ."

She promised to send him every well-written book she could find on the subject of finance, strange reading for this social butterfly. "I cannot help being diverted at the avidity I express for whatever relates to this subject." It was not so much "a source of amusement," she declared, but rather "of interest." She was too sad to send him agreeable news or gossip, but "I can at the very least give you a History of my Mind, which is at present very much occupied by a very great, and a very amiable personage."

Soon her playful jealousy would extend to his absorption in the work of the new government. She was determined to share all that concerned him. "I am impatient to hear in what manner your Budget has been received, and am extremely anxious for your success." Sometimes she feared that "you now forget me, and that having seen me is like a dream which you can scarcely believe." But no, she tried to resist "this idea of being lost in the tumult of business and ambition." She would always be "your devoted Angelica."

II

(September 1789–January 1790)

On September 11, Hamilton moved without ceremony into well-appointed space in Federal Hall. From a long-standing bill which he owed to L'Enfant, it appears that Hamilton engaged the architect to design furniture, which was then fabricated by

the skillful cabinet-makers of New York in that day. Two arm-
chairs and two side chairs, both of mahogany with elegantly
carved leaf finials, or pinnacles, and fluted sides and legs would
follow Hamilton to his various offices and homes. He was particularly attached to a desk of mahogany veneer and satin-
wood.

Hamilton had not waited for a formal setting to get to work
on national finance. For some weeks, it appears, he had been
busy both at the Wall Street office and at Fraunces Tavern,
where the Confederation board of treasury had stored its
records. A bewildering mélange of military and civilian accounts confronted the Secretary. The central government owed
a grand total of close to $80 million. That broke down into debts
of about $12 million to foreign governments and banks; $40
million and more to American soldiers and their suppliers; over
$25 million of pledges for which the individual states were
responsible.

The House of Representatives requested him to prepare
recommendations for revenue-raising. It then adjourned till
January. Hamilton, by now accustomed to asking Madison's
advice, did so in a letter dated October 12. He thanked his
friend for the loan of a book, expressed regret at not having said
goodbye before the Virginian set out for home, and then got
to the point.

"May I ask of your friendship to put on paper and send me
your thoughts. . . . The question is very much, 'What further
taxes will be *least* objectionable?' Adieu, My Dr Sir. Yr Affec
& Obed."

Madison replied "With affect & regards" from Orange, Virginia. He recommended (as Hamilton had hoped he would) an
excise tax on home distilleries. Whiskey-making was by far the
most prolific cottage industry of the frontier and mountain
states. More important than anything else in the letter was
Madison's eagerness to please—"my unwillingness to disobey
your commands" was the way he put it.

Hamilton proposed to pay the government's running expenses by means of domestic taxes and tariffs. He would discharge the debt by the method he'd learned from Robert Mor-

ris—that is, by uniting the interests of wealthy investors with
the policies of government. The Treasury would "assume" and
"fund" all the paper-money obligations of the states. It would
sell government stock, which would increase in value as the
nation grew. But he must make all this acceptable to Congress.
The first task during those last weeks of 1789 was to prepare
a Report On The Public Credit, meaning the terms on which
a nation-state could borrow. He wrote:

"The Secretary of the Treasury, in obedience to the resolution of the House of Representatives . . . has during the recess
of Congress applied himself . . . with all the attention which
is due to the authority of the House, and to the magnitude of
the subject."

He was putting it all down on paper, a total of twenty-two
thousand words, but he did not anticipate that the Representatives would have to read it. He would give a verbal presenta-
tion, respond to questions, and resolve their perplexities, as was
done by the Chancellor of the Exchequer in the House of Commons. The House of Representatives, sixty-four members, was
about the size of the recent Poughkeepsie Convention, and he
had confidence in his persuasive powers.

"States, like individuals," he wrote, "who observe their engagements, are respected and trusted; while the reverse is the
fate of those who pursue an opposite course . . . the creation
of a debt should always be accompanied with the means of
extinguishment." This, the Secretary assured the House, "he
regards as the true secret for rendering Public Credit immortal."

He could guess where the concurrence and where the opposition would come from. As Madison wrote, "all hands" would
doubtless agree that the foreign debts should be discharged so
as to facilitate the selling of grain to Europe, where there had
been a crop failure. But men would argue over "funding" the
domestic obligations. They would call this money owed to "ourselves." Such was the argument for "repudiation," the way of
many revolutionary governments. Hamilton was determined
that America should be different.

By far the most difficult of the three classes of debts—foreign,

Congressional, state—would be the third. For one thing, assumption of these would bring some inequities. Southern states did not owe as much as Northern states. Also, hundreds of soldiers, farmers, and merchants in the states had already disposed of their pay-certificates. Hundreds more would sell their scrip for a few shillings on the pound to speculators who learned or guessed what the government was about to do. Hamilton's Report met this matter of speculation head-on. He stated the question thus: "Whether a discrimination ought not to be made between the original holders of the public securities, and the present possessors by purchase." He was coldly logical about public debt management. Sellers of the Continental scrip at a mark-down displayed a lack of faith in the country. Purchasers of the certificates—clever, unscrupulous, wealthy though they might be—were believers in its future.

The Secretary held it good policy to allow profits to men who had bought the scrip and thereby invested in "the stock of the country." To do otherwise, to pay off the faithless sellers, no matter how poor and ignorant, he contended, would be "unjust . . . impolitic . . . injurious . . . ruinous to the Public Credit . . . inconsistent with justice . . . a breach of contract—a violation of the rights of a fair purchaser."

He had won so many political debates, so many cases at law, that he was sure he could stand on the floor of the House and win again. Besides, he was counting on Madison's support.

But when Congress reconvened in January, Hamilton received a double blow. The House voted down a motion that the Secretary present the Report with "oral illustration." That way was too "English" for the Representatives. And Madison had developed serious reservations. On February 11, 1790, he delivered his opening speech against the Hamiltonian financial system. He opposed "assumption" of state debts. He favored "discrimination" between the original purchasers and the present holders of the scrip.

It was a definite cleavage. The affectionate colleague of Annapolis and Philadelphia turned against these crucial phases of the Secretary's plan. Indeed, within four weeks after the first break, Madison had divorced himself from Hamilton and attached himself inseparably to Jefferson, who by then had arrived in Philadelphia to join the Administration.

Madison's best explanation is found in a letter written long afterwards, May 31, 1857, by an acquaintance of Martin Van Buren, an avid collector of anecdotes on notables. Van Buren's correspondent, N. P. Trist of Philadelphia, quoted Madison on the suggestion that he had "jilted" Hamilton. Madison said:

"I abandoned Col. Hamilton—or Col. Hamilton abandoned me,—in a word we *parted* & upon its plainly becoming his purpose and endeavour to administration [*administer*] the Government into a thing totally different from that which he and I both knew perfectly well had been understood & intended by the Convention who framed it, and by the people in adopting it."

A much briefer and more sardonic clarification is the one by John Randolph, "Madison always was some great man's mistress—first Hamilton's—then Jefferson's."

III

(March–July 1790)

In March Thomas Jefferson was sworn in as Secretary of State, and the Cabinet was complete. Jefferson was the last aboard, as Hamilton had been the first. President Washington had Henry Knox as Secretary of War, and Edmund Randolph as Attorney General. John Jay was Chief Justice. It was a ministry of proven talent.

Jefferson, rangy, red-headed, and radical for the rights of man, had had a mountain-top experience as minister to France since leaving Congress in 1784. He returned to America just as Madison was warming to the session-long fight against the Treasury proposals.

To understand Hamilton's Report On The Public Credit required members of Congress to give it close reading. Very few did so. "I think it well calculated to keep us all in the dark except those . . . who thrive on speculation," said Jones of Virginia. Many Americans thought they knew how to thrive that way. Ships were leased and horsemen dispatched to Southern and Western regions. The speculators and their agents carried bags of specie with which to buy up the Morris notes and other scrip. It was a time when the gambler's itch was rampant. Many would gain and some would lose.

Hamilton avoided both these courses. He made no investments at all, and ordered his stock in the Bank of New York to be sold at a loss. He was dismayed that William Duer, whom he had appointed as his assistant at the Treasury, became involved in speculation and was subsequently disgraced. Hamilton saw that Duer must resign, but would not turn against a friend in trouble. "I count with confidence on your future friendship, as you may on mine."

Much of the plunging would have been averted if Hamilton's strong and repeated advice had been followed. He warned Congress in January to act promptly, because, he said, "Delay would sink the price of the stock," and "millions would probably be lost to the United States." Later, in September, he published an Address To The Public Creditors, advising all who held Continental certificates to continue to hold them. "You may be tempted to part with your securities much below their true value, and considerably below what it is probable they will sell for in eight or nine months from this time."

Meanwhile he drove himself into a frenzy in the effort to win House approval for his plan. Since he could not address that body from the floor, he took to the corridors of Federal Hall. He "spent most of his time running from place to place among the members," by one account. He enlisted helpers wherever they were to be found. Some friends from the Army joined up. So did Humphreys and Jackson of the President's staff, and some members of the clergy. One minister called on Speaker Muhlenberg and "argued as if he had been in the pulpit." At times, Hamilton would take members for a stroll, and give them his undivided attention. A lady recalled seeing him walk with Madison, "then turn and laugh and play with a monkey that was climbing in a neighbor's yard." Again, he met Senator Robert Morris "walking early in the morning on the Battery . . . as if by accident."

Morris remembered: "Mr. Hamilton said he wanted one vote

in the Senate and five in the House of Representatives; that he was willing and would agree to place the permanent residence of the Congress at Germantown or the Falls of Delaware if he would procure those votes."

He could make bargains with Morris but not with Madison. The Virginian had a shell—the pride of a shy and scrupulous man—into which he withdrew when pressured. A senator came to him with a compromise plan. "I read the resolutions. I do not think he attended one word of them, so much did he seem absorbed with his own ideas. . . . His pride. . . . The obstinacy of this man. . . ." Abigail Adams thought Madison was "acting a covered and artful part." But a male caller who tried to approach him through House Clerk John Beckley of Virginia decided, "I think I know him . . . if he is led, it must be without letting him know . . . in other words he must not see the string."

Another judgment on Madison was by Fisher Ames, who was so brilliant that he had been admitted to Harvard at the age of twelve. "I think him a good and able man . . . also very timid. . . . I see in Madison with his great knowledge and merit . . . much error and some . . . mischief." Ames, thirty-one when he joined the First Congress, would be Hamilton's tireless spokesman for many years to come, as Madison would be his careful but indomitable foe.

Hamilton and Madison were both feeling the strain of prolonged contest. One day the Senate adjourned, "and we went in to lower House to hear the debate. . . . Madison had been up most of the morning . . . seemed rather jaded." On another occasion Hamilton was described as "sombre, haggard & dejected . . . even his dress uncouth & neglected." He advanced upon the Madison-held chamber with "officers of government, clergy, citizens, Cincinnati and every person under the influence of the Treasury." Every vote was crucial. A homesick Federalist was consoled, a sick member and a lame one were helped to the floor, an absentee was recalled.

Secretary Jefferson could not but be an interested observer of Hamilton's furious campaign to win votes in the House. In the Confederation Congress of 1784 Jefferson had been floor leader for a measure close to his heart. He had proposed, as part of his legislation for governing the Northwest Territory, that after 1800 there should be "neither slavery nor involuntary servitude" in any new state admitted to the Union.

Jefferson's own situation was peculiar. He did not care to make the sacrifice of freeing his own slaves; but in his only book, *Notes on the State of Virginia,* he had advocated education, emancipation, and expatriation of the blacks. His proposition of 1784 was a lesser idea, but a momentous one launched at a propitious time in the progress of the Enlightenment. Had he won, slavery would have been cornered in the Southeastern states and the national agony over its expansion westward would have been averted.

Jefferson needed to carry seven states in the Confederation Congress, and he had had six. He would have had the seventh except that one member, John Beatty of New Jersey, was ill and absent, so that state lost its vote. Six years later, as he watched Hamilton's intensive drive for assumption of state debts, Jefferson must have wondered what history would have been made if he had mustered such leadership to stop the spread of slavery. Sick, lame, and slothful members did not inhibit the Secretary of the Treasury in his fierce drive to an objective.

On April 12, an equally determined Madison led a sortie and whipped assumption by two votes. "Speculation wiped a tear from either eye," wrote the caustic Senator William Maclay of Pennsylvania. Hamilton seemed to be stopped, but he had not given up. He would try again with better results.

IV

(May–September 1790)

Hamilton lost this skirmish to Madison, and a few weeks later he lost one to Jefferson. Some soldiers of the Virginia and North Carolina line had been inveigled by a talkative stranger into selling their pay certificates at a mark down price for money in hand. The salesman was James Reynolds of New York, who was subsequently to have an even greater impact on Hamilton's life. Reynolds was agent for the New York merchant, William J. Vredenburgh, having obtained the list of claims by an illicit transaction with Hamilton's friend, William Duer.

On May 21, 1790, both houses of Congress voted to restore the entire amount—about fifty thousand dollars—to the soldiers. Hamilton was outraged by this legislative intrusion into Treasury affairs. He felt no necessity to prove his patriotism by siding with the servicemen. In a lengthy paper he asked Washington to make his first use of the veto power to halt the repayment. Jefferson, in a paper of his own, protested.

It was a minor encounter, but one of principle. Jefferson argued for "giving the advantage to the party who has suffered wrong rather than to him who has committed it." Hamilton contended that "obligation of contracts" was at stake. The soldiers had parted with their certificates for a price. They should be held to the bargain unless they could establish fraud in a court of law.

Congress, he said, should not pass retroactive legislation, changing the rules after the fact. Let the soldiers take their case before a magistrate. Public credit would be compromised by the sort of political interference which, for the sake of a few individuals, "breaks in upon the great principle that constitutes the foundation of property."

But the politics of the case simply overwhelmed the principle. Hamilton was supporting money-changers against Revolutionary veterans. He was making a big to-do over a relatively small sum. He was opposed by the foremost Virginia Congressman and the Virginian Secretary of State, and the outcome rested in the hands of a President who was also from Virginia. The Old Dominion stood firm, and Hamilton lost again.

Jefferson professed at this point in his career to be naive about finance, though when he was a Congressman it had been one of his keen interests. His state paper of March 1774, "Notes on the Establishment of a Money Unit," was the original proposal for the dollar-decimal system. He had a blind prejudice against public debts and banks. He understood a good deal

about weights, measures, and coinage. Some of his first correspondence with Hamilton was on that subject. Jefferson offered
to obtain the services of Jean Pierre Dros, a Swiss citizen and
inventor of a machine for stamping images on the two faces and
the edge of a coin at one stroke. Hamilton sent "thanks for the
trouble Mr. J. is so obliging as to take." The two secretaries
were not well acquainted, but during that summer they found
they had two matters of common concern.

For one, Jefferson had not been paid for his services as minister to Paris. Three hundred fifty pounds were still due him. The
usual arrangement for payment of American envoys in Europe
was that they received their salary and expense settlements
from Holland bankers. Not knowing how to proceed, Jefferson
turned for help to the Secretary of the Treasury.

"You were so kind as to say you would write to our bankers
in Holland to answer my draught for a part of the balance due
me for salary etc. . . . They know that the diplomatic expenses
in Europe were paid on the funds in their hands, yet as I am
here they will naturally expect your instructions. . . ."

The other matter in which the secretaries shared an interest
was the hold-over Residency bill. Every city and every state
wanted the national capital, but there were conditions of eligibility. No city or state to the north of New York could be
considered geographically qualified, and even New York's title
was cloudy. Philadelphia was the sentimental favorite. But
considering how the mutineers had once put Congress to flight
from Philadelphia, Hamilton liked better the plan of a Federal
District, ten miles square. He wanted the Federal City to be
protected by national armed forces, with no need to rely on
state militia and timid governors.

He knew that the powerful Virginians would favor a location
on the Potomac. His old friend, Robert Morris, would help him
if Philadelphia were given consideration. Hamilton saw what
might be done by adroit political linkage. One June morning
he accosted the Secretary of State in the street. The Virginian
coveted the capital city; the New Yorker yearned for another
chance at Assumption. Jefferson again pleaded his ignorance

of finance. "I proposed to him, however," Jefferson wrote, "to dine with me next day, and I would invite another friend or two, bring them into a conference together. . . ."

V
(1790)

Jefferson would not dine with Hamilton very often, which was fortunate, for they seemed compelled to misunderstand one another. There was the time when, as Jefferson told it, "After the cloth was removed . . . conversation . . . was led to the British constitution, on which Mr. Adams observed 'purge that constitution of its corruption, and it would be the most perfect constitution ever devised by the wit of man.' "

At this point, Hamilton broke in to say, "Purge that constitution of its corruption, and give its popular branch equality of representation, and it would become an *impractical* government; as it stands at present with all its supposed defects, it is the most perfect government which ever existed."

Then there was another Jefferson dinner party when, "sitting at our wine . . . a collision of opinion arose. . . . The room being hung about with a collection of portraits of remarkable men, among them those of Bacon, Newton and Locke, Hamilton asked me who they were. I told him they were my trinity of the greatest men the world had ever produced, naming them. He paused for some time. 'The greatest man that ever lived,' he said, 'was Julius Caesar.' "

If Hamilton had set out deliberately to tease Jefferson—and perhaps he did—no better subjects could have been chosen than the empires of Britain and Rome. After these parties, if not before, Jefferson was convinced that Hamilton doted on monarchical corruption and dreamed of being a dictator. As Jefferson certainly knew, George Washington had a bust of Caesar standing in Mount Vernon. The mansion held busts of other conquerors—Charles XII of Sweden, Frederick of Prussia, and the Duke of Marlborough.

Had Jefferson wanted a true revelation of Hamilton, it was available to him in *The Federalist*, Number 72. In that paper

Hamilton had contended that there should be no limit on the number of terms a Chief Executive could serve. He was making his familiar points that "desire of reward is one of the strongest incentives of human conduct," and that "the best security for the fidelity of mankind is to make their interest coincide with their duty."

Perhaps Jefferson could follow Hamilton's logic that far, but the next step took them forever apart. Hamilton wrote that it was "love of fame, the ruling passion of the noblest minds, which would prompt a man to plan and undertake extensive and arduous enterprise for the public benefit. . . ." The passion of "ambition," in the minds of Washington and Hamilton, was not Caesarism; it was a desire to deserve the admiration of their fellow citizens.

This desire, to Jefferson's disapproval, would illumine Hamilton's entire career. Ambition drove him to seek fame, praise, and honor. It coincided with his duty to promote the greater glory of the nation. After Hamilton's death, Pickering commenced a never-finished biography by quoting the crucial passage of *The Federalist,* Number 72, adding, "That was his own ruling passion; & he sought for it in the ability and fidelity displayed in the contriving & executing of his public plans."

Fisher Ames, in another posthumous appraisal, asked of what Hamilton was ambitious. "Not of wealth; no man held it cheaper. Was it of popularity? That weed of the dunghill, he knew, when rankest, was nearest of withering. There is no doubt that he desired glory . . . [but] he thirsted only for that fame which virtue would not blush to confer, nor time to convey to the end of his course."

VI

(May–September 1790)

Jefferson's dinner for Hamilton this spring of 1790 hatched the most famous political bargain in American history. Philadelphia was to have the capital for ten years. After that the permanent site would be on the Potomac, quite close to Mount Vernon. But first, the House of Representatives would take another vote on Assumption. Madison, "afraid, even to timidity, of his state," Ames observed, would not switch; but he withdrew his opposition. Two other Virginia Congressmen went over to Hamilton. This time he had ambushed Jefferson and beaten Madison.

During July the necessary measures passed both House and Senate, and on the 17th of that month Hamilton completed an important transaction for Jefferson by a letter to Messrs. Willink, Van Staphorst and Hubbard, Amsterdam.

"Gentlemen, it being understood that you have retained in your hands a sufficient sum to discharge the balance of salary to Mr. Jefferson. . . . He, therefore, has informed me that he will draw upon you, on that account, for three hundred and fifty pounds sterling, to be expressed in Guilders, which I accordingly request you will be pleased to pay. . . ."

Madison and Jefferson accepted the terms graciously enough until they learned that the Virginia legislature had passed a resolution that "Assumption was repugnant," and until they saw the country in the full flush of speculation. Jefferson, feeling that Hamilton had gulled him, wrote bitterly of the affair:

". . . and so Assumption was passed, and twenty million of stock divided among favored States, and thrown in as a pablum to the stock-jobbing herd. This added to the number of votaries to the Treasury, and made its chief the master of every vote in the legislature which might give to the government the direction suited to his political views."

Hamilton, then, was "master" of government and not merely Secretary of the Treasury. Jefferson thought so, and many facts bore it out. Hamilton's friend Gouverneur Morris had been named envoy to London without consultation by the Secretary of State. Angelica's friend from London, Major George Beckwith, arrived in New York during the life of the First Congress. He discussed British-American affairs with Hamilton rather than Jefferson, a widower-beau to Angelica in his own right.

Beckwith was aide to Lord Dorchester, Governor-General of Canada, and was the counterpart of Morris, since there was no diplomatic recognition and no minister. In his opening talks with the Major, Hamilton sought to make Britain the anchor of America's European policies. "We think in English," Hamilton told him. He meant that Jefferson "thought in French," and would hardly understand Anglo-American partnership.

Like Jefferson and Madison and many other men in public life, Beckwith wrote his letters in cipher. He officially referred to Hamilton as Number 7. It was not a sinister numeral in an espionage code, as some Hamilton-haters have liked to think. In Beckwith's reports to his home government, Number 1 was William Samuel Johnson, Number 2 was Philip Schuyler, Number 3 was Henry Knox, and so on to Number 11, who was Gouverneur Morris. The numbering was in accordance with the order in which Beckwith made the acquaintance of important persons. He assigned no numeral to Secretary Jefferson.

Washington acquiesced passively in the British bypassing of Jefferson. Anglo-American relations became Hamilton's province. Although the path of communications was twisty—from New York, to Quebec, to London, and return—Hamilton had assurance that "the Cabinet of Great Britain entertained a disposition, not only toward a friendly intercourse, but toward an alliance with the United States." That would be going too far and too fast, in Hamilton's opinion. But Washington gave instructions "that the Secretary of the Treasury was to extract as much as he could from Major Beckwith and report to me. . . ." Secretary Jefferson was made "privy" to these matters, but that was about all.

Hamilton's authority seemed boundless. He increased the Treasury Department from thirty-nine workers in 1789 to seventy during 1790, and to ninety by the end of '92. He ordered the building of a fleet of revenue cutters; he nominated ship captains for commissioning; he submitted legislation for the postal service and a road-building program in that connection; he called for reports on all lighthouses and buoys; he volunteered ideas for a judicial system; he became purchasing agent for the Army; he informed the Academy of Arts and Sciences that the Treasury "from time to time" would require information on raw materials and manufactures. He made clear what was uppermost in his mind: "To the manufacture of Cannon, Arms and Gunpowder, the Secretary wished particular attention." He wanted the United States to have an arms industry.

First minister of Washington's Cabinet he certainly was in all but title. Suddenly, in May 1790, the question of title became of utmost importance. President Washington lay ill with pneumonia, and for six days his life was despaired of. "Most assuredly I do not wish for the highest post," wrote the Vice President's wife, who habitually echoed her husband's thoughts. "I never before realized what I might be called to. . . ."

If John Adams succeeded to the Presidency, who would be next in line behind him? The Constitution did not say, but Hamilton and Jefferson both had strong claims. The Treasury Department had been created by the Act of September 2, 1789, and the State Department by the Act of September 15. Thus Treasury was almost two weeks older. If seniority became a factor, and the successor was to come from the Cabinet, Hamilton would be next in succession to John Adams, aged fifty-five.

But this logic was not acceptable to the adulators of Jefferson. A counter-argument was that the State Department had originally been the Department of Foreign Affairs, created in 1781, and therefore predating the Treasury Department. Madison drew up a bill which designated the Secretary of State as the officer to succeed in the event of a double vacancy in the two executive offices. The bill would not be introduced until the Second Congress, but it then passed the House. It went to the Federalist Senate, where Jefferson was thoroughly detested and all sessions were secret. Representative Ames found out what happened behind the closed doors, and wrote with glee:

"The Secretary of State is struck out of the bill for the future Presidency, in case of the first two offices becoming vacant. His friends seemed to think it important to hold him up as King of the Romans. The firmness of the Senate kept him out."

As finally resolved by Congress, the Speaker of the House and the President pro tempore of the Senate were named, in that order, to succeed; but meanwhile Hamilton and Jefferson had become locked in a power struggle. To the relief of the eastern cities where the news of the President's illness had been published, Washington made a swift recovery. In June he led his warring secretaries on a three-day fishing trip off Sandy Hook.

The *Pennsylvania Packet* for June 10 noted:

"Yesterday afternoon the President of the United States returned from Sandy Hook and the fishing banks where he had the benefit of the sea air and to amuse himself in the delightful recreation of fishing. We are told he had excellent sport."

The President's principal guests did not enjoy the excursion, nor one another's company; their rivalry had become an open feud. There was no longer any doubt that George Washington was mortal. He talked so much about his loss of hearing and of memory that he could be taken for an invalid. Presidential politics advanced to being a continuous activity, not merely one of an election year. "I ran counter to Mr. Jefferson's wishes," observed Hamilton in a terse understatement of the rivalry. Exhilarated by the game of power, the toils of office, the responsibility, the success, and the prominence, he still could write to Angelica on September 2:

"I cannot let the packet go, my dear friend, without dropping you a line to prove that you are always of more consequence than the great affairs which you have so often represented as the rivals of all my friendships. . . ."

VII

(September 1790—January 1791)

Betsey was spending more and more time with the children at the comfortable family mansion in Albany. In New York, Hamilton was working hard and dining out, but on September 11 he wrote, "The Albany post is arrived and not a line from my dear Betsey. . . . This is a disappointment to me as I was anxious to learn how she & my dear children got up & how they were."

She had not improved as a correspondent; moreover, she had never missed him as he missed her. Hamilton, in all the years of military service, court circuits, Cabinet meetings, and Congressional battles, was never too busy to send frequent personal letters. "I am in good health, and in all respects as well as I can be without my very dear family—But there is a sad blank in their absence. . . . Adieu my Angel, take care of yourself."

Four days later he wrote again. ". . . I am tired of living alone. . . . But I leave the matter to yourself. If you feel anxious or uneasy, you had better come down. . . . If you knew, my beloved wife, how delightful it is to me to have you with me, you need not be told how irksome it is to be separated. . . . I have received but one letter from you, & this is my third."

The three letters to Angelica and to Betsey spanned less than a fortnight. It depressed him not to have the company of either of these two sisters who were so dear to him. But Washington and Jefferson were vacationing in Virginia, and Knox and Randolph were away. "I am the only one of the Administration now here. . . . It might be awkward for me to be absent also."

In addition to "putting into train of execution the laws of the last session affecting my department," Hamilton had to address himself to a written questionnaire by Washington on the Beckwith matter. He prepared a lengthy dissertation on international law as applied to relations with Britain and Spain. This was forwarded to Mount Vernon, and toward the end of September he was back in negotiation with the British agent, who was now pressing for the alliance against Spain and for protection of Canada. They talked in the manner of world statesmen:

"Beckwith: Do you wish to have a West India Island?

"Hamilton: I answer without hesitation. No, we do not, it is not in our contemplation. We wish the liberty of trading in that quarter. . . . We should consider the sovereignty of a West India Island as a burthen. Our territories are very extensive, and I can assure you that the idea of having possessions further to the north than our present boundaries would be esteemed an incumbrance, *with an exception to the Forts."*

Congress returned after the weather cooled, as did the executives, and Hamilton gathered material for further Treasury reports. By now many thoughtful persons, with varying viewpoints, could perceive the outlines of the Hamiltonian state. The indignant Patrick Henry saw it as a venture "to erect and concentrate and perpetuate a large monied interest in opposition to the landed interests." Not all agreed with Henry that this would hurl "agriculture at the feet of commerce" and prove "fatal to the existence of American liberty." On the contrary, the advance of industry and commerce, with the build-up of international respect, was already creating a balanced economy with no perceptible loss of freedom.

This would be the general theme of Hamilton's upcoming Reports. One was a second treatise on Public Credit, and would propose a National Bank. Another dealt with the Establishment of a Mint, and the enacting of Jefferson's plan for basing the American dollar on the decimal system. A third was the Report on Manufactures.

Hamilton was tiring, and he was not getting much support from Betsey. The Residency law of July 16, 1790, required that "prior to the first Monday in December next, all offices attached to the seat of government . . . shall be removed to . . . Philadelphia." Hamilton must find quarters there for the Treasury Department, but he might have expected his wife to help him select their home.

But in August he was writing to Walter Stewart, formerly of the Second Pennsylvania Regiment, "I thank you for the interest you are so obliging as to take in procuring for me a house." He would be given space for the Treasury in one of the public buildings, and told Stewart that he wanted a "house as near my destined office as possible." For the rest, "A cool situation & exposure will, of course, be a very material point to a New Yorker. The house must have at least six rooms. Good dining and drawing rooms are material articles. I like elbow room in a yard."

A week later he notified Stewart that the Department would be located at Chestnut and Third Streets, and that he had heard of a residential vacancy at Walnut near Third. Betsey showed no interest and shared none of the work of house-hunting. He could only hope she would like the house, to which they moved in October. As it turned out, she did not, and they had to move again.

The Department of the Treasury was listed in the city directory as 100 Chestnut Street, but was known as the Pemberton House, after its owners from 1745 to 1781. It was nearly a

century old, having been built in 1694 by the lawyer William
Clarke, who had the carpenters erect a two-story brick structure with a double front and hipped roof. Another Hamilton
family, no kin to the Secretary, had lived there before the
Pembertons, and three presidents of the Continental Congress
had occupied it during the war. Its immediate prior owner was
Tenche Coxe, and Hamilton referred to it on August 27, 1790,
as "the house of Mr. Coxe, formerly occupied by the President
of Congress." He requested Stewart "to procure one for me, as
near *that* as you can, having regard for the quality and situation of the house."

His office took the entire first floor of the house. A French
visitor found him, one day, at a common pine table covered
with a green cloth, amid documents piled on planks laid across
trestles. The Secretary's clerk was a man "in a long green linen
jacket." This was not the smart turnout the caller had expected. The Frenchman evidently did not know that other
members of Hamilton's staff were located on the second floor,
outside in the rear court, and in nearby houses. In all there
were some thirty clerks, a register, an auditor, a treasurer, a
controller, and an assistant secretary, as well as almost a thousand customshouse officers and workers. "Writing, Writing,
Writing in this department is the whole duty of man," a minor
Treasury functionary would comment.

Hamilton also worked at home, where Betsey, when she was
present, still helped at the copying. Neither of them cared for
the new capital city. ". . . Philadelphians have no great gayety
in their dress," noted James Kent, who visited there in 1793.
"The Quakers, who compose a large part of the city, probably
give a tincture to their manners. Their obstinacy and bigotry
are very manifest. . . ."

However, there were attractions for Kent that were never
mentioned by the Hamiltons. "I visited the celebrated Museum
of Peale," he wrote; "the principal attractions were a baboon
monkey, a white owl, a white-headed eagle, a hawk and a cow
with five legs."

When Betsey was in town she interested herself in charities,
with special attention to the refugee families from France and

French possessions. When her husband went into society it was often at Presidential levees. "They are every other Tuesday from three to four P.M. You enter, make a bow; the President and the company all stand with their hats in their hands, and after exchanging a few words retire *sans cérémonie.*"

But President Washington was a different person when dining among friends. Hamilton would reminisce in 1800: "Genl. Washington notwithstanding his perfect regularity and love of decorum would bear to drink more wine than most people. He loved to make a procrastinated dinner, made it a rule to drink a glass of wine with everyone at dinner, and yet always drank 3 or 4 more glasses of wine after dinner according to his company."

Before Hamilton left New York the Trustees of Dartmouth College wrote "to express their congratulations at the prosperous state of our national finances under your wise direction. . . . They beg, Sir, your acceptance of the Degree of Doctor of the Laws of Nature and of Nations." It was a time of life (1788–92) when academic honors poured in upon him. He had left college without graduating, but Columbia now bestowed on him the double degree of Bachelor of Arts and Doctor of Laws. Princeton, Harvard, and Brown gave him honorary doctorates. He was elected to the St. Andrew's Society, the American Philosophical Society, the American Academy of Arts and Sciences.

He could run the country, and his wisdom was widely acclaimed. But he could not run his family, and he had not always been wise in picking candidates. General Schuyler, unwell and often absent, had not been a satisfactory senator, and a move by the Clintonians brought about his replacement by Aaron Burr. Angelica wheedled at Hamilton to appoint her father to the London embassy, a premature thought, as Britain had not yet agreed to a formal exchange of ministers. Moreover, as Hamilton replied, "There is no proof of my affection which I would not willingly give you, [but] our republican ideas stand much in the way of accumulating offices in one family."

Had he been wise to accept the Treasury post, for all its opportunity and excitement? It paid him $3,500 a year, and he had a proved earning capacity of $15,000 in his private practice. Troup and Lafayette had questioned the wisdom of his acceptance, and he had admitted to Morris, "I hazard much." The universal fate of finance officers was to get into trouble. Of the several Army quartermasters he had known, only the fantastically pure New Englander, Timothy Pickering, was scrupulous about the money that passed through his hands. The imprisoned Duer was not likely to be the only political financier to go wrong. Senator Schuyler and one of his sons were deep in speculation, as was John Church, and there would come a time, after 1789–90, when these family connections would bring Hamilton to a disagreeable conflict of interests.

Robert Morris, now a senator from Pennsylvania, served Hamilton as a standing example of a finance minister who, with the permission of a grateful government, openly commingled his public and private business affairs. Morris, who had come up from poverty, enjoyed his riches with engaging gusto, and as a generous and lavish host shared his wealth with his friends—including George Washington, who lived in Morris homes both before and after becoming President.

The grand manner became Morris, and only a few spoilsports begrudged his success. He retained L'Enfant to build him a marble palace in Philadelphia, and Angelica wrote Hamilton to send her its specifications, explaining that she wished to compare it with the palaces of Europe.

Hamilton had only the magnificence of the Continental Financier to exemplify for him what could be made of such a post as the Treasury; it would have taken the gift of second sight to know what ruin lay ahead for Morris. He borrowed money with both hands and bought enormous tracts of land on credit. The future of the United States was so manifest that no investment was surer than land; but no calculation was less sure than the pace of onrushing history. War in Europe and on the seas, changing borders and cloudy titles, Indian uprisings and faulty maps, all could make it difficult for a heavy speculator to find ready cash for interest payments and pressing debts.

But nothing of an untoward nature had happened to Morris when he was there as a model for the new Secretary of the Treasury. Hamilton admired his rare genius for financial management. The younger man possessed the same unusual talent, but Morris's avarice was entirely absent from Hamilton's make-up. He liked what money could buy, and he enjoyed association with affluent persons. But the accumulation of wealth had no attraction for him, and his keen sense of personal honor removed the temptation to enrich himself in office.

In this he resembled Madison, who had a streak of the Southern puritanism that would show up later in such characters as John C. Calhoun and Robert E. Lee. When Madison needed money, he borrowed it without interest from an obliging lender, Haym Salomon, and he set rigid standards for the office he held. He had resolved early "never to deal in public property, and debts or money, whilst a member of a body whose proceedings might influence these transactions." Hamilton used similar language in his well-known letter to Henry Lee, who had naively asked for information "concerning the domestic debt. Will it speedily rise?"

Instead of taking offense, Hamilton answered Lee amiably (on December 1, 1789), as follows:

". . . you remember the saying with regard to Caesar's wife. I think the spirit of it applicable to every man concerned in the administration of the finance of a country. With respect to the conduct of such men, SUSPICION is ever eagle-eyed. And the most innocent things are apt to be misinterpreted. Be assured of the affection and friendship. . . ."

Something over a year after writing this letter, Hamilton was house-hunting in Philadelphia, and feeling the weariness of success. All of his Treasury plans were working out well. The negotiations with Beckwith were exhausting but rewarding. James Tillary, a Federalist, wrote from New York, "Long may you successfully fend off the Madisons of the South and the Clintons of the North. Good night & God bless you." That same month, January 1791, Hamilton published his intricate Report on the Mint, which had engaged him since April.

Now he was feeling the strain of a career, the loneliness of separation from his family, and the fear of making a misstep that would throw him at the feet of his enemies. It was easy to ask himself whether the satisfactions were worth the grinding travail. On the last day of January 1791 he told it all in a letter to Angelica in London:

"My official labors so far have not been unsuccessful though they have not issued exactly as I wished, but *it is said* much better than could reasonably have been expected. I look forward to a period, not *very* distant, when the establishment of order in our Finances will enable me to execute a favourite wish. I must endeavor to see Europe one day; and you may imagine how happy I shall be to meet you and Mr. Church there. God bless you. AH."

CHAPTER EIGHTEEN

The Affairs of Man

I

(February 1791)

Congressman Madison, still smarting from his defeat on assumption of state debts and discrimination in the matter of commerce, took fright over the National Bank bill that was submitted by Hamilton in December 1790. Madison had not signed himself "Yrs affectly" for more than a year. It was "Yrs. sincerely" on the rare occasions when he sent notes to the Secretary of the Treasury. A central bank, thought Madison, would add an impregnable turret to the monarchical castle of Federalism.

The Federalist party, Madison declared, consisted of "those . . . who are more partial to the opulent than to the other classes of society; and [have] debauched themselves into a persuasion that mankind are incapable of governing themselves. . . ." Federalists believed, he wrote, that the "stupid, suspicious, licentious" people could pronounce "but two words—Submission and Confidence."

Madison went to the House floor on February 2 to oppose the Bank bill. As everybody knew, he had attended every session of the Federal Convention. Not only was the Constitution silent on banks, but he "well recollected," Madison said, "that a power to grant charters of incorporation had been proposed . . . and rejected." Under the General Welfare clause, Congress could do many things for the people, but founding a bank was not one of them. "Reviewing the Constitution," Madison declared with authority, ". . . it is not possible to discover in it the power to incorporate a bank."

Perhaps not. But "unconstitutionality" was a new and awkward term. Madison feared another speculation spree if the bank were authorized, but others did not find the smell of money unpleasant. After the Senate, with little debate, had agreed to the bill, the House voted for it, thirty-nine to twenty, with most of the opposition coming from the agrarian South. So now the measure would stand or fall on the decision of one man, the President, who could give or withhold his signature. Washington wrote to Hamilton:

"Sir, . . . The Constitutionality of it is objected to. . . . As a means of investigation I have called upon the Attorney General of the United States. . . . His opinion is that the Constitution does not warrant the Act. I then applied to the Secretary of State for his sentiments. . . . These coincide with the Attorney General's. . . . I now require, in a like manner, yours. . . ."

The President enclosed Randolph's and Jefferson's opinions with his forwarding note. He did not say so, but he had asked Madison to draft a veto message. Hamilton had three of the great Virginians against him, and George Washington leaning their way.

Hamilton's opinion on the constitutionality of the National Bank runs thirty-three pages in his Collected Papers. The script was scratched and interlined with second-thought phraseology. It is incomplete, indicating that he may have dictated some passages from notes. "I sat up all night, and copied out his writing," Betsey told a visitor to her Washington home in 1853.

As Hamilton bent to his task, his first act was to study with the utmost concentration the opinions of Madison, Randolph, and Jefferson, all lawyers. He did not have access to Madison's proposed veto message, but it was a digest of ideas already expressed in debate. Madison had written for the President to say:

"I object to the bill because it is an essential principle of government that powers not delegated by the Constitution can not be rightfully exercised; because the powers proposed by this bill to be exercised are not delegated; and because I cannot satisfy myself that it results from any expressed power by fair and safe rules of implication."

As Hamilton mulled over Madison's objections, he must have remembered the Constitutional Convention with General Washington, silent but ever-observant, presiding through those long hot summer days. The General had come to Philadelphia only for one reason, as Hamilton knew well; and the reason was that Washington felt the states needed a strong central government to keep their freedom. Hamilton felt that the President would not believe the new Federal government to be as feeble as Madison contended. It could not be weaker than the Confederation which had chartered the Bank of North America, or the New York legislature which had incorporated the Bank of New York. The states' rights doctrine did not hobble the Constitution to this extent.

Madison's tiptoe caution seemed nonsense to Hamilton as he thought the matter through. In every covenant, such as the Constitution, there were implied powers as well as expressed powers. These implied powers could be directed by Congress to the act of chartering as well to any other activity. The only question, Hamilton believed, was whether the charter "had a natural relation to . . . the lawful ends of government." He asked, for example: Did the Constitution empower Congress to erect a corporation for policing this city of Philadelphia? No. For a city police force was not a national purpose. Did the Constitution permit erection of a corporation to collect taxes and to regulate trade? Yes. "Because it is the province of the Federal government. . . ."

Hamilton turned to the opinion of the Attorney General. Randolph was far less forceful than Madison. The Attorney General's argument acknowledged that only one section of the bill—"the clause of incorporation"—could be thought a violation of the Constitution. Thus, if Hamilton could blast this objection, he would demolish the President's reliance on the opinion of the Administration's ranking lawyer. He set out to do so:

"A strange fallacy seems to have crept into the manner of thinking & reasoning upon the subject. . . ." In Roman law, he said, a corporation was "a voluntary association of individuals at any time and for any purpose." The English usage connoted a group appointed to act for a larger number of persons. It could not be logically argued that the United States was without the sovereign power to appoint directors to manage a national bank.

Hamilton was contending that the Constitution was susceptible of broad, general interpretations, limited only by the covenant's chief purpose, that of doing good to society. All three of the Virginians opposed to Hamilton were contending for strict construction. The most threatening challenge to Hamilton's, to Washington's, to the nation's requirement for a forceful Constitution came from Jefferson. The Secretary of State was the only one among the four involved statesmen who had not attended the Convention. Hamilton's 15,000-word Opinion contained a detailed rebuttal of Jefferson's. The following are the major points at issue.

Jefferson: "I consider the foundation of the Constitution as laid on this ground—that all powers not delegated to the United States by the Constitution, nor prohibited by it to the states, are reserved to the states or to the people. . . ."

Hamilton: "It was the intent of the Convention to give a liberal latitude to the exercise of specified powers."

Jefferson: "To take a single step beyond the boundaries thus specially drawn . . . is to take possession of a boundless field of power, no longer susceptible of any definition."

Hamilton: "The expressions in the Constitution have peculiar comprehensiveness. They say, 'to make all laws necessary and proper for . . . the foregoing powers and all other powers vested . . . in the government.' "

Jefferson: "No. It was intended to lace all laws up straitly within the enumerated powers."

Hamilton: "On the contrary, those statutes, especially those which concern the general administration of affairs of a country, its finances, trade, defence, etc., ought to be construed liberally in advancement of the public good."

Jefferson: "It would reduce the whole instrument to a single phrase—that of instituting a Congress with power to do whatever would be the good . . . and as [Congress] would be the sole judges of the good and evil, [they] would also have a power to do whatever evil they pleased."

Hamilton: "Does the proposed measure abridge the pre-existing right of any State or of any individual? If it does not, there is a strong presumption in favor of its constitutionality."

He could not tell if he had out-argued Jefferson. The decision resided only in the mind of one man, George Washington. Twice during the War, this man had been voted the powers of dictatorship, and had returned them with the passing of the crisis. He had rebuffed Hamilton's suggestion of turning the discontented Army into a political force. He had wrathfully turned aside a proposal that he become a king. No great Chief could have been more solicitous than Washington of the people's will and the people's counsels. If Washington believed that a National Bank would, in Jefferson's language, be a "prostitution," would overthrow "ancient laws" and enthrone "evil," there could be no doubt that the President would give his veto to the bill.

On the other hand, Washington had no superstitions about banks, and had owned stock in the Bank of England throughout the Revolution. He detested the insolvency and inflation that came from want of fiscal controls. Nobody had suffered more than he from the feeble, feckless Congresses before 1789. It was beyond all doubting that the President would sign the bill if he could do so in conscience, even though he was half-committed to the negative by having ordered Madison to prepare the veto message.

In the last part of his Opinion, Hamilton dropped the pleading style, and began to assert his points:

All government is sovereign. The right to erect corporations is inherent in that sovereignty. The chartering of a bank is not an extension of the Constitution, merely an affirmation of it.

How well he knew how to appeal to Washington. Revenue and armed services were matters the Chief understood. Hamilton ended his report by expressing the hope that the President would perceive that the Bank had a natural relation to "the power of collecting taxes . . . of regulating trade . . . of provid-

ing for the common defense," and that any "objections taken
to this bill . . . are unfounded."

II

(February–July 1791)

Washington signed the Bank bill on February 25, and when
the shares went on sale in Chestnut Street on July 4, a mob
of buyers "rushed in like a torrent" and within hours had
engulfed all the four thousand shares available to the public.
It was as if "a golden mountain had been kindled, emitting
from its crater a lava of the purest gold."

Henry Lee, riding home to Virginia, wrote Madison: "My
whole rout presented me one continuous scene of stock-gam-
bling; agriculture, commerce & even the fair sex relinquished,
to make way for unremitted exertion in this favorite pursuit."

This was how Hamilton had planned it. Profits were being
made. Money was coming to the Treasury. Jefferson and the
farming interest feared what would happen to agriculture, but
not Hamilton. He had a letter from his Edinburgh bookseller
that told him: "Scotland alone owes all its improvements in
Agriculture, Commerce & Manufactures to the Institution of
Banks." The American agrarians soon would see new markets,
at home and abroad, for cotton, flax, tobacco, iron, copper, lead,
fossil coal, wood, skins, hemp, wool, glass, gunpowder, sugar,
paper, and even silk, of which "some pleasing essays are making in Connecticut."

The same letter entreated him to establish "bounties to Emi-
grants," so that "hard-wrought, half-fed inhabitants of
Europe" could come to the flourishing young nation. Recently
the brig *Havannah* from Ireland had brought 175 "manufacturers and farmers . . . from the oppression of Europe to settle
in this free country." Hamilton favored liberal immigration
policies, to attract both laborers and capitalists.

It would take a while for Americans to accommodate themselves to the convenience of banking. "In 1791," wrote a lawyer
of the time, "in most of the States a bank-bill had never been
seen. Beyond the mountains in the districts of Kentucky and

Tennessee, military warrants and guard certificates, horses and cows, oxen, cow-bells, and acres of land, constituted the money. . . . In western Pennsylvania whiskey was the circulating medium. In the South, every merchant and planter so fortunate as to have coin kept it securely locked in strongboxes in his own home. . . ."

The Secretary braced himself against the shock of transition. There was street-talk in the capital city. People were saying, "Bank scrip is getting so high as to become a bubble. . . . 'Tis a South Sea dream. . . . There is a combination of knowing ones at New York to raise it as high as possible by fictitious purchases." Enough of this was true to warrant countermeasures, and the surge of investment must be controlled. He had a way.

When Bank shares reached inflated prices, he went into the Treasury Department's Sinking Fund for $200,000, which was used to purchase stock and steady the market. He did not do this on his sole authority. It required action by the Sinking Fund Trustees, who were Jefferson, Adams, Randolph, Jay, and himself. He played Caesar's wife, exactly as he had promised Lee, by turning over his five shares in the Ohio Company to be evaluated by the Justice Department instead of his own department.

To be sure, there were rash speculators in the market, including some of his close friends—Duer and Macomb, Willing and Morris. But he did not approve of excess, and these friends were as subject as any others to the consequences of mistakes. " 'Tis time there should be a line of separation," Hamilton wrote, "between respectable Stockholders, and dealers in the funds, and mere unprincipled Gamblers. Public infamy must restrain what the laws cannot."

Rufus King wrote him that some of the losers and the fainthearted were spreading rumors against him. That was to be expected as mild periodic tremors shook financial centers, but Hamilton was not worried about such foes. He replied to King that "a bubble . . . is of all the enemies I have to fear . . . the most formidable." But there would be no Bubble. He was convinced of that, and events bore him out. King believed that the

discipline of the market would be instructive to amateur plung-
ers "and teach them contentment in their proper vocations."
Congressman Fisher Ames wrote from Boston that "all goes
well," adding:

"The people really prosper, and what is more, they know it,
and say it, and give credit to the General Government for the
change they have witnessed." Abigail Adams told her sister,
"Our public affairs never looked more prosperous." Jefferson
chimed in. "In general," he wrote in May '91, "our affairs are
proceeding in a train of unparalleled prosperity."

Prosperity! The word seemed on every tongue. The reality
was all about. It was spreading across the land, and President
Washington set out to see for himself. He left the capital in
April for a three-month journey through the Southern states.
He posted his itinerary with Hamilton, Jefferson, and Knox,
confident that his three Secretaries and the Vice President
could run the government in his absence. Britain and France
would be sending ministers in the autumn. The President had
reason to believe that America's foreign affairs were managed
as wisely as the domestic ones.

The time was approaching when the Chief must consider
whether to accept a second term. His illness in the summer of
1790 had forced him to think about a successor. Surely, that
person would come from among the surrogates whom Washington left in charge of the government during his absence. And
of these, the one Washington relied on most heavily was the
Secretary of the Treasury, whose skillful hand was in all four
departments and whose legislative program had succeeded in
every instance. There seemed to be nobody in sight who would
be able to beat Hamilton when the time came to choose a new
President—unless that impetuous man beat himself.

III

(May–December 1791)

Betsey liked Philadelphia summers as little as those of New
York City. At mid-May her indulgent and gouty father ("I have
hardly enjoyed a day without pain") wished "Eliza to let me

know when she would set out from Philadelphia, that I might engage a good and discreet master of an Albany Sloop to bring her to this place [with] all the children and their nurse." He begged Hamilton "to expedite her as soon as possible." No doubt the son-in-law was getting impatient at this presumptuousness. He could hardly call his wife and children his own.

He was "tired of living alone," he'd confessed in the previous hot summer, and now Betsey was leaving again just as they were changing houses once more. The only consolation was that an absent wife might give a man more time to read. The formidable Mrs. Mercy Warren sent him a volume of her poems, and he acknowledged gallantly, "Madam— . . . Not being a poet myself, I am in less danger of feeling mortification at the idea, that in the career of dramatic composition at least, female genius in the United States has outstripped the Male."

He also had a letter from James Riverton, printer and bookseller:

"I have now the Satisfaction to announce the Arrival of the first Volume of Hawkesworths Narrative, and the three least Volumes of Cooks Voyages, together with a large folio Volume of Chartes & Copper Plates applying to them; these, I trust, will serve to perfect the incomplete Set You had from me, previous to your Removal to Philadelphia."

These were splendid acquisitions for his library. Hawkesworth was the explorer of the southern hemisphere, and Captain James Cook's *A Voyage to the Pacific Ocean* was regarded in Europe as a masterpiece. He subscribed to the French journals *La Chronique Mensuelle, Le Trône Mensuel,* and *Journal Étoile.* He was improving his knowledge of French as late as 1794, with the aid of a tutor, M. Dornat. But he could not give all his leisure time to reading. Shortly before Betsey and the children were to depart, a woman called at the house and "asked to speak with me in private."

"I attended her," he recalled, "in a room apart from my family. With a seeming air of affliction she informed me that she was a daughter of a Mr. Lewis, sister to a Mr. G. Livingston of the state of New York, wife to a Mr. Reynolds . . . who for a long time had treated her very cruelly, had left her to live with another woman . . . desirous of returning to her friends, she had not the means; that knowing I was a citizen of New York, she had taken the liberty to apply to my humanity for assistance."

Such appeals were not unusual, as the Secretary of the Treasury was surmised to be wealthy. Actually he was so out of pocket at that time that, though he gave five pounds toward the burial of an old soldier, he also allowed some good friends to make advances on his large obligations. Robert Troup wrote from New York, on June 15:

"Your bill for 200 dollars was presented to me . . . & I paid upon being presented. You need make no arrangements for the repayment of this money. . . . I entreat you at all times without the least hesitation to make use of me as you please. It is amongst the pleasures I value most for me to contribute to your convenience, to your fame, or to your happiness."

Hamilton was equally generous when he had money to lend. "This letter . . . incloses 200 Dolls which I have been indebted to you for a most unconscionable length of time," James Tillary wrote to him on January 14, 1793. "You lent me some money to serve me at a time when an act of friendship had embarrassed me, & I now return it to you with a thousand thanks, the only interest I shall offer at present."

So open-handed in private finance was the Secretary of the Treasury that McHenry said to him of Betsey, "She has as much merit as your Treasurer as you have as Treasurer of the wealth of the United States." But having no money on him when the woman called, Hamilton agreed to get a banknote later and sent it to her address, 154 South Fourth Street. She departed, but the presence of Maria Reynolds stayed behind.

"This woman was common and sordid, but she was young and handsome . . . at once designing and seductive," Mrs. Atherton would explain in her biography of Hamilton; and she had just met a man "accustomed to easy conquest." When night fell his mood was such that he carried the banknote to her address. "Some conversation ensued from which it was quickly apparent that other than pecuniary consolation would be accepted."

Welcomed to Maria's bed on the first day of acquaintance, Hamilton confessed afterwards, "I had frequent meetings with her, most of them at my own home, Mrs. Hamilton with her children being absent on a visit to her father."

Thus began for the left-behind husband a voluptuous summer. But he did not neglect the absent Betsey. "I am again, my beloved Betsey, in the hot city of Philadelphia; but in good health," he wrote on July 27. "And you may depend I shall take all care in my power to continue so. . . . I have been to see your new house & like it better than I expected. 'Twill soon be ready and I shall obey your orders about papering."

After a while Maria confided that her husband wanted a reconciliation, and "I advised to it," Hamilton remembered. He also agreed to interview James Reynolds at the Treasury Department on Maria's word that "he could give information respecting the conduct of some persons in the department which would be useful." When Reynolds showed up, he said that Duer, the former assistant, had slipped him a "list of claims," useful in speculation. Since Duer had already resigned, Hamilton thought the information "was not very important—yet it was the interest of my passion to appear to set some value on it."

Fortunately Reynolds went off on a trip to Virginia, and "intercourse with Mrs. Reynolds continued," as did correspondence with Mrs. Hamilton, to whom on August 2 he wrote:

"I thank you, my beloved Betsey, for your letter announcing your safe arrival; but my satisfaction at learning this has been greatly alloyed by the intelligence you give me of the disposition of my darling James [their son]. Heaven protect and preserve him."

The other James, Maria Reynolds' husband, returned and "asked employment as a clerk in the Treasury Department." This put the deeply involved Secretary in a quandary. "The situation of the wife would naturally incline me to conciliate this man . . . but the more I learned of the person, the more inadmissible his employment in a public office became."

He would not hire Reynolds, and he wanted to break with Maria. It was the only way out, "yet her conduct made it extremely difficult to disentangle myself. All the appearances of violent attachment and of agonizing distress at the idea of relinquishment were played with an imposing art. . . . My sensibility, perhaps my vanity, admitted the possibility of a real fondness, and led me to adopt the plan of a gradual discontinuance. . . ."

While he pursued this disengagement plan, the good news came from Albany "that my dear James was better. . . . Never forget for a moment the delight you will give me by returning to my bosom. . . . Dear Betsey—beloved Betsey—Take good care of yourself." This was written in early August; Betsey was due home the first of September. On August 21 he declared that his concern for her health "will reconcile me to your staying longer. . . . But I do not believe that I shall permit you to be so long absent from me another time."

Autumn days came, his wife returned, and now it was more convenient to meet Maria in upstairs tavern rooms. Christmas approached, and to his dismay there arrived a note from Maria. Her husband had learned all about them! "Mr. has rote you this morning . . . and he has swore that If you do not answer . . . he will write Mrs. Hamilton. . . . I am a Lone and I think you had better come here. . . . Oh, my God. . . ."

Reynolds sent the accusing letter, and they met several times to negotiate. Hamilton was noncommittal on the charge, and offered him employment "as far as it might be proper"; then it was Reynolds who was noncommittal. They met again at the George Tavern, and Hamilton told him ". . . I was tired of his indecision, and insisted upon his declaration to me explicitly what it was he aimed at." On December 19 Reynolds sent another note:

"Give me the sum of a Thousand dollars, and I will leve the town. . . . I hope you won't think of my Request is in a view of making Me Satisfaction for the injury done me . . . there is nothing that you Can do will Compensate for it. . . ."

Hamilton paid this first blackmail demand in two installments.

IV

(April–May 1792)

Madison that spring was spending an inordinate amount of time in New York City. One purpose was to obtain the services of a writer for an anti-Federalist newspaper to be established in the capital. Madison was serving as the emissary of Jefferson. Three days after Washington's signing of the Bank bill, the Secretary of State had invited Philip Freneau, Madison's classmate and "poet of the Revolution," to leave the New York *Daily Advertiser* and take a job at $250 a year as translator for the State Department.

Freneau, failing to catch Jefferson's drift, declined the invitation. He did not know that the clerkship, at a pittance, was to be a cover. The main purpose of his moving to Philadelphia would be to edit the *National Gazette.* Madison explained this to Freneau who, in May, found himself with Madison and Jefferson at the Elsworth boarding house.

One reason why the Secretary of State wanted to control the *National Gazette* was that the Secretary of the Treasury controlled the *Gazette of the United States.* Hamilton had also obtained a New York editor, John Fenno, and was supplying him patronage through the printing for the Treasury and Senate. Two papers called *Gazette,* and two editors whose names began with F and sounded so alike, might be confusing, but there was nothing unclear about the political confrontation between the two secretaries.

Each was now the recognized leader of a "faction," or political party. And 1792 was a Presidential election year with the distinct probability that Washington would leave the office open. Indeed, by May 5, that was all but certain when the President sent for Madison and told him, in the latter's words, that "having some time ago communicated to me his intention of retiring from public life on the expiration of his four years, he wished to advise with me on the mode and time most proper for making known that intention." He asked Madison to write a farewell address.

The President had spoken also to Hamilton and Knox, and Hamilton reacted as Americans commonly do at a scent of the Presidency. He attacked his chief opponent. Hamilton jotted down, in the third person, that Jefferson saw him as "a formidable rival in the competition for the presidential chair . . . and therefore the sooner he can ruin him the better. . . ." Also, Hamilton recalled Jefferson's behavior at the time when Washington was near death two years before. "That melancholy circumstance suggested to him the possibility of a vacancy in the presidential chair, and that he would attract the public attention as a successor to it were the more popular Secretary of the Treasury out of the way."

Hamilton evidently intended having this published in the *Gazette of the United States* for national distribution, but thought better of it. He was not really "popular," just successful. Debt-funding and central banking were not activities that endeared him to the people. His lengthy Report on Manufactures in December 1791 actually alienated some, because it challenged agriculture as the sole way of American life.

Although the Report was widely discussed, there is some doubt as to whether it was widely read even after it became famous with scholars. In the 1920's Gertrude Atherton tried to study it in published biographies of Hamilton. "To put it plainly I couldn't understand a word; they might as well have been written in Chinese." But when she turned to a library copy of the original, "I had no difficulty. . . . Every word was like a wingéd arrow." If Hamilton had had a political platform it would have been this Report and these items from it would have been his principal planks:

Link machinery to agriculture. "Nations with both manufactures and agriculture are likely to possess more pecuniary wealth."

Institute government bounties. "The public purse must supply the deficiency in private resource."

Promote immigration. "Men reluctantly quit one course of occupation and livelihood for another unless invited to it. . . ."

Employ persons otherwise idle. ". . . women and children are more useful, and the latter more early useful, by manufacturing establishments."

Develop internal transportation, with roads and canals. "Of the former the United States stand much in need; for the latter they present uncommon facilities."

And, of course, introduce more banks, which have "a powerful tendency to extend the active capital of the country."

He rode out that spring among the purple and lavender iris,

which other travelers described though he did not, to inspect the new town of Paterson, New Jersey. This planned city was sponsored by the Society for the Establishment of Useful Manufactures. The state charter of the organization, called SUM, was drawn in Hamilton's handwriting. Major Pierre L'Enfant, architect of the projected Federal City, had drafted plans for "a cotton mill . . . the business of printing . . . spinning, weft and weaving . . . houses for the accommodation of workers." Legislation had passed in New Jersey to exempt these workers from military duties, and the investors from taxes, for ten years.

There was reality as well as a vision in SUM. Despite opposition, the Hamiltonian state was forming; it would be accepted. Regrettably, some reckless investors were drowning in the maelstrom of the stock market. However, a much larger number of small investors had advanced from the family chaise to the fashionable carriage. It was not an era in which great fortunes were made. The middle class increased, but the "triumph of American capitalism" awaited the nineteenth century. Hamilton knew there was no misery in America to compare with that among the lower classes of Europe, unless it was that of the black slaves under the Southern barons. He saw no threat to the national well-being, unless it lay in the continued hostility of the Secretary of State to the personality and the economic policy of the Secretary of the Treasury. Jefferson had stolen Madison's affections, and "aims with ardent desire at the Presidential chair," as Hamilton put it in a full-bodied letter dated May 26, 1792, to Colonel Edward Carrington of Virginia.

"I read him on the whole thus: A man of profound ambition and violent passions," he said of Jefferson.

V

(April–October 1792)

Hamilton should have smiled as he signed and sanded the Carrington letter. Pot was calling kettle black, one zealot was raging at the other's zeal. Federalist leader was charging Republican leader with engaging in party politics.

His friend, Gouverneur Morris, could see the humor of it, and sometimes joshed Hamilton about his partisanship. Aaron Burr, doubling that year as U.S. senator from New York and aspirant for the New York governorship, must have given a sardonic grin, for he was a party-switcher and an urbane cynic. But Hamilton and Jefferson were dead serious about it all. One philosophy or the other was to rule in America. One of these two irreconcilable parties was to guide the young nation after Washington stepped down. There was nothing amusing about it to the antagonists.

George Washington, in the judgment seat, never smiled over the enmity between his Secretaries, nor at their inconsistencies. He was the presiding angel, though not always objective. He saw that Hamilton was defending the regime, Jefferson attacking it. The General put on his spectacles and studied the two *Gazettes,* as well as other party organs. Beginning in April the Jeffersonian sheets exploited the people's normal spite against taxation. "The free citizens of America will not quietly suffer the *well-born few* to trample them under foot." There was a squib which declared that the debt-discharging funding system "is hereditary monarchy in another shape. It creates an influence in the executive part of the government. . . . It is the worst species of the *king's evil.*"

With the Administration getting the worst of the newspaper war, Hamilton considered what to do about it. Etiquette had its place. Niceties of conduct were all very well. But he had never cared for military staff work; he preferred combat. These were not mock battles in the two *Gazettes.* The future state of the Union hung on the outcome. Besides, Hamilton saw that Jefferson had a "pensioned tool," Freneau, who was a deadly satirist ("the First Lord of the Treasury," Freneau jeered), whereas Hamilton's own man, Fenno, was a well-intentioned dullard.

Assuming that Jefferson wrote or inspired the anti-Federalist *Gazette,* a trial of strength was in the making between the author of the Declaration of Independence and the author-in-chief of the Federalist Papers. Thereafter, beginning in July, Hamilton's *Gazette of the United States* began to whistle, swish, and boom with a series of editorials in a style that decapitated anti-Federalists several times a week. The author's true name was warranted to be on file, "if required." Such pseudonyms as American, Americus, Camillus, and the like would do to denounce Freneau and Jefferson. Both were in government pay, Hamilton wrote, and each was canine enough "to bite the hand that puts *bread in his mouth.*"

In September, the President intervened to prevent his Cabinet from blowing apart. He sent almost identical letters to Jefferson and Hamilton begging each to desist for the country's sake "whilst we are encompassed on all sides with avowed enemies and insidious friends." There was a war in Europe, an Indian massacre of nine hundred troups under General St. Clair in the Northwest Territory. "How unfortunate . . . that internal dissentions should be harrowing and tearing our vitals," the President exclaimed.

Neither secretary resigned, and neither recanted. But there was a third man, John Beckley of Virginia, clerk of the House, confidant of Madison and Monroe. Beckley closely followed all of Hamilton's activity, personal, political, and financial.

"His efforts, direct & indirect, are unceasing & extraordinary," wrote Beckley. There was incessant rumor of Federalist plots and irregularities at the Treasury, but Beckley thought he had something better than rumors.

"I think," he wrote, "I have a clew to something far beyond mere suspicion on this ground, which prudence forbids a *present* disclosure of."

Beckley was on the trail of Maria Reynolds.

CHAPTER NINETEEN

The Trials of Office

I

(December 1791–December 1792)

Hamilton was still going to Maria, here in this second summer of what he called his "indelicate amour." She was insatiable for him, and he admitted to being flattered. The variety of shapes which this woman could assume was endless. In one mood she would renounce her passion and set him free: "Yes Sir Rest assured I will never ask you to Call on me again. I keep to my Bed these two dayes and now rise from My pillow wich your Neglect has filled with the sharpest thorns. . . ." Then in another mood: ". . . all the wish I have is to see you once more that I may my doubts cleared up for God sake be not so void of all humannity as to deni me this last request. . . ."

She could not spell, but she could cast a spell of sorts: "My dear Col Hamilton on my kneese Let me Intreate. . . . oh I am distressed more than I can tell My heart Is ready to burst and my tears wich once could flow with Ease are now denied me Could I only weep I would thank heaven. . . ."

Man of business that he was, Hamilton filed her letters, as he did the receipts for $600 and $400 paid to James Reynolds in December '91 and January '92. All through the spring and summer, autumn and into winter, he continued his correspondence with James as well as Maria. At first it was hard to judge the character of Reynolds. Sometimes he wrote like a heartbroken husband who also was compassionate to the erring wife.

". . . it's Mrs. R. wish to see you, and for My own happiness and hers. I have not the Least Objection to your Calling as a friend to Booth of us, and must rely intirely on your and her honor."

Next, Reynolds would be in alarm over Maria's tantrums and

suicide threats and he would chide Hamilton. ". . . I do not
know what you think of me, but suppose yourself for a moment
in my setuation, that your wife whom you tenderly love should
plase her affections on another object, what would you do in
such a Case. . . ."

By June 1792, Reynolds was on rather amiable terms with
his wife's lover, and in an almost chatty letter asked for a loan
of three hundred dollars, with the assurance that "it will be
in my power to make it five hundred Before the Next week is
out." The Secretary pleaded that he didn't have it—his only
refusal—and Reynolds was back asking for fifty dollars toward
the end of the month. In August, the couple opened a boarding
house for the "genteel," and it required furnishing. "Now Sir,
if I can ask a favor once more for the loan of two hundred
dollars. . . ."

It was difficult to conduct the nation's business amid these
personal doings. Ames posted him a copy of a nettling satire
by Attorney General James Sullivan of Massachusetts, *The
Path of Riches,* but softened the sting with the comment, "You
have found the path for our Country, and it is advancing in it,
tho' you have not sought it for yourself." In January he heard
from New York of a plan to launch an institution called the
Million Bank. New Yorkers were making too much of a good
thing; two more banks were also being planned, the State Bank
and the Merchants' Bank. Hamilton took his usual stand for
fiscal moderation. He wrote Cashier William Seton, "These
extravagant sallies of speculation do injury to the Government
and to the whole system of Public Credit, by disgusting sober
citizens and giving a wild air to everything."

Also from New York came word in February of ominous
developments in the coming gubernatorial election. "On my
arrival here finding that a tide was likely to make strongly for
Mr. Burr," wrote Isaac Ledyard, "I grew more anxious. . . ."
This letter was delivered by Philip Schuyler, who traveled to
Philadelphia for consultation with his son-in-law. The Federal-
ist party must be planted firmly in their state, but first George
Clinton must be uprooted. They must decide whether Senator

Burr or Chief Justice Jay would make a better run against the Governor.

Another question in many Federalist minds was raised by James Watson. If Burr was thwarted, "will it not make him an ememy if he is not one now, and increase his enmity if he has any?" Troup, Hazard, Tillary, and Ledyard all feared for the Secretary if he opposed Burr, but Hamilton passed the word. A Federalist caucus nominated Jay, and Burr perforce withdrew.

Then there was the national economy, Hamilton's ward. The President kept inquiring about it among persons in the know. "They all agree that the country is happy and prosperous, . . ." Washington wrote from Mount Vernon; and then wrote again, in a letter marked "private" and signed with "sincere and affectionate regard":

"We have learnt . . . that you are in contemplation to take a trip this way. I felt pleasure at hearing it, and hope it will be unnecessary to add that it would be considerably increased by seeing you under this roof. . . ."

Many were invited to Mount Vernon (and many arrived uninvited); not many declined. "I have had it very much at heart to make an excursion to Mount Vernon, . . ." Hamilton answered. "But I now despair of being able to effect it. I am nevertheless equally obliged by your kind invitation."

Washington had written that the country was "prosperous," which was a commonplace word that summer of 1792. Not just a word, either, but a state of being that reached all areas of the country, all classes of society. In August, Tobias Lear reported from New Hampshire: "It is with pleasure I can inform you that everything in this part of the country wears the face of prosperity & contentment. The people appear to be quite happy under the present government, and speak of themselves as the most fortunate people in the world. . . . Not a man is unemployed unless he chooses to lead an idle life, and so few are in this class that they are in no repute."

In the flowery village on the Passaic River, the Society for the Establishment of Useful Manufactures had started a cotton factory which employed women and children as well as men. The industrial age was too far in the future for any questions about exploitation of factory labor to be raised. But the Indian tribes were an immediate problem, and Hamilton gave it more humane attention than did any other national figure. He wrote a passage into the President's November 1792 Address to Congress calling for "some efficacious plan . . . to protect them from extortion and imposition."

Two months later, January 8, 1793, Washington and Hamilton gave separate interviews to a man with a plan to help the Indians. He was the Reverend Samuel Kirkland, a Princeton graduate and a missionary to the Six Nations. Kirkland wanted to open a school that he named Oneida College, for the integrated education of white and Indian youths. After his interview with the Secretary of the Treasury, he wrote in his diary, ". . . Mr. Hamilton cheerfully consents to be Trustee of the said Seminary, and will afford it all the aid in his power. . . ." The school became Hamilton College.

II

(April–December 1792)

In Hamilton's possession was a confidential letter from Lord Hawkesbury, president of the powerful Board of Trade in London. "As long as Washington is head of the executive and the Federal party prevail, there will be no war with this country, as peace is the interest and wish of both governments."

The Secretary was often accused of assuming the interests of the Federalist party and the American Union to be one and the same—and he thought he had reason to do so. By doing some of Jefferson's work in diplomacy and keeping the foreign policy safely Federalist, he was healing wounds of the Revolution. And he believed that by persuading Washington to remain for at least some part of a second term, he would be serving the highest national cause. He wrote the President, ". . . your declining would be deplored as the greatest evil that could befall our country. . . . On public and personal accounts, on patriotic and prudential considerations, the clear path to be pursued by you will be again to obey the voice of the country which, it is not to be doubted, will be as earnest and unanimous as ever."

Hamilton was pretending to more confidence in a unanimous re-election than he actually felt. "While your first election was depending I had no doubt that you would see characters among the electors, who if they durst follow their inclinations, would have voted against you; but in all probability they could be restrained by an apprehension of public resentment."

He knew there were many more such "characters" now that the French Revolution had stirred up the American radicals. Besides, the Federalist party, keeper of the Union, guarantor of the peace, defender of Washington's reputation, was not so strong as formerly. Back in April, Clinton had narrowly defeated Jay in the disputed gubernatorial election. In Maryland, a Federalist member of Congress, John Mercer, accused Hamilton of trying to buy his vote for Assumption, and there was much correspondence about a duel. Valuable members of the party were dropping out of politics: Benson and Laurance of New York; Barnwell of South Carolina. In Pennsylvania the whiskey-making farmers were in a tax revolt that might require a military solution. Only George Washington could lead an expedition, and even he at the gravest risk to national unity.

"There would be a cry at once," the President wrote Hamilton. "The cat is let out; we now see for what purpose the Army was raised."

Hamilton drafted for the President a proclamation to the tax rebels, and it sufficed for a while. The Presidential race was crucial in every one of these crises. Washington would not declare himself, but his silence gave consent. Besides getting Washington unanimously re-elected, Hamilton had the anxious task of electing a suitable Vice President to stand behind a President who might not live much longer, and who in any case did not intend to stay in office for four additional years.

John Adams was difficult, but could probably be counted upon to defeat any of the three Republican aspirants to the Vice Presidency: Jefferson, Clinton, and Burr. All of these were unacceptable at a heart-beat's distance from the ailing sixty-one-year-old Chief, and Burr was unthinkable. Hamilton spread the alarm. "Mr. Burr's integrity as an individual is not unimpeached. As a public man he is one of the worst sort—a friend to nothing but as serves his interest and ambition. . . . In a word, if we have an embryo Caesar in the United States 'tis Burr."

Adams is "the man," wrote Hamilton. The Vice President "has his faults and foibles," he admitted. "Some of the opinions he is supposed to entertain, we do not approve—but we believe him to be honest, firm, faithful and independent—a sincere lover of his country—a real friend to genuine liberty. . . . No man's private character can be fairer than his."

One of the "foibles" of John Adams was his over-confidence, rooted in comical but deserved self-esteem. Hamilton wrote to warn the Vice President that Clinton is "your competition," and not to be lightly held. The prickly New Englander complained that he lost money in Philadelphia on his $5,000 salary, and much preferred living on his prosperous farm at Braintree. Hamilton respectfully urged him to return to the capital; ". . . it is the universal wish of your friends, you should be as soon as possible at Philadelphia."

Adams ignored the advice and stayed in the country. He was too proud to electioneer in any manner. Hamilton feared the race would be a near thing. Writing, conversing, advising, he fought the 1792 election contest harder than any of the candidates. In the event, the Electoral College gave Washington all of the 132 first-place votes. Adams defeated Clinton, seventy-seven to fifty-five, winning the second place.

III

(November–December 1792)

Even before the Electors cast their ballots, another accounting had to be faced. Reynolds was still marketing lists of soldiers with claims to military pay, and he had a partner in this enterprise named Jacob Clingman. They bribed a witness to give false evidence, and were arrested and held for trial.

Clingman raised bail and went for help to his employer,

Pennsylvania Congressman Frederick Muhlenberg, Speaker of the House and a Jeffersonian. Reynolds remained in jail, and got word to Oliver Wolcott, Jr., comptroller of the Treasury, who had brought the charges. Wolcott visited the prison, where Reynolds had a disturbing statement to make. "He affirmed he had a person in high office in his power, and had had for a long time past."

On November 13, Wolcott broke this news to Hamilton, who asked some anxious questions. Had Reynolds identified the person allegedly in his power? No, he hadn't used a name at first, but subsequently had said "that Wolcott was in the same department" as that person. This was enough "to leave no doubt that he meant Mr. Hamilton." Did Reynolds say what hold he had on the Secretary? Yes, he said that "Colo. Hamilton had made thirty thousand dollars by speculation, that Colo. Hamilton had supplied him with money to speculate."

There were several steps that could be taken at this point: drop charges against Reynolds; provide him with bail; get him out of town. A guilty Secretary might have followed some such course, and so would an innocent Secretary who wished to avoid unpleasant publicity. Had Reynolds become more specific? "He threatened to make disclosures injurious to the character of some head of a Department." At this point Hamilton ordered Wolcott "to take no step toward a liberation of Reynolds while such a report existed, and remained unexplained."

Hamilton had decided to ride out the storm. Nearly a month passed, and he hoped for the best if the case should come to trial. He did not know that in the interval Clingman had told Muhlenberg that Reynolds "had it in his power to hang Colo. Hamilton."

Muhlenberg was a just man, but a partisan politician. On December 12 he consulted with two fellow Jeffersonians, Representative Abraham Venable and Senator James Monroe, both of Virginia. These two went to the jailhouse to interview Reynolds. He repeated the accusations against Hamilton. So did his wife, that evening, when Venable and Monroe called at her home. Maria supplied some unsigned notes, which, she said, were Hamilton's, addressed to her husband.

Next day, December 13, Reynolds was not in his cell when Venable and Monroe came there for another talk. The case against Reynolds and Clingman had been dropped just the day before. Wolcott said the pair had agreed "to surrender the lists, to restore the balance which had been fraudulently obtained, and to reveal the name of the person by whom they had been furnished." Wolcott had cleared the release with Hamilton and the Pennsylvania authorities.

The three Congressmen were more suspicious than ever. They composed a letter to President Washington.

"We think it proper to lay before you some documents respecting the conduct of Colo. Hamilton in the office of the Secretary of the Treasury."

On second thought the Congressmen decided to give Hamilton a chance to explain. On the morning of December 15 they took their information to him. He told them he had the ability, "by written documents, to remove all doubt as to the real nature of the business." That night at his home, with Wolcott added to the gathering, Hamilton produced the Reynolds files. He was an adulterer, not an embezzler. He had broken the Seventh Commandment, but not the Eighth.

"We left him," the callers acknowledged in a joint memorandum drawn up by Monroe, "under the impression our suspicions were removed. He acknowledged our conduct toward him had been fair & liberal. He could not complain of it."

Two of them were apologetic for the intrusion, but Hamilton recalled how "cold" Monroe was at the parting. The Secretary had cleared his public honor; as for the rest—

"I had nothing to lose as to my reputation for chastity; concerning which the world had already fixed an opinion."

IV

(January–March 1793)

". . . I would not be fool enough," he had told Carrington, "to make pecuniary sacrifices and endure a life of extreme drudgery, without either opportunity to do material good or to acquire reputation."

Both the public good and his personal reputation were at stake at two night sessions of the House, February 28 and March 1. Galleries tossed with the gay colors of fashionable spectators who had come to attend the spectacular scene of the Secretary of the Treasury brought up for censure. The floor swarmed as never before. Visiting senators were there. House membership had been increased from sixty-five to one hundred five as a result of the 1790 census. The House of Representatives would decide whether or not Hamilton had abused his powers of office.

There was no doubt as to where the anti-Federalists found their leadership. Fisher Ames wrote in January: "Virginia moves in a solid column, and the discipline is as severe as the Prussian. Deserters are not spared. Madison is become a desperate party leader, and I am not sure of his stopping at any ordinary point of extremity."

Madison and Jefferson did not enjoy the open fight, but a fellow Virginian did. William Giles, untidy and loud, introduced nine resolutions, seven of them later found to be in Jefferson's handwriting. Giles would be floor manager of the attack, his second of the session. "*Hamilton delenda est*" was the anti-Federalist purpose.

The House wanted to examine records. Hamilton obliged *en masse* with sheaves of Treasury reports, dizzying columns of figures, extensions of remarks, rosters of persons paid salaries and indemnities. Nothing sufficed. The reams of data only perplexed and incited the anti-Federalists. At the outset of the inquest Giles had complained of "the embarrassments I have met with in attempting to comprehend. . . . These embarrassments have increased in proportion to the attention which I have bestowed on the subject."

It was thought that Hamilton would break under the strain. If the House went home without a vote of vindication, he would have to resign. No mortal could meet the ever-mounting demand, the pressure of deadline. Hamilton must crack, his foes believed; but they reckoned without the man. By laboring night and day, aided by Wolcott and other Treasury assistants, he brought forth still another mountain of documented rebuttal.

The accusers wanted to know how he ran the Treasury. Very well. He reported on "all unapplied revenues at the end of the year 1792 and on all unapplied monies . . . obtained by the several loans. . . ." as well as on "all public funds up to the end of 1792 and statement of what remains . . . on foreign loans . . . on loans negotiated . . . on revenues, appropriations, and expenditures. . . ." He delivered messages as to "the state of the Treasury at the commencement of each quarter during the years 1791 and 1792 and on the state of the Market in regard to the prices of stocks during the same years."

Amazingly the work was unmarred by haste. It was said that Jacques Necker, the famous French financier, could not match this American genius. "Even Necker's boasted account of the finances of France is inferior," declared a letter-writer to Fenno's *Gazette,* "although that was the result of long study and elaborate study, and Hamilton's the work of a moment. Poor fellow, if he has slept much these last three weeks, I congratulate him upon it."

But the anti-Federalists had come into court with a preconceived verdict. Jefferson drafted a crippling resolution for Giles to submit: "That the Secretary of the Treasury has been guilty of maladministration . . . and should, in the opinion of Congress, be removed from his office by the President of the United States."

Too strong by far, it was decided in Republican conclaves. If the House failed to concur, Hamilton would be cleared. Better to move more craftily at the same objective. Better to take advantage of calendar and clock. Adjourn, adjourn! Let the unresolved arithmetic fester in the public mind. The torment would drive Hamilton out of his senses. The President would ask for his resignation.

On February 27, in the shadow of the falling gavel, Giles sent up his bill of particulars. The Secretary "has violated the law . . . has deviated from instructions given by the President . . . omitted to discharge an essential duty in failing to give Congress official information in due time . . . did not consult the public interest . . . has been guilty of an indecorum to this House."

The final resolution, Number Nine, covered Jefferson's demand for censure and dismissal: "That a copy of the foregoing resolutions be transmitted to the President of the United States."

Hamilton's friends feared that Jefferson would kill him by harassment before Burr did so with a pistol. Some believed that his health was shattered by the mental exertion of nearly three weeks which climaxed in the night sessions. But against Madison and Giles, Hamilton had splendid Federalist debaters. The flamboyant, Jefferson-hating William Laughton Smith of South Carolina disparaged the charges. "There is present nothing . . . nothing that would sully the purest angel in heaven." William Vans Murray of Maryland, not always a Hamilton backer, came to his defense on these nights. Fisher Ames, ailing but ever loyal, called for facts, facts, facts. Where was the evidence of any crime?

Giles and Madison wavered; their supporters fled. No resolution got more than fifteen votes. The last four were abandoned. The House adjourned *sine die*. Hamilton stood vindicated.

V

(1793–1795)

Angelica held him captive, and so in a different way did Angelica's husband. When Hamilton became the Secretary of the Treasury, he turned over his law practice to Robert Troup, but remained the American agent for John Church.

In this capacity Hamilton processed many transactions and handled thousands of dollars for his overseas client. His books and correspondence do not show that Hamilton got paid for the work or enriched himself in any way. They do show that he borrowed heavily from Church and died in his debt; but the obligations were never treated as gratuities, and Hamilton also owed money to at least five other friends at his death.

Church was a secretive speculator whose explanatory letters are not extant. Some of Hamilton's correspondence, apparently relating to his work for Church, is missing. The Hamilton Papers, in a rare mood of insinuation, declare that "one can only surmise whether or not it was purposefully destroyed."

In the absence of contrary evidence, it is a permissible assumption that Hamilton minded Church's American business as a family obligation. The Schuylers and their interlocking relatives continuously exchanged favors and gifts. One of Hamilton's first cases was handled gratis for his mother-in-law. Angelica in London sent him books. General Schuyler contributed financial support and sent farm products for Hamilton's table. The circumstantial inference is that Hamilton could neither have refused to act for Church nor have charged for the services. It was all within the family.

Between 1791 and 1797, with Hamilton as *de facto* surrogate, Church worked in partnership with two men, Tenche Coxe and Robert Morris, whose financial reputations were not cloudless. As Hamilton's Assistant Secretary of the Treasury, later his commissioner of revenue, Coxe should not have speculated in land. There were laws against Federal officials using official information for private gain. William Duer was convicted under these statutes, but Coxe was not. Coxe was not considered dishonest, merely indiscreet. A volatile and winning person, he held financial positions under Presidents Washington, Adams, and Jefferson.

Hamilton's known dealings with Coxe centered on the loan of ten thousand dollars by Church to Coxe. The agreement was arranged by Hamilton. At one of several meetings with Coxe "it was verbally agreed that the Sum of 10,000 dollars should be forthwith invested in the purchase of lands in Pennsylvania on the joint and equal account" of Coxe and Church.

Hamilton delivered the sum "at different times" during 1793 on the understanding that the account would be closed, with "lawful interest," by December 31, 1796. Nothing untoward took place, though Hamilton found Coxe very mysterious and, at the end, very slow to settle up. However, Church was eventually paid in full.

Church also engaged in investment with Robert Morris, and did so through Hamilton while the latter was Secretary of the Treasury. Morris's land holdings and land claims went into the millions of acres, and his financial problems became virtually numberless. In May 1793 Morris purchased one hundred shares of bank stock from Church, and "in part payment for the said Bank stock," transferred some land to Hamilton, as

Church's agent. In the spring of 1797, after Hamilton had left the Treasury, Morris made a final report: "100,000 acres . . . mortgaged to Alexander Hamilton, for the use of John B. Church, to secure the pay of $81,679 . . . with interest, which I owed to him."

In addition to this, Hamilton loaned ten thousand dollars of Church's money to Morris in June 1794, and borrowed from another person to replace the sum. Although he dunned Morris for several years, Hamilton never recovered the loaned money. Coxe had a hard fight to avoid bankruptcy and Morris succumbed to total ruin. Morris had done so much for the country in its precarious years that he had a following of sympathizers when his luck went wrong. Washington made the gesture of taking dinner with him in the Prune Street debtors' prison where Morris was incarcerated in February 1798.

Taking into account Hamilton's close relations with Coxe and Morris, and the ferocious determination of the Republican investigators to incriminate him, the Secretary had to be lucky as well as innocent to escape serious damage. This may have been in McHenry's mind when he wrote, on February 17, 1795, a fortnight after Hamilton had left the Treasury:

"My dear Hamilton. . . . Few public men have been so eminently fortunate as voluntarily to leave so high a station with so unsullied a character and so well-assured a reputation, and still fewer have so well deserved the gratitude of their country and the eulogiums of history."

The best character reference for Hamilton is that none of his contemporaries seriously questioned his personal honesty. Madison, as an old man, in April 1831, virtually admitted that the several investigations of the Secretary were nothing but harassment.

"Of Mr. Hamilton I ought perhaps to speak with some restraint," he wrote James M. Paulding, "tho' my feelings assure me that no recollection of political collisions could control the justice due his memory. That he possessed intellectual powers of the first order, and moral qualities of integrity and honor in a captivating degree, has been decreed to him by a suffrage now universal."

PART THREE

HIS ONLY CLIENT WAS HIS COUNTRY

Hamilton was not a special pleader for the rich, constructing American institutions for the salvage and advancement of their claims. His only client was the entire country.
Broadus Mitchell: *Alexander Hamilton*

CHAPTER TWENTY

The Job Well-Done

I

(March–April 1793)

Washington's second inauguration was held quietly in the Senate chamber just three days after Hamilton's clearance by the House. Hamilton had reason for much satisfaction. His hard work had kept the Administration intact. His acquittal sent the opposition reeling home in confusion. Jefferson had said he would resign at the end of the year. Madison, as the Jeffersonian leader, had failed to destroy a party target. The Treasury and its Secretary's system were stronger than ever before.

Glasses were raised to toast him, as at Haut's Tavern in New York, where the toast was: "The Secretary of the Treasury—may his distinguished talents and integrity command universal respect." A tribute of a different sort entirely came from an unknown man of the people, Jonathan Ogden of New York—"Being a farmer, you will excuse incorrectness."

Ogden wrote that he had heard from many in his county and state "respecting your objects of revenue. I believe I speak safely when I say that not more than one person in five hundred disagrees in sentiment with the present plans. . . . These are the ideas of people universally here, and has no more acquaintance with your Self than I have. My sincere wish is that you may long continue to fill that august office you now occupy & your virtues be imbranced [sic] by those who labor to tarnish them—"

Hamilton endorsed the letter, "Answered April 1 with *thanks*." On July 13, another letter from another uneducated worker, John Walker, was sent him from London. "I Sir am a Callico Printer have been employ'd as Servant & Master in every department thereof above thirty years," wrote this stranger, who had read the English edition of Hamilton's *Report on Manufactures.* "I could not resist the immediate temptation of addressing myself to the Author of such critical and important Observation."

Walker wanted to immigrate, with his wife, daughter, and two sons, because "America appears to me, to be the only place in the whole world for the Protection of the Manufactoral Arts."

In Hamilton's mind, it could not be true that his policies were hurtful to the common people, or misunderstood by them. During his lifetime and afterwards, hasty and flippant opinions were given concerning Hamilton's regard for the populace. He stated it well in *The Federalist,* Number 71, and elsewhere. "It is a just observation that the people commonly *intend* the Public Good . . . and the wonder is they so seldom err as they do, beset as they continually are by the wiles of parasites and sycophants, by the snares of the ambitious, the avaricious, the desperate, by the artifices of men who possess their confidence more than they deserve it. . . ."

Historian Henry Adams, in a later generation, credited Hamilton with supreme contempt for the masses. "Compressing the idea into one syllable, Hamilton at a New York dinner replied to some democratic sentiment by striking his hand sharply on the table and saying, 'Your people, sir—your people is a great *beast.*' " But Adams was quoting a hearsay anecdote from a previous century. Even if authentic, the story showed Hamilton talking about generics and not persons. It was the human race, not any specific segments of it, that sometimes dismayed him. He had notorious quarrels at the top level of American society—with the first five Presidents of the United States, for example—but there is no record that he ever spoke rudely to a humble man or woman.

On the contrary, there are examples of his marked consideration toward persons of lesser social rank. On October 11, 1780, writing to Laurens about Benedict Arnold's treason, he recounted how André, the British spy, had attempted unsuccessfully to bribe three American militiamen to release him, and he scathingly compared the traitor Arnold to these rural soldiers.

"They rejected his offer with indignation; and the gold that could seduce a man high in the esteem and confidence of his country, who had the remembrance of past exploits, the motives of present reputation and future glory to cloak his integrity, had no charm for these three simple peasants, leaning only on their virtue and an honest sense of their duty. While Arnold is handed down with execration to future times, posterity will repeat with reverence the names of Van Wert, Paulding and Williams."

And on June 27, 1804, while exchanging dueling correspondence with Aaron Burr, Hamilton "was consulted by a poor illiterate man," and wrote to the man's employer, P. G. Stuyvesant: "Dear Sir: I should like to see you on the subject of a poor fellow, Peter Drinker, who says he has been employed by you, and appears unfortunate, which is his title to my attention. Yours truly, A.H."

Stuyvesant related: "I reproved the man for the freedom in which he had indulged and undertook to convince him of the impropriety of troubling General Hamilton with his concerns. His reply was,

" 'Oh, no, sir, he treated me very kindly.' "

By reading the straight Hamilton, instead of strictures about Hamilton and truncated quotations from his writings taken out of context, the generations may know the man. He believed in original sin, and in religious canons and civil laws to control it. "Take mankind in general, they are vicious, their passions may be operated upon . . . and it will ever be the duty of a wise government to avail itself of the passions in order to make them subservient to the general good." This is a restatement of his lifetime belief in the primacy of self-interest. He thought it should be harnessed to turn the wheels of government.

His opinion of "mankind" applied to the general run of men and women. "My Dear Girl," he had written Betsey in 1780, "there are very few of either that are not very worthless. You know my sentiments on that head." He believed that there was "universal venality in human nature," not confined to plebeians; and also that "there is a portion of virtue and honor among mankind." It was this small deposit of decency that made a republic the finest form of government, to Hamilton's mind, and a democracy the worst. A republic enabled the public to elect "a few choice spirits" as guardians of its interests. In stressful conditions the guardians, or representatives, provided "time and opportunity for more cool and sedate reflection."

Hamilton's enemies, then, were not the people, but the politicians who esteemed themselves the people's spokesmen, often for deceitful and specious reasons. For example, Southern politicians objected to one of Hamilton's luxury taxes, the one on horses and carriages, which they contended was discrimination against agrarians. In presenting this legislation, Hamilton specified, "Tax on horses kept or used for the purpose of riding or of drawing any coach, chariot, phaeton, chaise, chair, sulky or other carriage for the convenience of persons." He explicitly exempted "all horses usually or chiefly employed for the purposes of husbandry, or drawing wagons, wains, drays, carts or other carriages for the transportation of produce goods, merchandise and commodities or for carrying burthens in the course of trade or . . . military service of the United States." By levying a tax of one dollar per carriage horse on the one-horse family, and raising the tax by $2.50 per horse for each additional animal up to four, Hamilton was raising revenue from well-to-do families that kept large stables for traveling in private vehicles (or riding to hounds), while sparing the poor man whose horses supported the family by farm work or hauling. The tax applied equally to North and South.

Then there was the matter of the French debt, which the Treasury was paying off by agreed-upon installments. The Revolutionary Directory in Paris wanted the installments speeded up to help it pay for damages resulting from the Negro rebellion in Santo Domingo. Hamilton thought it unwise to accommodate the Directory. He argued that if the monarchy were restored, the United States might have to pay twice. But Jeffersonians interpreted this as proof that Hamilton opposed the cause of non-monarchical governments.

His best friends understood him. Elias Boudinot wrote on

March 26, referring to Hamilton's vindication by the House: "After passing through a fiery ordeal, I suppose you have a few moments to breathe a milder air. The part the country in general take in your triumph over the malicious and envious—enemies to the Government as well as yourself—must convince you that the influence of those beings extends but a little way out of their own narrow circle. . . . "Do not let those pompous, high-minded *would-be Kings,* though under the false garb of Republicans, draw your attention from the great objective; but look forward to those tranquil days when this child will be an Hercules. . . ."

There were those who, disagreeing in politics, still honored his motives and loved him. To Governor Light-Horse Harry Lee, restless in peace and desiring to offer his sword to Revolutionary France, affection for Hamilton overrode all. "Knowing you as I do," he wrote, "I should ever give your political conduct the basis of truth, honor & love of country, however I might have differed with you on some measures. . . ."

Hamilton appreciated this sort of masculine affection. It helped him to believe that the best people in America comprehended and shared his dream of a mighty nation, self-sufficient in agriculture and industry, bound to foreign nations by commercial treaties only, protected by vigorous men-at-arms such as Lee.

Ever since Yorktown, Hamilton and Washington together had been pressing Congress for a military Peace Establishment. State militia simply would not do, even to protect the frontier against the Indians. Congress agreed in principle to a regular force of five thousand, including cavalry and artillery; and now, with trouble threatened by both Britain and France, there must be a shipbuilding program too. Preparedness would cost money. That meant the usual outcry against taxation, but luckily there were men in sympathy with his efforts.

"You are, my good friend," Edward Carrington wrote on March 26 from Richmond, "too well acquainted with mankind, to expect that you are to proceed in an administration of an Office so efficacious in the operation of Government as yours, without being constantly exposed to attacks. All that you can do is to shield yourself, as you have done, against ultimate injury by the steady exercise of your best abilities, and manifesting in every act an integrity that even your enemies have not . . . ventured to call into question."

But in fact his integrity was always under attack, even after vindication. Truth was the best defense. He had asked Carrington to get "the final proceedings of the House of Representatives inserted into the most public and generally circulating paper of this place." Let Virginians read for themselves how Madison and Giles behaved. Carrington handled the matter in Richmond. He also sent the journal of Congress to Norfolk, Petersburg, Alexandria, and Winchester, "with a request through my friends at those places that they will be inserted in their papers, which will certainly be done."

Hamilton had women on his mind this spring. Girls, girls, girls—the subject of his earliest writing—managed to infiltrate the essays on foreign policy he was writing for his *Gazette*. He was trying to do a simple, explicit, patriotic article that would warn people not to take sides in the fracases of France and England, but Maria Reynolds and Angelica Church would not stay in the inkwell.

"A dispassionate and virtuous citizen of the UStates . . . will regard his own country as a wife, to whom he is bound to be exclusively faithful and affectionate, and he will watch with a jealous attention every propensity of his heart to wander toward a foreign country, which he will regard as a mistress that may pervert his fidelity, and mar his happiness."

Such "reflections," he declared, were suggested to him by a distressful tendency of persons to take the side of one or other of the foreign temptresses, France and Britain. "This effort is not prudent, is not commendable," he warned. All patriotic men "will scorn to stand on any but purely *American* ground." There were warhawks at large, but Hamilton was not among them. The French Treaty of 1778 required the United States to be a fighting ally, but Hamilton contended that this should not "uselessly expose the country to a great extremity" such as a war with England. By sound judgment based on love and fidelity to America, "we shall . . . avoid the terrible calamities of War. Which that God may grant, must be the fervent hope of every good Citizen!"

II

(April–August 1793)

He had appealed to the people, and now he needed to hear from the party chiefs. "All the cry here is for peace," he wrote Senator King. "How is it with you?" He asked James McHenry for word from Maryland, an important shipping state: "What say your folks as to Peace and War in reference to the UStates?" He queried Chief Justice Jay: "Would it be well to include a declaration of neutrality?" He got opinions from Carrington in Virginia, and from Smith of South Carolina, who was traveling the backwoods of that state and Georgia.

"We must not get entangled in this mad War," answered King, and so said all to whom Hamilton had written. There had been ten years of peace since the Treaty of 1783. With Europe at war, trade was such that "it is as much as we can do to find dishes to catch the golden shower," a newspaper noted. Hamilton dreamed of another decade of peace with prosperity. Neutrality—but armed neutrality.

Girls were still on his mind when he wrote Carrington about Jefferson and Madison: "They have a womanish attachment to France and a womanish resentment against Great Britain." The two Secretaries were irreconcilable opposites. Hamilton was a compulsive worker; he wrote and worried through the heat of city summers while Jefferson took three-month vacations at Monticello. Jefferson dabbled in abstractions of human freedom; he confused the principles of the American Revolution with the bloody terror in France. "Would to heaven the comparison were just!" exclaimed Hamilton. Jefferson rarely consulted with George Hammond, the British minister, but he found satisfaction in the arrival of Edmond Genêt, the fiery emissary of the Tricolor. The young Frenchman reached Philadelphia in May 1793. In July he made the error of appealing over the head of President Washington to the American people, and Jefferson had to ask the French government to recall Genêt as its envoy. It was one of the shortest envoyships on record.

Meanwhile, on April 22, 1793, Hamilton had got his way again, and the President issued the Proclamation of Neutrality, though the actual word "neutrality" was omitted at the insistence of Jefferson, who thought the document pro-British. Hamilton had—or believed he had—a cozy understanding with Hammond that the Royal Navy would respect American innocent passage through the sea lanes.

"Intelligence indicates thus far, an *unexceptionable* conduct on the part of the British Government toward the vessels of the UStates," Hamilton had written Washington at Mount Vernon early in the spring. But hardly sooner was the Neutrality Proclamation signed than the British ministry issued Orders in Council. English captains were "to stop and detain all vessels . . . bound to any port of France . . . except the ships of Denmark and Sweden."

Hamilton was outraged at what he considered a broken promise to exempt American ships. Hammond, in some alarm, wrote to London: "I have just had a conversation with Mr. Hamilton who regards it as a very harsh and unprecedented measure . . . particularly directed against the commerce and navigation of the United States." Soon there were reports of American ships taken, two hundred fifty in all before it ended; of American seamen captured and imprisoned, including the gallant Joshua Barney. Something had to be done. A special mission must be sent to London at once. Hamilton very much wanted to make that trip himself. On August 15, a dear friend had written him from the British capital:

" 'Are you too happy to think of us?' Ah, *petit Fripon,* you do not believe it. No, I am not too happy; can I be on this side of the Atlantic? Ask your heart and read my answer there. . . . You and Betsey in England. I have no idea of such happiness, but when will you come, and receive the tears of joy and affection? Your devoted Angelica."

III
(June 1793—June 1794)

As the war danger mounted, Hamilton saw an advantage in it. His chances of pressing military legislation and a shipbuilding program through Congress were much improved. England would understand the language of strength. That is what he would talk if dispatched to London. He did not doubt that the Federalist leaders—King, Ellsworth, Ames, Jay—would propose him as the representative, but the choice would rest with Washington, and that was a reason for finishing up his work at the Treasury.

"Considerations relative both to the public interest and to my own delicacy," he wrote the President on June 21, "have brought me after mature consideration to a resolution to resign the office I hold toward the close of the ensuing Congress."

Washington was not pleased, but he could scarcely object. The President himself had discussed stepping down and had received a letter from Gouverneur Morris, written that June, reminding him: "It is time enough for you to have a successor when it shall please God to call you from this world's theatre. . . . And do not imagine, my dear sir, that you can retire—though you may resign."

The same might have been written of Hamilton. He would not quit in the teeth of crisis. He would always be on call. There was much that needed his judgment this summer. If the Secretary's mind wandered from the menace of Britain and France, it lighted on Indian uprisings in Georgia and Ohio, on rumors of Spanish activities in the Mississippi Valley, on reports from Governor Clinton that Lord Dorchester was stirring up trouble from Canada.

Domestic unrest was also alarming. As Ames said, "the town is less Frenchified" with Genêt out of circulation. But Democratic Clubs, modeled on the Jacobin cells of Paris, were springing up in American cities. Merchants were grumbling and patriots angry at the British insolence.

In July 1793, deaths from a mysterious cause occurred in

Water Street, Philadelphia, and soon spread to more sanitary
parts of the city. An epidemic was acknowledged by the *Daily
Advertiser* on August 24, and identified by Dr. Benjamin Rush
and the College of Physicians as "billious remitting yellow fever." Dr. Rush, signer of the Declaration and local sage of
medicine, put out instructions: avoid fatigue, drafts, intemper-
ance; burn gunpowders to cleanse the air; take vinegar and
camphor.

Knox and Randolph were gone. Jefferson moved up his announced date of departure. President Washington sent the
Hamiltons a dinner invitation and learned that the Secretary
was down "with the reigning putrid fever." Betsey, Hamilton
informed him, was "in the disorder, contracted from me."
Washington wrote again, signing himself "always and affctly."
Martha wrote Betsey, "You have my prayers and warmest
wishes. . . ."

Jefferson diagnosed Hamilton's illness as nothing but fright.
He wrote Madison: "A man as timid as he is on the water, as
timid on horseback, as timid in sickness, would be a phenome-
non if courage of which he has the reputation in military occasions were genuine." The letter to Madison, one noncombatant
to another, was a final shot as Jefferson took off for Monticello.

Hamilton had sent his children off to their grandparents, and
was making a decision that probably lengthened his and Betsey's lives. With deaths in Philadelphia at one hundred a day,
he judged there must be something wrong with Dr. Rush's
prescription. Hamilton sent to New York for Ned Stevens, now
a physician, who was there on a visit. His old friend recommended hot rum and cold baths, the "West Indies treatment,"
very different from Rush's regime; and the Hamiltons quickly
recovered.

Although a notice in the *Federal Gazette* spoke of "the good-
ness of the plan recommended by Dr. Stevens," Rush wrote
Boudinot that "Colonel Hamilton's remedies are now as un-
popular in our city as his funding system is in Virginia and
North Carolina." Dr. Rush was convinced that Dr. Stevens, a
Federalist, had mixed medicine and politics.

Weak and shaken, Hamilton on September 11 passed along

his experience in a letter to the College of Physicians. He attributed his recovery, "under God, to the skill and care of my friend Dr. Stevens, . . . who has had the advantage of much experience both in Europe (having been in Edinborough some years since, when the same fever raged there) and in the West Indies where it is prevalent."

He sent the information and Stevens' Philadelphia address to Dr. John Redman, the medical school's president, who got Stevens to write a paper on the disease and its control. "Colonel Hamilton's letter has cost our city several hundred inhabitants," was Rush's unshaken belief, not widely shared.

News of the Secretary's recovery brought the same sort of response as his earlier exoneration by the House. The Reverend Henry Vandyke of New Jersey offered thanks "to the Supreme Disposer of All Events for this fresh instance of His Divine Favor to these United States in sparing your life. . . ." Vicomte Louis Marie de Noailles, an émigré from the Terror, expressed *"la joie que vos amis auront eu de vous voir échappé aux dangers. . . ."* Benjamin Walker of New York warned, "For God's sake, or rather for our sake, take care of a relapse." Olney of Rhode Island said, "I most sincerely hope a life so distinguished and essentially useful to the nation (as yours has proved) may under Divine providence be very long preserved." He heard in a like manner from Light-Horse Harry Lee, from the Commander's secretary, Tobias Lear, and from the master and mistress of Mount Vernon.

It was worth the brush with death to receive such messages of the heart. The reunion with Ned Stevens invited reflections on his youthful desire for fame. Had the prize been worth the chase? If he had died of the fever, would the country have mourned? As if to answer that vain question, he learned that rumors of his death were going the rounds. It was like a dead man come to life that he read a letter from Tobias Lear, who was in New York after a trip through New England: ". . . the estimation in which they hold you individually has lately been proved by the deep regret & unfeigned sorrow which appeared on the report of your death—and the marks of joy & satisfaction exhibited when the report was known to be unfounded.

That you may be long preserved in health & usefulness to your Country is the earnest prayer of your fellow citizens."

As Hamilton's strength returned, he prepared to take Betsey to the Schuyler mansion. "This journey must be planned with perfect safety to myself and to *others*," he wrote, since there was much fear of spreading the contagion. First he sought "assurance" from his physician. Then he and Betsey tested their strength and took the air on two or three carriage rides near home. Their personal linen was thoroughly washed. They discarded summer clothing that had touched their bodies and took along only winter garb. Hamilton planned to leave behind servants and vehicles before entering Albany. "This detail is of a nature to remove from every reasonable mind all apprehension concerning us."

They set forth on Sunday, September 15, but that night at a New Jersey tavern they encountered fugitives who demanded that they be turned away. On the approaches to New York City they were halted by guards "with orders to send back every person coming from Philadelphia." There was no boat at King's Ferry, so that day they drove on to Newburgh, nearly sixty-four miles. They were several times forced to keep going until eleven o'clock at night. At the outskirts of Albany, September 23, they had to submit to physical examinations. "Yet with all this fatigue and embarrassment, Mrs. Hamilton and myself are at this moment in better health than before we were attacked by the disease which is the subject of so much alarm."

Hamilton complained to Mayor Yates about the officious city authorities who had overstepped "the rules of reason, moderation & humanity. They are not at liberty to sport with the rights and feelings of a fellow citizen." He was as indignant as General Schuyler, who heard reports that "when I embraced my daughter on her arrival . . . I put a sponge dipped in vinegar to my mouth immediately after, and then left the room and washed my face and mouth." The General also protested to the Mayor.

This visit to the well-loved mansion, the reunion with the children, began badly and turned worse for Hamilton. At Albany he received a dunning letter from Andrew Fraunces, son of Washington's former steward and a one-time Treasury clerk. Fraunces demanded payment from the Treasury Department on two warrants which he claimed to have purchased from the Confederation's board of treasury. Proof of ownership was lacking, but Fraunces contended that Hamilton had allowed a similar claim by a friendly officer, Baron Peter William Jacob Ludwig de Glaubeck, and would be playing favorites if he refused to pay this one. The matter was entirely unrelated to the Reynolds matter, except for an interlocking acquaintanceship between Reynolds, Clingman, and Fraunces, but it was all very upsetting to the Secretary.

He lashed out at Fraunces: "Contemptible as you are, what answer could I give to your last letter?" He also wrote to a morning and an evening paper in New York. "One Andrew G. Fraunces . . . has been endeavoring to have it believed that he is possessed of some facts of a nature to incriminate the official conduct of the Secretary of the Treasury. . . . The Public may be assured that the said Fraunces . . . possesses no facts of the nature pretended; and that he is a despicable calumniator."

Fraunces retorted in the *Daily Advertiser:* "Be pleased to inform your friends that if I am a *despicable calumniator,* I have been unfortunately for a long time past a pupil of Mr. Hamilton's—and that it remains to be proved whether I do honor to my tutor or not."

Health and temper did not much improve under such stress. Hamilton stated his intention to be back at work in something more than a fortnight, which meant spending only about ten days in Albany. But he would not mend that fast. He found it awkward to run his Department from a distance, since many papers required his signature. By mid-October the President at Mount Vernon was restive.

"The calamity which has befallen Philadelphia & seems in no wise to abate," he wrote, "renders it more essential than ever for the heads of Departments to assemble, that proper measures with respect to the public Offices & Papers may be adopted." He needed Hamilton's opinion on whether the Chief

Executive could properly call a special session of Congress in some place other than the capital. "Would you advise me in this predicament?"

Then, there was a dispute at SUM (the Society for the Establishment of Useful Manufactures) which Hamilton was called upon to mediate. L'Enfant had proved unsatisfactory as the architect and had been replaced by Peter Colt, engineer. The jealous quarrel fell into Hamilton's lap while he was attempting to recuperate. Indeed, the whole SUM enterprise was on the rocks, much to Hamilton's annoyance. A cotton gin, which according to its promoter "required only the assistance of children," didn't work. The machine came to naught, and even the patent was never issued. The cotton mill superintendent had spent a year's salary, advanced to him by Hamilton, and soon would be begging a loan.

On top of all, there were concealed tensions between Betsey's husband and Betsey's father; between the father and the grandfather of the Hamilton children. Schuyler, host and paymaster, was gracious and generous but sometimes interfering. He kept the children after their parents headed southward, and did not want to give them up. When the Hamiltons were resettled in Pennsylvania and asked for the children to be sent on, Schuyler resisted.

"I have concluded that it would be improper to accede to your wish," he told his son-in-law. He agreed conditionally to bring down the baby, John Church Hamilton, born the previous year, "but the others, we all agree, must remain until Spring." Schuyler had become the benevolent family despot. "The children . . . afford us so much pleasure and real satisfaction, that we should part with them with infinite reluctance. . . . You must not therefore insist upon depriving us of them. They all join us in love to you & Eliza."

By October 24 Hamilton could write from the country home outside of Philadelphia, "Exercise and northern air have restored us beyond expectation." He had several relapses that autumn, but his mind focused on two events of the winter.

In December he wrote Washington's message to the Third

Congress, calling for preparedness. Included was a bill to construct six frigates, at a cost of six hundred thousand dollars. In March Congress passed a military appropriations measure of $1,457,936, the biggest ever. The President and the Secretary thought it the best answer to British hostility, and those who charged Hamilton with being pro-British were confounded.

With important public business taken care of, Hamilton wrote to Speaker Muhlenberg. He demanded that "a new inquiry into his official conduct be instituted in some mode most effective for an accurate and thorough investigation." The former inquest, Hamilton stated, was concluded "decidedly in a manner most satisfactory to me," but it had started late in the session and he resented suggestions that there was not time for due examination. He wanted the House to put him thoroughly to the test. "And I may add that the more comprehensive it is, the more agreeable it will be to me." Hamilton was not behaving as if he feared what an investigation of his work for John Church might bring out.

The Jeffersonians reacted cautiously to the challenge. William Branch Giles introduced resolutions in the House but did not press them. He said "it might be deemed a violation of delicacy" to proceed until the complaints against Hamilton by Andrew Fraunces were examined. But on February 19 the House acted to condemn Fraunces and commend the Secretary. At last Giles called up his resolutions. Between March 1 and May 22, 1794, Hamilton made nineteen appearances before his examiners. The result was full clearance.

Relief and satisfaction flowed throughout the entire Federalist establishment. "The report of the Committee to Congress," wrote William Heth from Shillelah, Virginia, "has turned out precisely as your friends here had predicted—'The more you *probe,* examine & investigate Hamilton's conduct, rely upon it, the *greater* he will appear.' "

Jay wrote on August 16, 1794, from London: "I am happy to find by a New York paper that the result of the late inquiry into your official conduct is perfectly consistent with the expectations of your friends. . . . Mr and Mrs Church are out of Town. . . . She is certainly an amiable, agreeable Woman."

CHAPTER TWENTY-ONE

The Well-Named Conqueror

I

(1793–1794)

"How long, Dear Sister, are the best of friends to be separated?"

In writing to Angelica just after Christmas of 1793, Hamilton anticipated that he would "break the spell" that held him at Philadelphia. "Nothing can prevent it at the opening of the spring, but the existence or the certainty of a war. . . ."

Now, spring had come and with it more war clouds. In April 1794 the British minister, mindful of American indignation against the seizure of ships, met with Hamilton and attempted to explain. "I was, however, much surprised, . . ." he wrote later, "that [Hamilton] did not receive those explanations with the cordiality I expected. . . ." Instead, Hamilton "entered into a pretty copious recital of the injuries which the commerce of this country had suffered from British cruisers." He was willing to renew negotiations, but first there must be "indemnification for all American vessels condemned in the West Indies."

Minister Hammond pleaded the necessities of war. "Here Mr Hamilton interrupted me with heat." The wrongs suffered by the United States were known in England, and he predicted that "a . . . powerful party might be raised in that nation in favor of this country." It had happened during the Revolution. The allusion to Edmund Burke's defense of the American colonies shook Hammond with "astonishment." He wrote his government that this "most moderate of the American Ministers" was caught up in the popular rage against Britain.

This was not so, but with the country arming, Hamilton chose to talk back to the British in the strongest terms. Hard-language conversations at the top level furnished the best means of peace, he thought, and he regretted it when Congress barged into the dispute. Madison introduced a trade program that would penalize the British, so that "our country may make her enemies feel the extent of her power." Blunderbuss diplomacy, Hamilton felt certain, would lead to war. Better hurry and send an envoy to London.

Seldom did political policy so nicely coincide with personal desire. "My own hope of making a short excursion to Europe the ensuing spring increases. . . ," he wrote Angelica. "I shall have the happiness of meeting you once more. But will not a few months afterwards give us the pang of final separation? Let us hope for the best. Adieu."

All the Federalist leaders agreed on the man for the mission to London. "Who but Hamilton would perfectly satisfy all our wishes?" exclaimed Fisher Ames. "He is *ipse agmen.*" On March 10, Rufus King called a meeting "at my house . . . to confer on the course most advisable to pursue." Since Hamilton was the point of discussion, he was not present. King's mind was already made up. He wished that Hamilton might "speedily go" because "then there would be some hope of our remaining at peace." The caucus sent Oliver Ellsworth of Connecticut to express their opinion to Washington. The President agreed that "An abler and honester man they cannot find," but the House was still investigating him and perhaps Hamilton "did not possess the general confidence of the country."

A crushing verdict! All considered, this was the bitterest rejection of Hamilton's career. He longed for Angelica, wished to visit the Old World, wanted so much to play a direct part in foreign affairs. "I am heartily tired of my situation," he told Angelica, "and wait only the opportunity of quitting it with honor, and without decisive prejudice to the public affairs."

By mid-April the President had settled upon John Jay as his envoy. Hamilton did not yet know this when he wrote Washington to "drop me from consideration . . . fix upon another character." Chief Justice Jay, he continued, was "the only man . . . and him alone would it be advisable to send."

Jay sailed off from New York on May 12 before a thousand

cheering citizens, with letters of instruction from both Washington and Hamilton in his luggage.

II
(1794)

The President had nominated a cautious man instead of an impetuous one, a bland character instead of one who was rarely out of controversy. Moreover, he had been warned by Monroe and other senators against nominating Hamilton, and he could readily anticipate what the opposition press would say about the appointment of a "monarchist" to plead in a royal court.

Perhaps the justification for not sending Hamilton overseas was that he was indispensable at home. Washington would not find in another man the gift of understanding money, the ready pen for partisan journalism, the mastery in Cabinet meetings, in the management of the military establishment and the sea power of the new frigates. Hamilton was atop every function of government, and he was driving Jay's peace-seeking chariot too with long reins. He wrote the envoy that "it will be better to do nothing than to do anything that will not stand the test of the severest scrutiny. . . . It is desirable, however, to push the British ministry."

Throughout the summer and autumn Jay sent home his reports. Officially he was obliged to communicate with the new Secretary of State, Edmund Randolph, and Jay did this; but he kept in much closer touch with the Secretary of the Treasury. He assured Hamilton that "appearances continue to be singularly favorable. . . . I will continue to accommodate rather than dispute; and if this plan should fail . . . must conclude the business of my mission."

Fair enough! Avoid wrangling! But let it be known that America's spokesman would come home rather than cave in. Hamilton learned that the country's regular minister in London, Thomas Pinckney, had been approached by emissaries of Denmark and Sweden to join the Armed Neutrality Convention of March 1794 against England. In writing to Edmund

Randolph about it on July 8, Hamilton sounded like the Secretary of State himself, addressing a subordinate—and indeed, that was essentially the case.

"Denmark and Sweden are too weak and too remote to render a cooperation useful," he wrote; "and the entanglements of a treaty with them might be found very inconvenient. The United States had better stand upon their own ground . . . the foregoing is the final result of full reflection."

When Hammond approached Hamilton on the same subject, the Secretary reminded the Minister that "it was the settled policy of this government . . . to avoid entangling itself with European connexions. . . ."

Once again, Hamilton associated himself with the word "entangle" to warn against getting into European quarrels. Hammond passed the message on to London. It was welcome there as a bargaining point for British negotiators, and ever after welcome to anti-Hamilton historians as proof of Hamilton's alleged un-Americanism. But he was only enunciating a respected and enduring principle of American foreign policy: No entanglements.

III

(June–August 1794)

Hamilton was now very close to being executive governor of the United States. Washington departed for Mount Vernon on June 17, leaving instructions for the Cabinet to take action on any matters on which there was unanimous agreement.

Hamilton had Secretary of War Henry Knox and William Bradford, the new Attorney General, in his pocket, and Secretary of State Edmund Randolph nearly so. For more than a year the Secretary of State had been hopelessly swamped in speculation and dunned for debts by merchants and shopkeepers. On April 3, 1793, he begged Hamilton to "accommodate me" on some overdue Treasury notes, in "a belief that I have not overrated the degree of friendship, which I have experienced from you."

Upon his appointment to the State Department, January 2,

1794, Randolph sent Hamilton a sycophantic note: "I have taken the oath of office which reminds me that I am brought in nearer relation to your department than hitherto." Later in the year Randolph would be touching Hamilton for personal loans, and thanking "your disinterested kindness." Hamilton, for his part, borrowed eighty dollars from Tenche Coxe on July 1. "The above is this day repaid to me, July 5, 1794," Coxe later recorded.

This year brought Hamilton the broadening experience of meeting Charles-Maurice de Talleyrand-Périgord. Angelica had made the introductions from London with a letter to Betsey. "I recommend to your most particular care and attention, my dear and kind Eliza, my friends, Messieurs de Talleyrand and de Beaumetz." These two were among dozens of refugees from the French Revolution, but Talleyrand would not be long in exile. "His patriotism," noted Washington Irving, "is a mere local attachment, like that of a cat who sticks by a house, let who will inhabit it." Talleyrand, ugly and clever as sin, was waiting for the Terror to subside, and meanwhile spying and speculating around America. To Hamilton, he was Machiavelli come to life.

"I am sorry," Angelica continued to her sister, "that you cannot speak French, or Mr. Talleyrand English, that you might converse with him." Little did Angelica know that the courtier's game was pretending ignorance of foreign tongues, the better to listen in. Years later, when Minister Martin Van Buren, the "red fox of Kinderhook," was in London, Talleyrand, then French ambassador to Great Britain, dealt with him through interpreters until the last day of their conferences. On that occasion Van Buren sent him a leg of venison as a farewell gift. When they met alone, the Prince "smiled and, without the slightest embarrassment and in very tolerable English, entered into conversation on various subjects, concluding by thanking me for the venison and inviting me to dine with him . . . and partake of it."

Hamilton delighted in such company, and Talleyrand lived to pay him a widely read compliment, in *Études sur la République:*

"Je considère Napoléon, Fox, et Hamilton comme les trois plus grandes hommes de notre époque, et si je devais me prononcer entre les trois, je donnerais sans hésiter la première place à Hamilton. Il avait deviné l'Europe." *

Philadelphia was feverish again this summer and Hamilton was touched with "a nervous derangement," which he called "the last vestige" of his previous illness. Schuyler said that, in consideration of "the danger which your health is exposed to, and the incompetent reward for the most arduous and important services . . . ," he felt that Hamilton should give up his office. But Hamilton replied that with a new revenue year commencing in July, he had appointments to make. Some were more important than the usual run because of the renewed rebellion against the Treasury's revenue collectors in the Alleghenies.

At midsummer four Pennsylvania counties erupted in arson and bloodshed. Hamilton told the President of Governor Thomas Mifflin's opinion "that the militia of Pennsylvania alone would be incompetent to the suppression of the insurrection. . . ." Adjacent states must therefore be called upon. "I would submit, then, that Pennsylvania be required to furnish 6000 men, of whom 1000 to be horse; New Jersey 2000 of whom 800 to be horse; Maryland 2000 of whom 600 to be horse; Virginia 2000, of whom 600 to be horse." He favored an imposing force that would "deter from opposition" and "save the effusion of blood."

The President hurried back to the capital. He signed the Hamilton-drafted proclamation. It deplored "acts which I am advised amount to treason, overt acts of levying war against the United States," and proclaimed that "I, George Washington, do hereby command all persons, being insurgents . . . to disperse and retire peaceably to their respective abodes."

Public support being essential, Hamilton went into print with a series of articles signed Tully (anglicized form of Tul-

---

* "I consider Napoleon, Fox, and Hamilton the three greatest men of our era, and if I had to choose among the three, I would without hesitation give Hamilton first place. He understood Europe."

lius, the immortal Cicero's name). The rebels numbered only "a sixtieth part of the community," he pointed out, and thundered, "How long, ye Catilines, will ye abuse our patience? . . .

"Let us see then, what is this question? It is plainly this— Shall the majority govern or be governed?"

Nobody in the administration needed to be reminded how grave and ironic it was to have to subdue rebellion inside a revolutionary nation. The President had seen it coming with those French-bred communes or Democratic Clubs—"self-created societies," Washington fumed, "to sow seeds of jealousy and distrust among the people." Three such clubs in the disaffected areas of Pennsylvania now emitted inflammatory addresses. French "liberty poles," symbols of defiance and terrorism, were a special annoyance to the President.

Washington would have been less vulnerable to the vituperations of living and future liberals if he had expounded the nature of the Jacobin organizations. An excellent summation, written June 9, 1794, reached Hamilton from an old acquaintance, Vermont's Chief Justice Nathaniel Chipman. The Justice had been misquoted in "detached sentences" which, he said, made him seem to endorse "the principles of anarchy instead of the principles of government." Chipman good-naturedly set forth his reasons for believing "such societies [as the Jacobin clubs] to be not only useless but dangerous." He wrote:

"Simple democracies, in which the people assemble in a body to enact laws and decide upon public measures, have from the earliest ages exhibited scenes of turbulence, violence and fluctuation. . . . No government has been able to exist under this form for any length of time. . . . Such is not the government under which we live. Our national government and the governments of the several states are representative democracies . . . calculated to give a permanent security to all the essential rights of man, life, liberty and property. . . ."

Chipman expressed himself in Hamiltonian phraseology that would have been useful to the President, whose censure of the Jacobin clubs some thought was—as Madison wrote Monroe—"perhaps the greatest error of his political life."

No amount of hand-wringing in Philadelphia could minimize

what was happening around Pittsburgh. Leaders were coming
to the fore. One was the Swiss-born Albert Gallatin, recently
found ineligible as a senator and unseated by the Federalist
majority. Gallatin disliked Hamilton, but was among the mod-
erates in the uprising. Less moderate was the lawyer Hugh
Brackenridge. But the radical and unmitigated hothead of the
western politicians was David Bradford. An onlooker described
him at a rally of seven thousand tax-protesters at Braddock
Field:

"David Bradford assumed the office of Major General,
mounted on a superb horse with splendid trappings, arrayed
in full martial uniform . . . with plumes floating in the air and
sword drawn, he rode over the ground and gave orders to the
militia and harangued the multitude. . . . The insurgents
adored him, and those who hated and despised him paid the
most servile homage, in order to be able to control and manage
him. . . ."

By the second week of September, Washington learned that
his proclamation had fallen flat. The Constitution put his duty
plainly: "[The President] shall take Care that the Laws be faithfully executed." Washington had procrastinated, but had never
disagreed with Hamilton on the principle of executive responsibility. Luckily, the indispensable aide was now doubly the surrogate. Knox had gone off to Maine on business, and Hamilton
was acting as Secretary of War as well as Treasury, signing
orders to the field in the name of the War Department.

Very well; the Commander in Chief authorized him to call
up 12,000 militiamen, volunteers, paid substitutes, and conscripts under the governors of Pennsylvania, New Jersey,
Maryland, and Virginia. Hamilton sent circular letters to these
officials, warning that the campaign would not be brief or per-
functory. Next day, the President put his name to another of
Hamilton's works, the second proclamation:

". . . now therefore I, George Washington, President of the
United States, in obedience to that high and irresistible duty
consigned to me by the Constitution . . . require all officers . . .
to bring under cognizance of the law all offenders in the premises."

Foot and horse marched through the city and headed west. Unless the danger quickly subsided, Washington must go along. Pennsylvania and New Jersey troops would assemble at Carlisle; Maryland and Virginia forces at Bedford, Pennsylvania, where the entire army would come together.

Presumably the government could not run itself. The Vice President was at his Massachusetts farm. Randolph's insecurity was known to Washington; no other than Jefferson himself had informed him on that score. Attorney General Bradford was a new man with only judicial experience. In every Congressional recess since 1789, it was Hamilton who had remained at the seat of government while others went on vacation. But now, on September 19, the President received a communication that may have drawn from him a nostalgic smile. It must have reminded him of a young staff officer who was always agitating to lead troops.

"Sir . . . in a government like ours, it cannot but have a good effect for the person who is understood to be the advisor or the proposer of a measure, which involves danger to his fellow-citizens, to partake in that danger; while not to do so might have a bad effect. I therefore request your permission for the purpose. . . .

"With perfect respect and the truest attachment. . . ."

The President granted permission.

IV

(September–November 1794)

At midday, September 30, 1794, Washington's splendid four-horse coach stood at the door of his Philadelphia residence. This vehicle and a predecessor carriage had long been the subject of controversy.

The "coach of state," with the President's monogram on the doors, was proof of majesty, but also it was proof of vanity. It was the proper equipage of a successful planter, of a conquering General, of the idol of his people—unless the beholder saw it as the affectation of a public surveyor who had married the richest widow in Virginia and won only one major battle in a long war, and that with the aid of a Bourbon King. The coach could be thought of either as America's sign of parity with all foreign governments, or as the puffed-up delusion of a figure-head ruler who ran the country as directed by flattering and venal subordinates.

For many years now, rolling through New York and Phila-delphia, along the route to and from Mount Vernon, on jour-neys into New England or into the Cotton South, Washington's coach had been cheered by adoring Americans—but it had also been ridiculed by Republican politicians and editors as an inde-cent imitation of European royalty. Many believed that Presi-dential dignity enhanced the young nation's status, but many others believed that it was a travesty on the principles of the Revolution. Friends and enemies alike regarded Washington as the irreplaceable man in the infancy of the new government, but there were skeptics who felt that he didn't know when a war was over, didn't understand that the people were self-governing, and was actually a dangerous anachronism in this Age of Enlightenment.

All these political misgivings about the General also at-tached to his aide, and in larger magnitude. Hamilton had proved himself brilliant and ruthless, powerful and indestructi-ble. He was a dandy in personal appearance, and had married the money that purchased his finery. His financial system had brought the country undisputed prosperity, but also much ill-feeling. He was the hero of a large following, but the villain of a growing coterie of emotional intellectuals who detected and hated his ambition.

There he was, Secretary of the Treasury and of War, old Washington's favorite, the scourge of Revolutionary France, the keeper of a compromising peace with Britain, the well-known pamphleteer for authoritative government at home. He represented Purse and Sword, Pen and Power. But whether he was for the general good of America, or for the special interests and schemes of empire, was a question for heated dispute.

In the glittering coach, this end-of-summer morning, Wash-ington sat at center, Hamilton on the left, a private secretary on the right. As the carriage rolled off, in the westward direction that troops had already taken, the tableau invited the judgment of onlookers, as it would of history. To a good many commanders it seemed preposterous for the President and his double Secretary to be taking the field against a rabble of disgruntled taxpayers in the far-off mountains. On the other hand, civil liberty seemed much better served by the attention of the top political leaders than it could be by sending some rough warrior like General Benjamin Lincoln, who had subdued the Shays rebellion.

Those who saw an authoritarian streak in Hamilton were not wrong. He had written in the Federalist Papers, "Energy in the Executive is a leading character in the definition of good government." He always believed that the central power, and that alone, bound the states in Union. This insurrection could hardly have come at a worse time. Jay in London was succumbing to social flattery, the occupational disease of diplomacy. Indian troubles, north and south, sizzled with the infusion of British, French, and Spanish intrigue.

Hamilton had personal problems that oppressed him— Betsey was pregnant again—but Washington's spirits rose as soon as the party cleared the city, and bounded when they reached open country. To their camp eight miles past Norristown, on the first night, messengers brought stirring news. On August 24, General Wayne had routed the confederated Indian tribes and some Canadian auxiliaries, at Fallen Timbers, south of Detroit.

Outdoor living further stimulated the President. On October first, he ordered an eleven-mile advance before breakfast, and then interrupted the march to inspect four locks at Tulkehocken Creek, the beginnings of a canal to join the Schuylkill and Susquehanna rivers. Engineering feats spoke to his memories, as did early morning rides. He fished the mountain streams and feasted on salmon and trout at campfire banquets. At Lebanon he admired the arched bridges and stone barns of the industrious German settlers, and at Harrisburg he heard the ceremonial salute of artillery.

Probably the salvos came from field pieces which Hamilton had sent on ahead. He had taken this precaution lest the rebels seize some of the forts and make heavy fighting. But instead of armed insurgents, the President's party met cheering citizens, who also cheered brightly clad units of the Philadelphia Horse Troop. At Carlisle, the governors of Pennsylvania and New Jersey joined the President at dinner and found him "in excellent humor, free and full of conversation."

Washington's party rode on, dipping into Maryland, where he greeted old comrades-in-arms, Light-Horse Harry Lee and Daniel Morgan. They swung back into Pennsylvania, and at Bedford joined the general rendezvous. Washington was reliving his youth. It was in these parts that he had fought his first battles as a British colonial, and had written to his brother, "I heard the bullets whistle, and, believe me, there is something charming in the sound."

There were no bullets now. The wilderness had given way to agriculture and settlements. But the President knew the frontier, as Hamilton did not. It pleased Washington when local delegations kept turning up to express loyalty as well as grievances. At one village ". . . he stopped his horse before the door of their lodging and called them to him—conversing with them some time in the street, and invited them to see him again in the evening, which they spent in conversation similar to that which had before taken place."

The President's simple pleasure in their reception did not extend to the nation's chief tax-collector. The air of innocence among the inhabitants did not alter what Hamilton knew to be true about the defection of this area. He had compiled, from the *Pittsburgh Gazette* and from his own inspectors, a thorough account of what he called "outlawry," 1791–94.

During these three years, Hamilton wrote, "the four western-most counties of Pennsylvania . . . have been in steady and violent opposition. . . . By formal meetings of influential individuals . . . by a general spirit of opposition (thus fomented) . . . by repeated instances of armed parties going in disguise to the officers of the revenue, and inflicting upon them personal violence and outrage . . . and by almost universal noncompliance with the laws, their execution . . . has been completely frustrated."

He had the names of places and persons. Seditious meetings had been held at Red Stone Old Fort, at Pittsburgh, at Pigeon Creek, at Mingo Creek, at Parkington's Ferry. Among others, Treasury agent Robert Johnson had been "seized, tarred and feathered." Treasury agent Wells had been "mistreated." A man named Wilson, "manifestly disordered in his intellect," had pretended to be a collector, and "was pursued by a party in disguise . . . inhumanly burnt with a heated iron . . . tarred and feathered." Witnesses to this crime and similar ones were seized "by armed banditti . . . to prevent their giving testimony." In one of several riots at courthouses, there had been gunfire, resulting in at least one death and several woundings. During the past summer, on July 25, armed insurgents had held up and robbed a mail coach. He also had names of many offenders who were still at large.

Hamilton was well aware that the use of a large force, in the absence of visible enemies, invited ridicule and accusations. He knew that the formation of Democratic Clubs and the raising of French liberty poles were called harmless expressions of political opinion. But unless it was merely a proper exercise of freedom for masked gangs to commit atrocities, and for courts to be disrupted by violence, Hamilton felt federal intervention was imperative. "It appears to me that the very existence of Government demands this course, and that a duty of the highest nature urges the Chief Magistrate to pursue it. The Constitution and laws of the United States contemplate and provide for it."

He had written this for Washington in August, back in Philadelphia; now the President's good humor was a positive hindrance to action. Luckily, by October 21, Washington decided to turn back and leave Hamilton and the governors in charge. The day before the President headed east, Hamilton obtained permission to write out full instructions to General Lee, the senior officer, and he made the most of it.

The objectives of the expedition had not changed. They were, he wrote: "To suppress the combinations which exist in some of the western counties of Pennsylvania in opposition to the laws laying duties upon spirits . . . and upon stills. These objects are to be effected in two ways:

"1. By military force.

"2. By judicial process and other civil proceedings."

With a troop of six horsemen, Hamilton ranged the countryside, constituting himself a mobile headquarters. He sent almost daily reports to Washington, who answered, "I hope you will be enabled by Hook or by Crook to send B____ and H____, together with a certain Mr. Guthrie, to Philadelphia for their winter quarters." David Bradford, the B____ of Washington's reference, fled to Louisiana, but Herman Husbands, the H____, was taken. Hamilton sent the President names of other captives: Corbly, Crawford, Sedgwick, Lock, Munn, Laughery, Gaddis, a sheriff called Hamilton, Wright, Holcroff, "the reputed Tom the Tinker, a colorful outlaw of the hills." The roundup was going slowly, but according to plan. No lives were lost. The show of force had the expected effect. "All announce trepidation and submission. . . . It does not appear that any great number have fled," Hamilton reported.

His letters were filled with picturesque frontier place names: Jones' Mill, Cherry's Mill, Roshaven, Budd's Ferry, Muddy Creek, Beaver Creek. There was a township named for Washington. Hamilton protected civilians from the soldiers by strict discipline. "A court martial sits today to try one or two riotous fellows, and one or two marauders." He was scrupulous in treatment of the accused. Hugh Brackenridge, confederate of Bradford, was brought in for interrogation, and Hamilton told him:

"Mr. Brackenridge, my impressions were unfavorable to you; you may have observed it. I now think it my duty to inform you that not a single one remains. Had we listened to some people, I know not what we might have done. Your conduct has been horribly misrepresented. . . . You are in no personal danger, and will not be troubled even with a simple inquisition by the Judge. . . ."

At another place, a large group of suspects were brought

before a magistrate for examination. An observer there was the Reverend Dr. James Carnahan, who wrote:

"The great number arrested made it impossible for a single judge to examine, within any reasonable time, the case of an individual. There were several persons not clothed with judicial authority, who assisted in making preliminary examinations. Among them, Alexander Hamilton took an active and distinguished part."

Hamilton never doubted that what the Federal government was doing had to be done. The Republican papers were in an uproar of protest and ridicule, but such stalwarts as John Adams and Edward Carrington approved. Out of many arrests came only two convictions; both men were pardoned. A republic able to maintain itself could afford to be merciful. Hamilton liked to think that, as he told Washington, "My presence in this quarter was in some respects not useless. And it is long since I have learned to hold popular opinion of no value. I hope to derive from the esteem of the discerning . . . the reward of these endeavors."

By November 19 his work was done, and he notified the President, "In five minutes I set out for Philadelphia."

V

(December 1794—January 1795)

Back at the seat of government he gave Washington the definite date of his departure from the Cabinet: January 31. He served notice on the Speaker of the House that he was prepared for any further investigation. He was proposed for governor of New York, and for Secretary of State, but after preparing a voluminous summation of his term in the Treasury Department, he felt he had come to the end of a chapter. Betsey had miscarried while he was away, and the Schuylers invited him to bring the family and stay. He would do that, and rest a while before returning to the practice of law. He wrote to Angelica:

"You say I am a politician, and good for nothing. What will you say when you learn that after January next I shall cease to be a politician at all? Such is the fact. I have formally and definitely announced my intention to retire and have ordered a house to be taken for me in New York."

Angelica feared that war would break out if Hamilton left the government, and wrote nervously to her sister:

"The country will lose one of her best friends, and you, my dear Eliza, will be the only person to whom this change can be either necessary or agreeable. I am inclined to believe that your influence induced him to withdraw from public life. That so good a wife, so tender a mother, should be so bad a patriot is wonderful."

Lavish and heartening honors awaited him along the way to private life. Mayor Varick and the aldermen of New York City, with elaborate ceremonies, extended the freedom of the city. The Chamber of Commerce authorized the painting of his portrait by Trumbull and tendered an enormous banquet. Considering what prosperity he had brought them, "a number of mechanics here have declared that they will build him a house at their own expense." Attorney General Bradford predicted his return to government: "You are made for a Statesman, & politics will never be out of your head." A group of American lawyers in London sent compliments "on the wisdom of your financial measures."

Best of all, in his possession was the carefully worded praise of George Washington's farewell letter: "In every relation which you have borne to me, I have found that my confidence in your talents, exertions and integrity has been well placed." Hamilton answered with affection: "As often as I may recall the vexations I have endured, your approbation will be a great and precious consolation."

Here, at the peak of his fame, says his grandson, Hamilton earned another nickname, "the little giant." William Sullivan of Boston, describing him this marvelous year of 1795, called him "under middle size, thin in person, but remarkably erect and dignified in his deportment. . . . When he entered a room it was apparent, from the respectful attention of the company, that he was a distinguished man." Then and always, many persons remarked on his unaffected social poise.

"He was expected one day in December, 1795, at dinner, and was the last who came. . . . The gentleman who received him as a guest introduced him to such a company as were strangers to him; to each he made a formal bow, bending very low, the ceremony of shaking hands not being observed. . . . In the evening of the same day, he was in a mixed assembly of both sexes; and the tranquil reserve, noticed at the dinner table, had given place to a social and playful manner, as if in this alone he was ambitious to excel."

Bathed in the adulation of both classes and masses, Hamilton had left the pack of political detractors far behind. They were unlikely in the mid-1790's to convince any except themselves that he loathed and was loathed by the people, that his foray into Pennsylvania had not served the general welfare, that his diplomacy had not preserved the blessings of peace, that his Treasury policies had not benefited the whole populace.

Historical judgments would be made upon the Hamiltonian State, 1790–1800, the combined tenure of the Washington-Adams administrations, when his financial methods were in full force.

"Hamilton," wrote Samuel Flagg Bemis, ". . . transformed almost overnight the credit of the United States from the worst to the best in the world." At no time did he take advantage of volatile monies to dodge America's obligations. In order to take up the eight-year arrears owed to France, he borrowed thirty-five million guilders from Dutch bankers, and used the new debts to discharge the old. Thus, Bemis attests, the United States "paid its just debts in specie, or equivalent, in value to the original loans." In 1793 Hamilton settled accounts with Spain to the penny.

On December 5, 1794, Minister John Quincy Adams at The Hague wrote to Hamilton, "It is with much pleasure I learn that in point of credit here, the United States stands upon a *higher footing* than any other power." Altogether, Hamilton's reputation was higher abroad than at home; European statesmen knew he had caused the United States to pay all debts in full and in an exemplary manner.

Hamilton's stimulation of prosperity did not cause overgrowth at home. New York, his home town in 1800, was said by Henry Adams to have been essentially unchanged a hundred years later—still a local market well served by its port and banks. Hamilton's promotion of domestic manufactures would not bring heavy industry during his lifetime.

He had private satisfactions to match the public triumphs. One of his quiet pleasures was his trusteeship at Columbia, where he was becoming the subject of legends. It was said that the faculty declined to graduate a student whose academic paper praised Jefferson, and that a clergyman at Trinity Church refused to baptize an infant named for the master of Monticello.

Hamilton had come into his own. It was the period of his life which justified the title of Gertrude Atherton's novel about him—*The Conqueror.*

CHAPTER TWENTY-TWO

The City He Called Home

I

(April 1795—May 1796)

In April Hamilton left Betsey and the children at Albany with her parents, and sailed for New York alone. "It is impossible to be happier than I am in a wife," he wrote on another occasion; but they were much apart. Once, when he had seen her off on one of many trips to her home, he "returned from the Sloop . . . very much out of spirits, and [she] was the subject of his conversation for the rest of the evening."

Despite all the successes, he was gloomy in these days of withdrawal from public life. "Am I a fool—a romantic Quixotic?" he soliloquized in a letter that expressed his post-Treasury moodiness. He was half persuaded that "there is something in our climate which belittles every animal, human or brute."

The cause of his depression was not in the state of the Union, which had seen far worse times, but in himself. It was the same black spell of dejection that had oppressed him when he complained to Ned Stevens of being locked into the dead end of the St. Croix clerkship, and when he had revolted from Washington because he felt trapped as a noncombatant soldier, and when he envied the gifted Major André's jaunty last hours. Angelica understood him. "Can a mind engaged by Glory taste of peace and ease?"

He drew a new will, and was further depressed to find that his debts probably exceeded his net worth. It hardly seemed to matter, for he was deluged with offers of help. The contractor Comfort Sands wrote, "As soon as your furniture arrives, I shall take care of it, and put it in my store . . . will arrange room for you for an office." James Greenleaf of the North

American Land Company offered him one-third of the company's five-million-dollar property and a partnership in a banking house if Hamilton would join up. While recognizing "expectation of large pecuniary advantage, . . ." Hamilton answered, "I think myself bound to decline the overture."

He wanted to walk wide of shady persons, and Greenleaf soon was exposed as a dishonest man. Hamilton also wished to avoid taking advantage of privileged information. Treasury intelligence would be particularly advantageous for speculation in public lands. Robert Troup, among others, thought Hamilton too fastidious.

"The lands of the United States like the lands of individuals in my opinion are fair objects of speculation," Troup wrote him in March 1795, "and I cannot attach any share of dishonor to this species of commerce. . . ."

Troup would gladly conceal Hamilton's part in such transactions, for he believed that material rewards of success were long overdue for his friend. "If you do not wish your name to appear I will cheerfully be your Trustee, and will execute to you a declaration of trust accordingly. . . . No event will contribute more to my happiness than to be instrumental in making you a man of fortune—I may say—a gentleman of you."

Troup was not discussing generalities here, for he had a rich investor in tow and a definite get-rich-quick offer for Hamilton. Troup went on, "I mean to embark for I see no risk. What will be expected from me will be principally advice & assistance in executing the plan if one is to be formed. The same will be expected of you."

Troup merely asked: Was Hamilton for sale? There is not in all of Hamilton's works a more explicit and less prudish declaration of conscience than his reply. He said to Troup that the proposed venture, "though very harmless to the *saints,*" would get ordinary mortals like himself "denounced as speculators, peculators, British agents. . . ."

He went on to say that the French Revolution and the European war "present a great crisis in the affairs of mankind [and] involve this country. . . . The game to be played . . . may be for nothing less than true liberty, prosperity, order, religion and, of course, *heads.*"

He had resigned but not retired from public service. He continued the reply to Troup, naming reasons for his decision to live as Caesar's wife:

"Because there must be some *public fools* who sacrifice private to public interest. . . .

"Because my *vanity* whispers I ought to be one of those fools. . . .

"Because I don't want to be rich. . . ."

Hamilton always was a puzzle to his friends. He tried not to sound lugubrious, but all he wished was "a moderate fortune, moderately acquired . . . to do nothing for my own emolument *undercover.* . . . I know it is pride. But this pride makes it part of my plan to *appear truly what I am.*"

With these resolves and self-evaluation, he commenced his return to private life.

II

(1795–1798)

In June, Betsey joined him in the small house at 56 Pine Street. They progressed to a larger establishment on Partition Street, and then to 26 Broadway, which was seventy-five feet wide. This became their city mansion. Hamilton had the delightful duty in October 1795 of house-hunting for Angelica. The Churches planned to come home in another year or so! She imposed on him shamelessly. "I am sensible how much trouble I give you, but you will have the goodness to excuse it, when you know that it proceeded from a persuasion that I was asking from one who promised me his love and attention if I returned to America." He answered in kind, and signed himself, "Yrs. as much as you desire."

Hamilton was back at fetch-and-carry, but he did not mind. The law business was rewarding and various. His cash books at a typical period in these years recorded fifty-five engagements for extra-legal settlement of disputes, one hundred twenty appearances in mercantile cases, and one hundred twenty-five in non-mercantile cases. "I am not worth exceeding $500 dollars in the world," he'd told two men before leaving Philadelphia. And Madison had written Jefferson, January 11, 1795, "Hamilton will probably go to New York with the word poverty for his label."

But in 1795–96 he was taking in handsome retainers from banks, insurance firms, and land companies. He was able, by May 1797, to write his uncle, the Laird of Grange, "Though I have been too much in public life to be wealthy, my situation is extremely comfortable, and leaves me nothing to wish for but a continuance of health. . . . It will give me the greatest pleasure to receive your son Robert at my house in New York. . . ." In 1798, as befitted a man of property, he increased his household staff, as an expense item shows: "Cash to N. Low 2 negro servants purchased by him for me, $250."

Among appointments offered to him when he left the Treasury was that of Chief Justice of the United States to succeed Jay, his nominee for governor. "Your squabbles in New York have taken our Chief Justice from us," Attorney General Bradford wrote, "ought you not to find us another? I am afraid that department 'as it relates neither to War, finance nor Negotiation,' has no charms for you: & yet when one considers how immensely important it is . . . it is not to be trusted to men who are to be scared by public clamor or warped by feeble-minded prejudices. I wish to heaven you would permit me to name you. . . ."

As next best, the Justice Department retained him to represent the government in the Supreme Court by defending the Carriage Tax of 1794. He relished the challenge of competing once more against a position held by Madison, who contended the tax was not authorized under the Constitution. In May, at the court in Philadelphia, Hamilton spoke for three hours and won the verdict. But he did not enjoy being in the capital city now that he was out of office. He saw that the hostile Albert Gallatin, now a Pennsylvania member of the House, was moving fiscal decisions away from the Treasury Department and into the Committee on Ways and Means, and it "puts my heart to torture," as he told Senator King.

In the spring of 1795 he had managed the Federalist campaign for New York state offices. His party brought in the absent Jay for governor, Betsey's brother-in-law Stephen Van Rensselaer for lieutenant governor, and both houses of the Legislature. At last the Federalist party ruled New York State. As the party leader, Hamilton went to the streets to speak for the Jay Treaty, and on July 18 in front of City Hall was met by a mob carrying French flags and accompanied by French sailors off the ships. Stones were flying. The demonstrators burned a copy of the Treaty and a caricature of Jay, and "they tried to knock out Hamilton's brains to reduce him to an equality with themselves," Cabot observed.

Jefferson liked what he heard of how the Republicans and their auxiliaries of "mechanics and laborers . . . not afraid of a black eye or broken head," routed Hamilton and some Federalist speakers. "The Livingstons appealed to stones and clubs and beat him and his party off the grounds," read the letter from Monticello.

During the street brawl Hamilton intervened in a personal fracas between a Federalist lawyer and the pugnacious sea dog, Commodore James Nicholson, father-in-law to Gallatin. Nicholson taunted Hamilton for being Tory-loving and pistol-shy, and two days later, July 20, there commenced the ritual of the Code.

Hamilton: "The unprovoked rudeness and insult which I experienced from you on Saturday leaves me no option. . . . I propose . . . Paulus Hook as the place . . . Monday next eleven o'clock as the time. . . ."

Nicholson: ". . . I entreat that it may not be postponed longer than tomorrow morning."

But neither contestant was as bloodthirsty as he sounded. After much discussion of time and place, and of who said what, some of the best legal talent in the state was put to work at the peace parley. DeWitt Clinton and Brockholst Livingston for Nicholson, Nicholas Fish and Rufus King for Hamilton, hung over three drafts of an apology-note that Nicholson finally signed a week after Hamilton's challenge.

While the dickering was going on, Hamilton made another false start toward the field of honor—his eighth of positive record. On a Saturday afternoon that July, "a number of gentlemen of [both] parties accidentally stopped at my door," Edward Livingston recounted. "We entered into conversation on the politics of the day, at first coolly and afterwards with some warmth. . . . Hamilton then stepped forward, declaring that if the parties were to contend in a personal way, he was ready, that he would fight the whole party one by one."

Internal evidence of spirituous liquor can be smelled through the braggadocio. Edward Livingston said he was about to accommodate Hamilton when a kinsman, Maturin Livingston, claimed the right. "—Maturin at this moment arrived, he stepped up and told him very coolly . . . that he accepted the challenge & would meet him in half an hour where he pleased. Hamilton said he had an affair on his hands already with one of the party (meaning a quarrel with Commodore Nicholson) & when that was settled, he would call on him."

Again, there followed an exchange of letters, not gunfire, and Hamilton "heard talk that I had acted with want of spirit on that occasion." Six months later he and Livingston were still performing the duello minuet of studied attitudes. Hamilton did other things much better. In this month of two unjoined duels (June–July 1795), he commenced publication, with Jay and King, of the thirty-eight-article series titled *The Defence,* and signed Camillus. It was a point-by-point support of the Jay Treaty. Hamilton wrote the first twenty-one numbers without a partner. Jay had not brought home the sort of pact that Hamilton wanted, but the choice was between a semi-satisfactory trade agreement and renewed warfare at sea. He urged acceptance because otherwise—

"There would be no security at home, no respectability abroad. Our constitutional charter would become a dead letter. The organ of our government for foreign affairs would be treated with derision whenever he should hereafter talk of negotiation or treaty. May the great Ruler of nations avert from our country so grievous a calamity!"

Nobody else in America could lift a dry subject and fly it like a banner. "Hamilton is really a colossus, . . ." Jefferson declared in a much-quoted letter to Madison. "Without numbers, he is an host unto himself. . . ."

July of 1795 was a bad time for the Jeffersonians. The British minister turned over to Wolcott some captured documents which indicated that Secretary of State Randolph during the Whiskey Insurrection had solicited a bribe from French Minister Fouchet. Since Randolph was opposing the Jay Treaty, it was clear enough to President Washington that he had a disloyal Secretary of State. There is some doubt about the shades of meaning in the French-language documents, but no doubt about Washington's opinion of Randolph. "A damneder scoundrel God Almighty never permitted to disgrace humanity!"

Washington asked Hamilton's advice on rebuilding the Cabinet. Pickering was moved to the State Department, and McHenry brought in as Secretary of War. The President also needed Hamilton's opinion on how to proceed with the Jay Treaty: "Aid me, I pray you, with your sentiments on these points, and on such others as may have occurred to you. . . ." Wolcott begged his advice on Treasury affairs, and Pickering on foreign affairs. McHenry implored, from the War Department, "My dear Hamilton, will you assist me, or rather your country, with some suggestions and opinions as may occur? . . ."

He was "master" still, in absentia. Jefferson thought of him as sailing the ship of state. "While all hands were below deck mending sails, and the captain in his cabin attending his log book and charts, a rogue of a pilot has run them into an enemy's port."

The man at Monticello grew increasingly disturbed as another Presidential election hove into view. If Washington did not run, the General's followers might nominate that Federal "colossus" in New York. Jefferson would rather have Adams. "He is perhaps the only sure barrier against Hamilton's getting in." The subject was also on Adams' mind. He doubted if the other politicians feared as much as they professed the time when Washington must depart. "None were truly sorry," Adams avowed. "One party . . . believed it a step toward the introduction of Mr. Jefferson, and the other . . . thought it an advance toward the election of Mr. Hamilton who was their ultimate object."

But none could make a move until the General removed himself. Hamilton had better information on this than the others did. In February 1796 Washington asked him to update the valedictory address written by Madison four years before. Hearing nothing further, Hamilton wrote on May 10, "When last in Philadelphia you mentioned to me your wish that I should *redress* a certain paper which you had prepared. As it is important that a thing of this kind should be done with great care, and much at leisure touched and retouched, I submit a wish that . . . it may be sent to me." Washington answered on May 15, and enclosed Madison's message, along with a foreword and an afterword of his own.

Hamilton opened the package in the office of his Broadway home. He was much relieved at the President's covering letter. It gave him permission "to throw the *whole* into a different form . . . curtailed if too verbose; and relieved of all tautology. . . . My wish is the whole may appear in a plain style, and be handed to the public in an honest, unaffected, simple part."

But the President wanted the message ready for release as soon as Congress should adjourn, presumably in June. In Hamilton's judgment that was much too early. From a literary standpoint, he needed time to take pains. From a political angle, he told Washington, "the declaration of your intention should be suspended as long as possible . . . two months before the time for the meeting of the Electors," which would take place in December.

Washington dreaded "the shafts which, it may be presumed, will be aimed at my annunciation." He feared that if he waited till a late hour the anti-Federalist press would say that he was quitting from "conviction of fallen popularity and despair of being re-elected." Hamilton disagreed. "I do not think it is in the power of party to throw any slur upon the lateness of your declaration."

Besides, there was the international climate. "If a storm gathers, how can you retreat?" Hamilton demanded. He had an alarming communication from Gouverneur Morris, who reported from London that a special French envoy was sailing, escorted by warships, and would demand "in a space of fifteen days a categorical answer to certain questions." In short, Morris predicted a French ultimatum against the Jay Treaty. Washington did not believe the report, but if it were true, he replied to Hamilton, ". . . my answer would be short and decisive, to the effect, 'We are an independent nation and act for ourselves.' "

Exactly. No other American could speak up in such a fashion to a foreign power. This was all the more reason "that you should hold the thing undecided to the last moment." Washington grumbled, but for once the aide was in command. Hamilton would take from May till September to prepare the Farewell Address.

III

(June–September 1796)

This time he knew that he was writing for the ages. It could not be otherwise in preparing the political testament of George Washington, a living legend. Hamilton assembled the materials at his writing desk in New York and called in a helper. Most of the work would be done after business hours, and the sort of help he needed was quite special. Years later, Betsey would tell about it in claiming authorship for her husband.

"The address was written, principally at such times as his Office was seldom frequented by his clients and visitors, and during the absence of his students to avoid interruption; at which times he was in the habit of calling me to sit with him, that he might read to me as he wrote, in order, as he said, to discover how it sounded upon the ear, and making the remark, 'My dear Eliza, you must be to me what Molière's old nurse was to him.' "

Washington had told him to write it "whole." That meant the address would say more than goodbye. It would be a state paper. It would review the nation's years of precarious existence. It would set forth the American doctrine of government, covering both domestic and foreign affairs.

Since the address would express Washington's sentiments and authority, it must be something to remember him by. The memorable utterances of the Revolutionary generation were Patrick Henry's orations, Jefferson's preamble to the Declaration, Tom Paine's stirring battlefield essays, Gouverneur Morris's prelude to the Constitution. Now Hamilton had his chance to become a national "stylist."

Madison's draft of 1792 was out of date, and Washington's suggestions lacked polish and sometimes taste. For example, the President thought the Farewell Address would give him an opportunity to retort to "infamous scribblers," some of whom had accused him of plotting a monarchy, and of enriching himself by public plunder. The President took several hundred words to say that he had never designed to answer such baseless slurs and to assert his guiltlessness. Hamilton proposed that he say, "I never abused the power confided to me—I have not bettered my fortune, retiring with it, nor otherwise improved than by the influence on property of the common blessing of my country."

Hamilton drew up an outline of subject matter, calling it an "abstract of points," twenty-three in number. He would tamper with his Chief's work only in phraseology, not in philosophy. Occasionally he added a germane passage. By introducing mention of "seamen of the North" and "interior communications," he showed that the Constitution made possible the negotiation not only of Jay's Treaty, which mostly benefited Easterners, but also of Pinckney's Treaty with Spain, which mainly concerned Westerners. Washington had denounced permanent alliances, and advised to "avoid connecting ourselves with the policies of any nation." Hamilton revised this to read, "as little political connection . . . as possible," thus leaving the way open for temporary alliances and commercial treaties when needed. Strangely, considering that the President was a church vestryman while his "ghost writer" was not even a church member, it was Hamilton who composed the much-quoted paragraph beginning: "Of all the dispositions and habits which lead to political prosperity, religion and morality are indispensable supports." Not strangely, Hamilton supplied the passages that stressed the self-interest of all nations, a favorite theme of his since student days.

At the end of July Hamilton was able to send the President what became known between them as the Original Major Draft, Hamilton's own handiwork. "I have endeavored to make it as perfect as my time and engagements will permit," he wrote his Chief. "It has been my object to render this act importantly and lastingly useful . . . to embrace such reflections and sentiments as will wear well, progress in approbation with time and redound to future reputation. How far I have succeeded, you will judge."

Hamilton offered to undertake any improvements proposed by Washington. In any event, he insisted that the President return the draft once more to New York for further polishing. Meanwhile, in order to give Washington a choice, Hamilton did some work on the Madison-Washington draft, which seemed "less eligible" the more Hamilton studied it. "There seems to be a certain awkwardness in the thing and . . . some ideas which will not wear well," he told Washington.

The President read both drafts, said he much preferred Hamilton's Original and only complained about sending it back for more "touching." Hamilton needed to test the complete address again on Betsey, for euphony. He dismissed Washington's compliments. "Had I health enough," he wrote on September 5, "it was my intention to have written it over, in which case I would both have improved and abridged." Ever since his experience with yellow fever, he had a spell of sickness each summer.

Hamilton did not expect the President to deliver the address simply as an oration to the people, or a message to Congress. He knew he was writing for newspaper publication, but he believed the document would live. He hoped some of its words would become familiar in American mouths. Thus he opened with the President speaking of his country, and greeting his "Friends and Fellow-citizens." The preamble soon led into the substance of the matter, with Washington announcing "the resolution I have formed to decline being considered for reelection." Then came the Molière touch: "Here, perhaps, I ought to stop." Did the audience want to hear more? In Hamilton's library, with Betsey the listener, the answer certainly was "Yes! Yes! More! More!"

Hamilton made the work warm and intimate by repeated use of the second person pronoun, "you." He had Washington speaking to "you" as "a parting friend . . . an old and affectionate friend." The Union "is . . . dear to you," the President said, because it makes "one people" of "citizens by birth or choice of a common country." And "the name of American . . . must always exalt the just pride of patriotism."

All free people have a right "to make and alter their constitutions of government," but the American Constitution could be amended only by lawful means. The people must beware of "innovations" and beware of "parties." To be sure, the spirit of partisanship "is inseparable from our nature, having its root in the strongest passions of the human mind," but it must not be permitted to disunite the country. Americans should cultivate "a respectful defensive posture," and never forget that "honesty is always the best policy." Hamilton was able, once again, to warn his countrymen not to allow their blessings to become "entangled" with European ambition, rivalry, interest, humor, or caprice.

The address closed on a sentimental note with the President wishing his people "good laws under a free government—the ever-favorite object of my heart and the happy reward, as I trust, of our mutual cares, labors and dangers."

The President's dependence on Hamilton was not lost on the opposition. It gave rise to many gibes that the Chief Executive had become a puppet. "Poor Washington!" Monroe wrote to Madison. "Into what hands he has fallen!"

The Address appeared in the *Advertiser* on Monday, September 19, 1796, with some of the language altered by Washington into his own idiom. Within a few weeks it was widely reprinted and praised, and was accepted then and ever afterwards as a great American document. Hamilton never asserted any share of the authorship, but after his death Betsey would spend years suing in the courts to establish that claim for the benefit of herself and their children.

IV

(1796–1797)

To the witty Fisher Ames the Farewell Address was "as a signal, like dropping a hat, for party racers to start." Politicians sprang from their tracks. Had Washington expressed any preference in the matter of a successor, the race would have provided little competition. Most Americans considered that the Revolution had switched their allegiance from one royal George to another. The country had enjoyed years of peace and plenty, despite many warlike threats and financial fluctuations. Designation of an heir apparent was the way of the eighteenth-century world; there was no easier and more normal method of insuring an orderly continuity.

True, the General had no natural son, but Colonel Hamilton had been his chosen aide in war and peace. You could hear it said of Colonel Hamilton that he was unpopular, but anybody who said so was forgetting much. No pamphleteer of the day approached him in productivity and readership. He had been openly elected to the New York Assembly and the Poughkeepsie Convention, and he had been a spellbinder in those bodies. He looked the part of the soldier-statesman. He and his wife were intimates of the Washingtons. Not one of the leading contenders—not Adams, not Jay, not Jefferson, not Madison, not Clinton, not Burr—had such qualifications.

Hamilton was so conspicuously the man best suited to follow Washington that this fact in itself was an obstruction. No man except the father of his country should be an automatic President. A Virginia editorialist wrote: "Hamilton, you have not triumphed yet. Long have you endeavored to improve the Constitution, and mould it to your standard. Yes—'Camillus'—a national debt, a funding system and speculation have been the cards with which you have played your political game. Wonderful indeed has been your success, but you have not triumphed yet."

There was another claimant to the title of heir apparent. Vice President John Adams read the Farewell Address in the Boston papers. He had reason to feel hurt that Washington had not designated him as his successor. Two terms of service in the faceless Vice Presidency ought to deserve some reward. Washington's administration owed its second citizen much. Twenty-nine times Adams had broken tie votes in the Senate in favor of Washington measures. He repeatedly had cooperated with the Secretary of the Treasury in making good use of the Sinking Fund. Adams had no love for the National Bank, but he did not join Jefferson and Madison in berating "stock-jobbers." To the big controversial subjects, Jay's Treaty and suppression of the Whiskey Boys, Adams gave his support, proving that he believed in a strong executive. He wanted to be President. He saw no fair reason why he should not be, now that Washington had withdrawn.

An obstacle in his way was that he had been such an excellent Vice President. At sixty-one, pudgy, toothless, in poor health, his sedentary job seemed fitting. Suggestions that he succeed himself in second place infuriated the crusty patriot. He would not blaspheme by bringing his Christian God into politics, but Jupiter, or Destiny, he said, "has given me an understanding and a heart which ought not, and cannot, and will not bow down under Jefferson nor Jay nor Hamilton."

Adams inclined to dismiss the first two that he named. The country was leaning Democratic, and had an emotional attachment to Revolutionary France, but it was not yet ready for Jefferson. The unpopularity of the Jay Treaty, regardless of hidden merits, just about eliminated the Governor of New York. That left Hamilton.

Adams frowned at the easy-going living standards of the dapper financier from the West Indies, but was not as yet much exercised about the other man's morals. The Vice President knew that he and Hamilton had much in common, beginning at the family level; Abigail Adams and Elizabeth Hamilton were both well-loved wives, with well-loved children. Both men were writers who were able to stir men's minds. Adams' "Discourse on Davila" had started a literary feud with Jefferson and Paine. Like Hamilton, Adams wrote much about the self-evident fact of human inequality, regarding it as a basis of freedom to rise or fall. Society was divided into "simplemen and gentlemen," wrote the Vice President. His hearty endorsement of business ("In short, commerce had made this country what it is") could have been a quotation from Hamilton himself.

Adams had been called "monarchist" almost as often as Hamilton had, and just about as often as Jefferson had been called "atheist." There were all sorts of derogatory stories in circulation about the Presidential rivals. One heard that Hamilton had stolen 100,000 pounds sterling from the government and invested the sum in English funds. Another canard was that Monticello was teeming with Jefferson-sired mulattos. A tall tale which amused Adams was that Washington had dispatched C. C. Pinckney to Europe to procure four pretty girls to serve himself and the Vice President as mistresses. "I do declare upon my honor," Adams commented, "if this be true General Pinckney kept them all for himself and cheated me out of my two."

All told, it was best not to believe much of what was said and written during this time about men in public life. Adams knew that, in time, the Federalist leaders—a vague group with no definite roster—would hold a convention of minds and select the party's two national candidates. The message that kept reaching Adams was that he should continue his admirable service as Vice President. He burst forth to Abigail, "I would be second . . . to no man but Washington."

The raw thriving country was full of men with such sentiments. Every white man in America sometimes felt he was born to be President. In 1796, however, the womb of that office was granted to be the Federalist national convention, a curious consensus in which decisions were arrived at by letters, conversations, and pamphlets. Hamilton, the acknowledged leader and the coziest confidant of Ellsworth, Jay, King, Pickering, Schuyler, Sedgwick, Wolcott, and the rest, was like everybody else in one respect—he was second to Washington. In short, Hamilton could advance anybody he wished for President, including himself, but only if the General did not disapprove.

" 'Tis all important to our country that [the] successor be a *safe* man," Hamilton wrote to a fellow Federalist. "But it is far less important who, of many men that might be named . . . than that it shall not be Jefferson." Side by side with Jefferson on Hamilton's proscribed list was Burr, who was openly campaigning for himself in five states. Since Burr had run with both parties, his affiliation was a puzzle. When Jonathan Dayton, the new Federalist Speaker of the House, proposed party support of Burr, Hamilton and Sedgwick instantly signaled with thumbs down.

But if Adams was to be kept in the Vice Presidency, and Jefferson and Burr denied the Presidency at all cost, Hamilton must have some other candidate. Then and later, there was the normal supposition that Hamilton wished to nominate himself. An assertion was made that he was secretly using the New York *Minerva,* of which he had been a co-founder, to put forward his name as a candidate. But Noah Webster, the *Minerva's* editor, later denied this with vehemence. The truth is that every member of the Federalist high command knew there were reasons why Hamilton could never be President. Twenty-two other men secured votes in the Electoral College between 1788 and 1804. The reasons why Hamilton never received a single vote require some examination.

CHAPTER TWENTY-THREE

The Presidency Was Not for Him

I
(1796)

Among the delegates to the Constitutional Convention, Hamilton, Robert Morris, and Pierce Butler were foreign-born. The eligibility of aliens to become citizens and members of Congress was thoroughly debated, but the qualifications as to place of birth for the Chief Executive were not.

Very late in the session, September 4, 1787, a select committee composed of Nicholas Gilman, Rufus King, Roger Sherman, David Brearley, Pierce Butler, and Abraham Baldwin (but not Hamilton) inserted the provision that the President must be a natural-born citizen or a citizen at the time of the adoption of the Constitution.

Although not debated, the item had been earnestly considered in committee, and apparently by Washington, at the instigation of a non-delegate, John Jay. The determining factor was a letter to Washington from Jay—who may have written also to others—and the opinion of scholars is that the purpose was to eliminate one man, von Steuben.

"Permit me to hint," wrote Jay on July 25, 1787, "whether it would not be wise and seasonable to provide a strong check to the admission of Foreigners into the administration of our national Government, and to declare expressly that the [position of] Commander in Chief of the American army shall not be given to, nor devolve on, any but a natural born citizen."

The leading authority on this point, Charles C. Thach, Jr., observed: "The name of von Steuben is not mentioned, but there can be little doubt that it was he, *'alieni appetens, sui profusus,'* with his sympathies for the followers of Shays, and his evidently suspected dealings with Prince Henry of Prussia, whom Jay had in mind when he penned these words. The silent insertion of the clause in the committee where matters could be managed quietly tends to confirm the conjecture."

In any event, Hamilton was left eligible for the Presidency. He need only live to "have attained to the Age of thirty-five years," and "have been fourteen years a Resident within the United States." He was in his thirty-first year in 1787, and had come to the American mainland in 1773, exactly fourteen years before the Convention. The Presidential eligibility clause may have been purposely written to include Hamilton, while excluding von Steuben.

Since there was no Constitutional bar against Hamilton, it is necessary to look elsewhere for reasons why the Federalists did not push him as the successor to President Washington. Among the lesser reasons was the floating scandal of Maria Reynolds. Every age is tolerant of the peccadillos of its great personalities, and the eighteenth century had many big men with accommodative morals. But it was too much to expect an ultra-conservative political party to pin its highest hopes for the highest office to a married man who, as Adams later wrote baldly, was sex-driven by "a superabundance of secretions which he could not find whores enough to draw off." No doubt thinking of Angelica Church's visits to New York and Philadelphia, Adams took note of Hamilton's "fornication, adultery, incest. . . ." Abigail saw him with a woman's eyes: "Oh, I have read his heart in his wicked eyes many a time . . . ," she wrote in this election autumn of 1796. "They are lasciviousness itself."

Even supposing that no other names than Angelica's and Maria's would be salaciously coupled with Hamilton's, there was also the fact, known to men of both parties, that Hamilton had on one occasion paid blackmail to a criminal, James Reynolds. It was a crippling vulnerability in a man up for consideration as President. Furthermore, Hamilton's financial policies and political philosophy were out of consonance with democratic agrarianism, as were those of John Adams. And no other prominent American of the time had such a variety of intellectual opponents and physical enemies as Hamilton. Women,

men, and his own vulnerability combined against him. Everything considered, it is easy to believe the subsequent disclaimer of Noah Webster:

"I never entertained an idea that Mr. Hamilton was a candidate for the presidency or vice presidency at the late election. I never uttered, wrote or published a hint or suggestion of the kind."

Webster might have added that Hamilton never expressed any desire for the Presidency. That in itself would be a strong reason why he never came close to getting it. Gouverneur Morris, who resembled Hamilton in his fascinated non-ambition for the Presidency, believed that his friend purposely blocked himself off from ever becoming a serious candidate. Hamilton, said Morris, held that public opinion absolutely dominated American political affairs. If there ever was a monarchy, Hamilton believed, according to Morris, that it would be one based on popular acclaim and not on military or aristocratic seizure of power.

"Our poor Hamilton," Morris wrote after his death, "bestrode his hobby to the great annoyance of his friends and not without injury to himself. . . . Hamilton was of that kind of man which may most safely be trusted; for he was more covetous of glory than of wealth or power. But he was of all men the most indiscreet. He knew that a limited monarchy, even if established, could not preserve itself in this country. . . . But although General Hamilton knew these things, from the study of history, he never failed on every occasion to advocate the excellence of, and avow his attachment to, monarchical government. By this course, he not only cut himself off from all chance of rising into office, but singularly promoted the views of his opponents who, with the fondness for wealth and power which he had not, affected a love for the people, which he had and which they had not."

In sum, Morris was saying that Hamilton, who loved the American people, did much to prevent himself from being carried into the highest office either on their shoulders or on those of his peers. He never advocated a monarchy, but the idea mightily intrigued him. All power fascinated him; kingly power fascinated absolutely. But he knew it was forbidden fruit.

Hamilton's own estimate of his role in American affairs bears examination. An accurate reflection of it was John Adams' memorable remark that Hamilton was Viceroy under Washington and he, Adams, was Viceroy under Hamilton. The role of America's Regent—the not-very-gray eminence—was most congenial to Hamilton. He did not care to become President, but he enjoyed wielding Presidential power. It is conceivable that Hamilton would not have rejected the Vice Presidential post behind a Chief Executive of his own choice. In that position, under the system established by Washington, he would have been in the midst of decision-making by the Cabinet, with a deciding vote in the Senate, which was then so small as to produce many tie votes.

But in Washington's two candidacies, a balanced ticket required a New Englander to balance a Southerner. The fact that Hamilton declined opportunities to run for governor of New York—though he regularly participated in trying to place his own candidate in that office—strengthens the supposition that he desired not to be an executive, but only to be the power behind one.

A still more subjective revelation of the role he preferred in American affairs is his choice of the many nom-de-plumes under which he pamphleteered. A monograph by the scholar Joseph Charles, *A Note on Certain of Hamilton's Pseudonyms,* goes into this matter, although for an ulterior purpose. Charles, an ardent Jeffersonian, was bent on proving that Hamilton had an obsessive distrust of the people. What he actually did prove was, at most, that Hamilton was affectionately and anxiously paternalistic toward the people. All his chosen pseudonyms suggest a worried sense of responsibility for the state and its citizens; not one of them is suggestive of despotism or dictatorship, but quite the opposite.

Hamilton's very first nom de plume, while he was still a collegian, was simply "A Friend to America." This was not mentioned by Charles. The most noted pseudonym, plucked out of Plutarch as were most of the others, revealed Hamilton in the mantle of Publius Valerius, hero of the Roman republic. Publius was second only to Lucius Brutus in overthrowing the tyrant Tarquin, known then as the last King of Rome, and in establishing a just and stable republic that lasted until the Caesars came.

When Hamilton wrote as Phocion, he chose the role of another estimable Plutarchian statesman. Phocion "never allowed himself from any feeling of personal hostility to do hurt to any fellow-citizen . . . he would befriend his very opponents in their distress and espouse the cause of those who differed most from him." He was especially sympathetic toward enemy prisoners of war.

Writing as Camillus in 1795, Hamilton borrowed a character from Livy to defend the Jay Treaty at a time of mob violence and public hysteria. Camillus was styled "the second founder of Rome," but demagogues "railed against him . . . as a hater of the people." As Titus Manlius in 1798, the time of troubles with the France of Bonaparte and Talleyrand, Hamilton was writing under the name of a Roman who advocated total war against Carthage. Tully (the popular name at that time for Marcus Tullius Cicero), which Hamilton used in 1794, was the denouncer of the corrupt and treacherous Catiline. Pericles, his nom-de-plume in 1803, was the premier statesman of Athens' golden age. He also wrote under the name of Lycurgus, father of Sparta's constitution, and that of Solon, whose name has become a synonym for a wise and skillful statesman.

By choosing such names to write under, Hamilton meant to strengthen whatever message he conveyed to the people at that juncture of national events. He may also have been expressing some wishful self-revelation. If so, what he wanted most of all to be in life was a wise and unafraid protector of the people's liberties and their republican form of government. He was speaking in the names of noble statesmen who put rectitude above popularity, and who were appreciated by posterity more than they were in their own times and countries. None of these declared heroes of his ever wore a crown or carried a truncheon.

Educated men of Hamilton's day knew what he was express-

ing through the allegories of his pseudonyms. "Alexander
Hamilton . . ." went a banquet toast in July 1802: "As like in
virtue as in suffering wrong, so may he prove the Camillus of
America, to drive from power, by fraud attained, the modern
Gauls and Vandals."

Although Hamilton won two open elections and lost none,
he scorned popularity while coveting fame, and undoubtedly
thought of himself as a patrician-who-knows-best. When Gouverneur Morris came to deliver his funeral oration, he stressed
Hamilton's faculty of warning the people against false friends,
often to his own hurt. This streak of paternalism in Hamilton,
benevolent but prone to be misunderstood, made him both aloof
from the people and apprehensive for the state. He did not
consider himself cut out to be Chief Executive, but rather to
be Keeper of the People.

Apprehensiveness, in the form of sporadic and profound pessimism, dogged him throughout his service to the American
state. He did not express this moodiness in his public writings,
which were purposely optimistic, but it marked much of his
intimate correspondence. The despair of winning the Revolutionary War, which he revealed to his fiancée and to his friend
Laurens, came out of the same melancholia which later caused
him to bemoan to Gouverneur Morris and Rufus King the
dreaded collapse of the Constitution.

It was not faint-heartedness by any means, much less was
it defection, as hostile historians desired to believe, else he
would not have been first over the Yorktown ramparts and
constant to the end. He overreacted to real and imagined
threats to the nation. There was a measure of deserved criticism in what John Adams said after receiving the news of
Hamilton's death on the field of honor at Weehawken:

"Mr. Hamilton's imagination was always haunted by that
hideous monster or phantom, so often called a *crisis,* and which
so often produces imprudent measures."

On this score of imprudence, Hamilton could be judged unfit
to be President, and Adams was not the only Federalist who
thought so. A more intemperate and unfair critic, John Quincy
Adams, called Hamilton's "ambition transcendent, and his dis-

position to intrigue irrepressible . . . he was of that class of characters which cannot bear a rival—haughty, overbearing, jealous, bitter and violent in his personal enmities, and little scrupulous of the means which he used against those in the way of his ambition." This diatribe disregards Hamilton's many close friendships, but attests to his ability to make enemies.

Again, there were Federalists who loved Hamilton, as the Adamses did not, and yet acknowledged him to be unreliable and headstrong. Despite admiration and affection, the Federalist consensus never seriously considered him for the Presidency.

Impatient of other men's faults, Hamilton was also sensible of his own. He was not a happy man, not stable, not secure. There are enough self-references to his alien birth and lack of American family background, enough emphasis on aristocratic relatives in Scotland and on membership in the Cincinnati, to suggest that his hauteur may have been a cover for a concealed unsureness. If so, few men ever succeeded so well under hidden handicaps. These misgivings, if they did exist in his mind, may explain why his ambition stopped before reaching toward civil supremacy.

Finally, the overriding reason why Hamilton never became a Presidential candidate was the veto of Washington. The General was an unshakable admirer of the younger man and took no stock in the alleged dangerousness of Hamilton's ambition. "That he is ambitious I shall readily grant," Washington wrote Adams of Hamilton in 1798, "but it is of that laudable kind which prompts a man to excel in whatever he takes in hand."

But the Federalist leaders knew by now that Washington regretfully believed that "Colonel Hamilton does not have the general confidence of the American people." If he was unacceptable as an envoy to Britain, for reasons already considered by Washington, he was manifestly unqualified to become President. The people expressed themselves ferociously in their newspapers and public meetings, but they had very little voting power. There was no popular mandate that could have stopped Hamilton from being confirmed as envoy in the Senate, or as President by the Electoral College. But the people's political

impotency was all the more reason for a paternalistic party like
the Federalists to protect them. Had all else been favorable to
Hamilton, the party leaders still would not name a man for
President over the disapproval of George Washington.

With himself out of the running, Hamilton looked again for
his candidate. Patrick Henry, he wrote Rufus King, should be
the first choice, but Hamilton rightly expected him to refuse
because he was sixty, and infirm. "I am entirely of the opinion
that, Patrick Henry declining," Hamilton told King, "Mr.
Pinckney ought to be our man."

King was enthusiastic about the minister in London. "Mr.
Pinckney has asked leave to return home and only waits for
permission. To his former stock of popularity, he will now add
the good will of those who have been peculiarly gratified with
the Spanish Treaty. Should we concur in him, will he not receive as great, perhaps greater Southern and Western support
than any other man?"

Thomas Pinckney for President? Hamilton wanted him.
King wanted him. Treasury Secretary Wolcott wanted him,
and said, "Mr. Pinckney is an honest man and cannot be made
the tool or dupe of faction." The Federalist convention was still
seeking its nominee.

Contrary to given opinions in the 1790's and afterwards,
Thomas Pinckney at forty-six was not unknown, subservient,
or provincial. Educated with his brother, Charles Cotesworth
Pinckney, in English private schools, he had served gallantly
in the Continental Army. Wounded and captured at the battle
of Camden, he wrote a spirited defense of his commander,
Horatio Gates, who was disgraced as the loser there.

Currying no favor with Washington and Hamilton by his
outspokenness, Pinckney came up through two terms as South
Carolina's governor. Both the Pinckney brothers were logical
choices for important foreign assignments because of their acquaintance abroad. As minister to London in 1794, Thomas
Pinckney did not enjoy playing second fiddle to Jay, so he accepted Washington's offer of a special mission to Spain. Going
by way of Paris, he angered French officials and pleased Hamilton by refusing to discuss the secret terms of the Jay Treaty.

It was quite deliberate on Hamilton's part that the Farewell Address alluded to the Spanish Treaty, popularly known as Pinckney's Treaty, which opened the Mississippi to American trade. "Pinckney from London is the man," Beckley informed Monroe.

Certainly he was Hamilton's man, rating well above John Adams. "New York will be unanimous for both. I hope New England will be so too." That was Hamilton's plan. If the party gave Adams and Pinckney equal support, the worst that could happen would be a tie vote, and that would be decided in the Federalist-controlled House of Representatives. But Federalist vote-splitting would be "most unfortunate," wrote Hamilton. "It will be to have *one* only of *two* against Mr. Jefferson."

Hamilton thought Adams neither politician nor statesman enough to be Chief Magistrate. With war against France or England more a probability than otherwise, Hamilton wrote that a "military character" in the Presidency was essential. When this word reached the Adamses, husband and wife, there was a male outburst against that "Creole bastard," and an opinion from Abigail that Hamilton was a combination of Julius Caesar and "spare Cassius." (Mrs. Adams was given to Roman allusions. She also called Gallatin "that specious, subtle, spare Cassius, that imported foreigner." Her family coach horses were named Caesar and Cleopatra.)

At one point Hamilton estimated that there would be eighty votes for Pinckney, enough to win. It was tight figuring where a little slippage might let Jefferson in, but Hamilton calculated the risk. Lacking a soldier as commander in chief, he wrote, the country would be better off with Jefferson than with Adams, since France would not attack a pacifist and democratic administration. But either such an administration, or an inept one under Adams, was much to be dreaded. Hamilton was saying all this as he worked at avoiding both.

He found French Minister Adet publishing vote-for-Jefferson letters in the Philadelphia *Aurora,* and announcing unrestricted warfare on American shipping. Hamilton was again President Washington's closest advisor. He told the President to maintain the chilliest possible air toward Adet. "France," he wrote to Washington, "has gone further than Great Britain ever did." He proposed a Jay-type commercial treaty to save the peace with France.

But there was hardly time for that, with the Presidential election rushing closer. There was only time to rally the country for peace through unity, something that Hamilton did better than anybody else. Adet filled the pages of the *Aurora* with bloodthirsty threats in the name of France—"a government terrible to its enemies, but generous to its allies." Adet wrapped himself in the tricolor and appealed to Revolutionary sentiments. "Oh, America covered with noble stars! Oh, you who have so often flown to death and to victory with French soldiers. . . . Let your government return to itself"—meaning that America should elect Thomas Jefferson.

Hamilton retorted with articles in the *Minerva,* signed Americus and sealed with his striking style and stirring images. *"The honor of a nation is its life,"* he wrote with emphasis. "There is treason in the sentiment . . . that we ought to bear anything from France rather than go to war. . . . The nation which can prefer disgrace to danger is prepared for a MASTER and deserves one."

Only one man in America could write with such spirit, and if Hamilton wanted Major Thomas Pinckney as President, there must be something in it. Unluckily, the essays were running behind the pace of the election season. Besides, the Electors and not the people would make the decision. The New England men could not bring themselves to vote equally for Adams and Pinckney. The Southerners were torn between Jefferson of Virginia and Pinckney of South Carolina.

New Year's Day was past before the final results were known: Adams 71 and Jefferson 68, with Pinckney third and Burr fourth.

II

(June–August 1797)

On a summer day in New York, Hamilton spread open Fenno's *Gazette* and read names he wished to forget. Maria

Reynolds . . . James Reynolds . . . Jacob Clingman. He turned
for help to Noah Webster, who immediately wrote to Timothy
Pickering, Secretary of State, in Philadelphia:

"Can you send me a copy of the History of the U. States,
Number V, advertized in Fenno?"

Webster's abbreviation was for James T. Callender's *American Annual Register, or Historical Memoir of the United States,
for the year 1796.* He and Hamilton had seen an advertisement
in the *Gazette* of Chapter V of this history. They needed to
examine Chapter V itself.

"Mr. Hamilton and myself wish to see it," Webster continued
to Pickering, "and one copy will answer for us both, as by the
advertisement we see it contains downright lies."

All too soon, Hamilton had before him Chapter V. Callender's account of the Presidential election of 1796 declared that
Hamilton had been the Federalist undercover candidate. Noah
Webster's name was also involved.

"During the late canvass for the election of a President," ran
the passage in Chapter V, "Webster in his *Minerva* gave hint
that Mr. Hamilton would be an advisable candidate. A person
in this city [of Philadelphia] who chanced to see this newspaper,
wrote immediately to a correspondent in New York. The letter
desired him to put himself in the way of Mr. Hamilton, and
inform him that if Webster should in the future print a single
paragraph on that head, the [Reynolds] papers referred to were
instantly to be laid before the world. The message was delivered to Mr. Hamilton, and the *Minerva* became silent."

The anonymous "correspondent in New York" sounded
much like Aaron Burr. If the story were true, Hamilton's noncandidacy would be further explained; his nomination had
been blocked by blackmail. But the story was "utter falsehood,"
Hamilton answered. "Does the editor imagine that he will escape the just odium which awaits him by the miserable subterfuge? . . . Till he names the author, the inevitable inference
must be that he has fabricated the tale."

Had Chapter V been all, it would have been enough. But
Chapter VI soon reached Hamilton. The new installment declared that he had connived at illegal speculation in Treasury

funds with James Reynolds, and had told Muhlenberg, Venable, and Monroe a black lie to cover up the offense. Adultery was not the sole subject of all those letters, said Callender. "So much correspondence could not refer exclusively to wenching. No man of common sense would believe that. . . . The solicitude of Mr. Hamilton to get these people out of the way is contrary to an amorous attachment for Mrs. Reynolds, and bespeaks her innocence in the clearest stile."

Hamilton knew what had to be done. First, Betsey must be told the story by loving persons before she heard from the other kind. Church paid a call on her, and wrote Hamilton:

"I am this instant returned from your house. Eliza is well; she put into my hand the newspaper with James Thompson Callender's letter to you. [But] it makes not the least impression on her, only that she considers the whole knot of those opposed to you to be scoundrels."

Betsey knew her man too well to be surprised. She understood him entirely, appetites and candor, affection and impulsiveness. She had to wait many years for a confrontation with Monroe, the chief tattler, and then, as only a great lady can do—she cut him dead.

As to her husband's love, Betsey never doubted that. He had spent over $1,100 to keep her from learning of his folly. He had written her hundreds of love-letters, as tender from the guilty husband as from the ardent suitor. "I am more than ever in debt to you," he wrote in this crisis, "but my future life will be more than ever devoted to your happiness." Yet in spite of sympathy and forgiveness, Betsey was hurt, and had need of the balm brought by her lively, worldly sister.

"Tranquilize your good and kind heart," wrote Angelica, who was clever enough to strike at Monroe while dispensing comfort. "I have the positive assurance from Mr. Church that the dirty fellow who has caused us all some uneasiness and wounded your feelings, my dear love, is effectively silenced."

Alas! the silencing of Monroe came too late, but Angelica wanted only to be the bringer of mercy and justification. She wrote on:

"Mercy, virtue and talents must have enemies, and are always exposed to envy. . . . My Eliza, you see the penalties attending the position of so amiable a man. All this you would not have suffered if you had married into a family less *near the sun*: but then you would have missed the pride, the pleasure, the nameless satisfactions. . . . Yours with all my heart and with redoubled tenderness."

Next to breaking the sordid story to Betsey, Hamilton felt it important to clear his public honor. For this it was necessary that Muhlenberg, Venable, and Monroe should declare that they still believed in 1797 what they had averred in 1792—that Hamilton was an honest public servant. Muhlenberg and Venable presented no difficulty, but Monroe was another matter. He had taken the original documents of accusation to Virginia and left them with a friend, while serving as minister in Paris. He had a letter from Clingman in which Hamilton was said to have invented the affair with Maria in order to cover up illicit transactions with her husband. All this made it doubly imperative for Hamilton to get a "certificate" of his *bona fides* from Monroe.

Accordingly, on July 11, Hamilton took along John Church and called on Monroe when the latter brought his wife, a former Miss Kortwright, to visit New York. They met at 46 Wall Street, in a stormy scene described by an eyewitness, David Gelston. When Monroe began to explain that he had nothing to do with the publication of the charges, Hamilton called this representation "totally false," and Monroe called Hamilton "a scoundrel."

"I will meet you like a gentleman," said Hamilton.

"I am ready," answered Monroe. "Get your pistols."

"Gentlemen, gentlemen, be moderate," Church pleaded.

It was decided to overlook the "intemperate expressions" until Monroe could return to Philadelphia and assemble some information to refresh his memory. He did not tell Hamilton what he subsequently told Burr, that it was another Virginian who had provided Callender with the Reynolds story.

"You know, I presume," Monroe said, "that Beckley published the papers in question. By his clerk they were copied for us. It was his clerk who carried a copy to H., who asked, as

Venable says, whether others were privy to the affair. B. told H. he considered himself under no injunction not to publish the business."

Hamilton also went to Philadelphia, the better to question witnesses, to collect documents, and to arrange for the publication by John Fenno of a unique political narrative with deep personal revelations. It carried the cumbersome title, "Observations on Certain Documents contained in Nos. V and VI of *The History of the United States for the Year 1796,* in which the charge of speculation against Alexander Hamilton, late Secretary of the Treasury, is fully refuted. Written by himself."

In this pamphlet Hamilton said much about the mischief brought to America by the French Revolution. He blamed the "spirit of Jacobinism" in the Jeffersonian party for the repeated efforts to destroy him. He published the memorandum of Muhlenberg, Venable, and Monroe, December 17, 1792, in which they had attested to their belief in his honesty. To this he added a deposition by Wolcott, July 12, 1797, declaring that the three members of Congress "severally acknowledge their entire satisfaction that the affair had no relation to official duties." Hamilton included the illiterate correspondence of Maria and James to prove his adultery and the blackmail. He confessed to the wound he had given his wife. "But that bosom will approve that, even at so great an expense, I should effectually wipe away a more serious stain from a name which it cherishes with no less elevation and tenderness. . . . I have paid pretty severely for the folly, and can never recollect it without disgust and self-condemnation. It might seem affectation to say more."

Expectably, the release of these "Observations" brought jeers from his enemies. What sort of man would make his home "the rendezvous of whoredom"? He was a Creole, and "even the frosts of America are incapable of cooling [his] blood." Such derision would have been more easily borne if he had received the corresponding support of his friends. But aside from the very closest, such as Troup and Church, the Hamilton followers took him at his own estimate—as "a Quixotic." His honesty seemed excessive, supererogatory. There was no need for humiliating confession when stony silence would have sufficed. The man who knew Talleyrand, admired Machiavelli, cited the scoundrel John Law and the cynic David Hume, should have been a better liar or equivocator. Webster spoke for many Hamiltonians when he wrote:

"What shall we say of a man who has borne some of the highest civil and military employments, who could deliberately . . . publish a history of his private intrigues, degrade himself . . . and scandalize a family, to clear himself of charges which no man believed . . . ?"

But if the charges were to be rendered entirely unbelievable, Hamilton must get an unequivocal statement out of Monroe. Hamilton pressed him in a protracted correspondence, but the other man avoided giving a categorical clearance. "—You imply that your suspicions are still alive, . . ." Hamilton wrote him on July 27. "The result in my mind is that you have been actuated by motives toward me malignant and dishonorable." This could be taken as a challenge, and Monroe properly accepted, though he said, "I have always stated that I had no wish to do you personal injury."

The highly mannered dialogue, in the form of letters, was carried on through June, July, and August.

Hamilton: "But the subject is too disgusting to leave me any inclination to prolong this discussion of it."

Monroe: "I have stated to you that I have no wish to do you injury. . . . I am ever ready to meet."

Hamilton: "I have authorized Major Jackson to communicate with you and to settle time and place."

Monroe: "My friend Colonel Burr . . . is authorised to give my answer to it, and to make such other arrangements as may be suitable. . . ."

Aaron Burr, connoisseur of the *duello*, thought he saw two men who did not wish to fight, and who had no good reason to do so. He acted as mediator, and the matter was dropped. Burr also did a decent and gentlemanly deed; he urged Monroe to exonerate Hamilton of any dishonorable conduct. He wrote to Monroe:

"If you and Muhlenberg really believe, as I do, and think you

must, that H is innocent of the charge of any concern in speculation with Reynolds, it is my opinion that it would be an act
of magnanimity and justice to say so in a joint certificate. You
expressed to me the same idea when we were together here."

Burr in fact drafted such a certificate for Monroe's signature,
but it was never signed.

CHAPTER TWENTY-FOUR

The Quasi War With France

I

(1797–1798)

Hamilton knew that Monroe wanted to fight him, but not with pistols. When the duel had seemed unavoidable, the Virginian stipulated a three-month postponement so that he might finish his book, *A View of the Executive,* an anti-Federalist diatribe against the administration of George Washington.

To Hamilton, all this bitterness in Monroe, Jefferson, and most of the Democrats meant that a French-type revolution was seething in America, and that French ships and troops might well arrive to hasten the eruption. He expected subversion and insurrection, possibly worse. "I think the overthrow of England & the invasion of this country very possible, so possible that any other calculation for our Government will be a bad one." He was writing to Rufus King, the new minister in London:

"You need not be told that every exertion, not degrading to us, will be made to preserve peace with France. . . . We shall not be dictated to. . . ."

He was thinking, when he wrote this, of his threefold policy for American independence. His financial system had brought freedom in that area. He could envision that useful manufactures would ultimately make the country self-sufficient, with a surplus of goods for export. But to be independent of foreign intrigue and aggressions required continuing efforts at separation from Europe. He was relieved when Congress, on July 1, 1798, finally rescinded the wartime French Treaty of 1778.

Hamilton made his New York law office a gristmill of patriotic essays, which was nothing new, and also a cornucopia which poured forth plans for running the government of the United States.

"Were I Mr. Adams, then," he wrote to Sedgwick, "I believe I would begin my presidency by naming an extraordinary commission to the French Republic. . . ."

Sometimes Hamilton did not preface his recommendations, "Were I Mr. Adams. . . ." In a letter to Secretary of State Pickering, for example, he called openly, in his own person, for ". . . an embargo. . . . Additional revenue for . . . a naval force . . . a provisional army . . . increase of our establishment in artillery and cavalry."

Dozens of such letters by Hamilton went to almost every living Federalist except John Adams. The President would receive the unsolicited advice promptly enough from Hamilton's fellow-alumni of Washington's Cabinet: Pickering, Wolcott, and McHenry. Moreover, these men would pass on to Hamilton requests from President Adams for advice on what to say in messages to Congress. Hamilton, providing the answers, became a hidden ghostwriter for John Adams.

Jefferson's defeat by only three electoral votes aroused the French Directory, which renewed sea warfare in earnest. Before the Atlantic battle dwindled three years later, French warships would have committed 1,853 acts of spoliation, with damages of $7.1 million, and America would have retaliated by sending forty-five Navy ships and 365 privateers against them. With the violence mounting, Hamilton pressed for a three-man mission to seek a trade treaty with France. General Charles Cotesworth Pinckney, brother of Thomas, was already in Europe, unable to get an audience with Talleyrand, who was now foreign minister in Paris. Hamilton would send a Republican and another Federalist to join him. This message reached Adams through the usual channels. To join Pinckney, he named Elbridge Gerry of Massachusetts and John Marshall of Virginia.

Hamilton approved of "General" John Marshall. The Virginia lawyer, although a Revolutionary soldier, had won his title of rank in a single postwar engagement. In 1794, on orders from Governor Lee, Marshall put on the epaulets, the cocked hat, the side arms, and the cavalry boots of a militia brigadier. He led an impressive force of foot, horse, and artillery to put down a pro-French demonstration in Isle of Wight County. Hamilton thought him a good man to send against Talleyrand.

Hamilton was once more behaving like the prime minister of a presidential cabinet. Surely there must have been business enough at the New York law office to occupy even an extraordinarily active mind. But a compulsion drove Hamilton to the action of governance. Fortune mattered not at all, and fame only as a by-product. What did matter was the desire for American independence of foreign money-lenders, diplomats, and producers. Involved here were the game of nations, and the hidden laws of chance, the quirks of fate, the historical forces at play, the consequences in human and national terms of winning or suffering loss.

In all this, the French Revolution was the big fact of the day. Its dynamics had caused a huge convulsion. Its ideas and armies had swept across Europe. Jefferson, in 1791, hoped that "so beautiful a revolution" would spread throughout the whole world. That was what Hamilton feared the Revolution's soldier of destiny, Napoleon Bonaparte, would bring about. Hamilton admired the master artillerist and the superb strategist—"unexampled conqueror"—and sought the means to repel him.

The French already had bases in the West Indies, and allied forces in the Spanish-held territories of Florida and Louisiana. Hamilton saw other threats. He deeply feared what the triumph of the Revolution's atheism would do to the peculiar genius of the American Republic. State after state, college after college, had been founded by the churches. Religious freedom came next to patriotism. In the spring of 1798 his writings burst out against the menace of ungodliness in "the disgusting spectacle of the French Revolution."

His newspaper series, "The Stand," in the *Commercial Advertiser,* warned of "a conspiracy to establish atheism on the ruins of Christianity—to deprive mankind of its best consolations and most animated hopes. . . . The proofs of this terrible design are numerous and convincing."

He went on to name the proofs out of reports on the Reign

of Terror in Paris: ". . . the object of supplanting the Christian Sabbath . . . the desire to discredit the belief in the immortality of the soul . . . a public courtesan decorated with the pompous title of Goddess of Reason . . . a new law of divorce . . . passed, which makes it as easy for a husband to get rid of his wife, and a wife of her husband, as to discard an outworn habit. . . . The pious and the moral weep. . . ."

An acknowledged and likeable atheist in New York these days was Aaron Burr. Defeated for re-election to the Senate, Burr was back in the Assembly and the spearhead of Jefferson's party, as Hamilton was of the Federalists. Often seen together in courtrooms and living rooms, Hamilton and Burr invited comparison. Benjamin Henry Latrobe marked the contrast between them:

"Hamilton tho' an insatiable libertine, talked of religion and order, and went to church from the bed of the wife of his friend. . . . Burr on the contrary pretended to no religion, and indulged in amorous excesses without disguise. . . ."

Whether Hamilton went to Angelica's bed or another's was no part of his politics, and no departure from his dedication and sincerity. Chastity has never been a requirement for genius.

II

(1798)

Out of the secret files in the summer of 1798 came the sensational documents called the XYZ Papers, their release doing great credit to the President's fortitude. Adams had known for some time that his peace mission of C. C. Pinckney, Marshall, and Gerry had been insultingly received by French authorities. Talleyrand's agents, to whom Adams gave the arbitrary initials, had demanded bribes. "No. No. Not a sixpence," Pinckney answered. When Marshall returned to Philadelphia in June 1798, and was honored at a Federalist banquet, the unforgettable toast rang through the nation:

"Millions for defense, but not one cent for tribute!"

What a rallying cry it was! "Hamilton's heart beat responsive to the throbbing of the nation's pulse," his son would write.

He shared the elation of an aroused country. That sort of defiance kept aggressors at bay. Hamilton tentatively put England too in this category, after hearing from Rufus King in London that Orders in Council were to be renewed. "It is the true policy . . . of our Government," Hamilton wrote Secretary of State Pickering, "to act with spirit and energy as well toward G Britain as France. I would mete the same measure to both [and risk] the extraordinary spectacle of a nation at war with two nations at war with each other."

Hamilton was pleased by the rise of C. C. Pinckney as a national figure, and he could claim some credit for it. It was Hamilton who had recommended this Pinckney brother to President Washington for the post of minister to France. Back in 1796, Washington's last year in office, the decision on the appointment had had unusual importance. Monroe's service in Paris had been a grave disappointment to Washington. The minister had brought to the post much of Jefferson's romantic liberalism and sympathy for the French masses, and he carried his enthusiasm to the point of seeming to care more for the French Revolution than the American one.

When Washington recalled Monroe, and asked Hamilton's advice on a successor, there were some obvious specifications. Monroe had been popular in France, and the next minister to Paris should somewhat resemble him. Hence a Southern liberal was indicated, yet he must be one in whom loyalty to the American government was paramount.

Hamilton, after consultation with Jay, wrote Washington that "General Pinckney is the only man we can think of who fully satisfies the idea." Pinckney was known as a provincial Carolinian, a states' rights man, and nominally a Jeffersonian. But on the way home from the Philadelphia Convention, he had stopped for a visit at Mount Vernon and had formed an admiration for its owner that was to be lifelong. Washington had offered him command of the American army in 1791, and the secretaryships of State and War on subsequent occasions. Pinckney had declined all of them, preferring to be a political leader at home, since his brother Thomas was abroad on diplomatic assignments. But in the late 1790's, with the country

near to war with two major powers, Pinckney felt that he could
not refuse to serve. He was exactly what Hamilton hoped to
get—"a friend to the government," as he assured Washington,
"and understood to be not unfriendly to the French Revolution."

Few of Hamilton's judgments on men proved better than this
one. Pinckney's intense patriotism gave America the representation that the young country needed in the tumultuous times.
When Pinckney had been on duty less than a year, it could be
seen that he was the direct opposite of Monroe in this post. He
felt that his country was being patronized by the French diplomats, and he considered America to be insulted by Talleyrand's
demand for bribes and by numerous slights.

To Hamilton's satisfaction, Pinckney did a full turnabout
from Monroe. He had set out to make peace with France; he
decided that America's honor called for war. He had accepted
the appointment as a restrained admirer of the French Revolution and a mild partisan of Jefferson's republicanism. But
Pinckney soon was persuaded that Revolutionary France was
a wild beast among nations, and that the party of Jefferson
came very close to being a treasonable conspiracy.

In the autumn of 1798 Pinckney was back in the United
States telling audiences, "If we would have peace with France,
it must be obtained not by negotiation but by the sword."

This was Hamilton's kind of man. Pinckney would be invaluable to the Federalist party and the country's leadership.
Hamilton himself was in demand, and he felt that he must soon
accept an official post. "Could anything prevail upon you to
take the War Department?" asked Harper of South Carolina,
one of the House leaders, and Hamilton answered in the negative. One of New York's Senate seats became open by retirement, and Governor Jay offered to appoint Hamilton, who answered revealingly in the summer of 1798, while the war fever
was high:

"There may arise a crisis when I shall feel myself bound once
more to sacrifice the interests of my family to the public weal,
but I must defer the change as long as possible."

There was just one sort of post for which Hamilton had inordinate ambition. The only office which he had ever clamored for was the combat command at Yorktown. Every man and woman who knew him well understood that part of his make-up. He would do almost nothing for political title, and he would do almost anything within honor for military glory. If there was going to be another war, he planned to be in the thick of it.

Just before adjournment in July 1798, Congress sent President Adams a bill which authorized him to appoint the following officers: Inspector General, with the rank of major general; Quartermaster General; Paymaster General; Adjutant General; Commander of the Army with the rank of lieutenant general.

"It is yet uncertain," Senator Henry Tazewell of Virginia wrote to Madison, "whether Washington will accept command of the army. Hamilton has been here eight or ten days, and it is believed that he will have the efficient command."

III

(1798–1799)

A man who had read, thought, and written as much as Hamilton had about government, and had lived at the center of military and political power for so long, might well find it downright impossible to practice law and go to dinner parties without a wondering mind.

He had written deeply about the Presidency in the Federalist Papers. The office had stringent limitations, surely. It did not control the national purse, and had only a limited veto over the laws. But the office had great potency, too. It commanded all the military forces. Except for the required confirmation every four years, it could be a lifetime position, and Hamilton in Federalist No. 72 had argued with his customary realism for unlimited terms:

". . . the desire of reward is one of the strongest incentives of human conduct . . . the best security for the fidelity of mankind is to make their interest coincide with their duty. Even the love of fame, the ruling passion of the noblest minds . . .

would, on the contrary, deter him from the undertaking when he foresaw that he would quit the scene before he could accomplish the work. . . ."

Yes, the Presidency could be a mighty office, and considering the increasing number of states—Kentucky being the fifteenth, in 1792, Tennessee the sixteenth, in 1796—and the growing population of North America, a man who was President of the United States could make himself the most powerful ruler on earth.

In Kentucky: James Wilkinson of Revolutionary notoriety had moved there in 1784 and become a politico-enterpriser in bringing off statehood and opening the Mississippi to American traders. Hamilton and Adams both had heard that Wilkinson was in Spanish pay and had tried to make a separate country out of Kentucky. But Wilkinson had fought well after returning to the American army under "Mad" Anthony Wayne. At Wayne's death in 1796 Wilkinson had been promoted by Washington to command of the Western Department.

In Tennessee: The state's lyrical name was proposed, it was said, by Andrew Jackson in the territorial legislature. Jackson, "the border captain," had made a name of his own, Hamilton noted. This backwoods lawyer, legislator, and militia leader personified the frontier, and the frontier personified the new nation, which had achieved a head-count of four million Americans in the census of 1790.

Wilkinson and Jackson represented the expansionist spirit that intrigued with red men and white men, plunged across boundaries, seized millions of acres of land—in the process acquiring individual wealth in the hundreds of thousands of dollars and threatening to drive Indians, Spaniards, Frenchmen, Englishmen off the map. Kentuckians and Tennesseans were a new breed of "monied men," building a slave-labor plantation society, supporting both the Jeffersonian democracy and the Hamiltonian programs for cavalry, cannon, and frigates. No writer and thinker in the 1790's could understand the American Presidency without understanding the West.

If you thought of the West, you thought of the European powers with their land claims and their imperial politics, so much at odds with the republican form of government. The United States would never be secure until the flags of Britain, Spain, France, and Russia were withdrawn from North America.

To think continentally was only a step from thinking hemispherically. The West Indies held a flanking position off the Southern states. It was known that Bonaparte, or the black general in Haiti who called himself Citizen Toussaint, had ideas of landing in the Carolinas and promoting a slave insurrection that would sweep to the Gulf of Mexico. "There can be no doubt of their arming our own Negroes against us," said Washington.

If you thought of Mexico, you thought of the whole of Spanish America, and Hamilton thought especially of Francisco Miranda, the would-be liberator of his native Venezuela, who had been a Revolutionary War officer under Lafayette.

Much depended on President Adams. He was getting the reputation of a "big Navy" man. He looked seaward, not westward. Amid the patriotic XYZ frenzy, and with Jeffersonians in partial eclipse, it was a time when John Adams could do no wrong. "I believe there is no want of firmness in the Executive," Hamilton told King, and went on to praise Adams' behavior as "manly and courageous . . . firm and magnanimous."

Hamilton saw that a man needed popular backing if he was to make the most of the Executive office. He saw how careful a President must be to keep the favor of the fickle public. For example, Adams scoffed at friendly advice. A Federalist warned that "public sentiment is very much against your being so much away from the seat of government." Adams regarded the warning as nonsense. "The Secretaries of State, Treasury, War, Navy and the Attorney General transmit me daily by the post all the business of consequence . . . nothing suffers or is lost." This President would be away from the seat of government for 385 days of his four-year term.

To Hamilton's dismay Adams committed a major *faux pas*

that could easily have been avoided. As February 22 of 1798 approached, the First Family were invited by a group of merchants to a "ball . . . in honor of the birth of George Washington." Adams brusquely marked the invitation "Declined" and did not attend.

Then, in the summer of the same year, Adams made a grosser blunder. He signed into law the four bills known collectively as the Alien and Sedition Acts. They lengthened the period for naturalization, gave the President power to deport non-citizens, allowed federal prosecution for seditious libel.

The measures were not without some justification in their time and place. There were estimated to be thirty thousand French nationals at large in the country, their loyalties unknown, and thousands of other immigrants from Europe and the West Indies with foreign ties. In addition there were overeducated intellectuals who postured as "citizens of the world," giving no fealty to America. Also, there were vicious journalists who hurled insults and malicious lies at the keepers of the American State. Whether it was nobler for the country and its leaders to endure all this, rather than turn the might of the central government against its tormentors, was a question to give pause to the thoughtful.

IV

(1798–1799)

Every Federalist in national office, without exception, supported passage of the Alien and Sedition Laws, as did George Washington in his retirement, along with Patrick Henry. Only two Federalists, Hamilton and John Marshall, took serious issue with some of the extreme proposals and provisions.

Marshall was not in office in June 1798, when President Adams signed the bills, but he was a candidate for the House in the autumn of that year, and commented on the measures. He said he would not have voted for them. He did not find them unjust, but, rather, "useless . . . calculated to create unnecessary discontents and jealousies."

This was Hamilton's position too. On June 7, 1798, he wrote

to Secretary of State Pickering concerning some naval matters, and continued:

"P.S. If an alien bill passes, I would like to know what policy, in execution, is likely to govern the *Executive*." Several versions of the bill gave Adams authority to deport undesirable non-citizens, and Hamilton was asking how the President would use this authority. "My opinion is," he continued to Pickering, "that while the mass ought to be obliged to leave the country, the provisions in our treaties in favor of merchants ought to be observed. . . ." He wrote this as many French merchants were leaving the country. He hoped the President would not cause an unselective exodus.

"There ought to be *guarded* exceptions of characters whose situations would expose them too much if sent away, and whose demeanour among us has been unexceptionable. There are a few such. Let us not be cruel or violent."

Typically, Hamilton was showing special concern for the mercantile classes. He believed these were of particular usefulness to the country and that they were generally attached to the Federalist party. He was showing also his often-expressed disinclination to see the innocent punished with the guilty. He would support the repressive measures, but his recommendations for amendment were all in the direction of moderation and leniency.

This attitude was more marked three weeks later in a letter to Secretary of the Treasury Wolcott on June 29. Hamilton said he had "this moment" seen a draft of the anti-sedition section. It troubled him, probably because the penalty clause called for capital punishment. He found the stringent provisions "highly exceptionable," and tending to "endanger" the country with "civil war." This was substantially the objection that Marshall would state even after the bill had been modified.

"I sincerely hope the thing will not be hurried through," Hamilton continued to Wolcott. "Let us not establish a tyranny. Energy is a very different thing from violence. If we make no false step, we shall be essentially united, but if we push things to an extreme, we shall give to faction *body* and solidarity."

Marshall, though he disliked the legislation, was fully satisfied that the Alien and Sedition Acts were constitutional. He
said as much in a written opinion on the Virginia Legislature's
resolution against the two acts. Sedgwick called Marshall's
paper a "masterly performance," and Albert J. Beveridge took
note of it in his biography of Marshall: "In no writing or spoken
word, before he became Chief Justice of the United States, did
Marshall so extensively state his constitutional views as in this
unknown paper."

Marshall expounded the same doctrine of implied powers
that Hamilton had used several times, notably in arguing for
the national bank. "It is essential to the common good," Marshall argued, to protect "the nation from the intrigues and
conspiracies of dangerous aliens . . . to secure the union from
their wicked machinations." The power of such protection "can
only be obtained by the cooperation of the whole . . . the government of the whole." Let the states attend to local matters.
Let the central government manage general affairs. This was
the meaning of the Constitution, in the opinion of Marshall and
Hamilton.

Neither man had a voting record on the controversial acts,
but it is fair to surmise from his silence that Hamilton consented. He neither protested the President's signature nor
recommended a veto. Had he strongly disapproved, his opinion
would have been made known to his intimate followers, who
wrote and promoted the legislation. But Harper and Otis in the
Senate, Ames and Sedgwick in the House, Pickering, Wolcott,
and McHenry in the Cabinet, were never set against the Alien
and Sedition Acts by their leader.

Henry Cabot Lodge, Hamilton's sympathetic and knowledge-
able biographer, would write with amusement: "There has
been a general effort on the part of biographers to clear their
respective heroes from all responsibility for those ill-fated
measures. The truth is, they had the full support of the congressmen and senators who passed them, of the President who
signed them. . . . Hamilton went as far in sustaining the principle of these laws as anyone." Having done what he could to
amend the worst features of the bills, "he was one of their
strongest supporters," wrote Lodge.

V

(1798–1799)

Hamilton had not changed his opinion that governors and presidents, when it became necessary, should always be swift to intervene against insurrection. He read the Virginia Resolutions of 1798 and the similar Kentucky Resolutions, drafted by Jefferson, as claims to nullify any offensive federal law, and therefore as proclamations for secession. In January 1799, he informed Jonathan Dayton, Speaker of the House: "The late attempt of Virginia and Kentucky to unite the State Legislatures in a direct resistance to certain laws of the Union can be considered in no other light than an attempt to change the government."

A month later, on February 2, he wrote to Theodore Sedgwick, who would be Speaker before the year was out, on the same point. Hamilton proposed that a House committee be appointed to study "the tendency of the doctrines advanced by Virginia and Kentucky to destroy the Constitution . . . and . . . to encourage hostile foreign powers. . . ."

Adams, after a strong start, was something worse than a weak President. He was an erratic one. In Hamilton's opinion, a vacuum existed in the chief magistracy after 1798. The country looked for something to which it had become accustomed through eight years of Washington's leadership and the first two years of Adams'. That strength was no longer there.

Hamilton could not but think how much better if the country had elected his candidate in 1796. Thomas Pinckney, militarily and gubernatorially experienced, would have been a better choice. War seemed more probable day by day, and letters flew fast between Hamilton's New York office and the Cabinet in Philadelphia. More significantly, they flew between Broadway and Mount Vernon.

Hamilton: "You ought to be aware, my dear sir, that in the event of an open rupture with France, the country will again call you to the command of the armies of your country."

Washington: ". . . I should like previously to know who would be my coadjutors, and whether you would be disposed to take an active part, if arms are to be resorted to."

Hamilton: ". . . I shall be willing to go into the Army. If you command, the place in which I should hope to be most useful is that of Inspector General, with a place in the line. This I would accept."

He remembered how much Baron von Steuben had done for the American army as its Inspector General.

There was something else to remember. Both Washington and Hamilton had said many times—in the Farewell Address and elsewhere—that military preparedness is the best way to avoid war. Now their maxim would be tested.

VI
(1798–1799)

On December 8, 1798, Major General Hamilton sat in the buttons-and-braid splendor of his new uniform at the side of Lieutenant General Washington, who wore his old buff-and-blue Continentals.

This last was only because the best tailor in Philadelphia was unable to find enough gold thread and had sent the Commander's ordered uniform off to London to be finished. Washington had requisitioned, through the War Department, "a blue coat with yellow buttons and gold epaulettes (each having three stars). . . . A white plume in the hat to be a further distinction." He was irate with both Secretary of War James McHenry and the tailor, for he believed in "a distinguished dress for the commander in chief of the armies of the United States." By bad luck, Hamilton had outdressed his superior officer.

The other major general, C. C. Pinckney—an imposing figure and a general officer since 1782—was also standing erect on the dais in Federal Hall, Philadelphia. Perhaps it was easy for the assembled Senate, House, and diplomatic corps to overlook the gnarled, crabbed, toothless Chief Executive, who should have been central and dominant here. When he entered the hall with his Cabinet in train, and took his place at the Speaker's podium, President Adams seemed diminished by the nation's chief citizen-soldiers.

No matter, for the hardy old patriot had a strong message

for the Fifth Congress. He gained stature and attention as he read, through his bare gums, without a lisp. His speech showed him to be in complete concurrence with the Farewell Address. The way to avoid wars and win negotiations was through military preparedness. Bonaparte and Talleyrand would be less obnoxious now that the three generals had put their uniforms on. The President warned: "Nothing is discoverable in the conduct of France which ought to change or relax our measures of defense." Never, Adams declared, would he send an envoy to France until assured that the minister would have a reception befitting this good and free nation.

Persons present in Federal Hall discerned that the absurdity fell away from one man and hovered ominously over another. Just as unfairly as Adams' appearance sometimes made him a figure of fun, so this day it happened to Hamilton. No matter how tall and straight he held himself, he looked ill-matched with the brawny giant from Virginia and the poised aristocrat from South Carolina. But Hamilton thought so well of his elegant uniform that P. T. Weaver's portrait of him as major general became the picture he liked best. The boyish vision of martial glory lingered with the man. It was the handicap all soldiers are under in peacetime.

Ridicule of Hamilton's military bent had held over from the Whiskey Insurrection, and had redoubled in the melée over the appointment of Washington's general staff. The old Commander accepted the call to arms, but with conditions. He would not take the field until the foe appeared, and he would be paid $500.42 a month while away from home. Also, he would choose his major generals and decide their ratings. Washington sent in the names of Hamilton, Pinckney, and Knox, but President Adams reversed the order in submitting them to the Senate, and Washington threatened not to serve. Senate, Cabinet, Mount Vernon, the Presidential household, and the national press, all reverberated with the quarrel. Hamilton, its central cause—the old General's favorite, the new President's abomination by this time, the brevet colonel jumped to major general and *de facto* commander—became everybody's example of ambition on a ladder.

In truth, Hamilton had strongly pleaded his case for promotion to the top, but had not made an ultimatum of his plea. "With regard to the delicate subject of the relative rank of the major generals, it is very natural for me to be a partial judge, . . ." he wrote his old Commander. But after giving every reason he could summon for outranking Knox and Pinckney, he concluded: "I stand ready . . . to submit the preference. It shall *never* be said, with any color of truth, that my ambition or interest has stood in the way of the public good."

Even so, the Jacobin press unmercifully taunted him as "Little Mars." He was the "Little West Indian" who aped the "Little Corsican." Abigail Adams wrote to her son-in-law of Hamilton: "That man . . . would become a second Bonaparty if he was possessed of equal power. . . ."

Abigail may not have remembered that her husband, no soldier at all, had dressed for his Inaugural with a sword draped around his large stomach. Or that when he addressed a group of patriotic students on May 7, 1798, he stepped to the balcony of his Presidential residence in full military regalia. As for Hamilton, he was inured to abuse, and it never deterred him. Many times during the envenomed nineties he was called a schemer for "monarchy," a conspirator who wished to steal the Presidential power that he was unable to win in an honest election, a militarist with the daft dream of conquering the hemisphere and putting himself at the head of the "empire" that he so often wrote about. Such characterizations of himself perhaps made him ruefully aware of the circumstantial evidence coming historians would build up against him.

There he stood in that incriminating uniform, with more power than any other American of the day. He was not President, but the principal Cabinet officers were in his pocket. He was not the supreme commander, but the army was under his personal command. When Adams went to his farm and Washington to his plantation, Hamilton stayed at or near the capital. He had soldiers at his heels. He had a Federalist majority in the Senate. He had a heavy score to settle with Madison, Monroe, and Jefferson, and this was his chance. With all this opportunity and motivation, an ambitious man almost had to be a Caesar, a Cromwell, a Bonaparte in the making. Thus the anti-Hamiltonians reasoned, in his time and thereafter.

The three generals had been at work for four weeks before the President's message. (Knox, who would have been the fourth, had refused to serve behind Hamilton and Pinckney.) As subordinate to civilian authorities, they set about to reorganize the army and navy in the manner desired by the legislative and executive branches. They fully understood the American repugnance for "standing armies"—how liberals feared that men-at-arms were a threat to liberty, how conservatives thought them tax-eaters. They wanted a small nucleus with a large reserve on call. There must be sufficient strength to deter Talleyrand or defeat Napoleon.

Hamilton soon had the preparation much to himself. Washington returned to Mount Vernon. Pinckney went off to take command of the exposed southern coast line. Hamilton tried for a while to do the double work of private attorney and Inspector General of the Army. He found himself neglecting his practice and losing clients.

He parceled out his business early in 1790, and gave still more time to the army. He brought in Captain Philip Church, Angelica's twenty-one-year-old son, as an aide, and asked to be considered as on full duty. President Adams in January put Hamilton on the payroll at $268.35 a month, retroactive to November 1798; this was about one-fourth of his average monthly earnings as a practicing lawyer.

His task of defending America was lofty, but it involved a mélange of trivia. Officers had to be commissioned, regulations drawn, manuals printed, pay rates set, pensions provided for, rosters accumulated. He had to make the decision that yellow buttons made uniforms smarter than buttons the color of tarnished silver. "Nothing is more necessary than to stimulate the vanity of soldiers," he noted to Secretary of War McHenry. He complained that "the Hats . . . received for our recruits are not three-cornered but round . . . sans buttons, loops, cockades or bands. . . ."

His policy was not just readiness; it was ever-readiness. Some day the nation might have to fight for its life, and he was laying out plans that would be good for the Adams administration, good forever. He drew up new legislation providing for a military academy, a naval academy, a Department of the Navy, munitions plants and arsenals. Special training was needed immediately for the new corps of engineers, artillery, and cavalry.

He wrote out, for introduction by Representative Harrison Gray Otis, "An Act for the Better Organization of Troops of the United States Army." He held long conferences with Senator Edward Gunn, chairman of the Military Affairs Committee. He inquired of a French officer concerning the best length and velocity for an infantryman's marching step, explaining, "I respect European precedents in a science which has been so much studied and practiced." He recommended the Ferguson rifle, a British Army weapon, for the American soldier. It was a newfangled breech-loader, easy to clean, and he reasoned that "if the shot of it be equally sure, or nearly so, those advantages entitle it to a preference."

President Adams grumbled about "Millions for Defense." He said, "I have always cried 'Ships! Ships!' Hamilton was always 'Troops! Troops!' "

But as former envoy to Admiral d'Estaing and a veteran of Yorktown, Hamilton could never be indifferent to sea power. He had agitated in Washington's Cabinet for the naval shipbuilding program. When the building went slowly under Adams, Hamilton solicited money from the city merchants to arm merchant ships. New York, Philadelphia, and Newburyport supplied funds. Abigail wrote John Quincy Adams, "We shall have a navy spring up like the gourd of Jonah."

But of course it could not happen that way. Rearmament meant heavy taxation, and Hamilton proposed to raise it by levying taxes on men of property. "My idea of revenue would be: A tax on buildings . . . $1,000,000." He would make the burden "fall light on inferior and country houses," but he "saw no impracticability" in making Southern slaveholders pay something on Negro cabins. He asked Congress for a poll tax on "male servants of the capacities by whatever name: *maître d'hôtel*, house steward, *valet de chambre*, cook, house porter, waiter, footman, coachman, groom, postilion, stable boy."

From June 1798 the Cabinet had a Secretary of the Navy, Benjamin Stoddert of Maryland, and he was seldom without advice from the Inspector General:

". . . Nicholson should be employed in superintending the building of one of the 74 Gun Ships. . . . Barry, the brave, seems to be and thinks himself too infirm for active service—perhaps employment may be found for him also on shore. . . . Truxton may be the senior officer in active service, Talbot next. . . . I trouble you with this view of Navy prospects in the hope that you will influence Talbot to serve. He is a man of too much merit to be lost to the service."

The Navy Secretary also learned that the senior major general had a number of deserving relatives. "Capt. Robert Hamilton, a first cousin of mine . . . is regularly bred to the sea, which he has followed since he was fourteen years old. . . . I venture with confidence to recommend him. I shall esteem his appointment a personal favor to myself. . . ."

Hamilton went to Pickering to get a Navy commission for "Capt. Van Rensselaer . . . a connection of our family . . . and may I add that he is of a *brave* blood." Another recommendation to the Navy Department was of Henry Seton, son of the late Cashier.

VII

(1798–1789)

Meanwhile, "the Army is progressing like a wounded snake," a Federalist complained, and Hamilton could hardly disagree. Since he was doing practically all the work, he attracted most of the complaints. People said he was second only to Washington. They forgot he was also second to President Adams, to the House and Senate, and to the Secretary of War. He knew better than anybody else that the build-up was going slowly, and he had a mental list of the reasons why.

Item: President Adams was back at his erratic behavior again. Shortly after the ringing message to Congress, he wrote McHenry that "there was no more prospect of seeing a French army here than in heaven," and that "regiments are costly articles."

Item: Genial James McHenry, poet and non-practicing physician, had done very well at the War Department when there was little to do, but no longer. "My friend McHenry is wholly insufficient for his place," Hamilton wrote Washington.

Item: Commissions were subject to political patronage and objections. Hamilton wanted the able Burr as a brigadier and quartermaster general. He wrote Wolcott expressing the hope that "the administration may manifest a cordiality to him. . . . I am aware there are different judges, but the case is worth the experiment." Washington rejected Burr as having "equal talents for intrigue," and Hamilton had to employ civilian agents to do the quartermastering.

Item: War with France would mean action in the Spanish territories of Louisiana and Florida. Wanted: a reliable Western commander. Available: General James Wilkinson. Hamilton "had heard hard things said of the General . . . never seen a shadow of proof." Washington thought the way to handle the able but ill-reputed Wilkinson was to "feed his ambition, sooth his vanity, by arresting discontent." It took time to sift so many opinions.

The Inspector General was kept crouching for long hours over his desk. At length, with relief, he would put on his dress uniform and go into society for relaxation. In the drawing room, it was noted by Troup, "he maintains an unequalled reputation for gallantry. Such at least is the opinion entertained of him by the Ladies."

Letters, diaries, printed items, and future memoirs all confirm that Hamilton enjoyed himself after staff work, and that he dallied in the "fields of Venus," since there were no "fields of Mars" to which he could gallop. Again, circumstantial evidence was being gathered against him by those who already had decided what sort he was, this friend of wealth, this dashing boudoir soldier.

In truth, however, the senior major general was as difficult to label as the young assemblyman had been many years before. He was thought the iron-hearted disciplinarian, but then across his desk came "a warrant for the execution of Sergeant Hunt," a deserter. "I incline to the side of forbearance," Hamilton wrote back to McHenry. "The temper of our country is not a little opposed to the frequency of capital punishment."

It did not mean he had turned soft on offenders and amenable to popular passions. Adams ordered Governor Mifflin to send five hundred Pennsylvania militiamen to put down the taxpayers' revolt led by John Fries; Hamilton was not consulted but he approved. "Whenever the government appears in arms, it ought to appear like a Hercules, and inspire respect by reason of strength."

He was not doctrinaire. He was flexible. He was an *ad hoc* decider of cases. Only those predetermined to think the worst of him fell into the conspiratorial theory. His maxim about a show of force to quell disturbances would be coupled in future books with the Napoleonic "whiff of grapeshot." Albert Gallatin, who had never seen a day of military service, told the House that Hamilton's peacetime army meant dictatorship.

Of more importance than guns and horses was the flotilla of seventy-five boats for military transport that Hamilton ordered General James Wilkinson to build on the western rivers. The flag must follow the frontiers. If war broke out with France, he was prepared to move into Louisiana and Florida. If the British Fleet struck at Spain in Latin America, he was willing to supply ground troops to aid the defenders but only on orders from President Adams. He made this point very firmly to General Miranda:

"The sentiments I entertain with regard to that object have long since been in our knowledge, but I could personally have no participation in it unless patronized by the government of this country."

His scrupulousness in such matters was taken for granted by those who knew him best. Gouverneur Morris, meditating in his diary after Hamilton's death, wrote of the man's ambition, ". . . but he was too proud, and let me add, too virtuous to recommend or tolerate measures eventually fatal to liberty or honor."

Hamilton ordered Wilkinson to come east for consultation, and they met in New York on August 1, 1799, for a full month of planning. Hamilton sent the plans to Mount Vernon, where they were approved but never executed, for John Adams' strategy for peace overtook all.

The President was craftier than his critics knew. Without consulting Congress or Cabinet, Washington or Hamilton, he appointed his son's friend, William Vans Murray, thirty-nine, who was minister at The Hague, to become envoy to Paris. Finally, in response to the near-frantic advice of the Cabinet, Adams added Chief Justice Oliver Ellsworth and North Carolina Governor William Davie as commissioners.

The President at no time admitted it, but he was about to test the Washington-Hamilton maxim that military preparedness is the best of all peace-keeping policies. By the Act of July 16, 1798, which made Hamilton the senior major general and Inspector General, Congress increased the authorized strength of the regular Army from 4,173 to 14,421 officers and men. Congress also authorized the President "to raise, in addition to the present military establishment, twelve regiments of infantry, and six troops of light dragoons to be enlisted for and during the continuance of the existing differences between the United States and the French Republic. . . ." This increment, used to patrol the southeast coast, the Mississippi Valley, and the Great Lakes region, was called the Additional Army.

In another Act to improve defense, Congress on May 28, 1798, had authorized the Provisional Army to be mobilized "in the event of a declaration of war against the United States or of actual invasion. . . ." This force, since war and invasion did not occur, existed only on paper, but it later became the equivalent of the modern Army of the United States, made up of infantrymen, riflemen, artillerists, engineers, and cavalrymen, to be deployed "in case war shall break out between the United States and a foreign European power."

As most friendly biographers claim and some hostile ones deny, Hamilton in Adams' administration, still under Washington's leadership, was the architect of the U.S. military establishment, just as he had been the architect of the financial establishment in Washington's. Both structures remain today much as he built them. In both instances, he literally made something where before there had been nothing.

All this increase of ground forces during 1798–1799, to say nothing of the superior American Navy, and despite annoying details of organization, did indeed convey a resounding message to France. Not-very-secret discussions of dispatching an American expedition to Santo Domingo also tended to put the French Directory off balance. There took place in Paris a distinct change of attitude toward the United States.

Adams was secretly in touch with Talleyrand and thought he had a bargain; but he refrained from dispatching Ellsworth and Davie until completion of three additional naval squadrons. John Adams, veteran negotiator, valued the position of strength, though he gave no credit to those who had brought it about. He said he wished engraved on his tombstone, "Here lies John Adams who took upon himself the responsibility of peace with France in the year 1800." He did not say that, in its first test, preparedness had kept the peace.

Adams' desire to be known as the one-man peacemaker was hardly stronger than his determination to assert his rank over Hamilton and to be finally rid of this incubus. In October 1799, with Hamilton pondering deployment problems, Adams left his farm to meet Ellsworth, Davie, and some of the Cabinet at Trenton, where the Administration had taken refuge from the Philadelphia fever. On Monday, October 14, the *Federalist & New Jersey Gazette* reported, "The President of the United States arrived in this city from Quincy on Wednesday last. . . . Same day arrived here Major General Hamilton from New York, and General Wilkinson of the western army."

Adams set up headquarters at the Phoenix Hotel. On October 15, the *New Jersey State Gazette* disclosed that the President "was immediately waited upon by the Heads of Department, Generals Hamilton and Wilkinson and a number of gentlemen of respectability.

"On Friday evening there was a handsome display of fireworks in honor of the President's arrival, in which Mr. Guimpe, the artist, exhibited much skill and ingenuity to the satisfac-

tion of a large concourse of spectators; the initials [J.A. and
G.W.] were displayed in coloured fires and received with shouts
of applause. . . .

"It is said that matters of great pith and moment are shortly
to engage the heads of the nation now in Trenton; the most
important of which are, probably, the question respecting the
sailing of our ministers, and the spoliation by British cruisers
on the American commerce which, we are reliably informed,
have strongly excited the sensibility of [the] administration."

It is uncertain whether Adams expected to encounter his
chief military officer; he was most certainly not amenable to
any advice from that source. Adams knew that Hamilton was
at the camp in Newark, and the President heartily wished he
would stay there "disciplining and teaching tactics to his troops
if he had been capable of it." Instead, Hamilton rode into Trenton to face fireworks of another sort—Adams' explosive temper—when they held their interview at the Phoenix.

"It was a strange meeting," observed the Adams biographer,
Page Smith, ". . . the Puritan and the Libertine, the short,
stout President, little more than civil, and the Major General,
gracious, charming and subtle." Hamilton predicted a French
monarchy by Christmas, and Adams quickly shut him off. He
did not believe the change would happen, and what if it did?
"We shall not be any worse off than at present." Adams by now
had divined who was running his Cabinet. He hated being
taunted as "President by three votes," and he knew who was
responsible for his tight squeak. He was more convinced than
ever that ". . . the British faction was determined to have a
war with France, and Alexander Hamilton at the head of the
Army and then President of the United States." He was more
than ever determined to make a personal truce with Talleyrand and Bonaparte.

Curtly and rudely, the President terminated the interview,
inflicting all the humiliation he could upon the other man. At
the end he pointedly turned his back and left his caller standing.

It seemed a risky exercise in pique on Adams' part. Elements
of Hamilton's army stood in arms only a few miles away. A

military man with dangerous ambition could be tempted and insulted just so far. If Hamilton was truly what Adams said of him, he never had greater incentive to live up to that elegant Major General's uniform and make himself master of America.

Instead, he rode back to New York, and confided his misgivings in a letter to Mount Vernon, where they met with full agreement. "The President has resolved to send the commissioners to France, . . ." Hamilton wrote. "All my calculations lead me to regret the measure. I hope that it may not in its consequences involve the United States in a war on the side of France with her enemies. My trust in Providence, which has so often intervened in our favor, is my only consolation."

Hamilton thought Adams a foolish man, and Adams thought him a treacherous one. Hamilton thought that the President was only getting deeper into the intrigues of European power politics. The President thought Hamilton the leader of a cabal for dictatorship. Adams meant to pass this judgment into history, for in July 1806, when Hamilton was two years dead, Adams sent John Marshall an item for the latter's *Life of George Washington:*

"There is the fact . . . which it will be difficult for posterity to believe, and that is that measures taken by the Senators, Members of the House, some of the heads of departments, and some of the officers of the Army to force me to appoint General Washington . . . proceeded not from any regard to him . . . but merely from an intention to employ him as an engine to elevate Hamilton to the head of affairs, civil as well as military."

Adams never relented toward Hamilton, but he did once write, in old age, when contemplating life-after-death:

"After all, I hope to meet my wife and friends, ancestors and posterity, sages ancient and modern. I believe I could get over my objections to meeting Alexander Hamilton and Tim[othy] Pick[ering], if I could see a symptom of penitence in either. . . ."

CHAPTER TWENTY-FIVE

His Last Fling at President-Making

I

(1799–1800)

Usurpation would have been awkward while George Washington lived. But there came a letter, dated in December 1799, from General C. C. Pinckney, telling of Washington's death at Mount Vernon on the fourteenth.

"My imagination is gloomy—my heart is sad," Hamilton replied. He could not bring himself, he told Pinckney, to dwell upon the subject of losing "our beloved Commander-in-Chief." He touched upon his private grief. "Perhaps no friend of his has more cause to lament on personal account than myself," but the "public misfortune" was still worse.

Hamilton's last work of writing for the Chief was in the form of a "General Order for the Ceremony to be used on the Interment of Washington." In it, he hailed the Commander as "Man of the Age," and said, "I equally mourn . . . the long-tried patron—the kind and unchanging friend." He wrote feelingly to the widow and to the private secretary, Tobias Lear. In these letters he spoke with a delicacy that went unnoted for many years.

In 1972, James Thomas Flexner, the General's Pulitzer Prize-winning biographer, more perceptive than his predecessors, observed that persons close to Washington in the second term, and perhaps the man himself, had resented the contemporary suspicion "that Washington was as president little more than a puppet of Hamilton's." In order to banish any such idea from the minds of Mrs. Washington and Lear, Hamilton chose words that have often been misinterpreted.

"I may, without impropriety, allude to the numerous and distinguished marks of confidence and friendship of which you yourself have been a witness," he told Martha, "but I cannot say in how many ways the continuance of that confidence and friendship was necessary to me in my future relationships."

Earlier he had written to Lear, who had been at the General's death bed, in a passage that has often been given a pejorative interpretation: "Perhaps no man . . . has equal cause with myself to deplore the loss. I have been much indebted to the kindness of the General, and he was an Aegis very essential to me."

Hamilton was assuring the widow that Washington "was necessary to me," rather than the other way around. This was something that she, of course, very much wanted to hear from the man alleged to have been her husband's puppet-master. There was no "singular infelicity," as has been written, in Hamilton's words; quite the contrary. In telling Lear that Washington had been an "Aegis"—the shield or breastplate of Zeus—to him, Hamilton was again giving reassurance to a grieving intimate of the deceased. He was saying that Washington had been the protector and, in the underlying meaning to Lear, never the protected.

Only six months before his death, Washington was importuned by Governor Jonathan Trumbull of Connecticut and by Gouverneur Morris to make himself a candidate in the Presidential election of 1800. There was little hope that Adams could win, or would govern well if he did, and Trumbull urged Washington to head off "a French President," Jefferson by name.

Trumbull later admitted he had showed the letter to two or more Cabinet members, and presumably had their approval. The conspicuous omission of Hamilton's name indicated that he either was not consulted, or did not approve. His hand in composing the Farewell Address showed that he had long ago abandoned the idea of a lifetime Presidency, and had since concentrated on the orderly succession of the headship of state, a rare event in the waning eighteenth century.

There is a strong signal that Washington to the end felt that this orderly succession should be left entirely to the people, even under the threat of getting the "French" Jefferson. The signal was given when, at the time Washington was drawing his last will, he decided to return to England a symbolic oaken box that had been sent to him as a gift by the Earl of Buchan. The box was said to be made of wood from a tree which had sheltered William Wallace after the battle of Falkirk in 1298. It had been sent to Washington by Lord Buchan with the request that Washington bequeath it (in the General's own words) "to the man in my country who should appear to merit it best."

Under the circumstances, writing his will with a premonition of approaching death, Washington had this last chance at President-making. Should he bequeath this emblem of his approval to Hamilton? To John Marshall? To Bushrod Washington, his nephew, heir to Mount Vernon and at that time Supreme Court associate justice?

No; it would not do for America to be touched by the slightest taint of monarchical succession. Nor for Hamilton, of all men, to be stigmatized by any such symbolic laying on of hands. "I recommit the Box . . . to his Lordship"; that was how Washington made his position clear.

But when the mourning for Washington had subsided a little, there stood Major General Hamilton, in full control of the American armed forces. The President drove Pickering and McHenry from the Cabinet, raging to the former that Hamilton was "an intriguant . . . a bastard . . . a foreigner." Here was more incentive for a *coup d'état* by Hamilton. The peace mission was in France, but Wilkinson had those invasion barges on the Ohio River. All the elements for a military take-over were present. Hamilton needed only to give the word for an advance against the weak Spanish forces downstream, to set it all in motion.

Of course it was a word that Hamilton was incapable of giving. He would have had to re-enter the womb and be reborn as another sort of nation-builder. He would have had to expunge several passages of the Federalist Papers in which the military authority was subordinated to the civilian authority of Executive, Legislative, and Judicial branches. He would have had to disavow the Farewell Address with its stress on national unity and order. He would have had to disappoint thousands of readers of those patriotic polemics, destroy his own image as protector of the Constitution, alter his association with the Federalist party aristocracy, and consort with such confederates as the venturesome Miranda, and Wilkinson, the "tarnished warrior."

Worst of all, perhaps, he would have had to eat thousands of his own written and spoken words in which he had declared that the American and French revolutions were nothing at all alike. The social revolution in France had committed regicide, devoured its own children, invaded its neighbors, put a dictator on horseback, reached across oceans for world conquest, and was swinging full circle from monarchy, to anarchy, to republic, to empire.

In contrast, the strictly political revolution in America had flourished under two opposing factions in bloodless competition, made a peaceable and lawful succession of Presidents, fought only a defensive war at sea, resisted the temptation to attack any neighbors. Though he was often pessimistic about the Constitution's longevity, Hamilton had had a hand in writing that covenant, and it was foreign to his nature to make a military move "unless patronized by the government of this country."

While awaiting orders from the civil authorities, Hamilton learned that President Adams had reprimanded McHenry for a report to the House in which the departed Washington was eulogized and Hamilton praised.

"Passing wonderful!" Hamilton remarked, "that a eulogy of a dead patriot and hero . . . should . . . be irksome to the ears of his successor! Singular, also, that an encomium on the officer first in rank in the armies of the United States, appointed and continued by Mr. Adams, should in his eyes have been a crime. . . ."

No signal was given to indicate Hamilton's military status. No officer ranked above him, and in that sense he felt "continued" in his present rank—not the same as being raised to Washington's rank of lieutenant general. "Who is to be Commander in Chief?" he asked Rufus King. "Not the next in command. The appointment will probably be deferred." He had made material sacrifices to build the armed forces which had made the peace come true. President Adams might have expressed thanks. But "I could not see . . . any proof of good will or confidence, or of a disposition to console me."

Gradually the negative message became all too clear. He was not wanted. His presence was not needed. Congress did not renew appropriations for the emergency, and the Army must be cut back to its Regulars, 3,500 in number. On May 13, 1800, Hamilton asked leave of the War Department to resign on June 1. This request was refused on the grounds that he should stay until it was certain that he had fully and safely disbanded the troops. Ultimately he submitted another resignation, written on June 13, to be effective July 2. In the intervening six weeks he traveled to the scattered eastern bases and carried out the demobilization. He observed the strictest formality, drafting the General Order in the President's name:

"Major-General Hamilton has it in command from the President of the United States to assure the officers and men . . . that he entertains a strong sense of the laudable zeal by which they were induced to take the field at the appearance of danger to their country. . . . The Major-General is happy to be the organ of this expression of the sentiments of the President."

Recalling the disgraceful aftermath of Revolutionary War demobilization, Hamilton followed up the General Order by adding more intimate farewells. He took his stand in front of the troops as he told them they deserved well of their country, and reminded them that they were returning to civilian life with training that might later be useful.

The personal appearances were appreciated. At Providence, Rhode Island, the soldiers were moved to weep, "not merely on account of this last interview with their General, but by the impressive sentiments which fell from his lips, enforced by the most charming eloquence and pointed diction." At Boston there was a triumphal turnout of clergy and officialdom, a testimonial previously reserved for George Washington.

Some accused the Inspector General of making the trip to electioneer against Adams. In any event, with armed men cheering him and citizens celebrating his coming, he was walk-

ing the paths which many a hero had taken toward dictatorship
and monarchy. But he was no more than ever capable of forcing
the hand of history against the letter or the spirit of the American law.

He had watched Adams muddle through a troubled term,
and was determined to do what had to be done about that in
a Constitutional manner. Adams must go.

"For my individual part, my mind is made up," he wrote
Federalist Samuel Dexter. "I will never more be responsible for
[Adams] by my direct support, even though the consequence
should be the election of *Jefferson.* If we must have an enemy
at the head of the government, let it be one whom we can
oppose. . . ."

Now, in his fourth round of President-making, Hamilton
surveyed the game and what it could win him. First, he wanted
to get rid of John Adams. Second, he would like to end the
national career of Thomas Jefferson. But the grand sweep-
stakes prize would be to make a President out of Charles Cotesworth Pinckney, elegantly educated at Oxford and Caen, a
military figure, a noted diplomatist, a signer of the Constitution, a negotiator who had scorned to pay bribes and had inspired the lasting motto, "Millions for defense, but not one cent
for tribute."

II

(January–February 1800)

Hamilton picked up his neglected law practice. His contemporaries by now regarded him as an intellectual prodigy; his
brethren at the New York Bar hung upon his words and actions
like mere mortals watching an Olympian.

James Kent, his hero-worshiper since the mid-eighties ("He
was my idol"), would live to write memoirs, and he could never
mention Hamilton without awe. "His mighty mind would at
times bear down all opposition by its comprehensive grasp and
the strength of his reasoning power." Kent selected two Hamilton cases "in which his varied powers were most strikingly

displayed." One of them was *Le Guen v. Gouverneur & Kemble,* Court of Errors, Albany, beginning in January 1800.

Louis Le Guen, French citizen and trader, had arrived in New York in 1794, unknown and unable to speak English, but with a large cargo of indigo and cotton from a French island off Madagascar in the Indian Ocean. As a sagacious stranger, he set about to learn who were the New Yorkers of the most prestige, and to put his business into their hands. His first move was to store his goods in the warehouse of the merchants Isaac Gouverneur and Peter Kemble, and to engage this firm as his agent, or factor. Le Guen's next move was to consign his goods, under a labyrinthine contract, to the ship *White Fox* for a try at the European market. The upshot was a running legal battle that went on from 1796 to 1800, comprising eight separate actions and providing precedents that became contractual doctrine in fifteen states, the last known citation being in New Jersey in 1948.

Once entangled in the law, Le Guen looked about for the New York lawyers of the highest standing. He engaged Hamilton as chief counsel, with Aaron Burr and Richard Harison as associates. Hamilton soon noted several ironies at play. He was defense counsel for a French subject at a time when he was arming the nation against France. Three persons involved in the cross-suits for fraud were referred to throughout the trials as "the Jews"; Hamilton's supposed mother had been married to a member of that race. Some ugly anti-Semitism developed, and Hamilton found himself defending the civil right of "Jews" to testify under oath in a Christian court.

As an attorney with a marked and reciprocated preference for wealthy, high-born, well-established clients, Hamilton was representing something else in Le Guen, and his service to this client brought him many similar ones. "His clients in these cases," noted *The Law Practice of Alexander Hamilton,* "were not the established merchants of New York, but the small businessmen, strangers and foreigners, agents, captains, supercargoes and free lances, who served or dealt with those settled merchants."

Hamilton was undertaking a case which made him the court-room opponent of some fast friends: Robert Troup, Gouverneur Morris, Brockholst Livingston. Opposed also was a new friend but an old acquaintance. This was Nathaniel Pendleton, "a gentleman-like, smooth man," by Hamilton's description. Virginia-born, a year younger than Hamilton, Pendleton had fought in the Southern campaigns under Greene; he had received for his gallantry one of those rewards that had always eluded the Little Lion—the official thanks of Congress. Pendleton set up as a lawyer in Savannah, became a non-serving delegate to the Constitutional Convention, and rose to be Georgia's chief justice; he moved to New York in 1796, during the early rounds of the Le Guen case.

From the outset Brockholst Livingston was nervous about opposing a lawyer of Hamilton's renown. He warned his client, Isaac Gouverneur, "I much fear you are marked out as a victim to the reputation of Mr. Hamilton."

Troup, whose feelings were easily injured, disliked going up against Hamilton, who treated a law court like a battlefield or a political contest. On February 7, Troup wrote: "Between us, Hamilton has pushed this cause to the utmost extremity, and in my opinion in the utmost animosity & cruelty against Gouverneur & Kemble."

Troup was testifying to his friend's intense will-to-win in any contest. This wholly commercial case did not hold the moral significance of others in which his ardor would be more explicable. "Hamilton was undoubtedly bitter, sarcastic and emotional in his appeal . . ." admits Goebel, the legal biographer, and puts it down to the need of discrediting witnesses who were accusing Le Guen of fraud. But the debate did not threaten to get out of hand until the appearance of a colorful personality, huge in body, pompous in language—Gouverneur Morris, the hearty roué of two continents.

Morris had a pecuniary interest in the case through his kinsman, Isaac Gouverneur, and he thought himself the intellectual match of Le Guen's chief counsel. But Morris had not practiced law for many years, certainly not since 1788, when he left this country for Europe, whence he had just returned.

He undertook to substitute rhetoric for argument, and literary ostentation for case histories. He thought he could blow Hamilton down by bluster. With a tactic that suddenly changed the nature of the contest, he pointed at Hamilton, who was standing near Burr, and declaimed that he intended to make the former cry out, "Help me, Cassius, or I sink."

Hamilton asked leave to answer the personal reference, and this was granted as the court adjourned for the day. Word spread of a battle between titans, and next morning "an immense auditory" was on hand. Hamilton by all accounts surpassed himself, using subdued satire that caused Morris to writhe as he listened, taking up the slurs against Le Guen and his Jewish partners, moving to bombast where it fitted his orchestration. He declared that "Justice . . . knew no birthplace, no dominion, no power on earth. Born in heaven, her home was and ever would be wherever right was to be administered—wrong redressed; and be the injured party, or Jew, or Gentile, or Christian, or Pagan, Foreign or Native, she clothes him with her mantle. . . ."

After three hours of somewhat savage badinage at the expense of Morris, Hamilton broke off. "But let us have done with this trifling," he said; and speedily summed up the case and asked for a verdict.

"We all thought we knew him," gasped an opposing counsel, "but we knew nothing of him."

"I thought myself something," observed Kent, who was one of the sitting judges, "but I find I am a pigmy."

Troup wrote a coverage of it all to Rufus King. "Our friend Hamilton never appeared to have his passions so warmly engaged in any cause. He was full of acrimony against Gouverneur and Kemble and . . . I think he was guilty of indelicacy toward me which my heart tells me I ought to forgive, but which my friends will not permit me as yet to bury in oblivion."

When court closed that day Hamilton went to Schuyler's house to dress for a dinner given by the patroon, Stephen Van Rensselaer. Referring later to Morris' painful humiliation in such a public place, Schuyler said, "I hope he will profit by it, for I very sincerely wish him well." It was expected that Morris would be among the guests that evening, and when they reached the patroon's home, Van Rensselaer met Hamilton at the door, "and to put him on guard, informed him that Morris was in a very bad humor."

Hamilton entered and boldly approached his sulking adversary, saying, "My friend, you will rejoice, I hope, that by Cassius' help I meet you here with our friends for dinner."

When the verdict was given shortly afterwards, it reached the dizzying height of $119,302.47. Agog with gratitude Le Guen went to Hamilton and offered him a fee of $8,000. Not for the first time by any means, Hamilton declined to take advantage of a client who was hysterical with thankfulness. He told Le Guen that he would accept no more than $1,000.

"Leaving General Hamilton," wrote a person who got it from the bewildered Frenchman himself, "Mr. Le Guen went to Mr. Burr's and made him the same offer, which he received without difficulty; and a few days later borrowed of him another eight thousand dollars, which he never repaid."

III

(1800)

Hamilton was now fairly back into his business. He welcomed the chance to catch up with his creditors (including John Church, whose loans he considerably reduced), renew acquaintance with his children, and sometimes talk of building the family a home in the country. But he did not know how to retire from public life.

No happening impressed him more than the emergence of C. C. Pinckney as a political force. On his return from France, the Carolinian and his wife were feted by citizens in Newark, Trenton, and Philadelphia; they were received warmly at Mount Vernon by the Washingtons, and at Richmond by John Marshall. Impressively mounted, Pinckney rode into Charleston in full major general's uniform, to be welcomed home by trumpet, horn, artillery salute, and infantry parade. Best of all for political purposes, the new celebrity was patriotism incarnate and a convert to Federalist politics, without a trace of jealousy or resentment toward Hamilton. "I know that his talents in war were great," Pinckney declared to McHenry, "that he is a genius . . . a spirit courageous and enterprising. . . ."

To Hamilton such a man as this seemed heaven-sent as a Presidential candidate to replace Adams and head off Jefferson. By far the best way to begin was for New England Federalists to drop Adams from the ticket, but this they would not do. Hamilton pursued the next best method. He recommended that a national Federalist caucus, meeting at Philadelphia in May of 1800, nominate an Adams-Pinckney ticket, which in due time he would try to reverse. In spirited correspondence with fellow-Federalists, Hamilton threatened to "withdraw from the party and act upon my own ground" if he could not have his will. He wrote to Sedgwick:

"The only way to prevent a fatal schism in the Federalist party is to support General Pinckney in good earnest. . . . If not I will pursue Mr. Pinckney as my single object."

New York State, as always, was his particular responsibility, and Aaron Burr his personal adversary. The April election for the legislature would choose delegates who in turn would name the Electors. After many years of indirect conflict, Hamilton found himself confronting at point-blank range the most resourceful political manager of the generation. The party which carried the city in large numbers probably would carry the state, and the state could well carry the nation.

As election day approached, Hamilton went from precinct to precinct and made his appeal. He rarely got there first, and was never uncontested. He and Burr would wait politely for each other to finish speaking. The contrasting styles, reputations, and personalities of the two men stood for judgment before the voters.

"They were much the greatest men in the state, and perhaps the greatest men in the United States," Erastus Root recalled thirty years later. Hamilton had met his match. Burr and the Democrats won big enough to claim all twelve Electoral votes for President.

One last foray might still snatch victory from the maw of disaster. There was time for the man whom Hamilton had placed in the Governor's chair to call a special meeting of the outgoing Federalist legislature, which could quickly pass a bill to have the Electors chosen in the districts by the people, thus giving Hamilton a second chance.

"It will not do to be over-scrupulous," he continued to Governor Jay. "It is easy to sacrifice the substantial interests of society by a strict adherence to ordinary rules." Dare to bend the rules, he urged the Governor, and take "a legal and constitutional step to prevent an atheist in religion, and a fanatic in politics, from getting possession of the helm of state."

But Machiavelli had come before Aristides the Just. Jay filed the request, noting, "This is a measure for party purposes which I think it would not become me to accept."

Hamilton found himself in a stricken ship. He could not defeat Burr nor conscript Jay, and soon it turned out that he could not control Pinckney. That elegant idealist positively would not consent to any double-cross of President Adams. Pinckney wrote McHenry that under "their agreement entered into by the Federal party at Philadelphia," the New England or "eastern States should be convinced of Mr. A's . . . unfitness to be President" before there could be any move "to substitute another Candidate in his stead." Pinckney continued:

"This event I do not think impossible, and his conduct and the critical situation of our Country may require it. But to preserve the Union, this must originate to the Eastward—the Middle States can then take it up, and the Southern ones with propriety may follow."

Hamilton had planned it quite another way. Let the South vote for two of its own, Jefferson and Pinckney, and this would split the ticket from Adams. But Pinckney still refused to win by chicanery. He wrote a public letter asking equal support for himself and Adams, and pledging that "his efforts would be directed to obtain for [Adams] . . . in So Carolina" as many votes as he should be given himself.

By a modicum of home-state manipulation, Pinckney could have made himself either President or Vice President; he had only to jilt his running-mate. "With singular good faith and honor," Fisher Ames reported, "he adhered to the compact and rejected the offer." James Gunn confirmed this in an after-the-fact letter to Hamilton, December 11, 1800, saying, "The double choice was lost in South Carolina, owing to General Pinckney refusing to give up Adams."

By now, Hamilton had reached midpassage in a Lucifer's fall. Pinckney's chivalrous behavior made political trickery look all the more shabby. Benjamin Stoddert saw that, if Pinckney "should defeat himself, he will gain by the defeat." Ames, fore-seeing Hamilton's plunge, advised him to consider that the "question is not . . . how we shall fight, but how we and all Federalists shall fall, that we may rise, like Antaeus, the stronger for our fall."

It was a time of Hamilton's life when his living friends and future admirers were to wish that he had acted otherwise. Troup, Ames, and Gouverneur Morris, who stuck by him in his embarrassment, and Noah Webster, who did not, were alike in refusing to find extenuation for Hamilton's faults, and there is no way or reason for a sympathetic biographer to differ from them. "We must take man as we find him," Hamilton had told the Federalist Convention. The advice was well given as it applies to Hamilton himself.

Late in the campaign, he saw that there was no way to defeat Jefferson and Burr except by resurrecting Adams. The party leaders must be re-rallied behind the President, and the only means of sending this message to Federalists in sixteen states was by pamphlet. Troup and others near him in New York urged an unsigned piece couched in the third person, but Hamilton refused. He chose the upright pronoun above his own signature, but agreed to private circulation, as there was no point in letting the Democrats in on Federalist party troubles. He squared away to compose a 14,000-word open letter with the salutation "Sir," and the title, *The Public Conduct and Character of John Adams, Esq., President of the United States.*

He was pleading for the pardon of a delinquent whom he had previously condemned. Even for a skilled attorney and writer, it was a difficult assignment. A mere informal screed such as he had in times past flung at George Clinton would not serve. The dignity of both the author and the object must be pre-

served. Hamilton had to justify an about-face on the choice for
the top Federalist candidate. He had to sketch President
Adams as a poor thing but America's own, much more acceptable than the opposing ticket of Jefferson–Burr, "of whose unfitness all sincere Federalists are convinced."

The President's oddities were well-known among those to
whom the work was addressed, and it could have done him
little harm. "I smile," wrote Fisher Ames, "to hear Hamilton
and his book condemned by men who go on to find fault with
the President at least as harshly." Unfortunately this limited
audience was widened, and the author ignominiously trapped,
by a man cleverer than himself. Aaron Burr, the early arriver,
got up at dawn on the morning of publication and intercepted
a printer's errand boy on the street.

"What have you there, my lad?"

"Pamphlets for General Hamilton."

Burr helped himself to a copy, and soon published the Adams
Letter far and wide. There is nothing to show that the embarrassment to Hamilton altered the election results. As Adams'
best biographer, Page Smith, points out, the President ran better than previously in every state except New York, and this
had been lost to him far back in April, six months before the
damaging article. The accumulated deficits of a party already
twelve years in power, the unpopularity of the Alien and Sedition Laws, the Millions for Defense taxation, the electioneering
skills of Jefferson and Burr, were all reasons why Americans
felt it was time for a change. The score: Jefferson and Burr
seventy-three votes each, Adams sixty-five, Pinckney sixty-
four, Jay one.

Adams, who always expected the worst, was not surprised at
his own defeat, only at the tie vote and the Constitutional crisis.
"What course is it we steer, and to what harbour are we
bound?" he asked.

Hamilton was dismayed but could not have been astounded.
From the first election in 1788 onward, he had mistrusted the
"defect" in the Constitution, and had feared that some day the
vote would bring in an unintended winner. Many times Hamilton himself had put his hand to rigging the vote. He might even

do so again. His party still held the balance of power in the House. The Constitution read, in Article Two, Section One, that if the Electoral College produced more than one claimant:

". . . the House of Representatives shall immediately chuse by Ballot one of them for President; and if no person have a majority, then from the five highest on the list, the said House shall in a like manner chuse the President."

The Federalists, then, had two means of electing a President, even though they had just lost an election. They could bargain with Jefferson and Burr on matters of patronage and policy, and pick the man who promised more. They could use delaying tactics in the House, prevent a majority vote, and thus have five candidates, three of them Federalists, in the competition. Jefferson, Burr, Adams, Pinckney, and Jay would all be eligible if there were more than one round of balloting in the House.

Far from Hamilton's home, in the new Federal City of Washington, the principals of the drama gathered without him. President and Mrs. Adams had moved into the unfinished mansion on the canal of mud called Pennsylvania Avenue. Vice President Jefferson had come to live in a crowded boarding house near the white marble Capitol. There, on the appointed day, he faced the assembled members of Congress, broke seals, made tallies, and announced the expected results: No candidate had a majority of electoral votes. Senators retired from the chamber and Representatives responded to the first roll call: six states for Jefferson, four states for Burr, six states with split delegations, nine states needed to elect.

Visitors and letters poured into Hamilton's home at 26 Broadway. Hamilton was besieged for advice on what the Federalists should do with their opportunity. Burr, the party-switcher, had once been a Federalist; he would bring military experience to the Presidency as Jefferson would not. And Burr would give the coveted office to New York. Hamilton's closest followers leaned toward Burr.

"I beg of you," Hamilton wrote Sedgwick, "as you love your country, your friends and yourself, to reconsider dispassionately the opinion you have expressed in favor of Burr. I never was so mistaken in my life as I shall be if our friends, in event of their success, do not rue the preference they give to that Catiline."

A dozen or more such letters went out from his hand. Burr, in his opinion, was "one of the worst men in the community . . . bankrupt beyond redemption . . . wicked enough to scruple nothing . . . has no principle, public or private . . . For heaven sake, my dear sir," he entreated Representative Bayard of Delaware, "exert yourself to the utmost to save our country from so great a calamity."

The same sort of letter went to John Marshall, Adams' new Secretary of State, who was now regarded as a top Federalist. Marshall replied on January 1, 1800, that he did not know Burr, "cannot bring myself to aid Mr. Jefferson," and that a personal reason would "deter me from using my influence (if, indeed, I possess any) in support of either gentleman." The personal reason, Marshall went on to say, was that any show of preference might "be suspected" as a move to keep himself in his $3,500-a-year post. He needed it after three years' absence from his law practice.

Hamilton could not know the effect, if any, that his appeals were having in Washington. The House in continuous session was casting five and six ballots a day without a majority. Jefferson never fell behind; Burr never gained a single vote. The Federalists of the House were ready to choose either man who would make suitable promises. Bayard, Hamilton's key man, later told him how it ended. "When . . . Burr was resolved not to commit himself . . . I came out . . . for Jefferson."

On the thirty-third ballot the deadlock broke and Jefferson was chosen. It was Hamilton's last fling at President-making.

PART FOUR

THE INEVITABLE HOUR

The boast of heraldry, the pomp of pow'r,
And all that beauty, all that wealth e'er gave,
Await alike th' inevitable hour.
The paths of glory lead but to the grave.
                                        Thomas Gray

CHAPTER TWENTY-SIX

The Garden of Contemplation

I

(1800–1802)

There were compensations. Hamilton would never be President, nor again promote a winner, but on May 7, 1800, the Society of the Cincinnati elected him President-General to succeed George Washington. At the same meeting, held in Philadelphia, the Society chose C. C. Pinckney as its Vice President. The two men, fellow-generals, fellow-Federalists, and now ranking officers of the Cincinnati, formed a friendship that was one of the last and warmest of Hamilton's life.

To another friend, Light-Horse Harry Lee, Hamilton wrote, following the Jefferson victory: "Believe me, that I feel no despondency of any sort. As to the country, it is too young and vigorous to be quacked out of its political health; and as to myself, I feel that I stand on ground which, sooner or later, will insure me a triumph over my enemies."

These enemies would have pounced on a recommendation for an hereditary-monarchical constitution, which Hamilton drafted about this time. However, he drew it up not for America, but, at the request of his old West Indian friend Ned Stevens, as the best form of government for Santo Domingo. Old James Hamilton's death in 1799 was another reminder of the West Indies days, and perhaps of Hugh Knox, who had always expected a great book from his former student.

Hamilton had begun to plan and discuss a major work on civil government. He saw its structure as that of the Federalist Papers. Once more he would undertake to be chief writer as well as editor in chief. The work was to be a study of world history and governments. James Kent, whom Hamilton consulted and whom he invited to be a collaborator, said the plan was modeled on the "inductive principles" of Francis Bacon, the philosopher-historian who had taken "all knowledge" to be his province. Hamilton had comparable scope, wrote Kent.

"His object was to see what safe and salutary conclusions might be drawn from an historical examination of the effects of various institutions hitherto existing upon the freedom, the morals, the prosperity, the intelligence, the jurisprudence and the happiness of the people."

He chose Richard Harison, John Jay, Gouverneur Morris, and Rufus King as "desirable coadjutors," along with Kent. There was to be a section on "ecclesiastical history" by the Reverend Benjamin Moore, by now president of Columbia College and Episcopal Bishop of New York.

Hamilton was continuing in his role of founder of American nationalism and its enlightenment. The surge toward cultural independence and "originality" (a word much used by American magazine editors of the period) had not halted, though progress was slow. "Political and literary independence . . . are two different things," Philip Freneau declared. "The first was accomplished in almost seven years, the latter will not be completely effected, perhaps, in as many centuries."

Hamilton's intimates knew that he thought and cared a good deal about humanity, the mark of enlightenment. "Honor is a great check upon mankind," he had written. "The science of policy is the knowledge of human nature," was one of his sayings. He believed that honesty was a product of the business world. Contracts and banknotes were the promises men lived by.

Besides, if America was becoming materialistic, that was not all bad. His friend John Trumbull said that economic well-being was necessary for the production of polite letters. Trumbull believed that cultural refinement would polish "that rugged ferocity of manners which is natural to the uncultivated nations of the world." Jeremiah Gridley said that artists required "easiness of mind and a competent fortune." There was not a professional man of letters in the country, unless it was young Washington Irving, who was the protégé of a wealthy brother and of Aaron Burr. John Quincy Adams, a dabbler in verse, insisted that his "poetic trifles" appear anonymously in the *Port Folio* because, he said, "it is impossible at once to be a man of business and a man of rhyme." There was as yet no commercial market for creative writers.

But if there was to be one, it was well understood that Hamiltonian prosperity would develop it. As a Columbia trustee and promoter, as a member of learned societies, as a patron of music and drama, as the owner of an excellent library, as a statesman whose legislative programs called for copyrights and patents and tax-free importation of textbooks, as a publishing partner with the grammarian, Noah Webster, Hamilton was granted a place among patrons.

True, his salon was not the equal of Burr's home, Richmond Hill, as a colony of striving young men. Both the Irving brothers frequented Richmond Hill, as did the artist John Vanderlyn, and Matthew Davis, one day to be his biographer; Martin Van Buren, a future President; Daniel Tompkins, who was to be twice Vice President and three times governor of New York—as well as foreign philosophers, scientists, émigrés, and travel-writers. No young woman of the time had so many suitors and accomplishments as Theodosia Burr, who was mistress of her father's lively mansion.

Yet Hamilton collected a fair share of cultivated company. It included Timothy Dwight, the Connecticut wit. It had epigrammatic Fisher Ames, who believed that the chief inducement to genius was not fees and royalties but applause. A Hamilton protégé was William Winstanley, the English landscapist, who in 1795 put his panorama of London on permanent exhibition in New York, the first of its kind. Hamilton had commended Winstanley to Pinckney: "He appears to have a warm passion for his present pursuit . . . and what is more to the purpose, *talent.*"

Living and dead, Hamilton would always be wrongly faulted as a purveyor of philistinism. Peter Markoe said the country was tainted by Hamiltonian love of gain, and was "to curs'd luxury unwisely prone." Joseph Dennie wrote of "Americans . . . [so] engrossed with Jewish bargains . . . and such great speculators that they neither know inventors and authors nor

command nor remunerate their services." The apathy of readers disgusted Joel Barlow, who cynically lamented the failure
of his verse to bring in profits: "I'll despite my literary labors
. . . and I'll boost my bank shares."

Hamilton was not unacquainted with disappointment himself. He had reached an upland of sapience in this closing phase
of his life. He had this to say to an unknown correspondent
about the obstruction of desires:

"Arraign not the dispensations of Providence . . . they must
be founded in wisdom and goodness; and when they do not suit
us, it must be because there is some fault in ourselves which
deserves chastisement; or because there is some kind intent,
to correct in us some vice or failing of which, perhaps, we may
not be conscious; or because the general plan requires that we
should suffer partial ill.

"In this situation it is our duty to cultivate resignation, or
even humility. . . ."

II

(1803–1804)

He had long felt that his city, to say nothing of his party, had
need of a high-class newspaper. In 1802 he and some Federalist
backers founded the New York *Evening Post,* under the editor-
ship of the talented William Coleman. In Hamilton's memory
was a disagreeable episode back in 1799, when the powerful
Philadelphia *Aurora* ran a story that the Inspector General
had attempted to buy that paper with six thousand dollars
supplied by the British minister. When the article was repub-
lished by the New York *Argus,* Hamilton brought suit against
the printer of the *Argus,* David Frothingham. He had previously treated slander by "repaying . . . hatred with contempt,"
but as senior major general he was not covered by the Libel
section of the Sedition Act; and he could not, in the circumstances, leave unanswered the charge that he was in foreign
pay.

The upshot was that the State of New York prosecuted the
case, convicted Frothingham, and sent him to jail for four

months with a $100 fine. This did not satisfy Hamilton at all. The purpose of his suit had been to prove that a free press should be a responsible press, publishing truth and excluding irresponsible falsehood. But the court ruled that, under common law, the truth or untruth of the slander was not admissible as evidence. The plaintiff had been damaged, and the culprit was punished, but proof of the plaintiff's innocence of the crime he had been charged with was excluded.

Hamilton wanted a newspaper that would espouse party viewpoints and yet would avoid personalities and scurrilities concerning public figures. At a time when President Jefferson was the target of mud-slingers, Hamilton entered a notice in the *Evening Post* declaring "his sentiments to be averse to all personalities, not immediately connected with public consideration."

The message was addressed to Federalist editors throughout the country. It was intended to reduce the output of political screeds, but it succeeded only in part. As a busy lawyer, often out of the city, Hamilton took unusual responsibility for what appeared in the *Evening Post*. Editor Coleman said:

"Whenever anything occurs on which I feel the want of information I state the matter to [Hamilton], sometimes in a note; he appoints a time when I may see him, usually a late hour in the evening. He always keeps himself minutely informed on all political matters. As soon as I see him he begins in a deliberate manner to dictate and I note down in shorthand; when he stops, my article is completed."

His life was warming in many ways. Angelica and her husband, John Church, returned to America for good in the summer of 1798. The Hamiltons and the Churches jointly rented a farmhouse for the season, though the Inspector General could not have been often there; but it was good to know that Angelica was, and that she was home to stay. Philip, eighteen years old in 1800 and a Columbia College student, had become his father's pride. At a campus speech delivered by the young man, Hamilton declared with relish, "I could not have been content to have been surpassed by any other than my son." For the afflicted second child, Angelica, he bought a piano and arranged for lessons. He had a deep, true voice of his own, the delight of the drawing rooms where he sang, and he joined the Philharmonic Society, which met in Snow's Hotel at 69 Broadway. He and Betsey often attended plays at the Park Theatre.

Together with his law practice and his newspaper, his most satisfying intellectual pleasure was the steadily accumulating library, which at this time received a windfall of 340 choice volumes in French bequeathed to him by a friend and client, William Constable.

Among the books left at Hamilton's death were: Hume's *Essays; The Letters of Pliny; Oeuvres Posthumes de Frédéric, Roi de Prusse; Traité Générale du Commerce; Oeuvres de Molière; Histoire de Turenne; Gil Blas; De la Félicité Publique;* Diderot and d'Alembert's *Encyclopédie Méthodique;* La Rochefoucauld-Liancourt's *Travels; Journal des États Généraux;* Plutarch's *Lives;* Hampton's *Polybius;* Lord Chesterfield's *Letters;* Voltaire; Winn's *History of America;* Cicero's *Morals;* Bacon's *Essays;* Ralt's *Dictionary of Trade and Commerce;* Montaigne's *Essays;* Cudworth's *Intellectual System; The Orations of Demosthenes;* Hobbes's *Dialogues;* Robertson's *Charles V;* Enticle's *History of the Late War; The Works of Laurence Sterne; The Works of Edward Gibbon; The Connoisseur;* Walpole's *Anecdotes; The Works of Sir Thomas Browne;* Goldsmith's *Essays; Hudibras; The Works of St. Anselmo; The Letters of Socrates;* and Ruthfurd's *Institutes.*

John Church Hamilton thought that his father's reading of Virgil's *Bucolics* had something to do with the family decision, first broached in 1799, to move to the country. As Hamilton put it shortly before he died, "To men who have been so much harassed in the world as myself, it is natural to look forward to complete retirement. . . ." As a beginning, he offered thirty pounds an acre for some land that he fancied nine miles north of the city. "If I like it, after another look at the premises, I shall probably take the whole at this price. But I can only pay one half down, a quarter in six months and the remaining quarter in twelve months."

He fancied the tract partly because it was on or near the battlefield of Harlem Heights, where he had first come to

Washington's attention, and also because the Albany coach passed, three times a week, the place where he intended to set his gate, and because he was learning to take recreation in tramping with a sporting iron and riding horseback on the court circuit. But most of all, he was drawn to this home site by its singular beauty. He liked the dense grove of forest trees—beech, maple, sycamore, and flowering tulip tree—and the delicate undergrowth of dogwood and hemlock. He found a grassy knoll, the ideal setting for a comfortable manor house. The elevation gave him a view of the Harlem River as it flowed into the Sound, and of the stately Hudson at a distance.

Another softening influence entered his life as politics and military interests faded out. Partly because of reading Paley's *Evidences of Immortality,* partly because of spending more time in the company of Nature, and, perhaps, because of premonitions, which he sometimes mentioned to Betsey, Hamilton was turning more than ever before to religion. "Genl. Hamilton has of late years expressed his conviction of the truths of the Christian Religion," Wolcott would write to his wife while Hamilton lay dying. He continued as unpaid non-member attorney for Trinity Church in New York, but when he worshipped publicly, it was with Betsey at the Dutch Reformed congregation to which the Schuyler family belonged. He conducted the Episcopal service on Sundays at his home, and with this, on weekdays, says the son, "he now united the habit of daily prayer, in which exercise of faith and love the Lord's Prayer was always a part."

In the late summer of 1800, he made some sketches of the house he wanted, square-structured, two stories high. The main entrance would face west; there would be verandas on both north and south wings, and two tall chimneys. His chief builder was Ezra Weeks. As a designer, he chose John McComb, who had worked with L'Enfant on Federal Hall, where the First Congress had met. General Schuyler was a constant advisor and benefactor.

"If the house is boarded on the outside, and then clapboards put on, and filled in the inside with brick, I am persuaded no water will pass to the brick. If the clapboards are well painted, and filled in with brick, [it] will be little if any more expensive than lath and plaister, the former will prevent the nuisance occasioned by rats and mice. . . ."

Schuyler promised that should the builder "be extravagant in his demand, I shall . . . go up and contract for the timber and purchase the boards and planks, and, if possible, I will cause the boards and planks to be put into water for two months, and then piled up with decks between them that they may be seasoned before they are worked up."

After living in so many rented houses, Hamilton, Betsey, and their eldest son, Philip, took joy in building a home. They would call it the Grange after the Hamilton place in Ayrshire. Construction went slowly. Hamilton enjoyed being present to watch the workers. He wrote from the circuit that his horse Riddle had gone lame, otherwise "I ought now to be further advanced." Details of internal construction delighted him; he spoke of "two Iron Cranes in the Kitchen fire place—& an Iron door for the oven mouth." He paid the designer to put up "two sets of Italian Marble in the octagon room, such as General Hamilton may choose—and six sets of Stone Chimney pieces for the other rooms."

Outside, he planted a circle of gum trees, thirteen, of course. The house construction would take the better part of two years. In August 1802 Schuyler would write, "I am anxious to visit you and to participate in the pleasure of your country retreat which I am informed is fast reaching perfection." In the following April, the old General sent the Hamiltons a team of work horses to replace their own, which had drowned when the wagon overturned. "If you cannot recover the paint," he wrote his daughter, "purchase no more as I will have the house painted."

Hamilton was making from twelve thousand to fifteen thousand dollars a year, but he had to start borrowing again to meet immediate expenses. He would pay McComb $875 for design, and Weeks 1,550 pounds for construction at the going rate of six shillings to the dollar. Construction costs did not include the pay of the workers, whom he hired on his own. Those mounting costs worried him (they would reach seventy-five thousand dollars), but he was determined to have his manor. He made a plan for debt retirement. It was to live "within the compass of four thousand dollars," aside from what he was putting into the house, and then at a chosen time "to lease that establishment for a few years" and pay off the mortgage. He was confident that, given a normal life span, he would be relieved of debt "by the progressive rise of property on this Island," and that the mansion "by the felicity of its situation [would] become more and more valuable."

His heart was given to the home-building. "Don't forget to visit the Grange," he wrote Betsey from the road. "From what I saw it is very important the drains should be better regulated. Leave, in particular charge of Philip, what you yourself cannot accomplish."

Philip, graduating from Columbia College in the spring of 1801, was shortly afterward incensed to hear his father savagely attacked in a Fourth of July address by a Democratic orator, George Eacker. The speech, subsequently published, charged the Hamiltonians with having, "under the pretended apprehension of a foreign invasion, created a military establishment in order to suppress the opposition by fear."

Four months later Philip, at the theater with a friend, saw Eacker and ridiculed the speech. The ridicule was repeated, insults were exchanged, and before the evening was done, Philip's friend, one Price, met Eacker at the noted dueling place on Weehawken Heights above the Hudson. Four rounds of shot were exchanged without damage, and satisfaction was expressed.

Now there was reason to hope that Philip would also walk away from the quarrel, and he very much wished to do so with honor. He chose as his second young Captain Philip Church, his cousin, and a formal challenge was sent to Eacker. Friends attempted to negotiate, and Philip confided his misgivings to others while concealing the matter from his parents.

His brother, who was only six at the time, but who reconstructed the affair from family memories, said that Philip considered that the original provocation had been on his part, and was willing to say so if Eacker would also retract some unpar-

donable language. The father's teachings were evident in
Philip's statement that he was "averse in principle to the shed-
ding of blood in private combat, anxious to repair his previous
fault as far as he could do so without dishonor, and to stand
acquitted in his own mind." For such reasons, "he determined
to reserve his fire, receive that of his adversary and then discharge his pistol in the air."

As was often the case, word that two parties of men had
started across the river to Weehawken raced through the community. That was how Hamilton, on the morning of November
22, 1801, heard of his son's involvement. His first thought was
to reach his friend and country neighbor, Dr. David Hosack,
and make him ready in case the worst should happen. In his
anxiety, his panic, his returning premonitions, and his love for
this gifted son, Hamilton felt his consciousness leave him as
he hurried to the doctor. He fell down in a faint, recovered,
staggered on. His fears had warned him all too well. Philip had
gone down, mortally wounded through the abdomen, at the
first volley.

"On a bed without curtains lay poor Phil," a Columbia classmate wrote, "pale and languid, distorted eyeballs darting. . . .
On one side of him on the same bed lay his agonized father, and
on the other his distracted mother . . . relatives and friends
weeping. . . ."

In the twenty hours that Philip lingered, Hamilton gave his
heart to his dying son. How well the boy had deported himself,
how bravely died, "chiefly anxious to conceal from his relatives
and friends the suffering he endured." Philip did not blame his
slayer nor lament the shortness of his life. Those at the bedside
would remark that Hamilton "in an undertone" spoke the com-
forting words of the Christian Creed. And when it was over,
writes the biographer-son, "a radiance spread over Hamilton's
face at the assured conviction of his son's resignation and
faith."

"The poor father was with difficulty supported to the grave
of his hopes," Philip's friend wrote after the funeral. Hamilton
soon had letters from friends on two continents. "Sacred be
your sorrow," wrote C. C. Pinckney. Sadness had to be set aside

for daily living, and Hamilton rallied; "but his countenance is strongly stamped with grief," Troup reported to Rufus King in London.

Since it concerns both human character and historical judgments, it must be stressed that the effect of personal tragedy on Hamilton was to deepen his identification with religion. In answering one of the letters of condolence, he wrote: "My loss is indeed great. The brightest, as well as the eldest, hope of my family has been taken from me. . . . But why should I repine? It was the will of heaven."

Betsey's eighth child, born six months after the tragedy, was christened Philip. In this way, and in returning to putter around in the unfinished home and its grounds where the first Philip had been a helper, the Hamiltons renewed their life. His detractors, some then as yet unborn, saw him depressed and defeated, not so much by the death in the family as by the Jeffersonian state now taking shape in Washington, where Gallatin was Secretary of the Treasury and Madison Secretary of State. Indeed, Hamilton must have been wrily quoting hostile opinion of himself when he wrote to C. C. Pinckney two years after Philip's death, "A garden, you know, is a very useful refuge of a disappointed politician."

There indeed was the "garden" with the "disappointed politician" in it, and it was easy for present and future critics to stuff him with appropriate sentiments and motives. The man who lived by the sword of partisan politics had seen his son die by that sword. To spiteful observers he was the fallen leader who jealously watched his foes feasting at the Presidential palace. Professional envy and personal tragedy drove him into "opportunistic religiosity," according to Jeffersonian dogma of the twentieth century.

But the chronology of his life and writings shows that from the outbreak of the French Revolution, Hamilton had regarded that cataclysm as inimical to the Christian Church as well as to the American Constitution. He wrote and thought like a religious man long before Jefferson's election and Philip's death.

In April 1802 Bayard asked him to assemble some thoughts

helpful to the party and the country. "I will comply with your invitation by submitting some ideas which, from time to time, have passed through my mind. . . . The present Constitution is the standard to which we are to cling . . . rejecting all changes but through the channel itself provides for amendments. By these general views on the subject have my reflections been guided."

He then proposed the founding of what he called the "Christian Constitutional Society." Its stated purpose was to employ "all lawful means in concert to promote the election of fit men," to establish charitable institutions "for the relief of immigrants" and schools to teach "the different classes of mechanics."

Nothing was new about Hamilton's desire for political organization that would bring "fit men" into government, nor in his encouragement of immigration and education. He had inserted the clause about "religion and morality" into the Farewell Address, proving that he was no parvenu in the spiritual realm of governance.

He had good reason to think the Constitution needed strengthening. The Presidency in 1801 had been up for auction in the House of Representatives. Next time the country might not survive such a crisis. In the spring of 1802 Hamilton was recommending two amendments to the new Senator from New York, Gouverneur Morris: "1st to discriminate the candidates for the presidency and vice presidency; 2nd to have the electors of these officers chosen by the people, in districts, under the direction of Congress. Both these appear to me points of importance."

Hamilton was writing on these political matters to Bayard and Morris less than six months after his son's death, and the state of his mind showed through. "I should be a very unhappy man if I left my tranquility at the mercy of the misinterpretations which friends as well as foes are fond of giving to my conduct," he told Morris. "What can I do better than withdraw from the scene? Every day proves to me more and more that this American world was not made for me."

Despite his hurt, he was not withdrawing, but striving as

hard as ever. But he felt downcast and forsaken; he was in one of his many periods of depression, so well known to his intimates. He bared his feelings to the man who understood him best. "You, friend Morris, are by *birth* a native of this country, but by *genius* an exotic. You mistake if you fancy that you are more a favourite than myself. . . ." He was feeling unloved by his country, estranged from reality, a failure in his life's work; but it was not in him to quit the fight.

Not just the Jeffersonians of his time and afterwards, but Hamiltonians as well, would read these letters without reference to his state of mind, and to his stated purpose of buttressing the Constitution after its severest shock. It was so easy to explain him as a prototype. He had moved to the country, had he not? He was growing flowers. He must, therefore, be an embittered and defeated exile who had lost the will to live and had abandoned faith in his country. One of his closest New England friends, George Cabot of Massachusetts, would in time have a descendant, Henry Cabot Lodge, the best of Hamilton's nineteenth century biographers. Lodge, drawing on family memories, explained Hamilton as having been virtually driven from his senses by the French Revolution, and impelled to a violent death out of a mad despair for his country. Aaron Burr would help him to a soldier's end, in this biographer's view, but only after the atrocities of France had cracked a noble mind. Lodge wrote:

"It is neither fanciful nor strained to regard Hamilton's death as a result of the opinions bred by the French Revolution. That terrible convulsion had many illustrious victims of all nations and creeds, but hardly one more brilliant or more uselessly sacrificed than the great statesman who fell before Burr's pistol that peaceful July morning."

Such conjectures have a certain poetic persuasiveness. But the stubborn fact is that in the period between Philip's death and his own, 1801–1804, Hamilton was far oftener in the courtroom than in the garden, much more engaged in writing than in mourning, a hero of his caste and never a recluse. He was undisputed leader of the New York Bar, chief proprietor of the best newspaper in America, continuing consultant on political affairs. He stood equipped with a powerful mind that was the envy and admiration of his associates, one that glittered with undiminished brilliance to the very end.

III

(1801–1804)

Hamilton plunged back into print a month after Philip's death. Writing as Lucius Crassus in the *Evening Post,* he opened an eighteen-essay serial described by himself as "Examination of Jefferson's Message to Congress of December 1, 1801." He flayed the new President's weakness with customary wit and sarcasm. Jefferson had told Congress that in a sea battle with the pirates of Tripoli, one of the enemy's ships had been captured—and returned with its full crew—because there had been no declaration of war by Congress.

What "a prodigal sacrifice of Constitutional energy!" raged Hamilton. What nonsense to contend that "there may exist a state of war on one side—of peace on the other." The corsair, liberated, would fight again. "What will the world think of the fold where such is the shepherd?" Hamilton demanded.

By June 3, 1802, Hamilton was lamenting to Rufus King, whom Jefferson had retained as minister to London: "No army, no navy, no *active* commerce; national defense not by arms but by embargoes, prohibitions of trade etc.; as little government as possible *within*—these are the pernicious dreams which, as far and as fast as possible, will be attempted to be realized."

Hamilton was positive that Jeffersonianism would not work. Only by the grace of God could a disarmed and undisciplined America survive in this ravening world. Jefferson carried religious freedom too far for Hamilton. The President allowed the first November of his term to go by without proclaiming the national Thanksgiving Day. For thirteen years under Jefferson and Madison this religious festival would lapse. Not only did Jefferson officially disregard the Deity, but he seemingly ignored another Being which Hamilton worshiped, the national Destiny.

Jefferson's followers and oncoming history would understand him far better than Hamilton ever could. The President was a private man in spiritual and patriotic affairs. He believed that God's Kingdom was "within." He was not indifferent to American expansion. He had been a draftsman of the Ordinance that organized the Northwest Territory above and beyond the Ohio. He took the larger nationalistic view when Kentucky and Tennessee were carved out of Virginia. He understood what would come to be called geopolitics. In 1802 Jefferson wrote his minister in Paris, Robert R. Livingston, that New Orleans was the "one single spot, the possessor of which is our natural and habitual enemy."

War was in the minds and correspondence of men in 1802. Hamilton, as always, examined the American self-interest. "The whole is, then, a question of expediency. Two courses only present: First to negotiate and endeavor to purchase; and if this fails, to go to war. Secondly, to seize at once on the Floridas and New Orleans, and then negotiate."

He was astonished—joyfully surprised—at the Louisiana Purchase, which was consummated in May of 1803. By acquiring territory on both banks of the Mississippi, Jefferson increased the American land mass by 846,000 square miles, approximately doubling the national area, and without so much as a skirmish. Almost every Federalist except Hamilton hated Jefferson's success. "At length," Hamilton wrote in the *Evening Post* of July 5, 1803, "the business of New Orleans has been terminated favorably for this county. . . . The navigation of this Mississippi will be ours unmolested . . . essential to the peace and prosperity of our Western country." He couldn't resist adding that "the acquisition has been solely owing to a fortuitous concurrence of unforeseen and unexpected circumstances, and not to wise and vigorous measures on the part of the American government."

But the size of the purchase price did not disturb Hamilton; he knew the nation's resources to be virtually boundless. There was the Constitutional question: How does a democratic republic "buy" people—the people of Louisiana? Hamilton dismissed it with a Machiavellian *mot:* "It will not do to carry the morals of a monk into the cabinet of a statesman." Jefferson took the

same line: ". . . the less is said about any constitutional difficulty, the better. . . ."

Thus, nearly three years after the earthquake election of
1800, the ironies were sifting themselves out for Hamilton. His
part in exchanging Jefferson for Adams had amounted in his
mind to substituting a lucky and crafty man for one who was
star-crossed and erratic. His choice of Jefferson over Burr in
the run-off election of 1801 was the choice of a befuddled theo-
rist over a sinister scoundrel. Hamilton would rather have had
General Pinckney as Chief Executive than any of the other
three (Pinckney would run against Jefferson in 1804); but he
could not deny that the pacifist President had achieved empire
without bloodshed.

CHAPTER TWENTY-SEVEN

Liberty of the Press

I

(February 1804)

They couldn't hold a quorum in the New York Legislature that day, February 17, 1804. The state's supreme court was sitting in the same building, the capitol at Albany, and Hamilton was pleading the case of his life.

Earlier, as he approached the city, "persons were seen waiting on the road to catch a glimpse of him, or to tender evidence of their respect." The streets and inns filled up. The courtroom became packed with luminaries of the bar and with spectators. After the other attorneys had addressed the bench, "came the great, the powerful Hamilton," noted a reporter. The legislative chambers emptied and poured their personnel into the courtroom. The state senate gave up and adjourned. The general assembly tried to do business, and sent the sergeant-at-arms to round up the delinquents.

"The Speaker of the House of Representatives requires every member to take his seat," the sergeant bawled. Hamilton suspended his address. "Order! Order!" called the sergeant. It was useless. A "transfixed" audience remained.

This was the case they would remember him by. "I have had a dozen Federalists with me," Schuyler had told Betsey a whole year before, "entreating me to write your General if possible to attend . . . at Claverack as Counsel to the Federal printer there who is to be tried on an indictment for a libel against that Jefferson. . . ."

The printer, Harry Croswell, was convicted, and motions for a new trial were denied. Hamilton held off entering the case until it reached the court of last appeal. He refused to take a fee. There was so much involved that the defendant almost

disappears below the horizon of immensities. Croswell is sometimes represented as an innocent victim in the battle of political giants. In fact, he was a mischievous provocateur, aged
twenty-five, printer and assistant editor of *The Balance and
Columbian Repository,* Hudson, New York. As a spare-time job
he printed a four-page weekly pamphlet, *The Wasp,* and wrote
for it as Robert Rusticoat. *The Wasp* carried the slogan, "To
lash the Rascals naked throughout the world." Croswell's foremost rascal was Thomas Jefferson. Quoting another editor in
a September 1802 issue of *The Wasp,* Croswell declared:

"Holt says, the burden of the Federal song is that Mr. Jefferson paid Callender for writing against the late administration.
This is wholly false. The charge is explicitly this:—Jefferson
paid Callender for calling Washington a traitor, a robber and
perjurer; for calling Adams a hoary-headed incendiary; and for
most grossly slandering the private characters of men who he
well knew were virtuous."

Since the Sedition Act, with its section on libel, had been
extinct since March 1801, Croswell was being tried under common law for "being a malicious and seditious man . . . intend-
ing . . . to represent . . . the said Thomas Jefferson as unworthy of the confidence, respect and attachment of the
people. . . ."

Without doubt, *People v. Croswell* carried major implica-
tions. The names of three Presidents were involved. So was the
unforgettable election of 1800. So was the scorpion-writer
James Thompson Callender, who had forced Hamilton to issue
the Reynolds Papers. With or without the Sedition Act, did the
Constitution permit citizens to be punished under any law for
the defamation of public men? From another viewpoint, did the
Constitution protect citizens from criticism that was malicious
and untrue?

Central to the Croswell case were letters by Jefferson to
Callender that would sustain the accuracy of that stinging
paragraph in *The Wasp.* There was the crux of *People v. Croswell*: Could the truth of the libel be admitted as evidence?
Hamilton addressed the New York supreme court for six hours,
an afternoon and a morning session. He carried with him an

outline of his points, but soon was soaring above it. The court-recorder let go his pen and sat mesmerized. Luckily, one of the supreme court justices, James Kent, took notes, and many others at the scene reported it in newspapers or in their anecdotes. The documentation takes up seventy-three large pages in *The Law Practice of Alexander Hamilton.*

"Two great questions," Hamilton told the court, "had arisen in this case: Can Truth be given as evidence? Are the jury to judge of the intent and of the law?"

He believed that there are very few absolutes in life. He did not believe in untrammeled license for the press. But the accuracy, the intent, the result were more important than the indignation of some injured public figure. He said this in full knowledge that writers would continue to abuse their liberty, as they had done against George Washington himself.

He raised his arm and pointed to a portrait of the first President, "the best of characters," at whom the most vile slanders had been hurled. "No, I do not contend for this terrible liberty of the Press; but I do contend for the right of publishing Truth with good motives, for justifiable ends, although the censure may fall upon the government, the magistracy, or individuals."

He wound into his subject, the audience sat enthralled, and half a dozen different listeners in time would comment: "Nothing ever equaled it. . . . He rose above himself, I had almost said above human nature. . . . It was a mighty effort in the cause of Liberty . . . to convince and persuade; to force the tear from the eye of the aged and the young; to agitate, to soothe, to calm them at pleasure is the test of true eloquence. This he did. It was a day of triumph for virtue and talents."

Hamilton did not get the new trial for Croswell that he sought. The supreme court cast a tie vote, and the sentence stood. As in *Rutgers v. Waddington,* however, Hamilton's plea had propounded a political philosophy, and the New York legislature subsequently wrote this philosophy into law. Truth became a defense in libel suits. Juries were permitted to decide both the fact and the law. But Hamilton's contribution to justice carried beyond and above mere legislative statutes. It came to be written into the New York Constitution. The unemotional

editor of *The Law Practice of Alexander Hamilton* (1964) remarks:

"Croswell's case and Hamilton's part in it were destined to
leave a mark upon the constitutional history of New York,
uneradicated to this day. For despite the fact that the legislature had for all practical purposes settled the question of law
in the terms urged by Hamilton and his associates, there remained the matter of placing this determination beyond future
meddling. This was to be done at the Constitutional Convention
of 1821, called by the People to amend the Constitution of
1787."

II
(February–June 1804)

Business kept Hamilton in Albany for the rest of February
and into March. The Croswell case, more exposition than competition, gave much light and little injury, and provided an
atmosphere for mending. At Hamilton's request, George Clinton, who was back in the governorship after a six-year lapse,
wrote a letter which put down the old canard that Hamilton
had schemed to implant a monarchy. The Governor dubbed the
charge "odious and disreputable."

"It became no man more to be the vindicator," Hamilton
replied gratefully. Clinton was already slated to replace Burr
as Jefferson's running mate in the November election, so New
Yorkers would seek a new governor. Vice President Burr for
more than a year had been lifting his glass with the cryptic
toast, "To the union of all honest men," which meant that he
wished to be the coalition candidate for governor.

Naturally, while asking the support of "honest" Democrats
and Federalists, Burr's own honesty in the election of 1800
must be attested, and this had prudently been done by Hamilton. He did so in the *Evening Post,* October 13, 1802, declaring
that "he had no personal knowledge of any negotiation between Colonel Burr and any person whatever, respecting the
elevation of himself to the chief magistracy."

Hamilton felt relieved to be able to make this avowal, and

he welcomed Burr's acceptance of it. He had long had a "strong and deep conviction that he should die by Burr's instrumentality." But now he told Betsey, "I may live twenty years, please God."

A few days after closing *People v. Croswell,* Hamilton, uninvited, dropped into a Federalist meeting at Lewis' Tavern, Albany. Party members had left him out of the caucus for good reason. They intended to nominate Burr to oppose John Lansing, the veteran Clintonian. Hamilton brought with him an eight-paragraph address headed, "Reasons why it is desirable that Mr. Lansing rather than Col. Burr succeed."

He had often castigated Burr in private correspondence, but this time he was speaking before a banquet-hall audience. The Federalists, he said, would be deluded if they endorsed Burr; "he will certainly not at this time relinquish the ladder of his ambition and espouse the cause or views of the weaker party." To elevate Burr to the governorship, he told his hearers, would be "to reunite under a more adroit, able and daring chief, the now-scattered fragments of the Democratic party, and to reinforce it by a strong detachment from the Federalists."

As governor, Hamilton continued, Burr would look further. He would look to New England, where there was open talk of secession since the Louisiana Purchase. The son and grandson of New England clergymen and college presidents, Burr envisioned himself "to be chief of the Northern portion, and placed at the head of the State of New York, no man would be more likely to succeed." Finally, he said that to choose Burr would be to "infuse rottenness in the only part of our country which still remains sound—the Federal[ist] States of New England."

Considering that he believed Burr to be plotting a Northern secession, Hamilton's words at Lewis' Tavern were surprisingly moderate. He said that sentiments in New England were leading "to an opinion that a dismemberment of the Union is expedient. It would probably suit Mr. Burr's views to promote this result."

He was using restrained language because it was probable that the speech would carry beyond this audience. As it turned out, two Burrites were hidden under a bed in the next room, and the address was soon published in the *Morning Chronicle*. But Hamilton had succeeded in his purpose—the Federalist caucus took his advice and withheld endorsement of Burr.

This was intended to be Hamilton's last activity in the race for governor, and he allowed Schuyler to announce as much by a notice in the *Albany Register*. But that was before the Vice President, headquartered in his fine mansion, Richmond Hill, began to show extraordinary strength among the Sons of Tammany and other elements that had served him well before. By this time Lansing had withdrawn and the Democrats had settled on Chief Justice Morgan Lewis, a worthy and colorless candidate. New England dissidents were boisterously toasting Burr: "Aaron's Rod—may it blossom in New York."

At Albany, as the election approached, Hamilton dined one evening at the home of Judge John Taylor, along with James Kent, Stephen Van Rensselaer, and others. All those present favored Justice Lewis over Vice President Burr, and they talked freely, as among friends. But Judge Taylor had an indiscreet son-in-law, who wrote a letter dated April 12 to Andrew Brown of the village of Berne, foolishly quoting both Hamilton and Kent. They had agreed, Charles Cooper wrote, that Burr was "a dangerous man, and one who ought not to be trusted with the reins of government."

This letter, entrusted to a messenger, was "embezzled and broken into," and turned up in the *Albany Register*. Cooper, unwilling to leave ill enough alone, wrote on April 23 to Philip Schuyler, explaining how his words had got into print, and repeating many of them in the process. The second letter was also purloined and printed, and it contained a passage of subsequent importance:

"It is sufficient for me, on this occasion, to substantiate what I have asserted," Cooper rambled on. "I have made it an inveterate rule of my life to be circumspect in relating what I may have heard from others; and in this affair, I feel happy to think that I have been unusually cautious—for really, sir, I could detail to you a still more despicable opinion which General Hamilton has expressed of Mr. Burr."

CHAPTER TWENTY-EIGHT

Eve of Combat

I

(April–June 1804)

The three-day election for governor ran from April 24 to 26, and on the closing day, Federalist Kent feared the worst. "The election is nearly over," he wrote his wife, "and the Burrites are sanguine and appear flushed with the laurels of victory. They claim a decided majority in this city. The Federalists have been generally bought out. The cold reserve and indignant reproaches of Hamilton may have controlled a few, but they are but few."

Final results became known on May 1—defeat for Burr, after all. He had carried New York City as expected, but the upstate Federalist counties fell on him like a landslide, and clearly showed that Hamilton's time in Albany had not been wasted. Since the election results of 30,829 to 22,139 were so pronounced, there was no dispute. "*Tant mieux*," Burr wrote to his daughter—so much the better.

The May days slipped by, and by mid-June there was no known trace of bad blood left from the election. The paths of Hamilton and Burr crossed constantly, for the circuit court was sitting in New York, where both of them lived and practiced.

Then at eleven o'clock on the morning of June 18, a young caller was announced at the small house which the Hamiltons kept in town, at 52 Cedar Street. He was William Peter Van Ness, called Billy, a protégé of Aaron Burr, and he handed a note and a newspaper clipping to Hamilton. In the note, which was from Colonel Burr, the writer stated that the clipping, "published some time ago, has but recently come to my knowledge." He said that Van Ness would point out a passage that required a "prompt and unqualified acknowledgement or denial." Hamilton, with Billy watching him closely, read the blundering words of Charles Cooper about "a still more despicable opinion which General Hamilton had expressed of Mr. Burr."

Under different circumstances Hamilton would have smiled over "more despicable." He had called Burr "an embryo Caesar . . . a bankrupt in property and reputation . . . a profligate . . . a voluptuary . . . an adventurer *à la* Buonaparte . . . as true a Catiline as ever met in midnight conclave." Both he and Kent had been quoted in this same newspaper as calling Burr dangerous and untrustworthy. Burr had not selected a prima facie fighting epithet. He had brought up a phrase so vague that any good lawyer would be remiss not to quibble at it.

Hamilton wanted to think it over. Having examined the materials, according to Billy Van Ness, "Genl Hamilton . . . remarked that they required some consideration, and that in the course of the day he would send an answer to my office."

For better than two hours that morning, Hamilton put off any decision. "I was certainly desirous of avoiding this interview," he wrote, but it would be difficult. He could not plead conscientious objections this time. He had challenged Monroe, and Burr knew it; and he had challenged Nicholson. On the other hand, he had fought nobody, and had an unbroken string of side-stepped duels behind him. In addition to Monroe and Nicholson, Hamilton had got out of meeting J. S. Eustice, Samuel Chase, Charles Lee, William Gordon, Aedanus Burke, and John Mercer. All this was reason for confidence that he could evade this one more.

There was coming at this time of Hamilton's life another of those episodes that were to embarrass his best friends. His conduct, beginning with the receipt of Burr's curt note, reveals another side of the bold stormer of Redoubt 10, the scrupulous man of public and private business, the patriotic nation-builder. He was now revealing the character in which he had tempted Charles C. Pinckney to double-cross Adams, and advised Jay on how to nullify the people's vote. "All's fair" might do as a code for political chicanery, but it seemed not to fit the *code duello.*

Yet explanations can be found. If Hamilton can be called the challenged party at this point, he had the choice of weapons, and he elected to use those of the lawyer and the author for a while. He would wrangle and write as a means of staying away from the field against Burr. There was some extenuation for this behavior. The Vice President, though a gentleman, was a discredited one, with bad debts and desperate schemes. None of the American leaders of the day trusted him. The idea that he had a good name to defend was far-fetched. Dueling was an amateur sport—literally a game to be played for the love of it—and Burr violated that spirit. He had trained himself since his nonage in handgun marksmanship, and trained his daughter too. He was another "disappointed politician" in a "garden," but instead of growing flowers, he was often to be seen at pistol practice on the grounds of Richmond Hill.

He won regularly at impromptu shooting contests that took place around the courthouses and at outdoor parties. Burr had a slave named Harry who tossed up apples for him, and Harry liked to boast: "De Colonel would hit 'em almost every time, but d'other gentlemen couldn't hit 'em nowhar." A respectful guest at Richmond Hill declared, "There was hardly ever a man could fire so true."

The Colonel did not always shoot at inanimate targets. John Church had a shaking experience in 1798, when he dropped a careless remark about Assemblyman Burr's taking bribes from the Holland Land Company.

"This is an absolute and abominable lie," was the Colonel's answer. It brought him together with Angelica's husband soon afterwards. Burr turned over his ornate Irish-made set of dueling pistols to his second, John Burke. The guns, which he had acquired from a client in lieu of a fee, were finely balanced instruments, and Burr was disturbed when he looked around and saw Burke hammering home the ramrod with a stone. Upon examination, Burr saw that the load was not in place.

"I know it," said Burke. "I forgot to grease the leather, but you see your man is ready. . . ." Burr replied lightly that if he missed him, he would hit him with the next shot. He stood there with a defective weapon, received Church's bullet, which went through his coat, and reached for the other pistol. But Church declared his honor satisfied.

On a later occasion, one of Hamilton's followers, Samuel Bradhurst, thought of a way to meet Burr without risking the pistols. He had no trouble provoking a challenge, and he used his choice of weapons to decide on sabers, with which he was presumably expert. Bradhurst perhaps had not heard of a certain episode several years earlier, when young Colonel Burr was sent to replace officers of a mutinous regiment at a Valley Forge outpost, and to restore discipline. Learning of a plot to assassinate him, he secretly removed the ammunition from the muskets, and ordered a midnight turnout. Burr was ready when a soldier leaped from the ranks with leveled musket, yelling, "Now is the time, my boys!" The young colonel's sword flashed, biting into the mutineer's arm, which next day had to be amputated. Burr may not have had a blade in hand in the intervening years, but he cut up Bradhurst and walked from the field the victor.

Any tactic short of groveling dishonor seemed permissible to escape this violent man and a hopeless fight. Hamilton had many reasons to wish for a normal lifetime. There was his unpaid-for mansion, his unwritten masterpiece. He loved his wife, children, friends, and occupation. As a fellow-soldier, he might have answered Burr in a passage such as one attributed later to John Trumbull—one of many Connecticut gentlemen who believed that Hamilton should have declined the challenge:

"Sir, a duel proves nothing but that the parties do not shrink from the smell of gunpowder or the whistling of a ball. On this subject you and I have given too many proofs to leave any necessity for another, and therefore, as well as for higher reasons, I decline your proposal."

But Hamilton dismissed this forthright method of refusal, believing, so he wrote, that he could not "be in the future useful" with any cloud on his manhood. Instead, he would try to avoid the death sentence by showing it to be unwarranted. Accordingly, at half-past one on this same Monday, June 18, Hamilton called at the Van Ness home, saying that "a variety of engagements would demand his attention during the whole of that day and the next," but that on Wednesday he would furnish an answer to the Colonel's note.

Hamilton's 607-word answer, delivered on Wednesday, began by refusing to disavow the offending phrase. It ended by saying that he "must abide the consequences" unless he could bring the Colonel "to see the matter in the same light with me." But between the opening and closing passages, Hamilton pettifogged and caviled: " 'Tis evident, that the phrase 'still more despicable' admits of infinite shades, from very light to very dark. How am I to judge of the degree intended?"

He delivered the letter at eight o'clock that night. Van Ness handed it to Burr on Thursday, and had a written reply before the day was out. The Colonel succinctly dismissed the quibbling, and told Hamilton that his letter of April 20 "has in it nothing of that sincerity and delicacy which you profess to value."

Hamilton was brought up short. In all his other brushes with duel-minded men, there had been intervals of weeks and months between harsh words, and elaborate explanations of alleged insults. But Burr minced no words, nor would he permit them to be minced by another. He again demanded "a definite reply," and he demanded that it be delivered promptly.

Hamilton tried for a week, by conversations with Billy Van Ness and by additional letters to Burr, to procrastinate, to bluster, and to negotiate. It was useless. Burr would not be put off or placated. By Wednesday, June 27, the ominous words "time and place" entered the dialogue.

The ritual had been a frighteningly rapid one, as such things went. Only nine days, which included a weekend, elapsed between the first encounter and the agreement to meet. It was Burr who did the pressing and Hamilton the backing off. Even when they had agreed through their emissaries on the principle of a meeting, there would be another fortnight to wait. This was because Hamilton asked for a delay through the court session, to accommodate his clients, and beyond that, "a little time to make some arrangements respecting my own affairs."

Burr had become snappish with impatience. He agreed

unwillingly—"anything," he said, "so we but get on." When the
date was set for July 11, he told Van Ness, "I should regret to
pass over another day." He would hold no direct discussions
with Hamilton, saying, "I don't see the necessity of *his* presence
in order to ultimate arrangements."

Hamilton had failed in his first endeavor to escape. But he
would make some other tries as the summer days went by.

II

(June 1804)

Early in the proceedings, on June 22, Hamilton engaged the
services of the transplanted Virginian, Nathaniel Pendleton,
to be his second. As a relatively new friend, Pendleton may not
have known Hamilton's proclivity for walking to the brink of
personal combat and halting just in time. Pendleton was one
of many who wrote accounts from their separate viewpoints of
the Burr-Hamilton affair. At no time did he seem aware that
Hamilton was using him, not so much to dignify and expedite
the duel, as to abort it. Yet such was the case. It was Hamilton's
plan to stop somewhere short of pistol point. He was seeking
Burr's sympathy by asking for additional time to serve in the
court and to make personal arrangements. Translated, this
request said that Hamilton's family and creditors needed the
fees and that he did not expect to survive a meeting.

Burr was unmoved. Next it was Pendleton's turn to make a
pacifying approach. This effort took a complicated form. Pendleton drafted a letter for Hamilton's signature. This message
would be a reply to a proposed note to be drafted for Burr by
Van Ness. In it the Colonel would simply ask "to know in
substance" whether Hamilton had imputed any "dishonorable
conduct" in the words given to the newspaper by Cooper. Pendleton wrote his reply on April 23, and had "several conversations" with Van Ness, until they had a satisfactory product by
April 25.

This odd document was destined to remain unsigned by
Hamilton and unanswered by Burr. It contained pleas of a bad
memory. "General Hamilton," Pendleton's draft began, "says

he cannot imagine to what Doctor Cooper may have alluded. . . . Genl H⸺ cannot recollect distinctly. . . . The expressions are entirely forgotten . . . the specific ideas imperfectly remembered. . . ."

The unsuccessful ruse to find a solution only served to harden Burr. He instructed Van Ness to say that negotiations were "concluded" and that no more verbal messages were to be exchanged. In a harsh demand for Hamilton's compliance or total surrender in writing, Burr proposed a humiliating statement for his opponent's signature. In this document Hamilton was asked to say that he "frankly & explicitly disclaims & disavows the use of any expressions tending to impeach the honor of A. B. . . . fully and explicitly withdrawing them & regrets having employed [them]."

These were conditions of the groveling dishonor which Hamilton could not accept, and were written by Burr in that knowledge. But Hamilton did not give up trying to make use of Pendleton. He sent his second to Burr's second with the request that Dr. David Hosack, who had attended Philip Hamilton's deathbed, should accompany the challenged man to the field.

While it was not unusual in these affairs to have a doctor standing by, the inference may fairly be drawn that Hamilton again was seeking a soft spot in Burr. Dr. Hosack was a Hamilton family friend, a reminder of a Hamilton family tragedy. Burr assented sourly to the arrangement, remarking to Van Ness that "H⸺k is . . . unnecessary"; afterwards he said that he had intended to kill Hamilton instantly in order to have "spared him needless pain."

Finally, Pendleton was utilized in a way that was totally at variance with the strict rules of the dueling code. Hamilton mentioned to his second on July 1 that it was probable he would "not return Mr. Burr's first fire." Pendleton said he "remonstrated against this determination, and urged many considerations against it." He called it foolishly dangerous to Hamilton, and out of keeping with this case, in which Burr had been offered every ground of accommodation not humiliating to Hamilton. At length, Hamilton agreed to think it over. Subsequently, on the eve of the encounter, "he informed Mr. P. that he had made up his mind *not to fire at Col. Burr, but to receive his fire and fire into the air.*" Again Pendleton remonstrated, and Hamilton answered:

"My friend, it is the effect of a religious scruple, and does not admit reasoning, it is useless to say more on the subject as my purpose is definitely fixed."

Hamilton had put the same statement into his Remarks, which he had written for circulation in case of his death. It is really believable—as it was from other events and testimony—that he did not intend to shoot. Considering his attitude toward capital punishment as well as dueling, his decision could be construed as admirable. The impropriety lay in telling it to anyone. If the intention were relayed to Burr, the Colonel would be placed in the intolerable position of shooting a non-resisting opponent, or giving up the satisfaction of his honor.

It is hard to avoid the suspicion that Hamilton had this plan of escape in mind. He told Pendleton, who told Dr. Hosack. The physician might well have thought he had a duty to inform Burr or Van Ness in a move of mercy, to save a human life. Pendleton had numerous opportunities to tell Van Ness. Had either Hamilton's second or Hamilton's doctor breathed the secret, Hamilton for the ninth time would have evaded a meeting of honor. There is every reason to accept his word that he sincerely disapproved of taking life except in war, but he was violating the rules of *duello* after engaging to play by them when he revealed his intention to his friends.

Another Virginian of the time, John Randolph, gave a classic opinion of the contrasting behavior of Hamilton and of Burr at this stage of their approach: "On the one side, there is labored obscurity, much equivocation, not unmixed with a little blustering; on the other, unshaken adherence to his object, and an undeviating pursuit of it not to be eluded or baffled. It reminded me of a sinking fox, pressed by a vigorous old hound, where no shift is permitted to avail him."

The judgment of John Randolph makes the worst possible case against Hamilton, and for that reason ought not to be omitted from a sympathetic biography. However, it is the language of sportsmanship, and is narrow. Hamilton was something more than an animal fleeing for its life.

At no time was he actually without recourse. Burr had offered him a paper to which his signature would buy back his life. Moreover, nothing could physically prevent Hamilton from deciding not to attend the event that was now scheduled to take place on the heights of Weehawken, New Jersey, on July 11. He feared for his life. He had used his wits at some cost to his reputation in an effort to prolong it. But he would not go so far as to run away, or turn away. He literally chose death before dishonor.

There is something else to be said for Hamilton. On every useful occasion, and in unmistakable language, he had warned that America would be injured, perhaps fatally, by Aaron Burr. "I feel it my religious duty to oppose his career," he had written twelve years before. By Hamilton's standards it would be cowardly far beyond the disciplines of a shooting match or sword play to allow such a man to become President or governor or head of some secessionist movement in the states. Many a time he could have allowed Burr to succeed by merely doing nothing. He could have decided to see no evil, when evil went armed. Figuratively speaking, Hamilton could have asserted his "alien" birth and consigned the American republic to its decline and ruin very early in its existence. But he would not do this to save his life.

Respected historians would appear much wiser in retrospect if Hamilton had indeed taken some life-saving course. They liked to interpret him (though not the Swiss-born Gallatin) as a "foreigner." "His breeding was not of the colonies," wrote Woodrow Wilson. "His thinking marked him of the culture that belonged to the other side of the sea." And long before Wilson, as sapient a man as Martin Van Buren was so imbued with the Jeffersonian dogma as to misname Hamilton's birthplace. "I allude," wrote Van Buren in a passage meant to be complimentary to Hamilton, "to the case of Alexander Hamilton . . . it may well be doubted whether his native country—England—has ever produced one who was, at all points, a more finished orator."

Hamilton would have lived longer had he deserved the low opinion of his many detractors. But he would not have lived, and died, by the light of his own nature.

III

(July 4–10, 1804)

On July Fourth there were patriotic celebrations around the city. Amid the sounds of holiday gunfire, beneath the starry banners, were the taverns and private homes that Hamilton and Burr had often frequented. There were old streets where they had met, first as young soldiers, then as fellow members of the campaign committee against George Clinton, and later as rival orators for Presidential electors. There were the court-rooms. There were the drawing rooms. And there were the memories—the battles of Manhattan and Monmouth, the winter at Valley Forge. Hamilton and Burr had shared many acquaintanceships, including those with Madison (whom Burr had introduced to Dolley Payne Todd, his future wife) and with Jefferson, the indestructible democrat.

The Society of the Cincinnati held its usual banquet in honor of the nation's birthday. Few other than the principals and their seconds knew that the duel was set for a week from this day, but several who attended the affair would afterwards recall how the men had behaved. "Burr, contrary to his wont," Trumbull wrote, "was silent, gloomy, sour; while Hamilton entered with glee into all the gaiety of a convivial party, and even sang an old military song." It may have been Hamilton's all-but-final appeal to Aaron Burr's adamantine heart.

Hamilton spent the weekend of July 7–8 at the Grange. He had as guests Colonel and Mrs. William Smith (she was John Adams' daughter), and Smith was surprised to learn that his host no longer permitted bird-shooting over his land. It was a quiet time, with Hamilton reading the Episcopal Church service on Sunday morning and sunning himself with others of the family in the afternoon.

On Monday, July 9, at the Cedar Street town house, he sent for three impersonal witnesses to a newly written will, and completed papers for the power of attorney to John Church. The court had adjourned on the first day of the month. Pendleton and Van Ness had ridden out to inspect the grounds at Weehawken. Hamilton did some work with Gouverneur Morris on the Constable estate, observing the *sang froid* that was expected of duelists, much as he disliked being one.

On Thursday the tenth, the eve of the engagement, he dropped in at the office of Egbert Benson, and went into its library, where he found a copy of *The Federalist.* The master of the place was away, but his nephew, Robert Benson, permitted the familiar visitor to make himself at home. Hamilton sat and listed the Papers by number, noting those written by himself, by Madison, by Jay. He inserted the slip of paper into a volume of Pliny, and it was later pasted into Benson's copy of *The Federalist.* In his list, the proud author, not unprecedentedly, claimed a somewhat larger share of the credit than his collaborators or critics allowed him.

After the evening meal at home, he heard the prayers of his ten-year-old son John, and returned to his writing desk. At ten o'clock he wrote:

My beloved Eliza. . . . This is my second letter.

The scruples of a Christian have determined me to expose my own life to any extent rather than subject myself to the guilt of taking the life of another. . . . The will of a merciful God be done.

Once more adieu, My Darling wife.

It was on this night too that he wrote a letter which he knew would be read after his death. It was a message from the grave to the men who were still plotting a northern confederacy divorced from the new union. But because of his death at the hands of Aaron Burr it would be read and noted by the whole nation. It was his last chance "to be in future useful whether in resisting mischief or effecting good."

I will here express but one sentiment, which is, that dismemberment of our empire will be a clear sacrifice of great positive advantages, without any counterbalancing good; administering no relief to our real disease which is Democracy, *the poison of which by subdivision will only be more concentrated in each part, and consequently the more virulent. . . . God bless you!*

Pendleton had drafted "Regulations For The Duel," and these were before Hamilton that night: "1. The parties will leave town tomorrow morning about five o'clock. . . ."

CHAPTER TWENTY-NINE

The Final Accounting

I

(July 11, 1804)

Pendleton, with Dr. David Hosack and with John Church's English-made pistols, called at Hamilton's Cedar Street house in the light of dawn. The three men walked down to the river, where a barge awaited them. Hamilton had already consigned to Pendleton a packet which contained the will as well as an untitled document that began, "On my expected interview with Col Burr, I think it proper to make some remarks. . . ."

Here, in his last piece of public writing, Hamilton declared again his religious and moral scruples against the practice of the duel and announced his intention to withhold his fire. "It is also my ardent wish," he wrote concerning Burr, "that I may have been more mistaken than I think I have been, and that he by his future conduct may shew himself worthy of all the confidence and esteem, and prove an ornament and blessing to his country."

Again, as the executor of this paper, Pendleton was being used in a manner not countenanced by the code. Hamilton had resolved against any last-moment "explanation" on the dueling grounds. He was as sure as a man could be that he was going to his death, and he had also made sure that the man who killed him would be marked for life. Again, Hamilton was using Pendleton and others in a manner which they could forgive but not condone. Intentionally or not, Hamilton had plotted a posthumous revenge, and this was outside the bounds of honor.

When four friends called for Vice President Burr somewhat earlier that morning, they found him, stripped to shirt sleeves and stocking feet, "in a very sound sleep" on the library couch. On the table lay his will, "six blue boxes of love letters," and notes to his daughter Theodosia and her husband. Creditors had hounded him since his loss of the election, and he had sold off all but four acres surrounding his mansion. What he had to leave above his debts was mostly books, portraits, and a connoisseur's collection of artifacts. But he did manage a small cash gift for Peggy the cook and Leonora the mistress, and mementos for the young men whom Theodosia called his Tenth Legion. "Give each of them . . . some small token in remembrance of me." Lastly, "If it should be my lot to fall . . . yet I live on in you and in your son" (Aaron Burr Alston).

Burr had read of an English girl, shot on the breast and saved by a silk bodice which caught the bullet in its folds. The coat that he donned that morning was made of silk, said to be tailored especially for the occasion. He chatted easily with the four—John Swartwout, Matthew Davis, Marinus Willett, and Billy Van Ness—entrusting the case and its handsome Irish-made pistols to Van Ness. Swartwout would remain behind to spread the word of an expected victory among other young protégés, as well as the Sons of Tammany. Davis and Willett went along to hide in the bushes and observe the sport. Van Ness would be his hero's second. They timed their crossing of the Hudson River so as to reach the site ahead of the other party.

The Jersey shore was a wall of summer greenery, broken by a few riverfront homes. Three miles upstream, as Burr and his party traveled, was a sandy landing place, visible among the rocks only at low tide, and from there rose the woodland called the Heights of Weehawken. Twenty feet above the river ran a narrow shelf of flat ground, bounded by high rocks at one end, overhanging the river at the other.

Burr and Van Ness made the climb and busied themselves at clearing foliage and trampling undergrowth. It was six-thirty when they saw Hamilton's barge, rowed by two or more boatmen and assisted by a sail, making its approach.

Leaving the doctor and the boatmen below, Hamilton and Pendleton climbed the steep path. The two seconds shook hands. Hamilton pointedly did not speak to the impassive Vice President. Brief formalities began with the drawing of lots, and

Hamilton was twice the winner. He drew the right to choose his position and the right to have his second give the instructions as well as the signal.

After the ten paces were measured off, Hamilton chose a position that placed him in a cavity of rocks, the perfect background for a target. He also was positioned to face into the glare of the sun, which at this hour was at eye level. He and Burr took their positions, while the seconds loaded the pistols in each other's presence. Pendleton had this last chance to tell Van Ness that Hamilton intended not to fire at Burr. "It was most scrupulously and I think correctly withheld from me," Billy said later. Pendleton brought the gun to Hamilton. "When he received his pistol, after having taken his position," Pendleton recalled, "he was asked if he would have the hair spring set? —his answer was,

"'Not this time.'"

In the Remarks that he had prepared for public consumption, Hamilton had given a previous intimation that there might be more than one exchange of shots. "I have resolved," he wrote, "if our interview is conducted in the usual manner, and it pleases God to give me the opportunity, to *reserve* and *throw away* my first fire, and I *have thoughts* even of *reserving* my second fire—and thus give a double opportunity to Col Burr to pause and to reflect."

He was still hopeful of saving his life. He had one more device for playing on the feelings of his opponent. He stood there and stared into the blinding sun while Pendleton stolidly read off the regulations.

". . . shall loudly and distinctly give the word 'Present'—If one of the parties fires and the other hath not fired, the opposite shall say one, two, three, fire, and he shall then fire or lose his shot. A snap or a flash is a fire."

"The gentlemen . . . ready?"

With aching tension each second fixed his eyes upon his principal. Pendleton and Van Ness were there to certify that all the niceties were observed. Each must watch his own man for the first flash of gunfire, perhaps for the fleck of the incoming bullet.

"Stop!"

Hamilton, on the mark and holding his pistol high, had broken the awful silence. "In certain states of light one requires glasses." Van Ness saw that "Gen Hamilton elevated his [gun], as if to try the light & lowering it said,

"'I beg pardon for delaying you, but the direction of the line renders it necessary.'

"At the same time," Billy continued, "feeling his pockets with his left hand, & drawing forth his spectacles, put them on."

Burr watched this delaying action with contempt. "He looked like a convicted felon, . . ." the Colonel would declare, "oppressed with the horrors of conscious guilt. . . . I was sure of being able to kill him."

"Gentlemen . . . ready?" Pendleton repeated.

Yes, ready. He had forced Burr at the last moment to think again about killing him. There was nothing more to be done.

"Present!" called Pendleton.

One shot rang out, then another. According to Billy Van Ness's account, he saw his principal stagger. The Colonel's foot, he learned later, had slipped on a rolling pebble. Burr himself recounted that "the smoke of G H's pistol obscured him for a moment." This moment, in Billy's estimation, amounted "only to five or six seconds of time intervening." If these two accounts are accurate, Aaron Burr had that much time to take dead aim and fire at a man whom he thought to be holding an empty pistol.

Pendleton, whose eyes naturally had been fixed on Hamilton, *his* principal, saw a different sequence of events. When the first shot sounded, Pendleton also saw a staggered man, as Hamilton spun around and collapsed on the ground with his back to his rival. As Pendleton reported it, Hamilton had withheld his fire, and only clutched the trigger in mortal agony as Burr's bullet tore into the right side of his breast, sending his own ball into a cedar branch high above Burr's head. Pendleton and Church would later retrieve the bullet-severed branch as evidence.

Burr, through the smoke of his own pistol, saw Hamilton fall, according to Pendleton, "then advanced toward General

H_____n with a manner and gesture that appeared to General Hamilton's friend [*i.e.*, Pendleton himself] to be expressive of regret." But the surgeon and the bargemen were running up the path, and Billy needed to get his man out of sight of witnesses. He hid Burr under an umbrella, brought for that purpose. "I must go & speak to him," said Burr, but Billy "insisted on immediate departure," and hurried the victor to his boat. Later, when he reached Manhattan, Burr dispatched a note to Dr. Hosack, asking him "to inform him of the present state of Genl H. and of hopes which are entertained for his recovery."

The man he left lying on the ground on Weehawken Heights looked up at the surgeon and said, "This is a mortal wound, Doctor."

II

(September 1976: A backward glance)

Four men, the two principals and their seconds, were the only legitimate witnesses to the Burr-Hamilton "interview." Dr. Hosack had withdrawn and waited to give any needed medical services, and it is just as well to exclude from consideration the Tammany Hall snoopers who watched from the bushes. In a case where eyewitnesses, especially interested parties, give contradictory accounts of the same event, both a courtroom jury and a fair-minded public would refer back to impeccable reference material: the testimony of moral character and reputation for honor.

This method of decision may seem to stack the deck against Aaron Burr. He was a charming scoundrel, a "proud pretender," a dishonest man before the duel, a disloyal man afterwards. He was vicious enough to have slashed off a soldier's arm at Valley Forge, and violent enough to merit Randolph's analogy of the ruthless foxhound pursuing the "sinking" quarry. Burr never admitted any regret for having killed Hamilton, nor forgave him for his posthumous "victory." But years after the meeting, a fugitive, an exile, a high-headed pauper, Burr chanced upon the passage in *Tristram Shandy* where Uncle Toby carefully puts the fly out the window with the remark that the world is wide enough for both of them. Burr said, perhaps wistfully, to a visitor: "If I had read Sterne more, and Voltaire less, I would have known the world was wide enough for Hamilton and me."

Billy Van Ness, Burr's second and protégé, was of much the same mold as his hero. Not to be confused with other more prominent bearers of the family name, Billy was a frequenter of Tammany Hall (known to Federalists as "the pig pen"), and probably was among the members who held an impromptu celebration at the news of Hamilton's fall.

Judge Nathaniel Pendleton, Hamilton's second, was a man of the highest probity. His fealty to Hamilton, carried to the point of holding back the deadly secret that his principal did not intend to fire at Burr, put Pendleton and Van Ness at an equal level of loyalty. Each was apt to see it all through the eyes of his friend.

The fourth witness to the duel, Hamilton himself, stood high in public respect. He had been downright quixotic in his determination to publish the Reynolds materials rather than leave the American people in any doubt as to his trustworthiness. Even his political chicanery had the patriotic flair of an attempt to save the Republic from "atheists" and "fanatics."

Dr. David Hosack was one of the eminent practicing, teaching, and founding physicians of his century. While Dr. Hosack did not witness the actual shooting, he was soon at the side of the fallen man, exchanged several sentences with him, and remained beside him till the end.

The story of the Weehawken duel, from that day to this, has had many emendations by past and present persons who were not there. Burr has been described as leaving the field in gales of demonic laughter, and ballads were sung telling how he "hid behind a bunch of thistle, and shooted him down with a great hoss-pistol."

A recent examination of the John Church dueling pistol case in the Chase Manhattan Bank of New York purportedly shows an intricate hair-trigger in both of the pair of guns used by Hamilton. But the pistols were fired in anger at least once by Church against Burr, once by Philip Hamilton against Eacker, and once by Hamilton against Burr. None of these shots drew blood.

Manifestly, the closest we can come to a true account is the story told by each witness, weighed and offset against his reputation, credibility, and character. There is no need, and no excuse, to call any of the men a liar; each saw the event from a different viewpoint.

Burr was positive that Hamilton fired first, but did not attempt to explain why the shot carried into the overhead foliage. Van Ness saw his principal stagger at the sound of a shot, but the stumble was over a rolling pebble, as Burr acknowledged, and Hamilton's bullet clipped a cedar branch at least seven feet above the head of Burr, its putative target. Hamilton, on the other hand, caught the impact of a pistol ball full in the chest, and it spun him around and hurled him to the ground. Judge Pendleton, his second, hurried to his side and was half supporting his body when Dr. Hosack hastened to the scene. Dr. Hosack heard Hamilton call it a mortal wound, and quickly confirmed that fact.

Each man told his own story in conversation, in newspapers, in judicial testimony. Immediately after the duel, Van Ness and Pendleton collaborated in preparing a joint account, each telling what he saw and heard, but ending with the following sentence:

"We conceive it proper to add that the conduct of the parties in that interview was perfectly proper as suited the occasion."

In the barge that bore him back to Manhattan, Hamilton twice gave a dying man's word that he had not fired at his adversary. Hamilton makes, one must believe, the most reliable witness of them all.

III

(July 11–12, 1804)

But he would live another thirty-one hours. It was time enough to learn anew how much he was loved for himself, for his labors, for his projection into futurity. The barge landed him back on Manhattan Island near 52 Jane Street, where

William Bayard, warned by a servant of the outward voyage, waited in trepidation. At sight of "his poor friend lying in the bottom of the boat, he burst into a flood of tears and lamentations." The bad news spread fast. Angelica Church sent a note to her brother: "The town is in consternation, and there exists only the expression of grief and indignation."

Carried to a bedroom in the Bayard home, Hamilton became the center of sorrow and adulation. Dr. Hosack had found him half sitting on the ground, supported in Pendleton's arms, able to say those despairing words before losing consciousness. Unable to detect signs of pulse or breathing, the doctor considered him to be "irrevocably gone." But fifty yards from shore, either the fresh air or the ammonia applied to his skin and poured into his mouth revived the stricken man, "to our great joy." He was able to warn a bargeman that one of the pistols was still loaded and cocked, and Hosack would remember that he also said:

"Pendleton knows"—attempting to turn his head toward his second—"that I did not intend to fire at him."

"Yes," said Pendleton, understanding the importance that this matter had attained. "I have already made Dr. Hosack acquainted with your determination as to that."

From then onward, Hamilton commanded the last march. Aided by pain-killing fomentations applied to the body, by small doses of laudanum, and by Dr. Hosack's knowledge of his physique, Hamilton fought his way through "sufferings . . . almost intolerable" to regain the management of what little life he had left. He ordered a message sent to the Reverend Benjamin Moore, the Episcopal Bishop of New York and Hamilton's friend. It was a request, said Moore, "that I would come to him for the purpose of administering the Holy Communion. I went."

Bishop Moore, however, had other considerations beyond friendship and compassion. Hamilton had violated the laws of both New York and New Jersey against dueling; he belonged to no church; he had participated in a custom which the clergy thoroughly abhorred. Although Bishop Moore intended to comply with his request if possible, he would not be rushed.

He left the bedside, and Hamilton summoned another cleric, Dr. John Mason, Betsey's friend and probably her pastor, a minister of the Dutch Reformed Church. Mason had to tell the dying man that he was not permitted to give private communions. But at one that afternoon, Bishop Moore returned, and Hamilton was able to greet him with composure.

"My dear sir, you perceive my unfortunate situation, and no doubt have been made acquainted with the circumstances. . . . It is my desire to receive the Communion at your hands."

"I must unequivocally condemn the practice which has brought him to his unhappy condition," Bishop Moore said to others present. But he extracted a promise from Hamilton that, if he should recover, he would do his utmost to "discountenance this barbarous custom," and asked him if he repented his part in the deed and forgave his adversary.

"With the utmost sincerity of heart, I can answer those questions in the affirmative," said Hamilton. Bishop Moore then administered the sacrament.

Meanwhile, the men had sent to the Grange for Betsey. "No one dares tell her the truth," admitted Bayard; "it is feared she would become frantic." Dr. Hosack called in a colleague, Dr. Wright Post. The French commercial consul, Gabriel Rey, summoned gunshot specialists from frigates in the harbor. Their diagnosis, later confirmed by autopsy, was that the bullet had broken some ribs, punctured the liver and diaphragm, and was lodged in the spine. The case, all agreed, was utterly hopeless, as Hamilton had believed from the first impact.

But Hamilton asked Hosack to bring in "my beloved wife and children." There were seven of the latter, the youngest of them, the second Philip, only two years old. At sight of them at his bedside, Hosack reported, "his utterance forsook him; he opened his eyes, gave them one look, and closed them again until they were taken away."

Hosack thought it "a proof of his extraordinary composure of mind . . . that he alone could calm the frantic grief of their mother. 'Remember, my Eliza, you are a Christian,' were the firm expressions with which he frequently, with a firm voice, in a pathetic and impressive manner, addressed her." The doctor had seen many men die, but Hamilton's "words, and the tone in which they were uttered, will never be effaced from my memory."

On the second day he was weaker but more free from pain, and the doctors consented to admit more visitors. Among them were his college mates, Robert Troup and Nicholas Fish; his political colleagues, Gouverneur Morris, Rufus King, and Oliver Wolcott. He could not speak, but smiled faintly at them.

The dying man's smile overwhelmed Morris. "The scene was too powerful for me, so that I am obliged to walk in the garden, to take breath. After having composed myself I return and sit by his side till he expires." Also present was Bishop Moore, to whom Hamilton expressed faith in God's mercy "with his last faltering words. . . . I remained with him till 2 o'clock this afternoon," the bishop wrote later, "when death closed the awful scene—he expired without a struggle, and almost without a groan."

IV

(July 12–14, 1804)

Morris, stylist of the American Constitution, was chosen to give the funeral oration. "I promise to do so if I can possibly command myself enough," he told William Smith, Hamilton's weekend guest, "but express my belief that it will be utterly impossible. I am wholly unmanned by this day's spectacle."

The day after the deathbed watch, July 13, Morris needed to talk. Money would have to be raised for the funeral and family, he knew. But Morris conjectured that wealthy Federalists would acknowledge, when solicited for funds to sustain the widow and children, that Hamilton's policies had made their fortunes possible. Morris took the attorney Richard Harison out to dine. "Discuss the points which it may be safe to touch tomorrow," the Morris diary plunges on, "and those it will be proper to avoid. To a man who could feebly command all his powers, this subject is difficult."

With the ceremonies set for the following day, July 14, he complained that there would not be time enough to write out his address or to memorize it. Morris, vain and conscientious about such matters, had delivered the eulogy at St. Paul's Church after Washington's death. Some hearers and readers criticized that address as verbose, and it certainly did not measure up to Light-Horse Harry Lee's memorial address on Washington in Congress, in which he used the unforgettable phrase: "First in war, first in peace, first in the hearts of his fellow countrymen." This time Morris wanted to come up to his own highest standard. He needed time for preparation, but delay was out of the question. "The corpse is already putrid, and the funeral procession must take place tomorrow."

While the temperamental orator fumed and complained, arrangements went forward for a state funeral such as had never before been tendered to an American—far beyond Washington's modest burial at Mount Vernon. The city council readily agreed to pay the expenses and declare a public holiday. The mood of the people demanded much, and this made another difficulty for Morris.

"Their indignation amounts almost to a frenzy, and words must be chosen that will not excite to any outrage on Colonel Burr." On the other hand, "something . . . must be said to excite public pity for his family, which he has left in indigent circumstances." Some believed that "a subscription will not go down well, because the children have a rich grandfather." Only a few persons were aware that the land-poor Schuyler "owes money and has no funds at command."

There was much in Hamilton's life story, Morris felt, that must be omitted or elided. "The first point in his biography is that he was a stranger of illegitimate birth; some mode must be contrived to pass over this handsomely." The same of "his domestic life; he has long since foolishly published the avowal of conjugal infidelity . . . ," and though "he was in principle opposed to duelling . . . he has fallen in a duel."

Much of his politics was controversial, as were the financial policies on which his reputation rested. As a personality, "he was indiscreet, vain and opinionated; these things must be told, or his character will be incomplete." Morris despaired. "All this must, somehow or other, be reconciled."

At ten o'clock on the morning of the funeral, Morris arrived at Angelica's house on Robinson Street, where the body lay. He still did not consider that he had an acceptable speech in mind. Ships in the harbor boomed their guns, church bells tolled, flags hung at half-mast. Morris learned the order of the two-hour march to Trinity Church, and his place in it. It was to be as follows:

The military units, the Society of the Cincinnati, the clergy of all denominations.

The body of General Hamilton.

The General's horse, with empty saddle and reversed boots.

The family, the physicians.

The judges of the Supreme Court.

Gouverneur Morris, the funeral orator.

The ministers, consuls, and residents of foreign powers; the officers of the Army and Navy of the United States; the officers of the State Militia.

Presidents, directors, and officers of banks; the Chamber of Commerce; the city merchants.

The Marine Society; wardens of the port of New York; masters and officers of the harbor.

The president, professors, and students of Columbia College.

The citizenry in general, including the Sons of Tammany, the Society of Mechanics and Tradesmen, various other societies.

Morris rode in his carriage with a heavy heart. "While moving in the procession I meditate as much as my feelings will permit, on what I am to say. I can find no way to get over the difficulty which would attend the details of his death. It will be impossible to command either myself or my audience."

Shaken and uncertain, he mounted the outdoor stage under the portico of Trinity Church. John Church was beside him. At his feet sat four of Hamilton's sons, the eldest sixteen and the youngest six. The coffin was placed at the front of the stage, and Morris began.

He had much ground to cover—all of Hamilton's years in America; and many representative groups to address—the Columbia students, the Cincinnati, the clergy, the Bar. He must eulogize Hamilton the patriot, the friend, the Christian. He feared that the subject, so close to his own heart, could not be conveyed to this vast gathering. Especially, he grumbled, "since my voice is lost before it reaches one-tenth of the audience." He did not learn until later how his words went home.

Among the gathering, sitting on the church steps, was a fifteen-year-old boy, John W. Francis, who was to study medicine under Dr. Hosack, and to become a noted physician. Young Francis later told of hearing Morris heroically struggle to make the central point of his eulogy: that man brings nothing into the world, takes nothing out of it, but can leave much behind —and that Hamilton had done so, in patriotic service and example.

"Bear this witness to the memory of my departed friend. I CHARGE YOU TO PROTECT HIS FAME. It is all that he has left—all that these poor orphan children will inherit from their father. But, my countrymen, that Fame may be a rich treasure to you also."

The boy observed with awe that a grown man nearby, William Coleman of the *Evening Post,* was weeping. That night Coleman consulted his notes on the oration. He found them useless for the article he must write, and threw them away. He went to the orator himself and asked for help.

Morris received the editor in a wretched humor. "I find that what I have said does not answer the general expectation. . . . It must ever happen to him whose duty it is to alloy the sentiment which he is expected to arouse. How easy would it have been to make them, for the moment, absolutely mad!" How easy to have played Marc Antony!

Morris was flattered that his visitor "speaks very highly of the discourse, more so than it deserves." He promised the editor that "if he will write what he remembers, I will endeavor to put it into the terms which were used."

Only when his words appeared in print was Morris to know that he had not failed the dead hero whom he had set out, under many restraints, to praise.

AFTERWORD

I tamely attached a reference number to every quotation in the first draft of this book, and footnoted the source. My typist lost track of them, and I lost patience. I would have abandoned the footnote farce by the second or third draft if I hadn't been scared of what sarcastic professors always say about that sort of undress in a biography.

By the fourth draft, or thereabouts, I became more scared of my own hypocrisy than of other men's snobbery. With rare exceptions, I was using published source materials. Occasionally I went to photostat copies of manuscript and of old newspapers. But I had neither sought nor found any "quaint and curious volumes of forgotten lore." Footnotes, I concluded, are for the admired works of such dedicated scholars as Fawn Brodie, Julian Boyd, and Irving Brant (all of whom answered my letters), and James Flexner (who didn't bother). To festoon my book with page references to secondary sources would be, I came to feel, academic affectation.

Luckily I found a superb precedent. In the author's note for her masterful *Miracle at Philadelphia,* the late Catherine Drinker Bowen said this: "Because my book reveals no undiscovered material and attempts no new interpretations, I have kept scholarly apparatus to a minimum." By using no footnotes she had taken me off the hook. "A good one to follow, a hard one to beat," is a saying that applies admirably to this wonderful lady.

As I had previously written biographies of Aaron Burr and Martin Van Buren, the politics and materials of early New York State history were familiar ground to me. Visits to Nevis, St. Croix, Yorktown, Trinity Church, and the Bank of New York fed the mood more than the mind in regard to Hamilton. The technology of modern and devout Library Service, notably Xerox, has changed the work habits of biographers. In the 1930's I had to travel to local libraries and historical societies;

in the 1970's the custodians of those institutions would send me "burn copies," often gratis, never costly. I visited repositories only when it was convenient—the Library of Congress, the National Archives, the Treasury Department Library, the Firestone Library at Princeton University, and a few others. But person-to-person long distance phone calls worked many wonders.

As a legitimate and aesthetic substitute for numerals and footnotes, I made a practice of dubbing my source into the text, in the absence of any such reason not to as awkwardness or unnecessary affront to some anti-Hamiltonian. Beginning in the Foreword, I cited authorities: "The biographer Nathan Schachner says . . ." and "John Church Hamilton, the son-biographer, says. . . ." It is a simple matter for the curious reader to match the name with the title in the Bibliography, and for any doubter to write me a letter. The *Papers,* the *Works,* and the *Law Practice* of Alexander Hamilton are referred to throughout the book.

However, some Notes (not footnotes) on the Foreword and the four Parts are in order, and these follow.

NOTES

Hamilton left nothing but business letters about the slave system of the West Indies. But Lord Macaulay's father, Zachary, became a bookkeeper at a sugar plantation on Jamaica when he was not yet seventeen. In 1785, a dozen years after Hamilton had left the West Indies, Zachary Macaulay wrote that he had placed himself "in a field of canes, amidst perhaps a hundred of the sable race, cursing and bawling, while the noise of the whip resounding on their shoulders, and the cries of the poor wretches, would make you imagine that some unlucky accident had carried you to the doleful shades."

* * *

Part One: Chapters One Through Nine

Major Eustice's name is sometimes spelled Eustace.

* * *

Any reader of Jefferson's *Notes on the State of Virginia* will recall that he expressed an even more patronizing opinion of the Negro than did Hamilton.

* * *

Mrs. Bowen disclaimed any "new interpretations" in her book, but I am going to be less modest. No other writer, I believe, has spotted Angelica's birth date—premature to say the least—as a possible reason why the Schuylers did not hold Hamilton's illegitimate birth against him. There are other new interpretations in my book, but I shall mention only one and let the reader find the rest. I have in mind my expressed belief that it was Major André's hanging that turned Hamilton against capital punishment—but not, as has been written, against Washington.

* * *

I had finished the book when I heard Leo Rosten, on a TV talk show with Eric Sevareid, express his belief that it was almost immoral for writers and teachers not to be optimistic about the times they and their struggling contemporaries were living through. Mr. Rosten subsequently sent me the exact quotation, in a letter dated September 8, 1975: "The darker the times, the more one has a moral obligation to be optimistic." Beginning with Hamilton's letters to the Committee of Correspondence, I had already noted this as a lifelong habit of his.

* * *

In walking the battlefield I was disappointed to see how deeply the York River had bitten away the bank behind Redoubt 10.

In my small book, *Washington and Lee,* I described General Washington as being unbeatable because of his will to win, and General Lee as destined by character to be a noble loser. Much later I was pleased to read that both Tom Paine and Voltaire agreed with me about General Washington.

* * *

The following lists were provided to the author by the research department of the Library of Congress in a letter dated May 10, 1971. The list of aides-de-camp of General Washington is complete and includes states of origin. The list of foreign nationals who served as officers in the Revolutionary Army is only partial, and a large majority of the persons named are Frenchmen.

Aides-de-Camp
   Hodijah Baylies, Massachusetts
   George Baylor, Virginia
   Richard Cary, Virginia
   David Cobb, Massachusetts
   John Fitzgerald, Virginia
   Peregrine Fitzhugh, Virginia

Caleb Gibbs, Massachusetts
William Grayson, Virginia
Alexander Hamilton, New York
Alexander Contee Hanson, Maryland
Robert Hanson Harrison, Virginia
David Humphreys, Connecticut
George Johnston, Virginia
John Laurens, South Carolina
George Lewis, Virginia
James McHenry, Maryland
Richard Kidder Meade, Virginia
Thomas Mifflin, Pennsylvania
Stephen Moylan, Pennsylvania
William Palfrey, Massachusetts
Pierre Penet, France
Edmund Randolph, Virginia
Joseph Reed, Pennsylvania
William Stephens Smith, New York
Presley Peter Thornton, Virginia
Tench Tilghman, Maryland
John Trumbull, Connecticut
Jonathan Trumbull Jr., Connecticut
Richard Varick, New York
Benjamin Walker, New York
John Walker, North Carolina
Samuel Blatchley Webb, Connecticut

(During the Yorktown campaign John Parke Custis served as a volunteer aide, but without rank, pay, or appointment, so that he cannot properly be included in the above list.)

Foreign Officers:

Augustin Mottin de la Balme
Jouis-Saint-Ange Morel, Chevalier de la Colombe
Philippe Tronson de Coudray
Louis le Bègue de Presle Duportail
Pierre Charles L'Enfant

Joseph-Pierre-Charles, Baron de Frey
Jean-Baptiste de Gouvion
Charles-François Dubuysson des Hays
Louis-Casimir, Baron de Holtzendorff
Michel-Gabriel Houdin
Johann Kalb, known as Baron de Kalb
Tadeusz Kosciuszko
Marie-Joseph-Paul-Yves-Roch-Gilbert du Motier, Marquis de
    Lafayette
Jean-Baptiste-Joseph, Chevalier de Laumoy
Jean-Bernard-Bourg Gauthier de Murman
Charles-Albert de Moré de Pontgibaud
Louis de Pontière
Casimir Pulaski
Armand-Charles Tuffin, Marquis de la Rouérie
Friedrich Wilhelm August Heinrich Ferdinand, Baron von
    Steuben
Jean-Louis-Ambroise de Genton, Chevalier de Villefranche

* * *

Part Two: Chapters Ten Through Nineteen

Contrary to anachronistic sketches and advertising pamphlets, Hamilton was not present at Fraunces Tavern, December 4, 1783, when Washington bade farewell to his officers.
Hamilton was out of the city on business at the time.

* * *

Hamilton's political career and philosophy from 1780 on-
wards would be Schuyler-oriented. Gilbert L. Lycan wrote to
the author, May 25, 1973: "It is interesting to speculate on how
the history of the United States might have been different had
Hamilton married a Livingston."

* * *

Hamilton's monarchism became an immortal myth. John
McClaughry wrote to the author, February 8, 1973:

"I have already had occasion to argue Hamilton's view of monarchy, and as far as I am concerned the evidence is incontrovertible that Hamilton explicitly favored monarchy for the United States, by name. I refer you to his *Works,* Federal Edition, H. C. Lodge, ed. (New York: G. P. Putnam, 1904).

"In Hamilton's address to the Constitutional Convention of June 18–19, 1787, he urges an 'executive for life' which he terms an 'elective monarch'; he defends the British hereditary monarchy as a model—'the only good one on the subject'; points out the 'excellency of the British executive'; claims that 'nothing short of such an executive can be efficient.' (pp. 390, 392, 401)

"Barrington, in *Main Currents of American Thought* I, ch. 3, says:

"'The only effective way of keeping democratic factionalism within bounds, Hamilton was convinced, lay in the erection of a powerful chief magistrate, who "ought to be hereditary, and have so much power, that it will not be his interest to risk much to acquire more," and who would therefore stand "above corruption."' (Citation: *Works,* II, p. 415)

"This interpretation is corroborated by Van Doren's *The Great Rehearsal,* and by Russell Kirk, who writes, 'American hostility to [Hamilton's] proposal for a powerful magistrate, preferably hereditary, grieved and rather surprised him, and with pain he relinquished this plan.' (*The Conservative Mind,* Ch. 3, pt. 2)

"This is weighty evidence, Holmes, and if you contest the point I will expect to see even weightier evidence adduced to the contrary."

In that same letter, McClaughry observed: "It is true as you suggest that many poor people became prosperous due to Hamilton's financial plan. Many rich people became even more prosperous, which is not altogether a bad thing, of course. . . . As Madison wisely foresaw, the accumulation of wealth in a few hands would either incite the masses to overthrow Property in the name of socialism, or fall under the owners of great wealth."

*   *   *

Jefferson's hatred of Hamilton has descended to Hamilton biographers, according to one of them. Gilbert L. Lycan wrote to the author, July 16, 1973: "I seriously warn you that every writer for several years past has been attacked for writing an *objective,* balanced and fair book about Hamilton. People who review books are generally liberals, and American liberals have long since resolved to categorize H. falsely, and they defy anybody to write truthfully about him."

*   *   *

With regard to the original whereabouts of the Treasury Department, I am grateful for a copy of the following letter:

UNITED STATES
DEPARTMENT OF THE INTERIOR
NATIONAL PARK SERVICE

In reply refer to Federal Hall National Memorial
15 Pine Street
New York, N.Y. 10005

H 2215

Mr. Donald J. Lehman
Information Officer
Public Buildings Service
General Services Administration
Washington, D.C. 20405

Dear Mr. Lehman:
   It was good to hear from you again. I see where you have made great strides toward the completion of your project. I found your draft excellent and most interesting. I have made just one minor addition, as you can see on the last page of your draft. Your query concerning the location of the Department of the Treasury raises a question that we have been trying to solve for some time. The evidence we have found up to now is not conclusive.

Records are fairly accurate in pinpointing the offices of the Board of Treasury during the period of the Confederation when the Continental Congress was meeting in New York. The Board of Treasury, predecessor to the Department of the Treasury, had either all or part of its offices, including the Treasurer and Register, in the old Fraunces Tavern at the corner of Pearl and Broad Streets. Another part of its office, possibly the three members of the Board itself, utilized a house, no longer existing, on the East side of Broadway, at the corner of King Street, now Pine Street, until April 30, 1788. At that time it moved to another location, which is not known. The records are silent on this score, but it could be that it moved to Fraunces Tavern. It should be noted that on May 1, 1788, both the Department of Foreign Affairs and Department of War moved out of Fraunces Tavern. It is possible that the rest of the Board of Treasury moved into Fraunces Tavern now that there was room for it.

We know positively from the records that rent was paid for the Tavern by the Board until April 30, 1789. However, whether the newly established Department of the Treasury, successor to the Board, continued at that location cannot be determined since the records are silent.

Rufus Wilmot Griswold, in his *The Republican Court* (New York: D. Appleton and Company, 1867), noted that in 1789–1790 the Secretary of the Treasury occupied a house at the corner of Wall and Broad Streets, almost opposite to Federal Hall. This is substantiated by the Hamilton Papers, in which Alexander Hamilton has himself listed as living in house "No. 58" on Wall Street.

It was the practice in those days for many government officials to use their residences as places of business. If this was true, it may not be too difficult to suppose that all or part of the Treasury Department was located on Wall Street where Hamilton lived. It may also be true that all or part of the Department continued to use Fraunces Tavern. Unfortunately, evidence to corroborate both these statements is lacking.

I do not know how much help I have been to you, but I do hope that I have given you some information. If in the process of my researches I come across additional evidence, rest assured that I will call it to your attention. In the meantime lots of luck to you on your project.

> Sincerely yours,
> (signed) LOUIS TORRES
> Supervisory Historian

* * *

I regard John Randolph's comment on Madison rather as a risqué witticism than as a homosexual slur (otherwise I would have omitted it, as I was tempted to do), but Madisonians hate it. Irving Brant wrote to the author, December 10, 1970:

"You ask who it was that said 'Madison was always mistress to some great man.' I never heard of that characterization, but someone must have said it, and he must have been an ignoramus of the first order, with a gift of expression."

"Gift of expression" fits the sardonic Randolph. The quotation was used by John Church Hamilton and repeated by Gertrude Atherton. I tried but was unable to trace its origin through several authorities on Virginia biography.

* * *

The Rev. Alexander Hamilton's letter to the author follows, in full:

> Threadbare Manor
> An Olde New England Homestead
> Route 1, Box 290
> Kennebunkport, Maine 04046
>
> 7 June 1973

Mr. Holmes Alexander
1391 National Press Bldg.
Washington, D.C. 20004

Dear Mr. Alexander,
    Fred Hunt did indeed write to me. Of course I am glad to help his friend and our fellow member of the Cincinnati.

Alexander Hamilton's Life, by Alice Curtis Desmond, is worth your study. While the book is written as other than straight history, Mrs. Desmond has done her research well. For myself, I have always understood that the Hamilton-Schuyler wedding was a formal military affair. I am inclined to suggest that nobody had any other clothes in those days. Whoever was in Albany was there, I am sure. The Schuyler mansion was the center of the social life of the day, and a very hospitable place (e.g., dinner for Burgoyne after he lost the battle).

I have no material to copy for you. Columbia University got everything I had, in 1967. Sorry.

Please feel [free] to ask me about any point. My best.

Sincerely,
(signed) ALEX. HAMILTON

*   *   *

Part Three: Chapters Twenty Through Twenty-Four

Despite the revolutionary ardor which brought about his recall and replacement as France's envoy, Edmond Genêt chose not to return to France and the Reign of Terror. Instead he remained in America for the rest of his life, marrying Governor Clinton's daughter and becoming a naturalized citizen.

*   *   *

Samuel Flagg Bemis, in *A Diplomatic History of the United States,* commented as follows on Hamilton's part in the Jay Treaty: "It is not an exaggeration to believe that Jay's Treaty, which was really Hamilton's Treaty, saved American nationality in an hour of crisis."

*   *   *

The mission to London which Hamilton did not obtain marked his third disappointment of a diplomatic assignment.

Schuyler had tried to send him to Paris in 1781, and Lafayette had wanted Congress to make him envoy to London in 1784.

* * *

E. Richard McKinstry, Reference Librarian, the New Jersey Historical Society, wrote to the author, May 10, 1973: "John Adams' headquarters was at the Phoenix Hotel . . ." at Trenton in mid-October 1799.

* * *

Part Four: Chapters Twenty-Five Through Twenty-Nine

"I wish I had the principal here," said DeWitt Clinton as he left the field of honor after having put a bullet in the leg of John Swartwout, Burr's political lieutenant.

The wonder is that Burr and Clinton, bitter enemies, did not fight. J. C. Hamilton writes that in June 1804 Burr called a meeting of his so-called Tenth Legion, or Little Band, and had them vote on who was to be challenged—Hamilton or Clinton.

* * *

It is the romantic legend that Angelica Hamilton, Philip Hamilton's younger sister, was stricken insane at the sight of him on his deathbed. I think she was already afflicted, and that it is not medically possible for a normal person to be driven mad by a single shock.

* * *

During the Republican administration that began in January 1969, there was some build-up of Hamilton. A ceremony proclaiming the Treasury Building a national historical site was held in Alexander Hamilton Place, where his statue stands south of the building. A plan was set in motion to buy up Hamilton furniture and make a replica of his original office for the use of the Secretary of the Treasury. I wrote to former Secretary Connally, asking him for details, but the idea apparently had not reached his level, for he replied:

VINSON, ELKINS, SEARLS, CONNALLY & SMITH
Attorneys at Law
First City National Bank Building
Houston, Texas 77002

December 31, 1973

My dear Holmes:

I wish I had said it, but I didn't. The idea of a room at the Treasury to resemble Hamilton's original office in New York is a superb one, and I could kick myself for not having thought of it.

My best wishes for a healthy and prosperous New Year.

Sincerely,
(signed) JOHN B. CONNALLY

Mr. Holmes Alexander
1391 National Press Building
Washington, D.C. 20004

* * *

In his fourth and final report on Public Credit, his valedictory on leaving the Treasury, Hamilton summed up his financial system: (a) Discharge past obligations by planned and phased reductions toward a specified date; (b) avoid further debt by pay-as-you-go taxation. In his words, with his own emphasis: "True patriotism and genuine policy cannot . . . be better demonstrated . . . than by improving, efficaciously, the very favorable situation . . . for extinguishing, with reasonable celerity, the actual debt of the country, and for laying a foundation of a system . . . which, if possible, may give IMMORTALITY TO PUBLIC CREDIT."

* * *

In addition to risking undeserved disgrace, financial officers courted unearned hostility and the danger of yielding to demands for public service that would require fresh borrowing.

Possibly thinking of the Whiskey Tax Rebellion, Hamilton
wrote in January 1795: "To pay taxes . . . is always, more or
less, unpopular . . . it is no uncommon spectacle to see the
same men clamoring for occasions of expense . . . yet vehe-
ment against every form of taxation. . . ."

*   *   *

Washington's signature on the national bank bill has to be
ranked among his master strokes. "The Bank of the United
States proved to be a safe depository for government funds, an
important aid in collecting taxes and in providing a uniform
circulating medium for the country, a source of loans in time
of emergency, an aid to foreign exchange operations of the
Treasury, a healthy restraint on unsound banking practices,
and a much needed source of capital for investment in industrial enterprises. . . ." (Jacob E. Cooke)

*   *   *

Of course, Inspector General Hamilton recruited and obtained commissions for others than his relatives. Washington
wrote him to "devote a good deal of your time to the business
of recruiting *good* men—and the choice of *good* Officers."

*   *   *

Knox was hurt and disgruntled at being rated militarily behind Hamilton, but Pinckney responded generously, writing to
McHenry about Hamilton: "I declared then, and still declare,
it was with the greatest pleasure I saw his name at the head
of the list of Major Generals, and applauded the discernment
that placed him there. . . . I therefore without any hesitation
sent him word, by Major Rutledge, that I rejoiced at his appointment and would with pleasure serve under him."

*   *   *

Other statesmen were well ahead of Hamilton in plans to
liberate the Spanish colonies in Latin America. Minister Rufus
King in London recounted a conversation with Foreign Minister Lord Grenville "which treated of the practicality and the

means of effecting the measure tending to shew me . . . a future connection with the United States and the independence of the Continental Spanish colonies." King also wrote Secretary of State Pickering: "As England is ready she will furnish a fleet and military stores and we should furnish the army. . . ."

* * *

Washington wrote to Secretary of War McHenry on the subject of military dress, December 13, 1798: "The uniform of the Commander in chief to be a blue coat with yellow buttons and gold epaulettes each having three silver stars with linings, cap and cuffs of buff, in winter buff vest and breeches, in summer a white vest, & breeches of nanken. A white plume in the hat to be a further distinction.

"The Major General to be distinguished by two silver stars in each epaulette and except the Inspector General by a black and white plume. . . . The Inspector General . . . to be distinguished by a blue plume."

* * *

From October 1798, Burr and Hamilton served together on the Military Committee of New York City, which arranged to fortify the harbor and city.

* * *

Larger-than-life statues of the two great foreign-born Secretaries of the Treasury flank the Treasury Department. Hamilton stands south of the building in what tourists might think of as the back yard—but, perhaps appropriately, facing the Washington Monument half a mile away across the Ellipse. Gallatin dominates the north entrance, which faces Pennsylvania Avenue, the route of Inaugural parades and of the heaviest visitors' traffic. Few historians have been able to give an objective judgment on the relative achievements of these two masters of national finance, so personally hostile to one another, so philosophically unlike. Which, if either, was "successful?"

Although Hamilton skillfully absorbed the national wartime debt, established world-respected national credit, spread prosperity, and increased the federal government at a time when that was imperative for its survival, the Hamilton era, 1789–1801, ended with a Treasury deficit of $900,000—considerably offset, however, by the Treasury's cash balance and its ownership of stock in the Bank of the United States.

After 1801, the Republican administrations, with Gallatin leading the chorus, verbally abused Hamilton and Hamiltonianism. But little was done to alter the system, although the responsibility for deficit budgeting and financial panics (none of the latter occurred under Hamilton) was shared by the Treasury and the House Ways and Means Committee, both Gallatin strongholds.

*   *   *

Although Hamilton was one of five board members who directed the sinking fund, he was the dominant figure and anticipated American financial history. "Indeed, he possessed half the power over credit given to the Federal Reserve Open Market Committee a century and a half later. Moreover, he could also support the market price of government bonds, a power which was not to be given to another Secretary until World War I." (*Financial History of the United States,* by Paul Studenski and Herman E. Kross.)

*   *   *

This Note is out of sequence because I did not meet Professor Julian Boyd for questioning until well along in my book. I finally encountered him at a Library of Congress ceremony, and later put my question in a letter to Princeton, where Dr. Boyd is in charge of the Jefferson Papers.

Dr. Boyd replied on August 7, 1975, saying, on the subject of Beckwith's cypher numerals: ". . . George Beckwith had no cypher numeral for Jefferson but always referred to him by name or as Secretary of State. . . . Washington, Jefferson, Madison, and other persons holding office who declined on principle to hold conversations with an unaccredited agent were referred to in Beckwith's reports either by name or by office."

* * *

In a letter to the author dated August 2, 1975, Fawn M. Brodie said on the subject of Jefferson's attitude toward Bonaparte: "He was grateful to Bonaparte for the Louisiana Purchase. Save for that all the writings are unfavorable except for a brief period after Elba, in which Jefferson momentarily believed him when he learned that Napoleon had promised to return liberty to France."

* * *

Although the author entertains no doubt that, next to Washington, Hamilton stands as our greatest American to date, it seems fair to seek a consensus.

Objective reviews of Secretary Hamilton's performance were mixed but generally favorable. "On the whole, the record of the Federalist administration in the development and management of the national finances was one of solid achievement. A comprehensive national financial system was established, national credit was placed on a firm foundation, every debt obligation was met and great encouragement was given to the development of commerce. However, the record also had its weak spots. . . . Indeed, no clear statement of the debt was ever presented by Hamilton or by Wolcott. . . . In short, Hamilton's administration demonstrated brilliance and executive genius, but it lacked the ability to supervise efficiently the unspectacular administrative details entailed in operating a Treasury Department." (Studenski and Kross, *op. cit.*)

* * *

In addition to correspondents previously mentioned, I received encouragement and material assistance from Hunter Alexander; Nicholas J. Anthony; U.S. Senator Robert C. Byrd and his assistants, Ethel R. Low and Frank A. Pietranton, Jr.; Carl Charlick; Mrs. Caroline M. Courbois; Frederick Drum

Hunt; Donald McCammond; Henry K. McHarg; the late U.S. Senator Karl Mundt, chairman of the Alexander Hamilton Bicentennial Commission, 1957; Sid Sanders; J. G. Sourwine; Mary Stewart; E. Berkeley Tompkins; Herbert Waite; Howard Wehmann; and J. Harvie Williams. Broadus Mitchell graciously granted permission to use the quotation from his biography of Hamilton which appears as a headpiece for Part III. Thanks are also due to the U.S. Treasury Department for the photograph which is used as the frontispiece of the book.

Any unintentional omission from this listing is regretted.

HOLMES ALEXANDER

National Press Building
Washington, D.C. 20045

922 Twenty-fifth Street, N.W.
Washington, D.C. 20037

1970–76

BIBLIOGRAPHY

Douglas Adams and Harvey Martin. "Was Alexander Hamilton a Christian Statesman?" *William and Mary Quarterly,* April 1955.

Ephraim Douglass Adams. *The Power of Ideas in American History.* New York, 1913.

Henry Adams. *History of the United States* (9 vols.). Boston, 1889–91.

John Richard Alden. *The American Revolution.* New York, 1954.

D. S. Alexander. *A Political History of New York* (4 vols.). New York, 1906.

Holmes Alexander. *Aaron Burr: The Proud Pretender.* New York, 1937.

G. Allen. *Our Quasi War with France.* Boston, 1967.

Bower Aly. *The Rhetoric of Alexander Hamilton.* New York, 1941.

Harry Ammon. *James Monroe.* New York, 1971.

J.-J. Antier. "La Bataille de Yorktown." *TAM: Terre, Air, Mer,* No. 208, November 1–15, 1971.

Aristotle. *On Man in the Universe.* Roslyn, New York, 1943.

Col. Robert Arthur. *The Sieges of Yorktown: 1781 and 1862.* Fort Monroe, Virginia, 1930.

Gertrude Atherton. *Adventures of a Novelist.* New York, 1932.

———. *The Conqueror.* Philadelphia, 1902.

Charles A. Beard. *The Idea of National Interest.* New York, 1934.

Samuel Flagg Bemis. *A Diplomatic History of the United States.* New York, 1936.

Peter M. Bergman. *The Chronological History of the Negro in America.* New York, 1969.

Andrew S. Berky and James P. Shenton. *The Historians' History of the United States.* New York, 1966.

Albert J. Beveridge. *The Life of John Marshall* (Vols. II and III). Boston, 1916, 1919.

"Alexander Hamilton: 1755–1804." *William and Mary Quarterly,* Vol. XII, No. 2, April 1955.

Alfred Hoyt Bill. *Valley Forge: The Making of an Army.* New York, 1952.

George A. Billias. *George Washington's Generals.* New York, 1964.

The Black Book, or Book of Misdemeanors in King's College, New-York, 1771–1775. New York, 1931.

448   *To Covet Honor*

Catherine Drinker Bowen. *Miracle at Philadelphia.* Boston, 1966.

Claude G. Bowers. *Jefferson and Hamilton.* Boston, 1925.

————. *Jefferson in Power.* Boston, 1936.

Allen Bowman. *The Morale of the American Revolutionary Army.* New York, 1943.

Julian Parks Boyd. *Alexander Hamilton's Secret Attempts To Control American Foreign Policy, With Supporting Documents.* Princeton, New Jersey, 1964.

H. M. Brackenridge. *History of the Whiskey Insurrection.* Pittsburgh, 1859.

Irving Brant. *James Madison* (6 vols.). Indianapolis, 1941–61.

Fawn M. Brodie. *Thomas Jefferson, An Intimate Biography.* New York, 1974.

F. M. Brewer. "Succession to the Presidency." *Editorial Research Reports,* Vol. II. Washington, D.C., 1945.

Carl Bridenbaugh. *Cities in Revolt.* New York, 1955.

Van Wyck Brooks. *The World of Washington Irving.* New York, 1944.

James Bryce. *The American Commonwealth.* New York, 1913.

Edmund Burton, editor. *Letters of the Members of the Continental Congress.* Washington, D.C., 1934.

Martin Bush. *Philip Schuyler: Revolutionary Enigma.* New York, 1970.

H. Paul Caemmerer. *Pierre Charles L'Enfant.* New York, 1920.

Allen Daniel Candler and Clement A. Evans. *Georgia: Surprising Sketches of Counties, Towns, Events, Institutions, and Persons, Arranged in Cyclopedic Form* (3 vols.). Atlanta, 1906.

John A. Carroll and M. W. Ashworth. *George Washington* (Vol. 7). New York, 1957.

Ernst Cassirer. *The Philosophy of the Enlightenment.* Princeton, New Jersey, 1951.

Chase Manhattan Bank. "What You Should Know About Money." *The Chase Manhattan Bank Public Affairs,* No. 2, Vol. VIII (March 25, 1968).

Joseph Charles. *Origins of the American Party System.* New York, 1956.

Marquis de Chastellux. *Travels in North America in the Years 1780, 1781 and 1782.* Edited by Howard C. Rice Jr. Williamsburg, Virginia, 1963.

Donald Barr Chidsey. *Victory at Yorktown.* New York, 1962.

Carter C. Chinnis. *The American Road to Yorktown: A Study in Command.* Thesis submitted to the faculty of the College of Arts and

Bibliography

449

Sciences of the American University in partial fulfillment of the requirements for the degree of Master of Arts, History. March 22, 1969.

V. L. Collins. *President Witherspoon.* Princeton, New Jersey, 1915.

Jacob E. Cooke. *Alexander Hamilton.* New York, 1967.

——, editor. *Alexander Hamilton: A Profile.* New York, 1967.

Cecil B. Currey. *Road to Revolution: Benjamin Franklin in England.* New York, 1968.

William Eleroy Curtis. *The True Thomas Jefferson.* Philadelphia, 1901.

William P. Cutler and Julia B. Cutler. *Life of Rev. Manasseh Cutler* (2 vols.). Cincinnati, 1888.

Alexander Deconde. *The Quasi War.* New York, 1966.

William H. S. Demarest. *A History of Rutgers College, 1766–1924.* New Brunswick, New Jersey, no date.

James Orr Denby. *The Society of the Cincinnati and Its Museum.* Washington, D.C., 1967.

Alice Curtis Desmond. *Alexander Hamilton's Wife.* New York, 1953.

Mabel E. Deutrich. *Preliminary Inventory of the War Department Collection of Revolutionary War Records.* Washington, D.C., 1970.

Dictionary of American Biography (22 vols.). New York.

H. J. Eckenrode. *The Story of the Campaign and Siege of Yorktown.* Washington, D.C., 1957.

Max Farrand. *The Framing of the Constitution of the United States.* New York and London, 25th printing, paperback, 1970.

Max Farrand, editor. *The Records of the Federal Convention of 1787* (Vols. I, II, III). New Haven, Connecticut, 1911.

Don R. Gerlach. *Philip Schuyler and the American Revolution* (Vol. I). New York, 1964.

Felix Gilbert. *To the Farewell Address.* Princeton, New Jersey, 1961.

F. J. Gould. *Thomas Paine.* London, 1925.

Francis Vinton Greene. *The Revolutionary War and the Military Policy of the United States.* New York, 1911.

Rufus W. Griswold. *The Republican Court.* New York, 1867.

Ira D. Gruber. *The Howe Brothers and the American Revolution.* New York, 1972.

Philip Guedalla. *Fathers of the Revolution.* New York, 1926.

Louis M. Hacker. *Alexander Hamilton and the American Tradition.* New York, 1957.

——. *The Triumph of American Capitalism.* New York, 1940.

Hamer's Guide. Lehigh University.

Alexander Hamilton. *Alexander Hamilton: A Biography in His Own Words*. New York, 1973.

———. *Alexander Hamilton and the Founding of the Nation*. Edited by Richard B. Morris. New York, 1957.

———. *Alexander Hamilton Reader: A Compilation of Materials by and Commenting on Hamilton*. Selected and edited by Margaret Esther Hall. New York, 1957.

———. *Alexander Hamilton's Papers on Public Credit, Commerce, and Finance*. Edited by Samuel McKee Jr. New York, 1934.

———. *Alexander Hamilton's Day Book*. Edited by E. P. Panagopoulos. Detroit, 1961.

———. *Basic Ideas of Alexander Hamilton*. Edited by Richard B. Morris. New York, 1957.

———. *Law Practice of Alexander Hamilton* (Vols. I and II). Edited by Julius Goebel Jr. New York, 1969.

———. Manuscripts at Columbia University.

———. Manuscripts at Library of Congress.

———. Manuscript in Maryland Historical Society.

———. Manuscripts in New York Historical Society.

———. Manuscripts in New York State Historical Association.

———. Manuscripts at National Archives.

———. Manuscripts in Princeton University Library.

———. Manuscripts in Treasury Department.

———. Manuscripts in Virginia Historical Society.

———. Manuscripts in William L. Clements Library, University of Michigan.

———. *Papers of Alexander Hamilton* (19 vols.). New York, 1961–73.

———. *Papers of Alexander Hamilton*. Edited by Jacob E. Cooke. New York, 1964.

———. *Works of Alexander Hamilton* (7 vols.). Edited by John Church Hamilton. New York, 1857.

———. *Works of Alexander Hamilton* (12 vols.). Edited by Henry Cabot Lodge. New York, 1885–1903.

———. John Jay, and James Madison. *The Federalist*. New York, 1937.

Allan McLane Hamilton. *The Intimate Life of Alexander Hamilton*. New York, 1910.

John Church Hamilton. *Life of Alexander Hamilton* (2 vols.). New York, 1840.

Bray Hammond. *Banks and Politics in America*. Princeton, New Jersey, 1957.

J. D. Hammond. *Political History of New York State.* Syracuse, New York, 1852.

A. Barton Hepburn. *A History of Currency in the United States.* New York, 1915.

Peter P. Hill. *William Vans Murray: Federalist Diplomat.* Ithaca, New York, 1971.

Mary Hinsdale. *A History of the President's Cabinet.* Ann Arbor, Michigan, 1911.

Rupert Hughes. *George Washington* (Vols. II and III). New York, 1930.

David Hume. *A Treatise on Human Nature.* Baltimore, 1969.

Information Please Almanac, Atlas and Yearbook, 1971. New York, 1971.

Washington Irving. *The Life of George Washington* (4 vols.). New York, 1855.

Marquis James. *Andrew Jackson: The Border Captain.* New York, 1933.

———. *Life of Andrew Jackson* (2 vols.). New York, 1938.

Thomas Jefferson. *Life and Selected Writings of Thomas Jefferson.* Edited by Adrienne Koch and William Peden. New York, 1944.

———. *Selected Writings of Thomas Jefferson.* Edited by Adrienne Koch and William Peden. New York, 1944.

Journals of the Continental Congress.

James Kent. *Memoirs and Letters.* New York, 1970.

Adrienne Koch. *American Enlightenment.* New York, 1965.

———. *Power, Morals, and the Founding Fathers.* Ithaca, New York, 1961.

Samuel J. Konefsky. *John Marshall and Alexander Hamilton.* New York, 1964.

Ralph Korngold. *Citizen Toussaint.* Boston, 1944.

Stephen G. Kurtz and James H. Hudson. *Essays on the American Revolution.* Raleigh, North Carolina.

Henry Lee. *Memoirs of the War of '76.* New York, 1870.

Library of Congress. *Articles of Confederation Agreed to by Congress, November 15, 1777; Ratified and in Force, March 1, 1781.*

———. *Information Concerning Speakers of the House of Representatives.* Washington, D.C., 1972.

———. *Listing of Vice Presidents and the Votes They Cast To Break Ties in the Senate.* Washington, D.C., 1973.

———. *Section 9 of the Presidential Election and Succession Act of 1792.* Washington, D.C., 1945.

Henry Cabot Lodge. *Alexander Hamilton.* Boston, 1882.

David Loeb. *Alexander Hamilton.* New York, 1939.

George Elliott London. *Diary.* At North Carolina University Library. Item in entry for September 22, 1800, *in re* conversation with Hamilton.

Luman H. Long, editor. *World Almanac and Book of Facts.* New York, 1972.

Gilbert L. Lycan. *Alexander Hamilton and Foreign Policy.* Norman, Oklahoma, 1972.

"Lysander." *A Correct Statement of the Late Melancholy Affair of Honor, Between General Hamilton and Col. Burr, in Which the Former Unfortunately Fell, July 11, 1804.* New York, 1804.

Niccolo Machiavelli. *The Prince.* New York, 1952.

James Madison. Letter to Edward Carrington concerning power of removal of the President. At Virginia Historical Society.

Allan B. Magruder. *John Marshall.* Boston, 1885.

Jackson Turner Main. *The Antifederalists: Critics of the Constitution, 1781–1788.* Chapel Hill, North Carolina, 1961.

Dumas Malone. *Jefferson and the Ordeal of Liberty.* Boston, 1962.

———. Jefferson and the Rights of Man. Boston, 1951.

———. *Jefferson the President: First Term, 1801–1805.* Boston, 1970.

———. *Jefferson the Virginian.* Boston, 1948.

John C. Miller. *Alexander Hamilton and the Growth of the New Nation.* New York, 1959.

Clarence E. Miner. *The Ratification of the Federal Constitution by the State of New York.* New York, 1921.

Broadus Mitchell. *Alexander Hamilton* (Vols. I and II). New York, 1957, 1962.

———. *Biography of the Constitution of the United States.* New York, 1964.

Lt. Col. Joseph B. Mitchell. *Decisive Battles of the American Revolution.* New York, 1962.

Gouverneur Morris. *Diary of Gouverneur Morris.* Edited by A. C. Morris. New York, 1970.

John T. Morse Jr. *John Adams.* Boston, 1884.

———. *Life of Alexander Hamilton* (2 vols.). New York, 1876.

Museum of the City of New York. *Bulletin,* No. 2, Vol. II (January 1972).

National Archives, miscellaneous documents:
Miscellaneous Papers of the Continental Congress, 1774–89. Washington, D.C., 1962.

Papers of the Continental Congress, 1774–1789. Washington, D.C., 1971.

Records of the Constitutional Conference of 1787. Washington, D.C., 1972.

National Park Service:

Hamilton Grange. Prepared by staff of New York City group. New York, 1964.

Naval Documents Relating to the Quasi War Between the United States and France: Naval Operations from February 1797 to October 1798. Washington, D.C., 1935–38.

Allan Nevins. *History of the Bank of New York and Trust Company: 1784–1934.* New York, 1934.

New Jersey State Gazette. Various issues, 1799.

New York Red Book, Seventy-ninth Edition, 1970–71. An Illustrated Yearbook of Authentic Information Concerning New York State, Its Departments and Political Subdivisions and the Officials Who Administer Its Affairs. Albany, New York, 1971.

Roy F. Nichols. *The Invention of the American Political Parties.* New York, 1967.

Richard M. Nixon. *Six Crises: 1962.* New York, 1968.

Frederick Scott Oliver. *Alexander Hamilton.* New York, 1906.

George Pellew. *John Jay.* Boston, 1890.

Harold L. Peterson. *The Book of the Continental Soldier.* Harrisburg, Pennsylvania, 1968.

Philadelphia City Directory, 1797.

Plutarch. *The Lives of the Noble Grecians and Romans.* Translated by John Dryden. New York, no date.

Records of the Continental and Confederation Congresses and the Constitutional Convention.

Neal Riemer. *James Madison.* New York, 1968.

Clinton Rossiter. *Alexander Hamilton and the Constitution.* New York, 1964.

———. *The Grand Convention.* New York, 1966.

———. *Parties and Politics in America.* New York, 1960.

Rutgers University. Verification of marker for Alexander Hamilton's battery, erected by the class of 1899. Courtesy Harmony Coppola, secretary to the Archivist.

Robert Allen Rutland. *George Mason: Reluctant Statesman.* Charlottesville, Virginia, 1961.

Albert B. Saye. *Georgia: Government and History.* Evanston, Illinois.

454   *To Covet Honor*

Nathan Schachner. *Alexander Hamilton.* New York, 1946.

George F. Scheer and Hugh F. Rankin. *Rebels and Redcoats.* Cleveland, Ohio, and New York, 1957.

Marvin D. Schwartz. "Antiques: Alexander Hamilton's Chairs on Display." *The New York Times,* September 23, 1972.

Bernard W. Sheehan. *Seeds of Extinction: Jeffersonian Philanthropy and the American Nation.* Williamsburg, Virginia, 1973.

Emily E. F. Skeel. *Notes on the Life of Noah Webster* (2 vols.). New York, 1881.

Eric Sloane and Edward Anthony. *Mr. Daniels and The Grange.* New York, 1968.

Adam Smith. *The Wealth of Nations.* London, 1776; New York, 1970.

James Morton Smith. *Freedom's Fetters: The Alien and Sedition Laws and American Civil Liberties.* Ithaca, New York, 1956.

Page Smith. *John Adams* (2 vols.). New York, 1963.

Lt. Col. Walter H. Smith. "Alexander Hamilton, Artillerist." *Field Artillery Journal.* Fort Sill, Oklahoma.

Society of the Cincinnati. *Proceedings of a Triennial Meeting of the Society of the Cincinnati, Convened at the City of Washington, in the District of Columbia, on Monday, the Third Day of May, A.D. 1802.*

Benjamin T. Spencer. *The Quest for Nationality.* Ithaca, New York, 1957.

William C. Stinchcombe. *The American Revolution and the French Alliance.* Ithaca, New York, 1969.

John J. Stoudt. *Ordeal at Valley Forge.* Philadelphia, 1963.

Gerald Stourzh. *Alexander Hamilton and the Idea of Republican Government.* Stanford, California, 1970.

William Sullivan. *Familiar Letters.* Boston, 1934.

Howard Swiggett. *The Extraordinary Mr. Morris.* New York, 1952.

H. C. Syrett and J. G. Cooke. *Interview in Weehawken: The Burr-Hamilton Duel as Told in the Original Documents.* Middletown, Connecticut, 1960.

Charles C. Tansill, compiler. *Documents Illustrative of the Formation of the Union of the American States.* Washington, D.C., 1927.

Charles C. Thach Jr. *The Creation of the Presidency.* Baltimore, Maryland, 1969.

Milton Halsey Thomas. *The King's College Building with Some Notes on Its Later Tenants.* New York, 1955.

Alexis de Tocqueville. *Democracy in America.* New York, 1956.

———. "New America as Seen by Alexis de Tocqueville in 1831." *Saturday Evening Post,* Fall 1971.

Charlemagne Towers Jr. *The Marquis de La Fayette in the American Revolution.* Philadelphia, 1901.

Arnold J. Toynbee. *A Study of History.* New York, 1947.

George Trevelyan. *The American Revolution.* New York, 1903.

Trinity Church. Clipping from *Churchyards* booklet regarding monument erected to Alexander Hamilton. Courtesy of Helen Rose Cline, Parish Recorder.

Sylvanus Urban. *The Gentleman's Magazine, and Historical Chronicle, Vol. XLVI, For the Year MDCCLXXVI.* London.

"Valley Forge, 1777–78." *Pennsylvania Historical Magazine,* Vol. XXI, 1897.

Martin Van Buren. *Autobiography.* Washington, D.C.

Carl Van Doren. *The Great Rehearsal.* New York, 1948.

Clarence Hayden Vance. "Myles Cooper, M.A., D.C.L., L.L.D., Second President of King's College, Now Columbia University, New York City." *Columbia University Quarterly,* September 1930.

Arthur Hendrick Vandenberg. *If Hamilton Were Here Today.* New York, 1923.

———. *The Trail of a Tradition.* New York, 1926.

Harry R. Warfel. *Noah Webster.* New York, 1936.

Robert I. Warshow. *Alexander Hamilton: First American Business Man.* New York, 1931.

George Washington. Letter to Alexander Hamilton, 8 May 1791, from the George Washington Collection in Princeton University Library, and Alexander Hamilton Checklist in Princeton University Library.

Patricia Watlington. *The Partisan Spirit: Kentucky Politics, 1779–1792.* New York, 1972.

Howard H. Wehmann. "To Major Gibbs With Much Esteem." Prologue, *The Journal of the National Archives,* Winter 1972.

Thomas J. Wertenbaker. *Princeton.* Princeton, New Jersey, 1946.

Anne H. Wharton. *Salons Colonial and Republican.* Philadelphia, 1900.

———. *Social Life in the Early Republic.* Philadelphia, 1902.

Arthur Preston Whitaker. *The Mississippi Question: 1795–1803.* American Historical Association, 1934.

L. D. White. *The Federalists.* New York, 1948.

Gordon S. Wood. *The Creation of the American Republic: 1776–1787.* New York, 1969.

Marvin R. Zahniser. *Charles Cotesworth Pinckney: Founding Father.* Williamsburg, Virginia, 1967.

Index

TO COVET HONOR
A Biography of Alexander Hamilton
by Holmes Alexander

Life really began, for him, with the American Revolution. He was a brilliant teen-aged officer when Washington himself picked him as an aide-de-camp. Later he became co-author of "the most wonderful work ever struck off at a given moment by the brain and purpose of man," as Gladstone called the Constitution. He reached his golden maturity as writer — he was chief author of the Federalist Papers — orator, statesman, financier; as the first Secretary of the Treasury, and founder of the system of business and finance that was to make his adopted country prosperous and great. Through it all, Alexander Hamilton sought and won honor — not power, though he gained that too; not wealth, which he neither coveted nor won.

Holmes Alexander's friendly and informal biography shows Hamilton as his contemporaries saw him — his towering intellect and all-too-human weaknesses. It reveals him as the impetuous young man who blew into American history on the winds of a West Indian hurricane, and lived to write his name indelibly in that history — but not to grow old. Few remember that he was still a young man when he died in a dramatic duel.

The Englishman, Frederick Scott Oliver, saw Hamilton as a master statesman who belonged to the ages. Holmes Alexander shows him as that and more — a warm, lively, fallible, and charismatic human being.